Everyday Mathematics®

The University of Chicago School Mathematics Project

Teacher's Reference Manual

Grades 1-3

The McGraw·Hill Companies

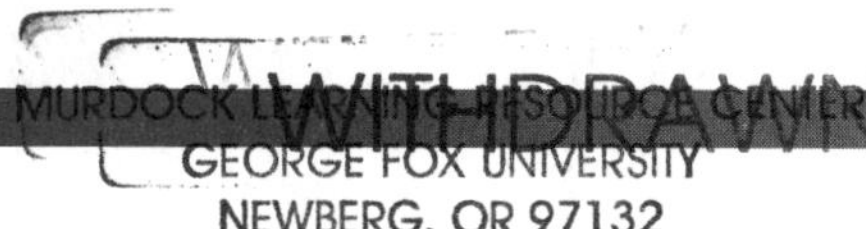

The University of Chicago School Mathematics Project (UCSMP)
Max Bell, Director, UCSMP Elementary Materials Component; Director, *Everyday Mathematics* First Edition
James McBride, Director, *Everyday Mathematics* Second Edition
Andy Isaacs, Director, *Everyday Mathematics* Third Edition
Amy Dillard, Associate Director, *Everyday Mathematics* Third Edition

Authors
Max Bell
Jean Bell
John Bretzlauf
Amy Dillard
James Flanders
Robert Hartfield
Andy Isaacs
James McBride
Kathleen Pitvorec
Peter Saecker

Technical Art
Diana Barrie

Photo Credits
© Lucien Carle, p. 209; © Getty Images, pp. iv, v bottom, 7, 22, 233, 243;
© iStock International Inc. pp. 118, 173, 243; courtesy Bill Lettow, pp. 75, 181;
© Punchstock, p. 1; with permission of Bob Thaves, pp. 26, 170;
courtesy of Kimble House, © Erika Yaffe, p. 144

www.WrightGroup.com

Printed in the United States of America.

Send all inquiries to:
Wright Group/McGraw-Hill
P.O. Box 812960
Chicago, IL 60681

ISBN 0-07-604594-3

8 9 10 12 11 10 09 08 07

The McGraw·Hill Companies

Table of Contents

Mathematical Strands and Threads

Change
Start ?
$1.50
End $6.50

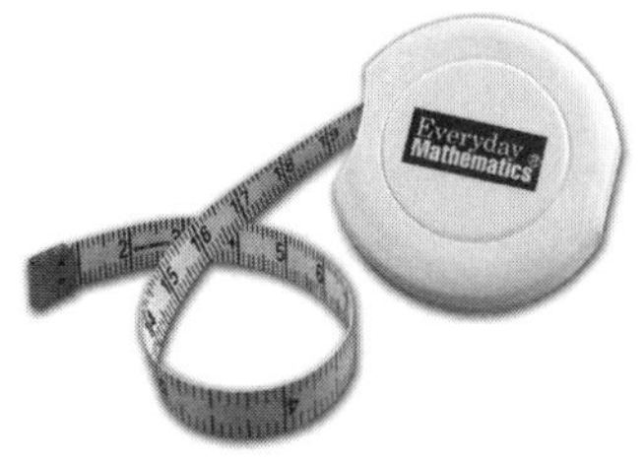
Everyday Mathematics

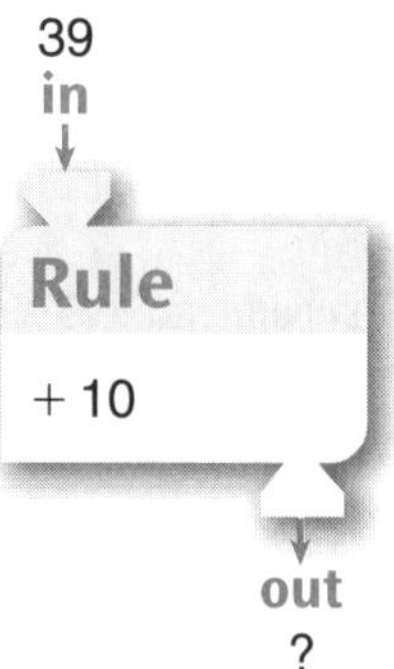

39
in
Rule
+ 10
out
?

Introduction

NOTE: Although this is a reference manual for Grades 1 through 3, many of the routines and games, as well as all of the mathematics in the strands and threads, begin in Kindergarten activities. Therefore, you will see many references to Kindergarten through Grade 3 and specific references to the Kindergarten materials in this manual.

i How to Use this Book

This *Everyday Mathematics Teacher's Reference Manual*™ has three main parts: an eight-chapter Management Guide, ten chapters discussing Mathematical Strands and Threads, and a Glossary. The Management Guide includes suggestions on implementing the *Everyday Mathematics*® program; ideas for organizing the curriculum, the children, and the program materials; and descriptions of important program features. The Mathematical Strands and Threads chapters contain reliable information on the mathematics in the curriculum. *Strands* are the familiar topics of mathematics such as numeration and geometry; *threads* are ways of thinking about mathematics that cross the strands, such as problem solving and estimation. These chapters are followed by a detailed Glossary of mathematical and special terms used in *Everyday Mathematics.*

In order to familiarize yourself with the program's features and routines, you may find it helpful to read all eight chapters of the Management Guide before you begin teaching with *Everyday Mathematics*. This reading will also help you decide on organizational strategies for your classroom. Then, as the school year progresses, you may want to refer to some sections again in order to gain further insights.

The ten Mathematical Strands and Threads chapters do not have to be read in their entirety or in any particular order. The topics presented in each chapter are summarized in a table of contents at the beginning of the chapter. You can skim the chapter, consult its table of contents for a specific topic, or read it straight through.

Selected terms in the Glossary refer to sections in the 18 chapters of the manual. For example, the Glossary defines *fact power* as "the ability to automatically recall basic arithmetic facts." The definition is linked to Section 16.3.2: Basic Facts and Fact Power, which details how *Everyday Mathematics* approaches the basic facts, why basic facts are so important, and how the program works to ensure that all children achieve fact power.

Every effort has been made to make this manual easy to use. The authors hope you find it worthwhile and invite your suggestions on how it could be improved.

ii The *Everyday Mathematics* Program

Everyday Mathematics is a comprehensive Pre-Kindergarten through sixth grade mathematics curriculum embracing many of the traditional goals of school mathematics as well as two ambitious goals for the 21st century:

- To substantially raise expectations regarding the amount and range of mathematics that children can learn;
- To support teachers and children with the materials necessary to enable the children to meet these higher expectations.

Philosophy

Children need a mathematics curriculum that is rigorous and balanced and that:

- Emphasizes conceptual understanding while building a mastery of basic skills;
- Explores a broad mathematics spectrum, not just basic arithmetic;
- Is based on how children learn and what they're interested in while preparing them for their future mathematical needs.

An ever-increasing demand for mathematics competence and problem-solving agility both in and out of school requires us to continue to change both the mathematics we teach and how we teach it. Beginning in Kindergarten, *Everyday Mathematics* makes these changes by introducing children to these six major mathematical content domains: number sense, algebra, measurement, geometry, data analysis, and probability. The program helps children build and maintain basic skills, including automatic fact recall, while helping you use everyday, real-world problems and situations to nurture their higher-order and critical-thinking skills.

Everyday Mathematics differs from traditional, textbook-centered instruction in a number of ways.

- It is consistent with how children actually learn mathematics as it builds understanding over a period of time, first through informal exposure and then through more formal and directed instruction. Because learning proceeds from the known to the unknown, new learning needs to be connected to, and built upon, an existing knowledge base.
- Mathematical content is taught in a repeated fashion, beginning with concrete experiences. Children using *Everyday Mathematics* are expected to master a variety of mathematical skills and concepts, but not the first time they are encountered. It is a mistake to

proceed too quickly from the concrete to the abstract or to isolate concepts and skills from one another or from problem contexts. Children also need to "double back" by revisiting topics, concepts, and skills and then relating them to each other in new and different ways.

- Pacing is important. Children learn best when new topics are presented briskly and in an interesting way. Most children will not master a new topic the first time it is presented, so *Everyday Mathematics* allows children to revisit content in varied contexts, integrating new learning with previous knowledge and experiences. When newly learned concepts and skills are periodically reviewed, practiced, and applied in a wide variety of contexts, they are better retained.

It is important to note how the differences between *Everyday Mathematics* and other programs may affect your day-to-day planning and teaching. Daily routines and games are a necessary part of the program, not optional extensions. Routines and games are designed to build conceptual understanding and ensure mastery of basic skills in authentic and interesting contexts. *Everyday Mathematics* also differs from other programs in that it is designed for the teacher. Rather than being centered on a student textbook, it offers materials that provide children with a rich variety of experiences across mathematical content strands and threads.

Because language, communication, social interaction, tools, and manipulatives all play important roles in helping children acquire skills, *Everyday Mathematics* employs cooperative-learning activities, Explorations, and Projects. The program gives guidance on how to set up your classroom to accommodate group work and on how to help children work together without direct supervision.

For more information, see Chapter 4: Organizing Children.

Through a comprehensive approach to differentiating instruction, *Everyday Mathematics* provides a variety of ways to help children and teachers manage different learning backgrounds, styles, and pacing needs. Mental Math and Reflexes exercises, games, and Math Boxes are just three features included to help children practice skills to keep them sharp throughout the year and into future years. Advice on how to adjust activities for children with different needs is integrated throughout the *Teacher's Lesson Guide*™.

For more information, see Chapter 6: Differentiating Instruction and the *Differentiation Handbook.*

In *Everyday Mathematics,* assessment is closely linked with instruction. While some formal assessment is necessary, a balanced approach including less formal, ongoing methods provides a more complete picture of each child's progress. A number of assessment tools are built into the *Everyday Mathematics* program to help you get feedback about your children's instructional needs and information you can use to assign grades.

For more information, see Chapter 7: Managing Assessment and the *Assessment Handbook.*

In summary, *Everyday Mathematics* is committed to establishing world-class mathematics standards for our nation's schools. The program assumes that virtually all children are capable of a much greater understanding of and proficiency in mathematics than has been traditionally expected, so it provides the features and materials you need to help them meet those higher expectations.

iii Program Highlights

Highlights of the *Everyday Mathematics* program include:

- *Problem solving in everyday situations* Research and experience show that children who are unable to solve problems presented in purely symbolic form often have little trouble solving them when they are presented in everyday contexts.
- *Developing readiness through hands-on activities Everyday Mathematics* offers many suggestions for Explorations and Projects on which children work together. These activities pave the way for the introduction of new mathematical ideas.
- *Establishing links between past experiences and explorations of new concepts* Ideas that have been explored with concrete materials or pictorial representations are revisited through oral descriptions and symbolic representations. Children learn to shift comfortably among various representations and to select models that are most appropriate for given situations.
- *Sharing ideas through discussion* Children gain important insights about mathematics by building on each others' discoveries—one idea leads to another or to refinements of a child's own understanding. Discussion promotes good listening habits and fosters a receptive attitude to the ideas of classmates. Because verbalization often clarifies concepts, talking about mathematics is an important part of thinking about mathematics.
- *Cooperative learning through partner and small-group activities* Children discover that working together is usually more enjoyable and stimulating than working independently. Moreover, as children learn to work as a team, cooperation replaces competition and the less-skilled among them benefit by drawing support from the more-skilled.
- *Practice through games* Children need frequent practice to master a skill. Unfortunately, drills become monotonous and lose effectiveness over time. Games, however, relieve the tedium of rote repetition, reduce the need for worksheets, and offer an almost unlimited source of problem material because, in most cases, numbers are generated randomly.
- *Ongoing review throughout the year* It is rare that children master something the first time they encounter it. For this reason, repeated exposure to key ideas presented in slightly different contexts is built into the *Everyday Mathematics* program. In addition, Math Boxes provide opportunities for cumulative review or assessment.
- *Daily routines* The program suggests routines that children can perform on a regular basis. Tasks such as keeping the daily schedule, class calendar, weather and temperature records, and attendance chart are learning experiences in themselves.

Other regular classroom tasks help children develop a sense of order, initiative, and responsibility while reinforcing numerous mathematical concepts.

- *Informal assessment* In addition to independent review exercises, *Everyday Mathematics* provides many suggestions for small-group activities to help you assess children's progress. Through your interactions with small groups of children, you obtain a clearer understanding of individual strengths and weaknesses.
- *Home-and-school partnership* Optimal learning occurs if it involves the child, the teacher, and people at home. The *Home Connection Handbook*™ offers many suggestions for this. Family Letters help inform parents and guardians about each unit's topics and terms, offering ideas for home-based mathematics activities that supplement classroom work. Also, parents or other caregivers are invited to participate in their child's mathematics experiences through Home Links.

iv Mathematical Content

First through *Third Grade Everyday Mathematics* is organized into the following content strands:

- Number and Counting
- Operations and Number Models
- Data and Chance
- Geometry
- Measurement
- Reference Frames
- Patterns, Sequences, Functions, and Algebra

Woven throughout the content strands are three important mathematical threads:

- Algorithms
- Estimation, Mental Arithmetic, and Number Sense
- Problem Solving

Special emphasis is placed on:

- Establishing links between new and past experiences through activities with concrete materials, pictures, oral statements, and symbolic arithmetic statements. For example, children might act out a problem or talk about it to get a feel for what is happening. Or they might draw simple pictures or diagrams, or do some mental arithmetic, which eventually leads them to write a number model.
- Discussing and sharing ideas. *Can you tell us how you do that? Why do you think so? Does everyone agree?*
- Using and comparing equivalent expressions. *What other ways can we say or write . . .?*
- Expressing quantities and measurements in context by including labels or units. *Five what?*
- Learning about the reversibility of most things: put in, take out; add, subtract; take apart, put together; go away, come back;

expand, shrink; spend money, earn money; positive, negative; and so on.

- Using calculators as tools for counting, displaying numbers, developing concepts and skills, and solving problems—especially real-life problems in which numbers are not always "nice."

By becoming a part of everyday work and play, the lessons, exercises, and concepts in *Everyday Mathematics* gradually shape children's ways of thinking about mathematics and foster the development of their mathematical intuition and understanding.

Management Guide

Contents

management guide

1 Managing the Curriculum

Perhaps the single greatest difference between *Everyday Mathematics* and other programs is that *Everyday Mathematics* is written for you, the teacher, rather than focused on a student textbook. Student materials are supplements to facilitate your use of the program. This section discusses features of the curriculum and describes materials that support its instruction. Central to the *Everyday Mathematics* approach is the introduction and management of three general types of routines: *Daily, Program,* and *Math-Modeling.*

▶ 1.1 Daily Routines

Children learn a great deal of mathematics through the daily routines they perform both independently and as a class. These include making an Attendance Chart, keeping a Class Calendar, creating and extending a Class Number Line, and performing classroom jobs.

For specific suggestions on how to set up and maintain daily routines, see Chapter 5: Organizing Daily Routines and Displays.

Most of the daily routines in *Everyday Mathematics* should be introduced in the first unit and then maintained throughout the year. Although these routines require special attention and extra time at the beginning of the year, you will find that investing this time will make teaching easier in the long run. Once routines have been established, they become self-sustaining, as much by the children's energy as by your efforts. Learning becomes much more efficient and effective.

▶ 1.2 Program Routines

Program routines are mathematical activities built into lessons in the *Teacher's Lesson Guide* and maintained across units and grade levels. They are described here in alphabetical order.

1.2.1 Explorations

In *Everyday Mathematics, Explorations* are time set aside for independent, small-group activities. In addition to providing the benefits of cooperative learning, small-group work lets all children have a chance to use manipulatives that are limited in supply, such as a pan balance or base-10 blocks.

If there are enough materials for everyone, you may have the whole class work on one Exploration at a time. However, it is more likely that you will want to have small groups of children working on several Explorations simultaneously. With a little planning, you can manage several different activities at the same time. Parent volunteers can be very helpful in these situations.

The Explorations have been designed so that you can position the various activities at different stations around the room and have groups rotate among the stations or rotate the materials among the groups. You might find it helpful to organize the materials for each Exploration by keeping them together in a small plastic tub, pan, bin, bucket, or box. After the Explorations have been completed, you can make the materials available for review and free-time activities.

Each lesson of Explorations suggests three activities, with the option of adding others. Decide how many stations you will need to accommodate groups of three to five children each. Each station should have one kind of material for children to share. To ensure that you have enough stations for all of your groups, you may want to set up two stations for each Exploration activity or set up additional familiar activities or games for children to complete independently while other groups are working on Explorations.

Exploration A focuses on the main mathematical content of the Exploration lesson and requires the most involvement by you at the outset. Try to spend most of your time at this station and only briefly visit other stations. Alternatively, if parent volunteers are not available or when children are less independent at the beginning of the year, remain at one station as children rotate through it. This allows you to work with every child in a small-group setting and to use the task at that station as an informal assessment opportunity.

To promote a cooperative environment, you might make and display a poster of Rules for Explorations, such as the one shown in the margin. Until children become accustomed to the rules, discuss them prior to each Exploration lesson, along with any other rules that you or the children want to add.

Rules for Explorations

1. Cooperate with others.
2. Move about quietly.
3. Keep voices low.
4. Treat materials as tools, not as toys.
5. Give everyone in the group a chance to use the materials.
6. Straighten up when finished. Put materials back where they belong.
7. Try to settle disputes quietly within the group. If necessary, one person can go to the teacher for help.

Beginning in first grade, instruction masters for the Explorations activities are supplied in the *Math Masters*™ book. These masters aim to make groups more independent and to incorporate reading into the Explorations. The groups will need a great deal of help and attention at the beginning of the year, but they will become increasingly independent as children become stronger readers and grow more familiar with the activities. You may want to mount the instructions on tagboard and/or laminate them for use throughout the year.

Set aside enough class time for all children to experience the Explorations. They are as important as any other lesson in *Everyday Mathematics,* so do not set them up as optional centers for children to use when they have finished other work. If you do that, children who could most benefit from these activities will get fewer opportunities to participate in them. The activities are not optional because they introduce, review, and/or deepen mathematical concepts.

1.2.2 Games

Many parents and educators make a sharp distinction between work and play. They tend to "allow" play only during prescribed times. However, children naturally carry their playfulness into all of their activities. This is why *Everyday Mathematics* sees playing games as an enjoyable way to practice number skills, especially those that help children develop *fact power.*

For more information, see Section 16.3.2: Basic Facts and Fact Power.

Games are an integral part of *Everyday Mathematics* rather than the optional extra activities that supplement traditional programs. Make sure that all children have time to play games, especially those who work at a slower pace or encounter more difficulty than do their classmates. As with Explorations, if children play games only after finishing other work, those who could benefit the most will have fewer opportunities.

Because the numbers in exercises are generated randomly, games make fact practice more fun than arithmetic worksheets. Also, the game format eliminates the tedium typical of most drills. Here are some suggestions for integrating games into your classroom:

- Include games as part of your daily morning routine.
- Devote the first or last 10 minutes of each math class to playing the games specified in the unit.
- Designate one math class per week as "Games Day." Set up stations that feature the games in the current unit. Ask parent volunteers to assist in the rotation of children though these stations.
- Set up a "Games Corner" of favorite games. Children can get additional skills practice while playing games of their own choosing during free time. Rotate games often to keep the Games Corner fresh and interesting.

For more information, see Section 16.3.4: Games for Fact Practice.

Competition

Some people are concerned that including games in the curriculum promotes competition between children. As one teacher writes, "I prefer to have children work in cooperative groupings, staying away from win-or-lose games. I can't think of a quicker way to turn a child off to the concept one is trying to teach than to inject the emotional disaster of 'I've lost!' into the experience."

It is true that many of the games in *Everyday Mathematics* are competitive. Fair and friendly competition can generate many good things, such as excitement, determination, independence, and challenge. However, game rules may also be changed to fit player and teacher needs for fairness, harmony, and equality. It is possible to modify most of the games so that children practice the same number skills while working cooperatively. The challenge and excitement can come from working together, making joint decisions, and doing one's best while having fun.

To demonstrate how a competitive game can be modified to make it noncompetitive, consider *Multiplication Top-It*. In this game, children use a 40-card deck of 1 through 10 number cards with four cards of each number. Each child turns over two cards and calls out the product of the numbers on them. The player with the highest product takes all the cards played in that turn. The player with the most cards at the end of the game wins.

Suppose, however, that two or three children are asked to play the same game but are given this group objective: *Play until all 40 cards are used, putting all the used cards into a single discard pile. Time the game. Play again until all 40 cards are used. Try to beat your best time to play the whole deck.*

This modified game allows practice of the same multiplication skills but does not declare winners and losers. Instead, the focus is on the group objective of achieving a faster time.

As written, many of the *Everyday Mathematics* games identify the winner as the player with the highest total after a certain number of turns. Here are some strategies for converting these games to relatively noncompetitive games:

- Have the children take turns as usual, but ask them to record their results for each round on the same sheet of paper. A game total will then represent the combined efforts of all group members.
- Redefine the game objective. For example, ask groups to play a sequence of games and report the highest and lowest single game totals. This modification may inspire some measure of healthy competition among groups, but the one-on-one competitive nature of the standard game will be reduced.

NOTE: If finding the sum is beyond children's comfort ranges, have them use a calculator or calculate the total for them.

These are only examples. The best ideas for modifying games are likely to come from your own classroom experiences. Involve the children in the revisions. If they realize that their input improves the games, they are likely to become more eager players and learners.

The Everything Math Deck

The Everything Math Deck is a deck of 54 number cards used for a variety of *Everyday Mathematics* games and activities. The deck can be purchased through the publisher. It has four of each card for the numbers 0 through 10 and one of each card for the numbers 11 through 20. On the reverse of the 0-through-10 cards are fractions represented in a variety of ways.

To transform an ordinary deck of 54 playing cards to function like the whole-number side of an Everything Math Deck:

- Change the four queens to 0s.
- Remove the four jacks, four kings, and two jokers. Label each of these ten cards with one of the numbers from 11 to 20.
- Change the four aces to 1s.
- Let all number cards represent their face value.

For more information, see Section 16.3.4: Games for Fact Practice.

1.2.3 Home Links

Home Links® are the *Everyday Mathematics* version of homework assignments. Each lesson has a Home Link which can be found in the *Math Masters* book. The next lesson has a follow-up to the previous Home Link. Home Links consist of active projects and ongoing review problems that show parents what the children can do in mathematics. You are also encouraged to make custom Home Links to fit your individual needs.

1.2.4 Math Boxes

Math Boxes are a main part of review and skills maintenance in *Everyday Mathematics*. Originally developed by *Everyday Mathematics* teacher Ellen Dairyko, Math Boxes are an excellent way to help children review material on a regular basis. Once this routine has been introduced in each grade level, every lesson includes a Math Boxes page in the *Math Journal*™.

Math Boxes problems are not intended to reinforce the content of the lesson in which they appear. Rather, they provide continuous distributed practice of skills and concepts that children have seen up to that point in the program. The Math Boxes page does not need to be completed on the same day as the lesson, but it should not be skipped.

The first four or five problems on a Math Boxes page are about mathematics in the current and previous units, including those from previous grades, and the final problem or two preview the math found in the next unit. Paired or tripled problems are included to give repeated practice on selected mathematics concepts and skills.

Math Boxes in the Progress Check lesson summarize all the preview problems in the unit. Children's performance on these problems informs you of their preparedness for the mathematics in the next unit.

NOTE: Although Math Boxes are designed primarily as an independent activity, at times it may be useful to have children work through some problems with partners or as a class.

Math Boxes are designed as independent activities, but expect that your guidance will be needed, especially at the beginning of the school year when some problems review skills from prior years. If children struggle with a problem set, it is not necessary to create a lesson to develop these skills. You can modify or skip problems that you know are not review for the children, knowing that the necessary skills will be revisited in subsequent lessons. Math Boxes also provide ongoing assessment information on skills.

1.2.5 Math Messages

Beginning early in first grade, a *Math Message* is provided at the beginning of each lesson. The Math Message leads into the lesson for the day. Children should complete the Math Message before the start of each lesson.

You can display Math Messages in several ways:

- Write them on the board, the Class Data Pad, or overhead transparencies.
- Post them on the bulletin board.
- Duplicate them on quarter-sheets of paper to hand out.

You may find it useful to have children record their answers to the Math Message. In some classrooms, children keep a daily Math Journal in which they enter Math Message questions and answers. In other classrooms, children record their answers on quarter- or half-sheets of paper, which teachers collect from time to time.

Although the *Teacher's Lesson Guide* contains many suggestions for Math Messages, you are encouraged to create your own, designed around the needs of the children and the activities that take place in your classroom. You may also want to provide a Suggestion Box into which children can put their own Math Message, number story, or other math ideas.

1.2.6 Mental Math and Reflexes

Mental Math and Reflexes exercises help children:

- Get ready to think about math;
- Warm up the skills they need for the lesson;
- Continually build mental-math and reflex skills;
- Inform you of their skill and concept development.

As shown in the example below, each exercise is given at three levels of difficulty to help meet children's individual needs.

Mental Math and Reflexes

Pose addition facts and extended facts. 

●○○		●●○		●●●	
	6 + 1 = 7		6 + 7 = 13		50 + 50 = 100
	8 + 0 = 8		8 + 4 = 12		20 + 30 = 50
	4 + 4 = 8		7 + 9 = 16		60 + 80 = 140
	9 + 2 = 11		5 + 8 = 13		90 + 90 = 180

Mental Math and Reflexes problems are typically answered orally, with body language, or on slates. A session should be brief, lasting no more than five minutes. Numerous short interactions are far more effective than fewer prolonged sessions.

For more information, see Section 1.2.10: Slates.

The *Teacher's Lesson Guide* suggests several kinds of Mental Math and Reflexes problems for Grades 1 through 3, including:

- *Choral counting routines* such as counting on or back, skip counting with calculators, stop-and-start counting, or problems on a number grid;
- *Place-value problems* such as writing the largest number from a set of dictated digits, identifying a particular place value in a dictated number, or recording dictated numbers and comparing them using > and < symbols;
- *Mental computation problems* with some or all of the four basic arithmetic operations both in and out of the contexts of number stories;
- *Mental estimation and approximation problems* such as making ballpark estimates for sums and products in number stories or rounding whole numbers and decimals to dictated place values.

The *Teacher's Lesson Guide* suggests Mental Math and Reflexes exercises for every lesson except the Progress Checks. You are encouraged to use these exercises based on the children's needs and your classroom activities. If the suggested exercises do not meet the needs of your class, feel free to substitute.

For more information, see Section 16.3: Mental Arithmetic.

1.2.7 *Minute Math*+

Minute Math®+ is a collection of short mathematics activities that require little or no preparation, can be done anywhere, and are brief enough to do in about five minutes. They can be used with large or small groups of children at any time of the day.

Minute Math+ activities provide children with:

- Reinforcement and continuous review of mathematics content;
- Preparation for a variety of testing situations;
- Practice with mental arithmetic and logical thinking;
- Opportunities to think and talk about mathematics and to try out new ideas;
- Experience with the problem-solving process and sharing strategies with others;
- Increased time learning and reviewing mathematics without increasing lesson time.

Minute Math+ activities give children an opportunity to solve a variety of number, operations, geometry, data, probability, and measurement problems. Each page of *Minute Math+* begins with a basic activity followed by suggestions for extending the problem when appropriate for various age and ability levels.

1.2.8 Museums

Everyday Mathematics encourages the development of classroom museums using a bulletin board or table where related items can be collected, categorized, and labeled. For example, first graders assemble a *Numbers All Around Museum,* using examples of uses of numbers from home. Other museums include:

- *Fractions Museum* Children bring halves, fourths, and other fractions of nonperishable things from home.
- *Hundreds Museum* Children collect sets of 100 things for display, such as 100-piece jigsaw puzzles or 100 baseball cards.
- *3-D Shapes Museum* Children collect 3-dimensional shapes and pictures of 3-D shapes.

Everyday Mathematics museums are often supplemented with posters of 2-dimensional representations of items. The posters help children to categorize the solid objects they manipulate and to connect concepts across dimensions.

If you take your class to a museum in your community, encourage the children to look for the uses of mathematics that abound there. Examples include statistics about objects in exhibits and ways of categorizing those objects that often have some underlying frame of reference, such as size or time.

1.2.9 Projects

The Projects suggested in *Everyday Mathematics* cover a wide array of mathematics activities and concepts created around themes that interest children. Project ideas are found in the Projects Appendix of the *Teacher's Lesson Guide* for each grade. Project Masters are found in the Teaching Masters section of the *Math Masters* book.

The Projects are cross-curricular, drawing on and developing skills and concepts in reading and language arts, social studies, art, and especially science. They often include the following science processes:

- Observing
- Communicating
- Identifying
- Collecting, organizing, and graphing data
- Using numbers
- Measuring
- Determining patterns and relationships

Some Unit Organizers in the *Teacher's Lesson Guide* suggest Projects that are appropriate at particular points during the school year. You are given enough ideas in Projects for you to choose those that interest the children, and you are encouraged to add your own as well. Unlike the short activities in the Explorations, projects may take a day or more to complete. Please take the time to do these important parts of the curriculum that are memorable to children.

NOTE: You can consider many Projects and other activities suggested in the *Everyday Mathematics* program to be a part of other areas in your curriculum including reading, language arts, social studies, art, and science.

1.2.10 Slates

Most children and teachers genuinely enjoy using slates. They afford an excellent opportunity for everyone to answer a question quietly and simultaneously, and they help you to see at a glance which children may need extra help. They also save paper. Two kinds of slates are particularly easy to use:

- *Plastic Write-On/Wipe-Off Slates* Children write on these small, white slates with dry-erase markers. They can store both the markers and the slates in their tool kits or stack them on a counter or shelf for easy distribution when needed.
- *Chalkboard Slates* Chalk may be kept in old socks that can also double as erasers. Small rug scraps or pieces of cloth also make good erasers; one teacher recommends small, cotton-quilt cosmetic pads.

Establish a routine for using slates. To help prevent confusion, you might want to use a procedure with 1-word cues, such as *Listen, Think, Write, Show,* and *Erase:*

- Tell children to *Listen*. Explain each exercise aloud. If children find the problems too challenging, you may want to write them on the board or an overhead transparency.
- Be sure to give children time to *Think*. Have them work problems mentally.
- Instruct children to *Write* their answers on their slates and keep them covered.
- When most children have written their answers, tell them to *Show* their slates at the same time by holding them up facing you. When appropriate, take a few minutes to have the children share their problem-solving strategies.
- Have children *Erase* their slates.

You can use laminated tagboard and dry-erase markers as an alternative to slates, or simply have children fold a piece of paper into fourths, giving them eight cells in which to write answers.

Instead of doing oral and slate assessments with the whole class, you might work with one small group of children per day over several days. While you do this, the rest of the class can work on Assessment Masters. When children use slates, it is not necessary to record each child's performance on every problem. You primarily need to keep a record of children who are struggling. At a later time, you can record positive comments for children you know were doing well.

NOTE: Unlike journals, both *My Reference Book* and the *Student Reference Book* are nonconsumable resources.

1.2.11 *My Reference Book/Student Reference Book*

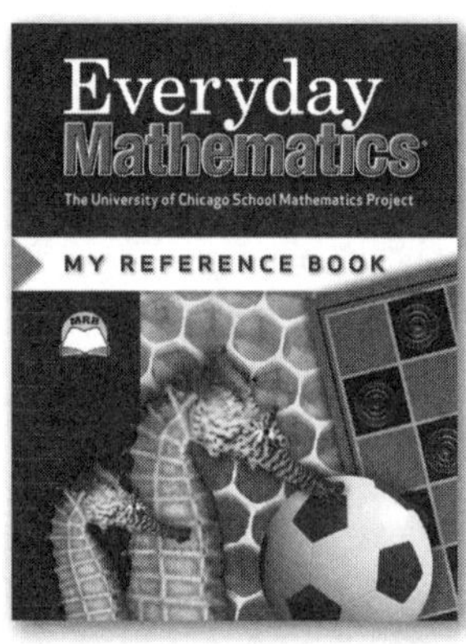

My Reference Book™ is an *Everyday Mathematics* resource for children in the second half of first grade and throughout second grade. Children can look up and review major mathematical topics, find rules for many popular games, and get tips on using a 4-function calculator. Although children may learn to use the book on their own, they most often use the book with teacher guidance. Because Math Boxes and Home Links are cross-referenced to *My Reference Book,* both teachers and parents may appreciate this resource.

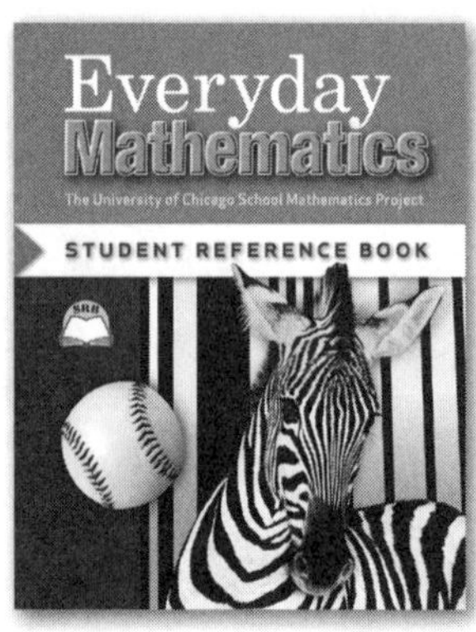

In Grades 3 through 6, students use a progressively more comprehensive *Student Reference Book*™. In addition to the information in *My Reference Book,* the mathematical-topics sections have many worked examples, and there is a Glossary of mathematical terms. In the Grade 3 *Student Reference Book,* a Data Bank includes weather, census, and animal data, as well as "stores" and "vending machines" that children use in many activities throughout the year. The Data Bank corresponds to the World and American Tours found in the fourth- and fifth-grade reference books. As in Grades 1 and 2, Math Boxes and Home Links are cross-referenced to the *Student Reference Book*.

1.3 Math-Modeling Routines

This section briefly summarizes the major *Everyday Mathematics* routines for children to practice mathematical modeling. Detailed descriptions of the routines and how they are used throughout *Everyday Mathematics* are included in the 10 Mathematical Strands and Threads chapters later in this manual.

1.3.1 Fact Families/Fact Triangles

A *fact family* is a collection of four related facts linking inverse operations. For example, the four equations in the margin symbolize the fact family relating 8, 9, and 17 by addition and subtraction.

$8 + 9 = 17$ $9 + 8 = 17$
$17 - 9 = 8$ $17 - 8 = 9$

Fact Triangles are the *Everyday Mathematics* version of flash cards to help children develop their mental arithmetic reflexes. Fact Triangles are more effective than traditional flash cards because they emphasize fact families. An addition/subtraction Fact Triangle has two addends and a sum; a multiplication/division Fact Triangle has two factors and a product. Examples are on the next page.

For more information, see Section 16.3.3: Fact Practice.

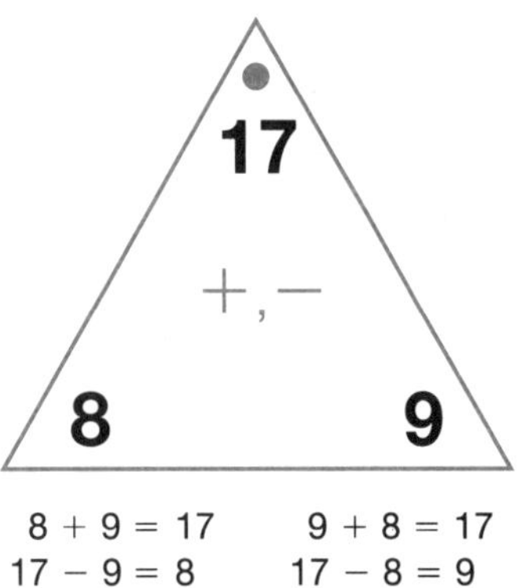

8 + 9 = 17　　9 + 8 = 17
17 − 9 = 8　　17 − 8 = 9

An addition/subtraction Fact Triangle

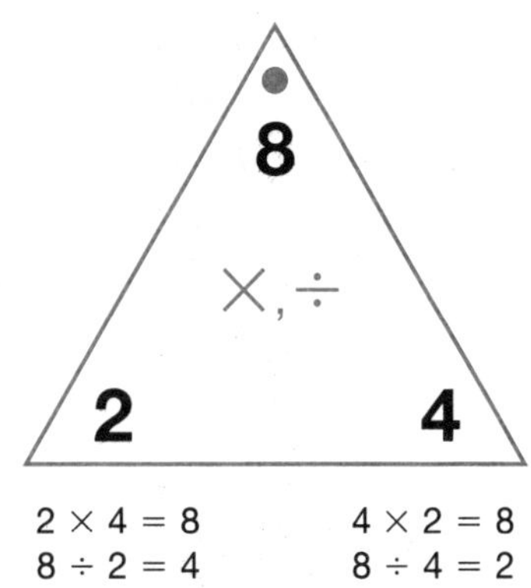

2 × 4 = 8　　4 × 2 = 8
8 ÷ 2 = 4　　8 ÷ 4 = 2

A multiplication/division Fact Triangle

1.3.2 Frames-and-Arrows Diagrams

Frames-and-Arrows diagrams help children organize their work with sequences. Each frame contains a number in the sequence, and each arrow represents a rule that defines the number that goes in the next frame.

For more information on Frames-and-Arrows, see Section 17.1.3: Sequences.

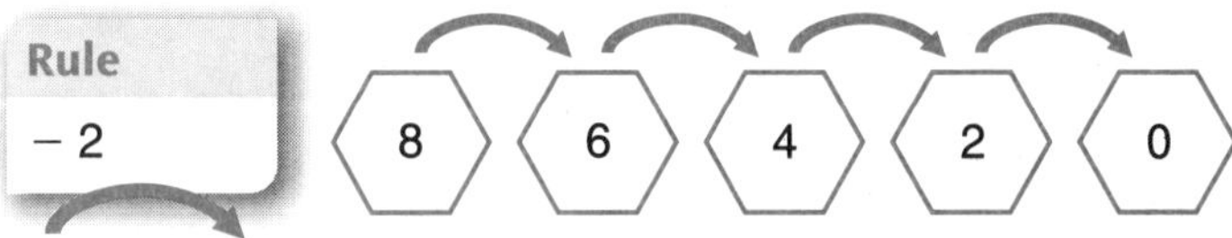

1.3.3 Name-Collection Boxes

Name-collection boxes offer a simple way for children to experience the idea that numbers can be expressed in many different ways. In Kindergarten through third grade, a *name-collection box* is a box with a label identifying the number whose names are collected in the box. For example, the box shown in the margin is a 16-box, a name-collection box for the number 16.

16

XVI
dieciséis
10 less than 26
20 − 4
4 + 4 + 4 + 4
(2 × 5) + 6
sixteen
half of 32
116 − 100
8 twos
32 ÷ 2

A 16-box

For more information, see Section 9.7.3: Name-Collection Boxes.

1.3.4 Number Grids/Number Lines

A *number grid* is a matrix that consists of rows of boxes, ten to each row, containing a set of consecutive integers. Children use number grids to explore number patterns, reinforce place-value concepts, and calculate sums and differences. By attaching grids of larger or smaller numbers to a starting grid, children make *number scrolls.*

−9	−8	−7	−6	−5	−4	−3	−2	−1	0
1	2	3	4	5	6	7	8	9	10
11	12	13	14	15	16	17	18	19	20
21	22	23	24	25	26	27	28	29	30
31	32	33	34	35	36	37	38	39	40
41	42	43	44	45	46	47	48	49	50
51	52	53	54	55	56	57	58	59	60
61	62	63	64	65	66	67	68	69	70
71	72	73	74	75	76	77	78	79	80
81	82	83	84	85	86	87	88	89	90
91	92	93	94	95	96	97	98	99	100
101	102	103	104	105	106	107	108	109	110

A number grid

For more information, see Section 9.7.2: Number Grids, Scrolls, and Lines.

A *number line* is a line on which points correspond to numbers called *coordinates*. There is one point for every number and one number for every point. Children use number lines when counting and skip counting, performing measuring activities, and adding and subtracting. Number lines are also used as the axes in coordinate graphing systems.

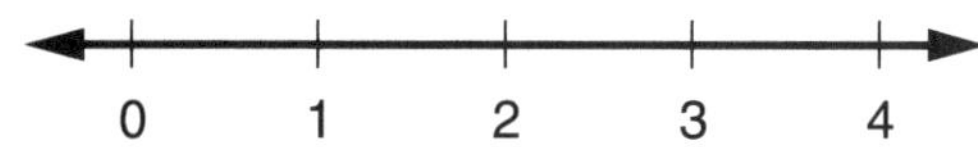

1.3.5 Situation Diagrams

For more information, see Section 10.2: Use Classes and Situation Diagrams.

In *Everyday Mathematics,* children are encouraged to use *situation diagrams* to help sort out various kinds of problem situations. These diagrams organize the information in simple 1-step number stories. Examples include the *parts-and-total, comparison, change,* and *rate* situations that are diagramed below. Diagrams do not have to be fancy, and you can omit or change words, as in the rate diagram.

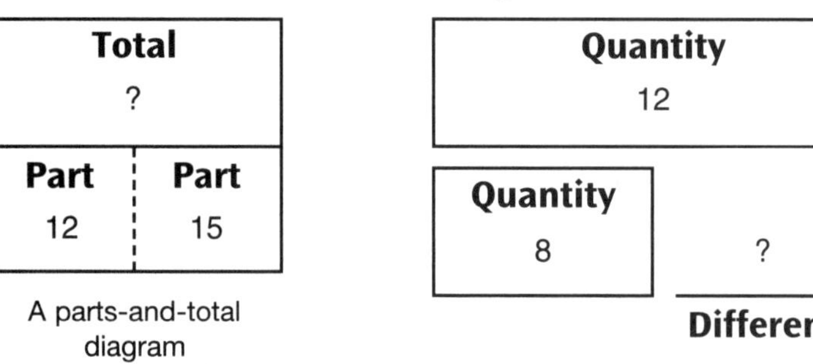

A parts-and-total diagram

A comparison diagram

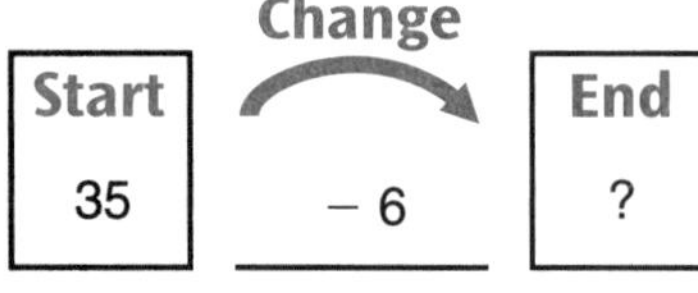

A change diagram

children	cards per child	cards
4	?	24

A rate diagram

1.3.6 Unit Boxes

A *unit box,* such as the one in the margin, is a rectangular box that is displayed next to a problem or a set of problems. Unit boxes contain the labels or units of measure used in the corresponding problem(s). Unit boxes help children to think symbolically by encouraging them to see numbers as quantities or measurements of real objects.

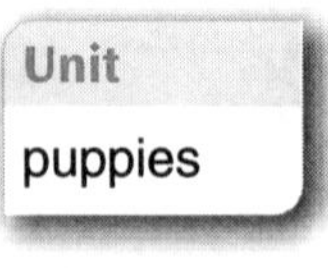

A unit box

1.3.7 "What's My Rule?"/Function Machines

"What's My Rule?" is an activity in which children analyze a set of number pairs to determine a rule that relates the numbers in each pair. The data are often represented using a *function machine,* an imaginary device that receives inputs and pairs them with outputs.

For example, the function machine below takes an input number and outputs 10 more than the input. The input/output pairs can then be displayed in a function table.

For more information, see Section 17.1.4: Functions.

in

Rule

+ 10

out

A function machine

in	out
15	25
4	14
7	
	63

A function table

1.4 Support for Substitute Teachers

Substitute teachers can handle many *Everyday Mathematics* lessons, especially if they let the children think things through for themselves. However, the program's approach may be unfamiliar to some of the substitutes, so it is wise to prepare additional materials for when you are absent. Here are some suggestions:

- Reserve the Math Boxes from several lessons or create extra Math Boxes of your own. Frames and Arrows and "What's My Rule?" routines can also be included. Use the blank masters in the *Math Masters* book.
- Games Days are easy for substitutes to manage. If necessary, move the week's planned Games Day to the day you are absent.
- Prepare suggestions for practice with Fact Triangles. Children can sort the facts by the different strategies they use to verify them or into facts that they know and those they still need to practice. Partners can take turns quizzing each other. Known facts can be recorded in the Math Journal.
- Make an "emergency box" with activities to be done on days when your absence is unexpected. As you teach, identify activities from *Everyday Mathematics* that could be included.

2 The Importance of Problem Solving

In *Everyday Mathematics,* problem solving is much more than solving word problems. Problem solving is a process of building a *mathematical model* of a situation and then reasoning with the model to draw conclusions about the situation. The process typically involves some or all of the following stages, not necessarily in the order presented:

- Identify precisely what the problem is.
- Analyze what is known and seek out further data as necessary.
- Play with the data to try to discover patterns and meaning.
- Identify mathematical techniques that can help a solution.
- Look back and ask *Does the solution make sense?*

This figure shows how these stages interact in the modeling process.

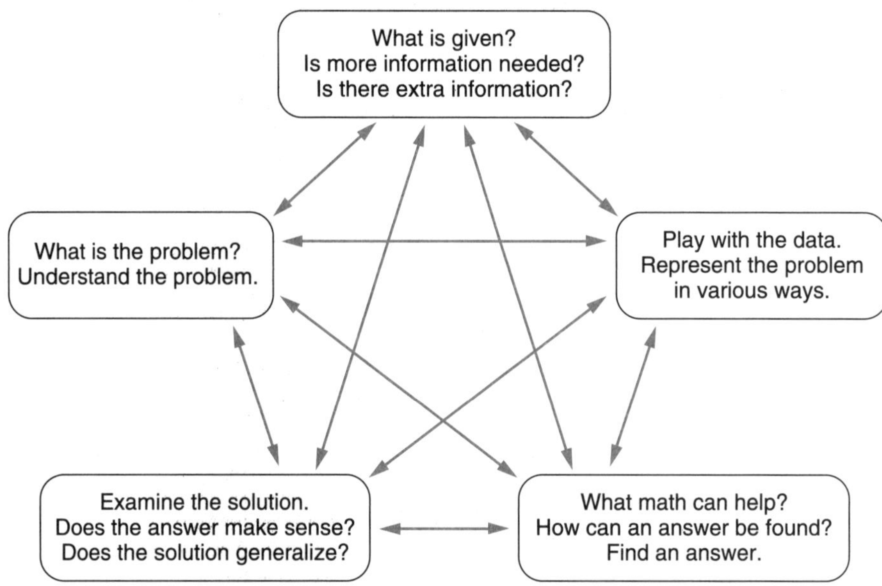

Stages in the mathematical-modeling process

The *Everyday Mathematics* approach to problem solving and mathematical modeling is described in detail in Chapter 18. The remainder of this chapter defines what the authors of *Everyday Mathematics* call *mathematical sense* and suggests ways to manage children's problem solving in your classroom.

2.1 Mathematical Sense

The range of experiences provided by *Everyday Mathematics* is designed to help children develop *mathematical sense,* which includes both an understanding of the body of mathematical knowledge and children's abilities to do mathematics to solve problems. Mathematical sense has the following principal components:

- *Number sense* is a feeling for where numbers come from and what they mean. Children need a great deal of experience using numbers of various kinds and sizes in order to understand which numbers make sense in a given situation. Number sense leads them to continually ask *What is a reasonable answer?* It helps children check the accuracy of answers whether they were obtained mentally, with pencil and paper, with a calculator, or by other means.
- *Operations sense* is a feeling for what addition, subtraction, multiplication, and division mean. For example, *Why is it that products of whole numbers greater than zero are greater than one or both factors, but products of fractions or decimals can be less than the factors?*
- *Measure sense* is a feeling for what measurement means, what kinds of measures and units are appropriate in different situations, and what range of results are reasonable to accept. *Is 20 square feet a sensible measure of the area of the backyard? Might my dog really weigh 800 kilograms?*

- *Data sense* is an appreciation of a collection of numbers as a whole. *How reliable are the numbers? How might they be used? What are the "spread" and "landmarks" of a collection, such as the range and middle value?*
- *Spatial sense* comes from extensive experience with 2-dimensional and 3-dimensional geometric objects and from hands-on constructions that apply geometric principles. *How many grocery bags will fit in the trunk of my car? Can I cover all the walls in my bedroom with a quart of paint?*
- *Function sense,* or *pattern sense,* comes from looking for visual and number patterns and predicting outcomes from applying a rule. It helps children develop multiple perspectives by relating pictorial, symbolic, verbal, and concrete representations of a pattern. *Which is better, doubling $2 every year or adding $50 every year?*

In addition to mathematical sense, *Everyday Mathematics* is committed to helping children recognize and develop their own common sense. By *common sense,* the authors mean an understanding of one's own basic ideas and how they are useful for judging among reasonable alternatives in everyday situations.

2.2 Sharing Children's Strategies and Solutions

Research indicates that children develop a variety of problem-solving strategies if they are given the opportunity to share their ideas with their peers. If this sharing takes place in an open, receptive environment, children will learn that inventing creative, innovative ways of solving problems is acceptable in mathematics. The practice of gathering together to share solutions after individual or group problem solving continues throughout *Everyday Mathematics.*

For more information, see "Exploring Mathematics through Talking and Writing" by Whitin and Whitin (2000). A full reference is on page 230.

Number stories are an excellent context for developing habits of sharing. Children can share their strategies, both correct and incorrect. They can record their solutions on the board, illustrating with pictures and number models. Children develop a better understanding of various mathematical processes when asked to think and strategize rather than when they are merely asked to repeat the steps of a standard written algorithm.

Discussing children's solutions can be extremely valuable, but care should be taken to ensure that children are not embarrassed if their efforts fall short. Children with correct answers are usually happy to share their models and strategies with the class, but discussing incorrect answers can also be very instructive. Here are several suggestions for dealing with wrong answers:

- Emphasize that it is OK to make mistakes. In fact, errors are inevitable. What is *not* OK is failing to learn from one's mistakes.
- Frame discussions of incorrect solutions by saying *Some children in last year's class did* _____ . [Describe the incorrect approach.] *Why do you think they did that? How would you help them see their mistake?*

management guide

- Emphasize that answers obtained using different methods should agree, so if there is not agreement, something must be wrong. Encourage children to resolve the dilemma.
- Compare and contrast different strategies and help children see advantages and disadvantages of each. An incorrect method may have some good ideas that can be used to improve another method.

At the beginning of each school year, *Everyday Mathematics* includes specific occasions for children to share strategies and solutions. Many other opportunities occur over the course of the year. With practice, children eventually become comfortable sharing their strategies and are able to talk about them freely and fluently, listen to one another attentively, and revise their own strategies and adopt new ones based on the discussions.

▸ 2.3 Problem-Solving Strategies for Beginners

The diagram of the mathematical-modeling process shown on page 20 generally fits what experts do when they solve problems, but is too complicated to be of much help for beginners. On the other hand, many elementary school mathematics textbooks include long lists of strategies and tips; but these lists are often little help even with simple real-life problems, and are essentially useless for dealing with complicated problems such as those found in the workplace.

Children need a guide that is more useful than a list of tips but simpler than a diagram of expert behavior. To this end, *Third* through *Sixth Grade Everyday Mathematics* outlines general guidelines for managing problem solving, such as the one for third grade shown in the margin.

Guide to Solving Number Stories

1. What do you know from reading the story?
2. What do you want to find out?
3. What do you need to do? Do it, and record what you did.
4. If you can, write a number model that fits the problem.
5. Answer the question.
6. Check. Ask Does my answer make sense? How do I know?

Because problems from everyday life are usually complicated, the first need is often to simplify the situation and figure out exactly what is known and what is to be found out. For example, problem situations in daily life often contain many irrelevant numbers. Sometimes relevant numbers are missing and must be inferred or derived from what is known. Often, the problem solver must deal not only with just a few counts or measures but also with large sets of data. Considerable effort may be required to make the data consistent in format and to devise a display that suggests useful patterns or interesting questions. The process seldom follows one predictable step after another.

3 Managing Tools

Tools are extremely important in the *Everyday Mathematics* program. The authors define tools broadly to include anything that can be used to facilitate mathematical thinking and problem solving. Calculators, rulers, manipulatives such as pattern blocks and geoboards, paper and pencil, slates, reference books, and the Internet are all mathematical tools. *Everyday Mathematics* helps children learn the skills they need to use these and other tools and to choose the proper tools to help solve a given problem.

By emphasizing the power of tools and helping children learn how to employ them intelligently, *Everyday Mathematics* is working to make doing mathematics in school resemble how mathematics is done in everyday life. Without this type of approach, school mathematics risks becoming abstract and disconnected from everyday life, a complaint that many adults make about their own mathematics education.

NOTE: Encourage children to respect and care for the tools in their tool kits just as doctors, carpenters, and others respect and take care of the tools they use.

The following sections focus on tools that are often used in *Everyday Mathematics*. More information about these and other tools can be found in some of the Mathematical Strands and Threads chapters, which link specific tools to the teaching, learning, and application of particular mathematical topics.

3.1 Electronic Tools

Electronic tools for mathematics education include calculators, computers, and computer peripherals such as probes, videodiscs, and CDs. Access to electronic tools is varied, and *Everyday Mathematics* is very conservative in its assumptions about which tools are available to every child. In fact, 4-function calculators are sufficient in Kindergarten through Grade 3, and scientific calculators are sufficient in Grades 4 through 6. Some links to Web sites are included in the materials, but none are required.

3.1.1 Calculators

In the more than a quarter-century since electronic calculators have become widely available, many researchers have studied their effects on how children learn. The preponderance of evidence from these studies suggests that the proper use of calculators can enhance children's understanding and mastery of arithmetic, promote good number sense, and improve problem-solving skills and attitudes toward mathematics.

Three summaries of this research are:

- "Research on Calculators in Mathematics Education" by Ray Hembree and Donald J. Dessart;
- "A Meta-Analysis of Outcomes from the Use of Calculators in Mathematics Education" by Brian A. Smith;
- "A Meta-Analysis of the Effects of Calculators on Students' Achievement and Attitude Levels in Precollege Mathematics Classes" by Aimee J. Ellington.

NOTE: For complete references to these studies, and information on other calculator research, see "Resources on Calculators" on pages 28 and 29.

The Smith and Ellington studies also conclude that calculator usage does not hinder the development of paper-and-pencil skills. Ellington recommends that calculators be used by children in Kindergarten through Grade 2 for experimenting with arithmetic concepts in problem-solving contexts.

Both teacher experience and educational research show that most children develop good judgment about when to use and when not to use calculators. *Everyday Mathematics* supports children's need to learn how to decide when it is appropriate to solve an arithmetic problem by estimating or calculating mentally, by using paper and pencil, or by using a calculator. The evidence indicates that children who use calculators are able to choose appropriately.

> **NOTE:** Neither the TI-108 nor the Casio SL-450 is required to use *Everyday Mathematics*. Any 4-function calculator will suffice.

Calculator A: the TI-108

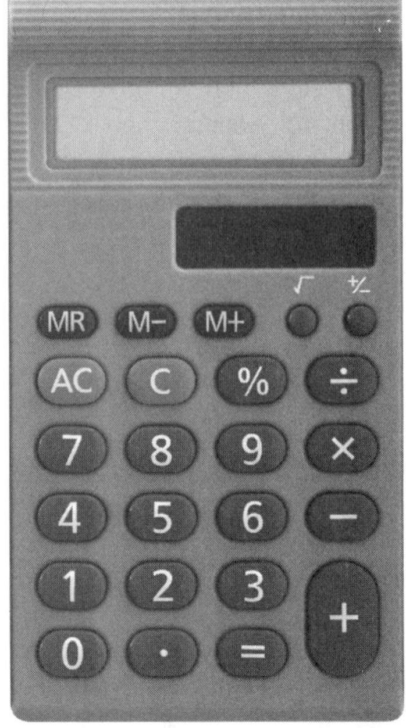

Calculator B: the Casio SL-450

Everyday Mathematics encourages children to think about developing algorithms as they solve problems. To foster this habit of mind, children need to study particular paper-and-pencil algorithms; but once the algorithms are understood, repeated use becomes tedious. One reason that calculators are so helpful in the mathematics curriculum is that they free both children and teachers from having to spend so much time on dull, repetitive, and unproductive tasks. Calculators also allow children to solve interesting, everyday problems requiring computations that might otherwise be too difficult for them to perform, including problems that arise outside of mathematics class. There is no evidence to suggest that this will cause children to become dependent on calculators or make them unable to solve problems mentally or with paper and pencil.

Before the availability of inexpensive calculators, the elementary school mathematics curriculum was designed primarily so that children would become skilled at carrying out paper-and-pencil algorithms. Thus, there was little time left for children to learn to think mathematically and solve problems. Calculators enable children to think about the problems themselves rather than focusing on carrying out algorithms without mistakes.

How the Authors Used Calculators when Writing *Everyday Mathematics*

In the second edition of *Everyday Mathematics,* one calculator was chosen as representative of all calculators for Kindergarten through Grade 3 materials and another for Grades 4 through 6. This choice allowed the authors to give examples of specific key sequences for a variety of calculations. However, having just one representative calculator led authors to explain features that were available only on the chosen machine and not on most other available calculators. To present a more balanced view, the third edition features key sequences for *two* widely available calculators.

By choosing two calculators, the authors have been able to define a "generic" calculator to support *Everyday Mathematics.* Only those functions that are on *both* calculators, and so likely to be on any other comparable calculator, are considered to be generic tools for problem solving.

For Kindergarten through Grade 3, the authors used TI-108 and Casio SL-450 4-function calculators. Both calculators offer the same functions. However, not all keys for common functions are the same on both machines, so *Everyday Mathematics* presents key sequences for both. Because of this, you should be able to find the help you need to use any 4-function calculator.

For political and other reasons, some schools cannot use student materials that mention specific brand names of products. Therefore, in *My Reference Book* and the *Student Reference Book,* the TI-108 is called "Calculator A" and the Casio SL-450 is called "Calculator B." Reminders of this convention are also given at appropriate places in the *Teacher's Lesson Guide*.

Types of Calculators

As with all electronic technology, the types of calculators and features they contain are always changing. There are calculators that print on paper; send data via infrared beam to computers or other calculators; and draw pictures, graphs, and geometric constructions. Who knows what they'll do tomorrow? At this writing, there are five general types of calculators: 4-function, scientific, fraction, and graphic calculators; and calculators bundled with computer, personal digital assistant (PDA), and cell-phone operating systems. Scientific and fraction calculators are used in *Fourth* through *Sixth Grade Everyday Mathematics,* but only the 4-function machines that children use in Kindergarten through Grade 3 are discussed here.

Four-Function Calculators These calculators originally got their name because all they did was add, subtract, multiply, and divide. Today, however, it is difficult to find a recently manufactured 4-function calculator that does only the four basic arithmetic operations. Most have at least a percent key and often a square-root key. Even most of the "credit card" calculators that are given as promotional items have a percent key. So today, 4-function calculators usually do more than four functions, but they are still referred to by that name.

NOTE: As recently as the mid-1960s, a 4-function calculator cost hundreds of dollars.

NOTE: Although most calculators have a percent key, the key does not necessarily work the same way on all of them. Students in Grades 4 through 6 learn about ways that different calculators find percents.

The authors encourage you to be less concerned with the number of available functions than with how a 4-function calculator works. Some 4-function calculators are programmed to follow the *algebraic order of operations,* while others are not. To find out whether or not a calculator is an algebraic calculator, try the following test:

- Enter 10 [−] 2 [×] 4 [=] into your calculator.
- If the result is 32, it is *not* an algebraic calculator.
- If the result is 2, it *is* an algebraic calculator.

A nonalgebraic calculator does the operations in the order they were entered: $10 - 2 = 8$ and $8 \times 4 = 32$. An algebraic calculator multiplies the 2 and 4 first and subtracts the result, 8, from 10. Both the TI-108 and Casio SL-450 are nonalgebraic calculators.

For more information on the order of operations, see Section 10.1.2: Reading and Writing Number Sentences.

Computer, PDA, and Cell-Phone Calculators There are several calculator applications or programs that run on computers. When you run the application, it looks like a calculator on the screen. MacOS X, Windows XP, Palm OS, and some cell-phone operating systems each come with a built-in calculator. Four-function-type calculator programs have been standard features of most computer operating systems since personal computers were invented. If you use computers with children, you might want to check if a 4-function calculator program is available and use the preceding comments to help determine how it works.

Calculator Basics and Key Sequences

Children begin using calculators in *Kindergarten Everyday Mathematics* both to display numbers and to count. If your class has had no previous experience with calculators, you may want to begin with a period of free exploration and then use some of the introductory exercises provided in the next section as a warm-up.

As with any tool, proper and effective use of a calculator requires instruction. Research has shown that without instruction, children using calculators do not calculate any better than children not using them. Whenever an operation that can be performed on a calculator is introduced, *Everyday Mathematics* includes an activity that introduces the new calculator key(s). It is recommended that you draw the new key(s) on the board or on an overhead transparency.

The order in which keys are pressed to perform a calculation is called a *key sequence.* In *Everyday Mathematics* key sequences, function keys such as [+] and [−] are written with square brackets or shown as pictures of actual keys. Numbers, including decimals, are not. For example, a key sequence to calculate 12 − 3 + 5 is 12 [−] 3 [+] 5 [=]. The authors recommend that you also use the square-bracket notation and encourage children to follow it when they are asked to write key sequences. Encouraging children to "discover" an appropriate key sequence is a suitable activity at any grade level and fits well into the *Everyday Mathematics* philosophy.

Using calculators may require children to learn alternative symbols for operations. For example, [/] means division on some calculators, but it is used to enter fractions on others. Also, not all calculators follow the conventional order of operations. For these and other reasons, it's advisable to try calculator activities ahead of time. Use the same model calculator the children use so that you will be familiar with all symbols and key sequences involved. Use your owner's manual to find answers to questions not addressed here or in the *Teacher's Lesson Guide*.

Introductory Exercises

Children who have had previous experience with calculators are wonderful resources for helping inexperienced children. Use the following exercises with first-time users or with small groups of children who have never used calculators.

> **NOTE:** Short-term memory is called remote access memory (RAM) on computers. Some people also refer to it as "available memory."

Entering and Clearing When you press a calculator key, some instruction or number is entered into memory. Almost all calculators have two kinds of memory, which in *Everyday Mathematics* are called *short-term* and *long-term* memory. Short-term memory stores the last number or function you pressed until you press [=]. Long-term memory stores numbers for later calculations using keys with an M on them.

FRANK & ERNEST® by Bob Thaves

Perhaps the simplest entry into a calculator is to turn it on. Another simple entry is to clear numbers from the display and short-term memory. When the calculator is cleared, you should see "0." in the display. Here are the keys and their purposes for the two calculators the authors used while writing the third edition of *Everyday Mathematics.*

TI-108	
Key	**Purpose**
ON/C	Turn the display on.
ON/C	Clear the display and short-term memory.

Casio SL-450	
Key	**Purpose**
C	Turn the display on.
AC	Clear the display and short-term memory.
AC	Clear the last entry during a calculation.

NOTE: In the third grade *Student Reference Book* and first and second grade *My Reference Book*, the TI-108 is Calculator A and the Casio SL-450 is Calculator B.

NOTE: None of the keys at left clear the long-term memory.

NOTE: "C" means "Clear"; "AC" means "All Clear"; "CE" means "Clear Entry."

Both calculators turn themselves off after a few minutes, so neither has an OFF key. If your calculator has an OFF key, it is wise to use it to avoid draining the battery.

Tell children that keys marked [ON/C], [AC], [C], or, on some calculators, [CE/C] function like erasers. Ask them to imagine that they are erasing a chalkboard so they can begin again. It is important for children to get into the habit of clearing the calculator at the beginning of each new calculator exercise. If they do not, they may obtain incorrect results.

Displaying and Reading Numbers One way to introduce calculator exploration is to ask *What if . . .?* questions. For example:

- What will happen if you do not press [ON/C] or [AC] before you start a new calculation? *(The new calculation might use a number already entered.)*
- What number will be in the display window if you press 3? *(3)*
- What number will be in the display if you press 3 again without first clearing the calculator? *(33)*
- What number will appear if you press 3 again? *(333)* And again? *(3333)*

Children can enter numbers they are able to read and then ask classmates to read the numbers in the displays. Some children may also want to display large numbers that they are unable to read; help them read some of these large numbers.

NOTE: Children in *Kindergarten* through *Third Grade Everyday Mathematics* "program" their calculators to skip count. For more information, see Section 11.3: Algorithms on Calculators.

Interpreting the Display

Calculators compute with programmed algorithms; they do not solve problems. The user must know which keys to press and how to interpret the results. As with any technology, calculators have their own unique challenges when it comes to displaying results.

Calculators often display more digits than are warranted in the context of a problem. For the primary grades, it's enough for children to be aware that not all the digits that a calculator displays are meaningful. A rule of thumb is that answers can have as many

NOTE: More advanced calculators have a *fix* function to fix the number of decimal places displayed. So fixing the display to two digits means that all decimals will be displayed as dollars and cents without the dollar sign.

meaningful digits as the original numbers. So if the numbers you calculate with have two digits each, then probably only the two leftmost digits in the calculator display are significant.

Another challenge is that calculators sometimes display fewer digits than are expected. For example, suppose a calculator is used to find the value of 36 nickels. The key sequence 36 [×] .05 [=] leads to a display of 1.8, not $1.80 or even 1.80. This cutting off, or *truncating,* of trailing zeros to the right of the decimal point can be confusing to beginning calculator users.

Perhaps the greatest challenge to interpreting calculator results is common to all forms of calculation, including paper-and-pencil algorithms. That is, sometimes the result is nonsense in the context of the problem being solved. Reasons for a nonsensical calculator result might include:

- The calculator wasn't properly cleared.
- A number or operation was entered incorrectly.
- The analysis of the problem was faulty and incorrect calculations were made.

Whatever the reason, sometimes a calculator's answer just doesn't make sense. When this happens, a user must determine whether an answer is reasonable by asking whether it makes sense in terms of the original problem situation just as he or she must after using paper and pencil or mental arithmetic.

Resources on Calculators

Campbell, P. F., and Stewart, E. L. (1993). "Calculators and Computers." In Jensen, R. (Ed.) *Research Ideas for the Classroom: Early Childhood Mathematics.* New York: Macmillan.

Demana, F., and Leitzel, J. (1988). "Establishing Fundamental Concepts Through Numerical Problem Solving." In Coxford, A. F., and Shulte, A. P. (Eds.) *The Ideas of Algebra, K–12: 1988 Yearbook.* Reston, VA: National Council of Teachers of Mathematics.

Groves, S., and Kaye, S. (1998). "Calculators in Primary Mathematics: Exploring Numbers before Teaching Algorithms." Morrow, L. J. (Ed.) *The Teaching and Learning of Algorithms in School Mathematics.* Reston, VA: National Council of Teachers of Mathematics.

Ellington, A. J. (2003). "A Meta-Analysis of the Effects of Calculators on Children's Achievement and Attitude Levels in Precollege Mathematics Classes." *Journal for Research in Mathematics Education 34(5)*: pp. 433–463.

Hembree, R., and Dessart, D. J. (1992). "Research on Calculators in Mathematics Education." In Fey, J. T., and Hirsch, C. R., (Eds.) *Calculators in Mathematics Education: 1992 Yearbook.* Reston, VA: National Council of Teachers of Mathematics.

National Council of Teachers of Mathematics. (2005). *Position Statement: Calculators, Computation, and Common Sense.* Reston, VA: Author. Retrieved from www.nctm.org/about/position_statements/computation.htm

National Council of Teachers of Mathematics. (2003). *Position Statement: The Use of Technology in the Learning and Teaching of Mathematics.* Reston, VA: Author. Retrieved from www.nctm.org/about/position_statements/position_statement_13.htm

National Council of Teachers of Mathematics. (1998). *Position Statement: Calculators and the Education of Youth.* Reston, VA: Author. Retrieved from www.nctm.org/about/position_statements/position_statement_01.htm

Smith, B. A. (1997). "A Meta-Analysis of Outcomes from the Use of Calculators in Mathematics Education." *Dissertation Abstracts International 58:787A.*

Waits, B. K., and Demana, F. (2000). "Calculators in Mathematics Teaching and Learning: Past, Present, and Future." In Burke, M. J., and Curcio, F. R. (Eds.) *Learning Mathematics for a New Century: 2000 Yearbook.* Reston, VA: National Council of Teachers of Mathematics.

3.1.2 Computers

Because computer access and availability vary widely across the United States, computer-based activities are currently not integrated into the core curriculum of *First* through *Third Grade Everyday Mathematics.*

Many existing software programs can be used with *Everyday Mathematics.* Some of these software programs are designed as instructional tools that can be used by teachers to model, demonstrate, or explain mathematical concepts. Children can use other software for concept development, practice, enrichment, motivation, and exploration.

NOTE: Optional computer activities are included in *Fourth* through *Sixth Grade Everyday Mathematics*. For example, students may work with spreadsheets in Grade 6 activities.

3.1.3 The Internet

As the Internet has become more widely available to the public and to schools, *Everyday Mathematics* has incorporated it into the program in a modest way. This section lists Web sites that seem destined to survive over the years and that supplement activities in a substantive way. At this writing, these include the Web sites listed in the following tables.

Mathematics Web Sites: Cross-Grade Resources

Organization	Web Site
UCSMP *Everyday Mathematics* Center	everydaymath.uchicago.edu
National Council of Teachers of Mathematics (NCTM)	www.nctm.org
The Math Forum	mathforum.org
Shell Centre	www.nottingham.ac.uk/education/shell

Mathematics Web Sites: Second-Grade Resources

Organization	Web Site
Yahoo! Search: Chinese New Year	dir.yahoo.com/Society_and_Culture/Cultures_ and_Groups/Cultures/Chinese/Holidays_and_Observances/Chinese_New_Year
Cosmic time capsule	www.iuinfo.indiana.edu/HomePages/120498/text/cosmic.htm

management guide

Mathematics Web Sites: Third-Grade Resources	
Organization	**Web Site**
Environmental Kids Club	www.epa.gov/kids
M.C. escher	etropolis.com/escher/index.html
National Watermelon Promotion Board	www.watermelon.org
SandLotScience	www.sandlotscience.com
Sunrise, Sunset Calendars and Local Time	www.sunrisesunset.com

3.2 Topical Tools

There is a variety of conceptual devices, manipulatives, and other tools that children use to help them understand *Everyday Mathematics* topics. This section summarizes them and discusses some management strategies. More information on each tool is then found in the last section of appropriate Mathematical Strands and Threads chapters.

3.2.1 Number and Counting Tools

Base-10 Blocks

For more information, see Section 9.7.1: Base-10 Blocks.

In *Everyday Mathematics,* children use base-10 blocks starting in first grade. Although these blocks have a variety of names, it helps to have a common vocabulary for discussions and written work with the blocks. In *Everyday Mathematics,* the following names are used: *cube* for the smaller 1-cm cube, *long* for the block consisting of ten 1-cm cubes (1 × 10), *flat* for the block consisting of one hundred 1-cm cubes (10 × 10), and *big cube* for the larger cube consisting of one thousand 1-cm cubes (10 × 10 × 10).

Sometimes you may want to make a written record of work with base-10 blocks. The shorthand shown below is handy for drawing quick pictures of base-10 blocks. Such pictures are often more convenient to use than are the actual blocks, especially the larger blocks, and can be useful for explaining and recording solutions.

2,045 in "base-10 shorthand"

Base-10-Block Shorthand		
Name	**Block**	**Shorthand**
cube		
long		
flat		
big cube		

Number Grids, Scrolls, and Lines

A *number grid* consists of rows of boxes, usually ten in each row, containing consecutive integers (positive and negative whole numbers).

−9	−8	−7	−6	−5	−4	−3	−2	−1	0
1	2	3	4	5	6	7	8	9	10
11	12	13	14	15	16	17	18	19	20
21	22	23	24	25	26	27	28	29	30
31	32	33	34	35	36	37	38	39	40
41	42	43	44	45	46	47	48	49	50
51	52	53	54	55	56	57	58	59	60
61	62	63	64	65	66	67	68	69	70
71	72	73	74	75	76	77	78	79	80
81	82	83	84	85	86	87	88	89	90
91	92	93	94	95	96	97	98	99	100
101	102	103	104	105	106	107	108	109	110

Number grids have many wonderful features that can help children with pattern recognition and place value. However, their original use in *Everyday Mathematics* was simply to solve the problem of number lines being unmanageably long. Number lines can be cumbersome even when stretched along a classroom wall, and it is nearly impossible to print them in children's books without breaking them into chunks. Number grids may be considered number lines that fit nicely on a page or a classroom poster.

Number scrolls are extended number grids. You can make them by adding single sheets of 100 numbers to existing sheets, either forward (positively) or backward (negatively).

A *number line* is a line on which points are indicated by *tick marks* that are usually at regularly spaced intervals from a starting point called the *origin,* the *zero point,* or simply 0. Numbers are associated with the tick marks, and the interval from 0 to 1 on the line is called the *unit interval.*

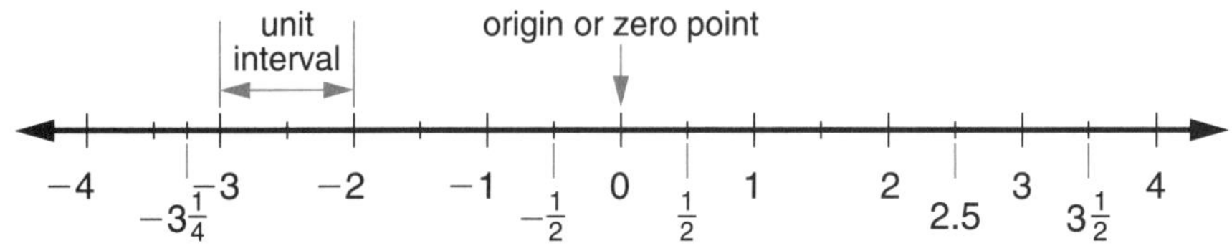

Children use number lines when counting and skip counting, performing measuring activities, and adding and subtracting. Number lines are also used as the axes in coordinate graphing systems.

For more information, see Section 9.7.2: Number Grids, Scrolls, and Lines.

3.2.2 Operations and Number-Models Tools

There are three main tools that children use to develop their skills for problem solving with operations and number models: paper-and-pencil algorithms, situation diagrams, and calculators. The summaries here are intended to put each tool in context. In-depth discussions of them are found in other parts of this manual as indicated by margin references.

Paper-and-Pencil Algorithms

An *algorithm* is a well-defined, step-by-step procedure guaranteed to achieve a certain objective, often with several steps that "loop" as many times as necessary. For example, an algorithm for multiplication will produce the correct product no matter what the factors are.

During the early phases of learning an operation, *Everyday Mathematics* encourages children to invent their own algorithms. Children are asked to solve arithmetic problems from first principles about situations in which operations are used, before they develop or learn systematic procedures for solving such problems. This helps them to understand the operations better and also gives them valuable experience solving nonroutine problems.

Later, when children thoroughly understand the concept of the operation, several alternative algorithms are introduced. Some of these algorithms are based on approaches that many children devise on their own. Others are less likely to be discovered by children but have a variety of desirable characteristics. Children are urged to experiment with various algorithms in order to become proficient at using at least one alternative.

For more information, see Chapter 11: Algorithms.

Everyday Mathematics designates one of the alternative algorithms for each operation as a *focus algorithm*. Focus algorithms are powerful, relatively efficient, and easy to understand and learn. All children are expected to learn the focus algorithm for each operation. In solving problems, however, children may use either the focus algorithm or any other methods they choose. The aim of this approach is to promote flexibility while ensuring that all children know at least one reliable method for each operation.

Situation Diagrams

For more information, see Section 10.2: Use Classes and Situation Diagrams.

In *Everyday Mathematics,* children are encouraged to use *situation diagrams* to help them sort the information in simple 1-step number stories. Examples include the *parts-and-total, comparison, change,* and *rate* situations diagramed below. Diagrams do not have to be fancy, and you can omit or change words, as in the rate diagram.

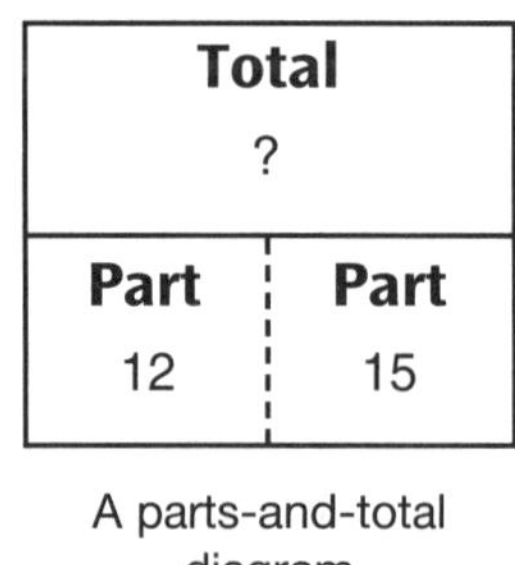

A parts-and-total diagram

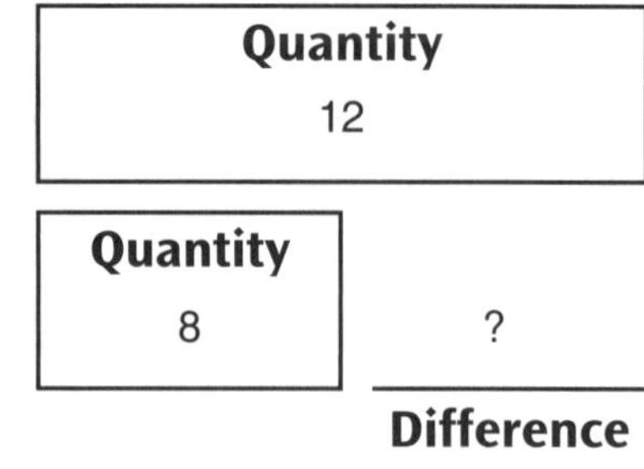

A comparison diagram

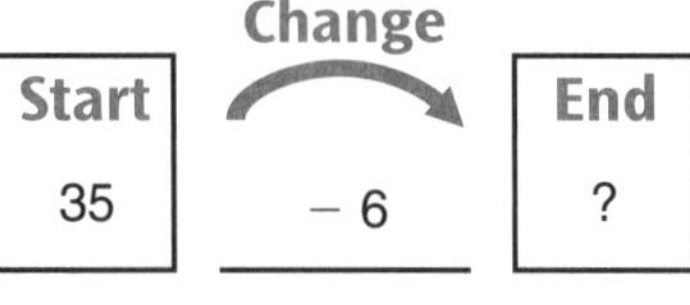

A change diagram

children	cards per child	cards
4	?	24

A rate diagram

Calculator Operations

Four-function calculators get their name from a shared ability to calculate using the four basic arithmetic operations: addition, subtraction, multiplication and division. Beginning in Kindergarten, *Everyday Mathematics* expects children to learn to operate calculators, to check results for correctness, and to think about whether using a calculator is appropriate or not. In Grade 4, students begin using scientific calculators.

For more information, see Section 3.1.1: Calculators.

3.2.3 Data and Chance Tools

Everyday Mathematics uses a variety of devices to generate random outcomes. These tools are integral to the success of many games. Often these devices do not generate perfectly random outcomes, but they are good enough for most purposes.

Random-Number Generators

Dice Use a regular die to generate the numbers 1 through 6. Use a polyhedral die (with 12 or 20 sides) to extend the range of numbers to be generated. Note that rolling more than one die and adding the resulting numbers of dots produces a *nonuniform distribution* of possible outcomes. For example, if you roll two standard dice, there are 36 possible ways for them to land.

For an example of a nonuniform distribution, see Section 12.4.1: Random-Number Generators.

Egg Cartons Label each egg-carton cup with a number. For example, you might label the cups 0 through 11. Place one or more pennies, beans, or centimeter cubes inside the carton, close the lid, shake the carton, and then open it to see in which cups the objects have landed. Randomness depends on how thoroughly the carton is shaken. This is probably the least random method of this list.

The Everything Math Deck This deck of cards consists of four sets of number cards 0 through 10 and one set of number cards 11 through 20. Fractions are on the reverse side of the 0 through 10 cards. You can limit the range of numbers to be generated simply by removing some of the cards from the deck. For a uniform distribution of the numbers 0 through 20, for example, use only one set of 0 through 10 cards and the set of 11 through 20 cards. To use the cards, simply shuffle and draw. The better the shuffle, the more unpredictable the draw will be.

You can transform an ordinary deck of 54 playing cards to function like the whole-number side of an Everything Math Deck as follows:

- Change the four queens to 0s.
- Remove the four jacks, four kings, and two jokers. Label each of these ten cards with one of the numbers from 11 through 20.
- Change the four aces to 1s.
- Let all number cards represent their face value.

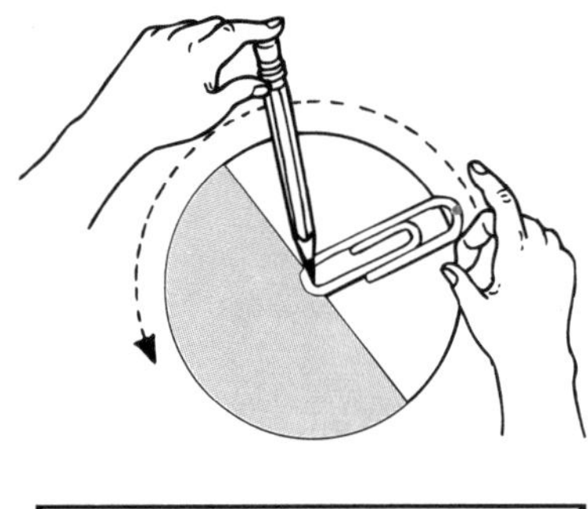

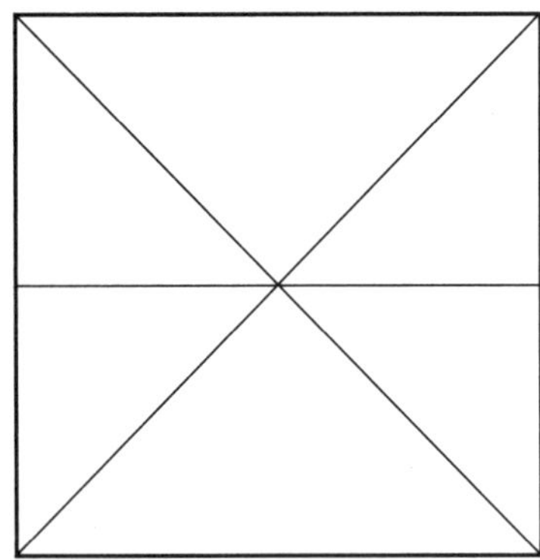

Spinners Spinners are used throughout *Everyday Mathematics,* usually in games. They are extremely useful for helping children visualize the idea of chance. There are many commercially available spinners, though it is not necessary to purchase them. Children can use a pencil and paper clip with a spinner mat as shown in the margin. Use either a large (about 2-inch) or standard (about 1-inch) paper clip for the part that spins. The larger size is preferred because it spins more easily. Make a mark as a pointer at one end of the paper clip using a permanent felt-tip marker.

The spinning mat may be drawn on cardstock or paper. Sometimes a mat is supplied as a master or journal page. If you make your own mat, start with a circle or square large enough to accommodate the paper clip. Mark the center of the circle, choose the number and sizes of the regions, and then measure and draw the appropriate angles. For example, six equal-sized regions would each measure $360° \div 6 = 60°$. You can use shapes other than circles for a spinner, and the regions do not have to be the same size, as in the square mat in the margin.

Before spinning, tape the mat to a level surface. You need only two small pieces of tape, one at the top and one at the bottom. To spin, place the tip of a pen or pencil on the center of the circle and within the paper clip as shown in the diagram. Flick the paper clip about halfway between the center of the circle and the tip of the paper clip, as flicking the paper clip near the pointer end will generate less of a spin.

Standard Playing Cards Use the 2 through 9 cards, the aces for 1s, and the queens for 0s. Draw one card to get a 1-in-10 chance for each one of the digits 0 through 9. Draw two cards to make 2-digit numbers, three cards for 3-digit numbers, and so on. If more than one card is drawn, you will need to decide whether to replace it before another card is drawn. If the first card is replaced in the deck and the deck is reshuffled, the probability will remain the same for each draw. If the card is not replaced, the chance of drawing that digit decreases.

3.2.4 Geometry Tools

There are many objects that can be used to explore geometric ideas, ranging from objects found around the house such as shoeboxes or marbles to elaborate kits sold by curriculum supply companies. Three simple tools that are readily available and relatively easy to manage are highlighted here.

Pattern-Block Templates

Pattern-Block Templates are used for exploring plane figures. Children are encouraged to use the templates to make designs in Explorations, Projects, and some lessons. For example, in first grade, children are asked to estimate how many triangles, squares, or other figures it will take to "fill up" a piece of paper. They check their guesses by drawing the shapes using the template. This informal introduction to area develops valuable background for formal definitions later. Children in Kindergarten through third grade also use their Pattern-Block Templates, rather than compasses, to draw circles.

Pattern Blocks and Geometric Solids

Pattern blocks help children learn the names and features of geometric objects. In Kindergarten and first grade, children identify categories of shapes and colors of pattern blocks. Beginning in first grade, children are encouraged to find different ways of categorizing blocks on their own, that is, to create multiple perspectives of a given set of blocks. This ability to think about the same things in different ways is important for many problem-solving activities. Science educators also identify classification as one of the most important processes of science.

For more information, see Section 13.4: Planes and Plane Figures and Section 13.5: Space and 3-D Figures.

Kindergarten Everyday Mathematics introduces children to measurement, in part, through the use of geometric solids and building blocks. In later grades, children use both metric and U.S. customary rulers to measure the lengths of block edges and the heights and lengths of structures they build using several blocks. Such uses of models of geometric solids continue through third grade as a basis for the study of 1- and 2-dimensional geometry.

Straws and Twist-Ties

Constructing 2- and 3-dimensional objects with straws and twist-ties is a popular activity beginning in *First Grade Everyday Mathematics.*

Teachers find that most children have little trouble constructing polygons with straws and connectors. The ends of the ties may need to be pinched a little to slide into the straws. If you have to use large-diameter straws, fold back an inch or so of the end of the connector for a tighter joint. To keep the size of polygons with more than five sides to sensible limits, use shorter straws. Except for triangles, polygons are easily twisted so that they don't lie "flat." When they are not lying flat, the figures are no longer in a plane and are no longer 2-dimensional figures. Have children make polygons on flat surfaces and encourage them to try to keep the polygons flat when picking them up.

For 3-dimensional figures, children can begin by putting two connectors, or one folded connector, into one end of a straw so that it can be connected to two other straws. When more than three straws need to meet at a vertex, additional connectors may be inserted as needed, or children can first connect several pairs of straws and then make a bundle of one straw from each pair held together with an additional connector.

For more information, see Section 13.10.3: Straws and Twist-Ties.

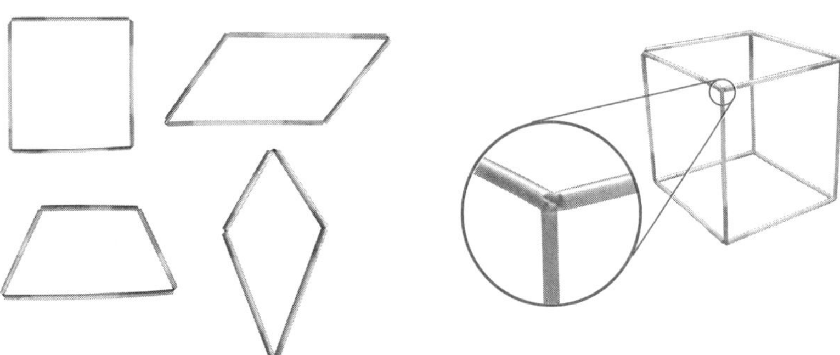

Straw constructions

3.2.5 Measuring Tools

Children in *Kindergarten* through *Third Grade Everyday Mathematics* use a wide variety of informal and formal tools for measuring. The informal ones, including body parts such as hands and feet or the edges of their journals, are relatively easy to manage. This section discusses some of the more formal, or *standardized,* measuring tools.

Rulers and Tape Measures

Children are introduced to standard units of measurement in Kindergarten, and rulers and tape measures are among the first tools children use. If the children use retractable tape measures, teach and enforce the "2-inch, 5-centimeter no-zap rule": Do not "zap" the tape measure until no more than 2 inches or 5 centimeters show. This will extend the life of these tools, as well as make your own life quieter and easier.

For more information, see Section 14.10.2: Rulers and Tape Measures and Section 14.10.3: Scales and Balances.

Scales and Balances

A scale is another historically old measuring tool. *Scales* are used to measure how heavy things are according to a standard weight. Different scales are used for different purposes, both in everyday life and in *Everyday Mathematics*.

Everyday Mathematics provides activities calling for children to weigh and then order objects by weight using pan balances, bathroom scales, and spring scales. Children use balances primarily in Explorations because of the limited supply of such tools. Activities begin with informal play in Kindergarten, when children first compare weights with their own hands and then with pan balances.

In first grade, pan balances are used to introduce the symbols for relations such as $<$, $>$, and $=$. Through third grade, children write number models using these symbols.

3.3 Tool Kits

A tool kit is designed to give children a sense of independence by giving them immediate access to basic tools. Every child in Kindergarten through Grade 3 can benefit by having a tool kit in which to store a calculator, measuring tools, and the manipulatives that are used throughout the year. Tools may be stored in the zippered bags especially designed for the *Everyday Mathematics* program or in some other container, such as a wooden box or a recloseable plastic bag. Use a permanent marker to write identification numbers on tool kits and on the nonconsumable items in the tool kits.

Early in the year, distribute tool kits with a few needed items. Hand out other items later, when they are first used in classroom activities. Eventually, the tool kit may contain a tape measure, ruler, calculator, play money, real coins, Pattern-Block Template, clock face, tangrams, dice, and other small items.

Encourage children to take care of their tool kits and to store each tool after use so that it is there when needed again. This practice will help children to develop a sense of responsibility that may be carried over to other activities. A periodic check of the contents might be a good idea, especially before vacation periods. You might also want to keep a classroom lost-and-found box.

4 Organizing Children

The following sections outline ideas for managing your classroom as children do mathematics.

4.1 Cooperative Groupings

Cooperative learning helps children by:

- Improving attitudes toward learning and academic achievement;
- Improving social skills and time spent on task;
- Helping develop speaking, listening, and writing skills;
- Creating an atmosphere for sharing ideas and problem-solving strategies that they may not have discovered on their own;
- Preparing them for real-life situations in which people often share responsibilities with others and need to cooperate and work together toward common goals.

The next few sections give suggestions for forming and managing partnerships and small groups.

Groups and Partnerships

For simplicity, the word *group* is used to refer to both partners and small groups. Learning becomes a dynamic process during group activities, as interaction among group members encourages an inquisitive spirit and introduces new avenues for exploration while instilling a spirit of teamwork.

Because *Everyday Mathematics* provides many group activities, both teacher-directed and independent, you may want to plan seating arrangements accordingly so that children can make the transition from whole-class work to group work with minimal disruption.

Use careful thought and planning when assigning children to groups. The best lessons can fail if groups are poorly formed. Having children work with their best friends does not always create a constructive learning environment. And if teams are formed at random, for example, children with the lowest skill levels could all end up in one group. Along with your personal knowledge of each child's skill level, the following teacher-tested strategies may be helpful:

- Make groups heterogeneous with regard to skill, gender, and race or ethnicity. The mixed achievement levels within groups allow for peer tutoring. Randomly selected groups or special-interest groups can be formed occasionally to vary the learning experience, but heterogeneous groupings usually work best.

- To arrange the class into groups, list the children from highest to lowest skill or achievement level. Take one student from the beginning of the list, one from the end, and two from the middle to form each group. When it is necessary to break a team into partners, match high with medium or medium with low achievers.
- A good size for small groups is four children, which also allows for pairs working together within the group. If the number of children is not divisible by 4, place one or two remaining children in a group that will best fit their needs. If three children remain, form another group.
- Keep group assignments for about six weeks. If situations impede a group's progress, make changes as necessary.

Team Building and Group Etiquette

For children to work cooperatively in groups, there often needs to be a team-building process to establish the team's identity, spirit, and responsibility to one another. If children don't know one another, "getting to know you" activities can help. For example, have children make lists of likes and dislikes, and then have them look for differences and common interests.

Even though children have worked in groups before, it is important that you take time during the first few weeks of school to review partner and small-group etiquette. The value of group study is diminished if social interaction replaces purposeful learning.

Post the three basic principles of constructive partner and group interaction: *Guide, Check,* and *Praise*. Then, during the first few days of the year, have children share what they think these terms mean. Guide the discussion to cover the following points:

Partnership Principles

1. Guide
2. Check
3. Praise

Guide

- Help and demonstrate what to do without telling or doing everything yourself.
- Take turns.
- Choose only one student to get help from the teacher if the group needs it.

Check

- Pay attention and listen to others.
- If someone makes a mistake, respond positively in a helpful way. (Supply a list of helpful phrases such as *Try again, Good try,* and *Close.*)
- Help fellow group members find correct responses.

Praise

- Let others know they are doing a good job.
- Praise others. (Help children compile a list of appropriate praise words and phrases.)

To establish a positive learning environment, have children brainstorm with you about a good set of general rules of behavior. Post these rules on the bulletin board so that you can refer children to them as needed. Such rules might include the following:

- Be polite to one another.
- Use quiet voices.
- Talk about problems, but don't argue.
- Do not let others do all of the work.
- Share materials.
- Move quietly.

Duties of Group Members

Each group member may be assigned a specific role that changes daily or weekly. Some roles can be eliminated or modified depending on the activity and grade level. This list suggests possible roles and duties:

Recorder Writes group answers and strategies used; can also act as the reporter for the group.

Reader Reads problems, text selections, directions, and so on.

Facilitator Makes sure that everyone is on task and encourages participation from each group member. Uses positive encouragement such as the following:

- *We need to work on problem 3.*
- *Which step is next?*

Gatekeeper Makes sure one person does not monopolize the activity and ensures equal participation. Uses positive questions such as the following:

- *Denise, how would you do this?*
- *Do you agree, Eric?*
- *What do you think, Shawna?*

Materials/Supply Handler Gathers and returns all materials needed for group activities.

Summarizer Sums up group solutions, opinions, or findings.

Duties of the Teacher

You may also want to share with children some specific classroom roles for the teacher such as those in the following list:

- Explains the activity.
- Monitors groups to make sure they are working in the right direction and that behavior is appropriate.
- Answers group questions and assists as necessary.
- Assesses group/individual skills.
- Provides closure for each lesson or activity.

Resources for Cooperative Learning

Artzt, A. F., and Newman, C. M. (1997). *How to Use Cooperative Learning in the Mathematics Class (Second Edition).* Reston, VA: National Council of Teachers of Mathematics.

Adrini, B., and Kagan, S. (1992). *Cooperative Learning and Mathematics.* San Juan Capistrano, CA: Kagan Cooperative Learning.

Johnson, D. W., and Johnson, R. T. (1991). *Learning Mathematics and Cooperative Learning.* Edina, MN: Interaction Book Company.

Johnson, D. W., Johnson, R. T., and Holubec, E. J. (1994). *The Nuts and Bolts of Cooperative Learning.* Edina, MN: Interaction Book Company.

Kagan, S. (1992). *Cooperative Learning.* San Juan Capistrano, CA: Kagan Cooperative Learning.

Shulman, J. H., Lotan, R. A., and Whitcomb, J. A. (Eds.) (1998). *Groupwork in Diverse Classrooms: A Casebook for Educators.* New York: Teachers College Press.

4.2 Group Responses

For more information, see Section 1.2.6: Mental Math and Reflexes.

Just as choral readings have proven beneficial for beginning readers, group-response techniques such as plain and fancy counting, calculator counting, and fact reviews can be equally beneficial for primary grade mathematics learners. Many Mental Math and Reflexes activities require group responses.

Group-response activities allow all children to participate at their own levels without being put on the spot. More-skilled children have the opportunity to lead while others hear them and are thereby strengthened in the concepts in which they are weak.

Establish a brisk rhythm, with responses given simultaneously and clearly. Keep group-response activities brief. If you have children work in small groups or sit around tables, you can focus on one group at a time, even if the whole class is responding. This will help you identify children who may need extra help.

4.3 Ideas for "Built-In" Mathematics

Teachers who piloted the *Everyday Mathematics* program contributed the following suggestions:

- When disputes between two children arise that could be settled in either one's favor, have each child choose a number between 1 and 100. Pick a number yourself and tell it to a third party or write it down secretly. Explain that the one who guesses closest to your number will be the "winner." After settling the issue, ask questions such as *Is this fair? What makes it fair?* You can extend or limit the range of numbers as appropriate for the situation or the grade level.
- Whenever the opportunity to choose an option presents itself, have the children vote. Tell them to vote for what they want but that they can vote only once. Be sure they understand that the option

receiving the most votes is the one by which they all must abide. Children can then tally, count, and compare totals. In the case of ties, ask the children to suggest a fair way to proceed.

- When you give directions, quantify as often as you can. For example, *Six children may use the Reading Corner, and five may use the Math Center.*
- Whenever possible, have children line up according to specified categories such as *everyone wearing something red, everyone wearing a belt,* or *everyone wearing brown shoes.*
- Alternatively, have children line up without revealing the category to them. For this version of "What's My Rule?" determine a category and then call out the names of children who fit the category. Then ask the class to explain why you chose those particular children. Don't insist on your rule if children see one that is equally valid. You might say *What I had in mind was . . ., but yours works, too,* or *I didn't think of yours.*
- Use lining-up activities to teach ordinal numbers. For example, have children line up and then give them directions such as *The first, second, and third children may walk to the door. The seventh child may walk to the door. The fourth child who walked to the door may sit down.*
- During the first few days of school, when books and supplies are distributed, you can use these distribution tasks to have children practice counting, make one-to-one correspondences, and do simple mental arithmetic operations. For example, ask someone to count the children in a row, at a table, or in a group, and then ask how many of each item being passed out will be needed so that every child will have one. Or you could ask a member of the group to figure out how many items their group will need before each distribution. Another idea is to give more or less than required of an item to a small group of children. After they have distributed the items among themselves, ask each group to describe the results. Encourage them to verbalize any problems with dialog such as *We needed __, but you gave us __. That's __ too many.*
- Dice and spinners are good random-number generators. You can make nonstandard dice by putting self-sticking number labels on standard dice or wooden cubes. Vary the numbers to make new games.
- When minor decisions need to be made or when you can't think of a way to perform a particular task, take a few minutes to have children think about the problem. Discuss their ideas, as they are often great. This also gives children a chance to solve real problems.
- If you have a Math Center, don't let it get too cluttered. Introduce new items and remove old ones to maintain children's interest.

5 Organizing Daily Routines and Displays

Most classes have routines for daily activities such as taking attendance or keeping track of the date. *Everyday Mathematics* strongly suggests that children take an active part in these routines, which provide many examples of mathematics in everyday contexts. The following sections contain general advice and tips from fellow teachers.

Semipermanent Chalk, a Useful Display Tool

There will be times when you will want to write or draw things on the board that cannot be erased with a standard board eraser. For example, you could draw a semipermanent array of dots to represent a geoboard. Figures drawn with regular chalk could be erased, leaving the array behind.

If you can't or don't want to buy semipermanent chalk, here are two ways to make semipermanent chalk drawings:

- Dissolve sugar in some hot water until the water can no longer absorb any additional sugar. Drop a piece of porous (not dustless) chalk into the sugar solution and let it stand overnight. The chalk will soak up the sugar solution and become resistant to erasure. When not in use, keep the chalk in a sealed container so that it stays moist. When you make a mark on the board with this chalk, the mark may not be visible at first. It will become visible when it has dried. Once dried, the marks can be easily erased with a wet cloth or sponge but not with a board eraser.
- Thoroughly wet the area where you want a semipermanent drawing. Draw with regular chalk while the board is wet. Let it dry completely. Now you will be able to write on the base drawing and erase a number of times without losing the base drawing. To remove the base drawing, simply wash it off with water.

▶ 5.1 Attendance Chart

Good mathematics activities can result from keeping track of which children are present or absent. Interesting activities can also be built around tracking lunch or milk counts. There are many ways to set up an attendance chart so that children can record their own arrival each day.

- Use a poster or wall chart with pockets containing name cards to be turned over by children when they arrive.
- Set up a grid on which children sign in daily with an X, as shown in the margin. Children's names can be numbered with the same numbers used to identify their tool kits and their nonconsumable tool-kit items. A stack of identical weekly grids can be posted and the used grid torn off to start each new week.
- A designated attendance person can pass around a class list on which children mark off their names.

You can also display attendance data in sentence form on a poster like the one shown in the margin. Or include lunch options in the posters. Over the year, vary the manner in which poster data are collected. Some suggestions are listed on the next page.

Attendance Chart

	M	T	W	T	F
1. John	✘	✘	✘	✘	✘
2. Gloria		✘	✘	✘	✘
3. Sara	✘	✘		✘	✘
4. Dave	✘	✘	✘	✘	✘

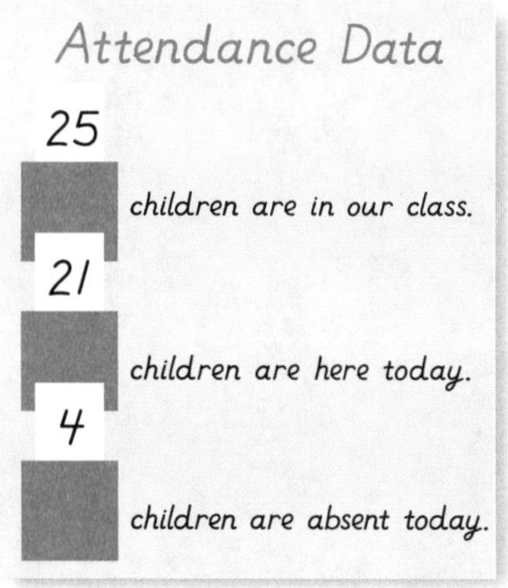

Attendance Data

25 children are in our class.

21 children are here today.

4 children are absent today.

- Gather children and have them count off, or have them count the class members to determine the number present. Help them determine how many children are absent. You could use a parts-and-total diagram to represent this situation.

For more information on parts-and-total diagrams, see Section 10.2.1: Addition and Subtraction Use Classes.

Total	
26	
Present	Absent
23	?

Total	
29	
Present	Absent
?	4

Parts-and-Total diagrams

- Later in the year, have children fill in the poster without help. Extend the job by having children help to fill out daily attendance slips.
- Children can use saved attendance data later in the school year. For example, they might make graphs to investigate whether certain weekdays or certain months have substantially more absences than others. This may lead to interesting discussions about possible reasons for the differences.
- Help children create number stories using the attendance data.

5.2 Class Calendar

Using the calendar every day helps children to quickly acquire calendar skills. *Everyday Mathematics* recommends that you buy or construct a large, reusable calendar and post it in your classroom. Laminated posterboard makes a good homemade calendar. Make a grid of six rows with seven cells in each row. Write the days of the week across the top and reserve spaces in which to write or post the month and the year.

September 2008

Sunday	Monday	Tuesday	Wednesday	Thursday	Friday	Saturday
	1	2	3	4	5	6
7	8					

Some teachers have a calendar in place at the beginning of each month, and children mark off the days with some kind of movable frame. Other teachers fill in the calendar as the month progresses, assigning to one child the job of placing a new number on the grid each school day. On the first school day after a weekend or holiday, that child also adds the missing days to the calendar.

You can place a number on the grid in several ways. Write the number directly on a laminated grid using a water-based marker, or write all the numbers 1 through 31 on cards or slips of paper that can be taped or tacked to the calendar. You might even cut the cards into shapes appropriate for the month and scatter them around for children to find and place on the grid.

In addition to recording the date, children can also record data such as weather conditions, temperatures, and special days and events.

At the beginning of each month, the class as a whole can work to dismantle the calendar for the previous month. Have children remove days of the month by identifying such things as:

- The 23rd day of the month;
- Pairs of dates whose sum is 20;

- The date in the fourth row and second column;
- Dates with a 4 in the ones place or a 2 in the tens place;
- The date equal to 1 ten and 4 ones or 1 ten and 14 ones;
- The date that is 10 more (or 10 less) than 16;
- The date that comes one week after the 8th of the month.

The possibilities for removal criteria are endless! Adjust them according to the abilities and interests of your class.

There is a blank blackline calendar master in the *Math Masters* for Grades 1 and 2. At the beginning of each month, make enough copies so that each child can have one. You might want to partially fill in the master before copying it.

Beginning early in first grade, date lines are provided on journal pages. Dating written work may be difficult for some children in the beginning but will become a habit over time. It helps to have the date posted daily on the board as either "October 3, 2007" or "10/3/07." Teachers have reported that following this procedure results in a tremendous payoff for younger children: Their understanding of days and months is greatly improved.

During a whole-group problem-solving session, some teachers have the class fill in the days by asking such questions as:

- How many days are in this month?
- If the first day is on a Monday, on what day will the 8th day be?
- If the 7th is on a Saturday, on what day is the 14th? The 28th?
- If the second Tuesday is the 9th, what are the dates of the other Tuesdays?

▸ 5.3 Class Data Pad

Throughout the year, you and the children will have opportunities to collect information that can greatly enrich the content of the *Everyday Mathematics* program. Data collected in and out of the classroom can be analyzed and graphed or used to make up number stories several times over the course of the year. For example, children might find the middle number for a collection of data, graph the data set at some other time, and compare it with a related set of data at still another time.

NOTE: You can save some data from year to year to explore changes over longer periods of time.

To use this data repeatedly, record it on a large pad of newsprint and call it the Class Data Pad. With the Class Data Pad you can save sheets on the pad for later use. If you label large stick-on notes and position them so that they extend over the edges of pages, you can easily index and retrieve stored data for children to write their own number stories or when you need information for problems.

NOTE: You could set aside a portion of a bulletin board or chalkboard to record data, but this might be inconvenient because both have limited surface area.

▸ 5.4 Class Number Line

A class number line has many possible uses:

- Tracking the school days in a school year;
- Providing a large visual display for rote-counting exercises;
- Focusing children's attention on specific numbers as they are introduced.

In Kindergarten, the authors recommend building a *growing number line* as the year progresses. In subsequent grades it is recommended that you display a labeled number line from the beginning of the school year. The growing number line is described here, followed by practical suggestions for making number lines in Grades 1 through 3.

Growing Number Line

Each day, Kindergarteners write the number of that school day and add it to a number line that grows around the room and is used throughout the school year. Three-by-five file cards are easy to use, posted in consecutive order high enough for the class to see. As the "1" for the first day of school is posted, children discuss the fact that because there was no school yesterday, "0" represents the day before school started.

The following are among many ideas that evolved from using a growing number line during the field-testing of *Kindergarten Everyday Mathematics*. You may be able to adapt some of these ideas for other grades as well.

- As one class reached school day number 101, a child observed that the number 101 was also on their classroom door. This led to a whole new activity of finding the numbers on other classroom doors and trying to figure out a pattern for that numbering.
- As another class began working with 10s, the teacher marked all the 10s on the number line with a different color, and then let the children figure out the pattern for those colored numbers.
- One class was learning to anticipate number order past 100. The teacher started each day by asking *What number should we put up today?*
- Many classes had "100 Day" celebrations, with children bringing in 100 of some object, such as buttons, pebbles, shells, or popcorn. The items were then displayed, weighed, measured, and discussed.
- Another class estimated what number would be on the number line at the point where it turned the corner of the wall—a possible activity for any fixed location in the room.

A Prefabricated Number Line

In Grades 1 through 3, it is worth prefabricating a number line before school starts with at least the number of days in your school year, usually about 180. You can make such a number line by combining a pair of commercial, classroom-size number lines and writing the missing digits for numbers greater than 100.

Mount the number line on a wall at a height that children can easily reach while standing on a sturdy stepstool or chair. You or another spotter can hold the chair steady and stand by to help if necessary. Alternatively, lower the current 10-day section of the line to a height convenient for children. The number line can go across windows or over door frames. One teacher made a number line by attaching the numbers to a string with paper clips and then strung the line around her room.

A prefabricated number line lends itself to many teaching opportunities. Besides being useful for numbering the school days, it can serve as a time line for recording special or memorable school events. Managing a time line can be the classroom job of *historian,* whose responsibilities include:

- Marking the current day on the number line;
- Choosing something noteworthy about that day or week;
- Drawing a picture or writing about the noteworthy event (with your help at first) and putting the picture or report on the number line.

By the school year's end, the historian will have generated a time line of the whole year.

The number line can serve as a frame of reference for counting and numeration activities throughout the year. Sample activities are:

- Find or read a number, and then add or subtract 10 (or 100).
- Skip count to or count on from any given number by 2s, 5s, 10s, and so on.
- Tell what number comes before or after a given number.
- Determine how many days there are until day n or from day n.

You can also use the number line as a starting point for discussions about specific numbers. On day 31, for example, ask questions such as:

- Where and when might the number 31 be used?
- What items or objects might you need 31 of?
- What will 31 cents buy?

5.5 Classroom Jobs

Children who perform classroom jobs can learn a good deal of mathematics. Many jobs present opportunities for practice in estimating, counting, measuring, and other mathematical skills. As an added benefit, children become increasingly independent and responsible, freeing you to devote your time and energy where most needed.

Although organizing these jobs requires special attention at the beginning of the year, taking the extra time to organize and explain the jobs then will pay off handsomely in the long run. Begin with two or three jobs, and add jobs as needed during the year.

Classroom jobs might include taking attendance, marking off days on the number line and calendar, recording the temperature, passing out materials, leading a line of children, delivering messages, keeping learning centers in good order, and performing jobs of your choosing.

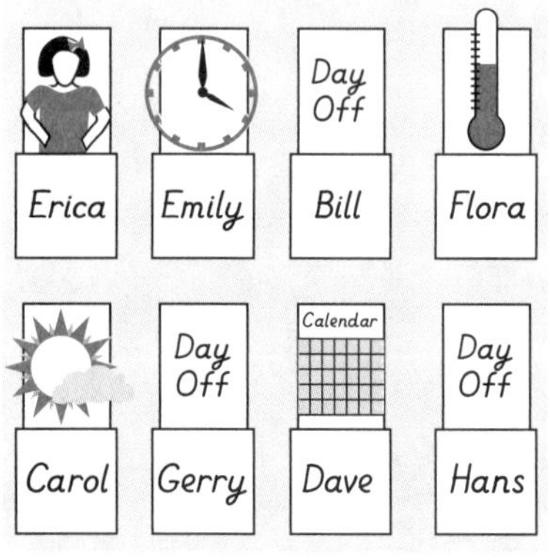

Job chart

Job Chart

You can keep track of job assignments with the help of a *job chart.* Staple or tape card pockets to a large posterboard and write a child's name on each pocket. On cards that fit into the pockets, write job titles and/or pictures or the words "day off," and insert the cards into the pockets. Change jobs by moving the cards across the rows of pockets in some regular pattern so that the children can anticipate their job assignments. Suggestions from field-test teachers include:

- Use library-card envelopes and file cards.

- On his or her pocket, tally the number of times a child has had each job assignment.
- Hold an election once a month to assign jobs.

Changing the job chart itself can be an assigned job.

5.6 Daily Schedule

Post a *daily schedule* or *time chart* such as the one below to acquaint children with each day's agenda. You can post small clock faces, rebuses, or sentence strips that can be changed as needed. Save one or more blank spaces for special activities. The schedule could also be displayed informally on a chalk, white, or bulletin board.

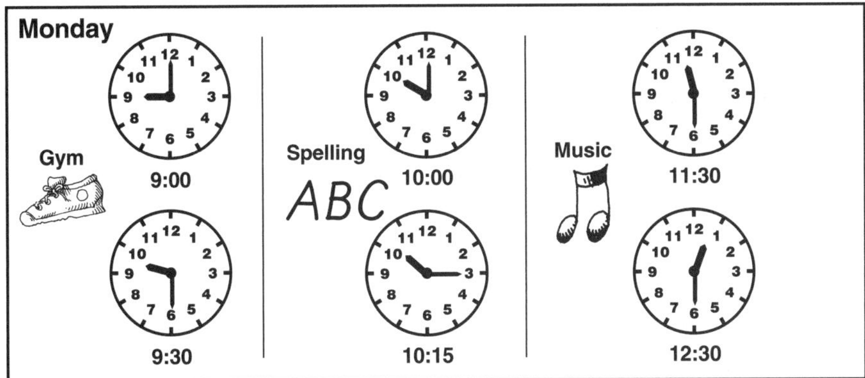

A daily schedule provides frequent opportunities for children to practice telling time. Whenever new opportunities arise, use the daily schedule and classroom clock to ask questions such as these:

- Does the classroom clock match *(a scheduled activity)* time? Is it *(a scheduled activity)* time?
- Where will the hour hand be for *(a scheduled activity)*? The minute hand?
- What activity takes place at this time? *(Show a time on a demonstration clock.)*
- If art class starts at 9:35 and ends at 10:15, how many minutes long is art class?
- How many minutes is it from now until recess?

5.7 Number-Writing Practice

Research has shown that young children who receive direct instruction while practicing the strokes for writing a number or letter quickly develop their own readable handwriting styles. If children are not instructed, they may develop an inefficient or illegible script that is often difficult to change when they learn cursive handwriting.

At young ages, children's motor skills and experience with writing vary greatly, so use your judgment on how rapidly to move through the number-writing activities that begin in *First Grade Everyday Mathematics.* The authors believe that it is beneficial to write correct forms of numbers earlier in the year than do typical handwriting programs.

Along with writing numbers in their journals and on blackline masters, children practice number writing on slates.

NOTE: If you choose to teach your own handwriting program instead of the *Everyday Mathematics* approach, tell the children to ignore the arrows shown on their journal pages.

For more information, see Section 1.2.10: Slates.

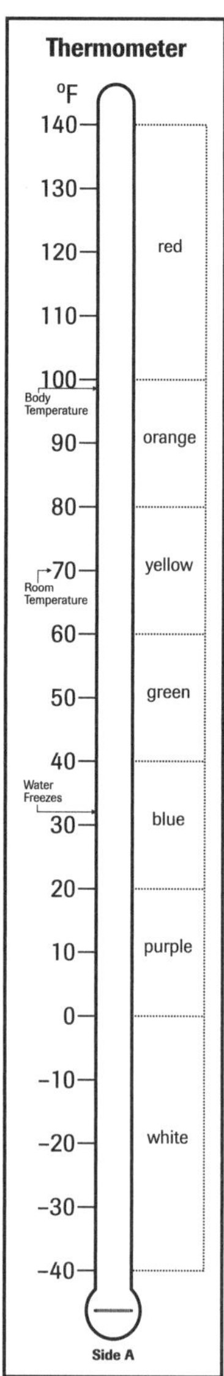

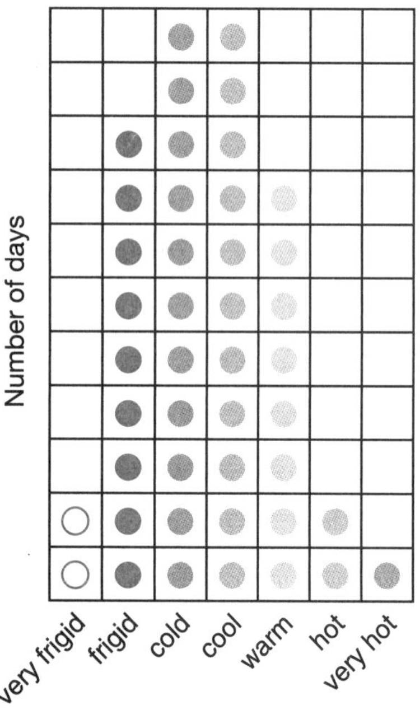

5.8 Temperature and Weather Records

Keeping daily temperature and weather records are regular routines in both Kindergarten and first grade. In second and third grades, children may continue to collect temperature and weather data during optional activities.

Temperature Record

At about the same time each day during the school year, have a child record the outside temperature. Pinpointing and reading the exact number of degrees on a temperature scale can be very difficult for young children. *Everyday Mathematics* suggests that you color-code a large outdoor thermometer with both Celsius and Fahrenheit scales using permanent markers, crayons, or colored plastic strips to mark temperature ranges. A marked Fahrenheit scale is shown in the margin. The table at right suggests some temperature-related words to go with the color codes.

Color Codes for a Classroom Thermometer

Color	Meaning
Red	Very hot
Orange	Hot
Yellow	Warm
Green	Cool
Blue	Cold
Purple	Frigid
White	Very frigid

Having both scales not only gives children an informal introduction to each scale, but it will also stimulate discussion about why we see temperatures recorded both ways.

At the beginning of each day, the child whose job it is to record the temperature should note the color zone on the thermometer and record it. Two ideas for recording are to:

- Put self-adhesive colored dots directly on the Class Number Line;
- Draw colored dots or put self-adhesive colored dots on a paper strip such as adding-machine tape and post it in the appropriate position below the Class Number Line.

Have the child also note the date or write it yourself. Paper strips can eventually be taped together and children can use the yearlong temperature record to observe seasonal trends. Analyzing the data often leads to discussion about the drop in temperature in the fall and the rise in the spring.

You might also want to construct a bar graph or line plot representing days with different temperature colors. Each day have a child add a region to a bar with the appropriate color or add another dot to a line plot.

As the year progresses, help children read the number of degrees Celsius or Fahrenheit and record this information as well as the appropriate color. The first day "below zero" will give you an opportunity to talk about the numbers less than zero, the *negative* numbers. At that time, you might want to add a few negative numbers to the class number line and point them out on the Number-Grid Poster.

Because the temperature changes continuously, later in the year the children might start taking second readings at lunchtime or before school lets out. Temperature data can be used throughout the year to make comparisons, create graphs, and generate number stories.

Temperature Maps

Another source of temperature data is the weather map from a daily newspaper. These maps often use a color scheme similar to the one described in the previous section. The maps are wonderful ways of showing the temperature changes across the country and of introducing children from warmer climates to negative temperatures. Weather maps also help children become familiar with the geography of the United States.

NOTE: Other sources of national and international weather data include the Weather Channel on cable television, on the Internet at www.weather.com, and on Web sites for local television stations.

You might want to use a weather map on a monthly basis so that children can observe how temperatures change greatly in some parts of the country and remain fairly constant in others. If possible, mount each map as it is used or keep the maps on the Class Data Pad so that the entire 9-month school period can be displayed and all the data compared.

If appropriate for your class, it might be interesting to find out where different children travel. For example, ask *Do more children go to warm areas or cold areas? To the mountains or the seashore?*

Weather Record

General weather conditions can be observed and recorded similarly to temperature data. Make it a class job to observe the weather outside and to tally it in an appropriate place. The title for this job could be *meteorologist*.

Children may help you choose symbols to pictorially represent the kind of weather your area experiences. Some suggested symbols are shown at right.

Different weather conditions can be tallied on cards hanging below the symbols on a chart, wall, or bulletin board.

Sunny		Cloudy		Rainy		Snowy		Partly Cloudy		Foggy	
HHT	HHT	//		///				HHT	//	/	
/											

A good skip-counting exercise is to count tally marks by 5s. By the end of the year, the class will know about how many days there have been of each type of weather. If the chart includes a grid with each square large enough for 5 tally marks, it is easier for children to record the tallies accurately. It is also fun to find out if the total number of tallies of the different weather types corresponds to the total number of school days in the year to date.

Weather often changes during the day. You may want to take this into account later in the year by having children take two readings per day and record the data by half-days. The data can be saved and used later in the year, or in following years, for graphing and comparison activities.

management guide

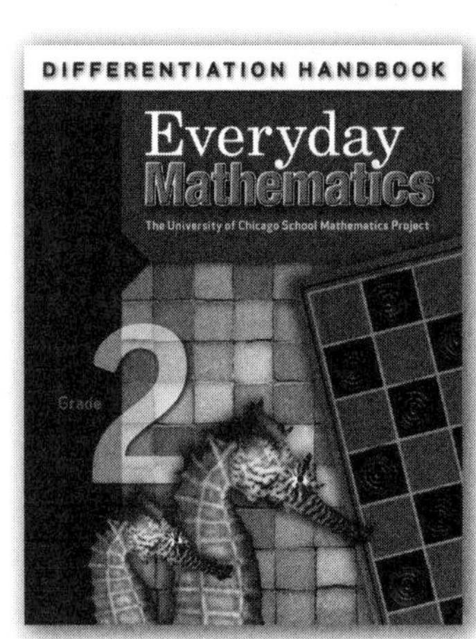

6 Differentiating Instruction

This edition of *Everyday Mathematics* includes extensive support for teachers to recognize and individualize the program for children with different learning needs. Major initiatives include:

- Adding Key Concepts and Skills tied to Year-End Goals to each lesson;
- Relating optional *Readiness* and *Enrichment* activities to the Key Concepts and Skills;
- Suggesting modifications to assessing children's performance on the Progress Check written assessments in the *Assessment Handbook*™;
- Providing more variations to games and routines;
- Highlighting opportunities for students to respond to open-ended questions and problems;
- Providing ideas for adjusting lesson activities;
- Highlighting assessment opportunities in a variety of forms;
- Providing ideas for supporting mathematical language in lessons.

For more information about managing your classroom to meet children's special needs and supporting English language learners see the *Differentiation Handbook*™.

Resources on Differentiation

Baxter, J., Woodward, J., and Olson, D. (2001). "Effects of Reform-Based Mathematics Instruction on Low Achievers in Five Third-Grade Classrooms." *The Elementary School Journal 101(5)*: pp. 529–547.

Garnett, K. (2004). "Math Learning Disabilities." *Reprint from the Division for Learning Disabilities Journal of the Council for Exceptional Children (November 1998).* Retrieved from www.ldonline.org/ld_indepth/math_skills/garnett.html

Gregory, G. (2003). *Differentiated Instructional Strategies in Practice.* Thousand Oaks, CA: Corwin Press.

Johnson, D. (2000). *Teaching Mathematics to Gifted Children in a Mixed-Ability Classroom.* Arlington, VA: ERIC Clearinghouse on Disabilities and Gifted Education.

Lock, R. (1996). "Adapting Mathematics Instruction in the General Education Classroom for Children with Mathematics Disabilities." *Reprint from the LD Forum: Council for Learning Disabilities (Winter 1996).* Retrieved from www.ldonline.org/ld_indepth/math_skills/adapt_cld.html

Tomlinson, C. (1999). *The Differentiated Classroom.* Alexandria, VA: Association for Supervision and Curriculum Development.

Usiskin, Z. (1994). "Individual Differences in the Teaching and Learning of Mathematics." *UCSMP Newsletter 14 (Winter 1994).* Chicago, IL: University of Chicago School Mathematics Project.

Villa, R., and Thousand, J. (1995). *Creating an Inclusive School.* Alexandria, VA: Association for Supervision and Curriculum Development.

Woodward, J., and Baxter, J. (1997). "The Effects of Reform-Based Mathematics Instruction on Low Achieving Children in Inclusive Settings." *Exceptional Children 63(3)*: pp. 373–388.

7 Managing Assessment

From the beginning, the philosophy of *Everyday Mathematics* regarding assessment has been clear. From the *Assessment Handbook*:

> Too often, school assessment tends to provide only scattered snapshots of student achievement rather than continuous records of growth. In *Everyday Mathematics,* assessment is like a motion picture, revealing the development of each child's mathematical understanding over time while also giving the teacher useful feedback about the instructional needs of both individual children and the class as a whole.
>
> For assessment to be useful to teachers, children, parents, and others, the *Everyday Mathematics* authors believe that . . .
>
> - teachers need to have a variety of assessment tools and techniques from which to choose so that children can demonstrate what they know in a variety of ways and teachers can have reliable information from multiple sources.
> - children should be included in the assessment process. Self assessment and reflection are skills that children will develop over time if encouraged.
> - assessment and instruction should be closely aligned. Assessment should assist teachers in making instructional decisions concerning both individual children and the whole class.
> - assessment should focus on all important outcomes, not simply on outcomes that are easy to measure.
> - a good assessment program makes instruction easier.
> - the best assessment plans are those developed by teachers working collaboratively within their own schools and districts.

The third edition of *Everyday Mathematics* provides teachers with extensive support in managing these assessment goals, including:

- Clearly articulated *grade-level goals* for the program organized by mathematics strands across all grades. Specific opportunities for assessment are identified throughout the lessons and are linked to grade-level goals.
- *Ongoing-assessment notes* to better support your understanding of the role of your grade-level mathematics content in the context of the grade-level goals. Specifically, these notes help you distinguish activities in which you can:
    - *Recognize student achievement* by collecting assessment data to monitor children's progress with respect to grade-level goals. These data come from a variety of sources, such as journal page problems, Mental Math and Reflexes problems, game record sheets, and Math Boxes.

For more information, see the *Assessment Handbook.*

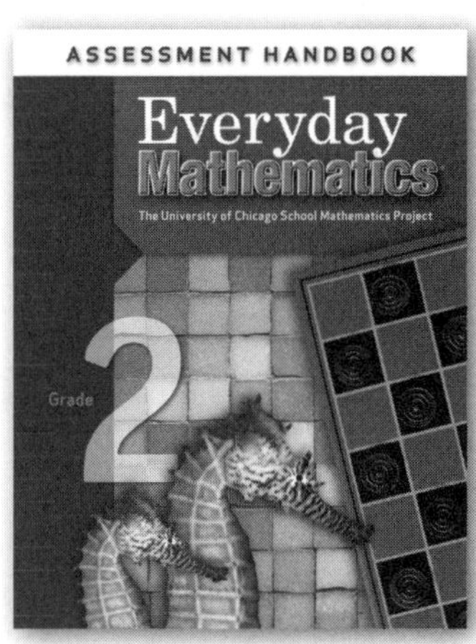

  - *Inform instruction* through tips that help you anticipate children's mistakes or misconceptions and highlight their successful solution strategies. Suggestions are given on how to evaluate children's performance and how to adapt your instruction to meet individual needs when appropriate.
- Improved support for *ongoing learning and practice* of mathematics skills by children through games, Math Boxes, and Home Links.
- End-of-unit *Progress Checks* are tied to grade-level goals that children studied in that unit and previous units. Progress Checks include student self-assessments, written assessments that distinguish between summative and formative understanding of concepts, oral and slate questions, and an open-response problem.

Resources on Assessment

Black, P., and Dylan, W. (1998). "Assessment and Classroom Learning." *Assessment in Education 5(1)*: pp. 7–74.

Black, P. and Dylan, W. (1998). "Inside the Black Box: Raising Standards Through Classroom Assessment." *Phi Delta Kappan 80(2):* pp. 139–149.

Bush, W. S. (Ed.) (2001). *Mathematics Assessment: Cases and Discussion Questions for Grades K–5.* Reston, VA: National Council of Teachers of Mathematics.

Glanfield, F., Stenmark, J. K, and Bush, W. S. (Eds.) (2003). *Mathematics Assessment: A Practical Handbook for Grades K–2.* Reston, VA: National Council of Teachers of Mathematics.

Kloosterman, P., and Lester, F. K., Jr. (Eds.) (2004). *Results and Interpretations of the 1990 through 2000 Mathematics Assessments of the National Assessment of Educational Progress.* Reston, VA: National Council of Teachers of Mathematics.

Kuhn, G. (1994). *Mathematics Assessment: What Works in the Classroom.* San Francisco: Jossey-Bass Publishers.

Mathematical Sciences Education Board/National Research Council. (1993a). *Measuring Up: Prototypes for Mathematics Assessment.* Washington, DC: National Academy Press.

Mathematical Sciences Education Board/National Research Council. (1993b). *Measuring What Counts: A Conceptual Guide for Mathematics Assessment.* Washington, DC: National Academy Press.

National Assessment Governing Board. (2004). *Mathematics Framework for the 2005 National Assessment of Educational Progress.* Washington, DC: U.S. Department of Education. Retrieved from www.nagb.org/pubs/m_framework_05.html

National Council of Teachers of Mathematics. (2000a). *Position Statement: High-Stakes Testing.* Reston, VA: Author. Retrieved from www.nctm.org/about/position_statements/highstakes.htm

National Council of Teachers of Mathematics. (2000b). *Principles and Standards for School Mathematics.* Reston, VA: Author.

National Council of Teachers of Mathematics. (1995). *Assessment Standards for School Mathematics.* Reston, VA: Author.

Shepard, L. A. (1995). "Using Assessment to Improve Learning." *Educational Leadership 52(5)*: pp. 38–43.

Stenmark, J. K. and Bush, W. S. (Eds.) (2001). *Mathematics Assessment: A Practical Handbook for Grades 3–5.* Reston, VA: National Council of Teachers of Mathematics.

Stiggens, R. J. (1997). *Student-Centered Classroom Assessment.* Englewood Cliffs, NJ: Prentice-Hall.

Webb, N. L., and Coxford, A. F. (Eds.) (1993). *Assessment in the Mathematics Classroom: 1993 Yearbook.* Reston, VA: National Council of Teachers of Mathematics.

8 Providing for Home-and-School Communication

Dialogue and discussion, as well as experimentation and discovery, are at the heart of *Everyday Mathematics*. Parents accustomed to conventional mathematics programs may think that because children are not bringing home daily arithmetic drill sheets, they are not learning or doing mathematics. The Home Links and Family Letters described below reassure them that this is not the case.

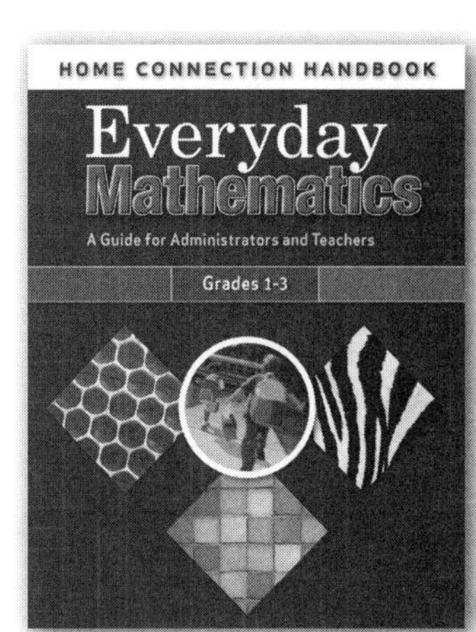

You received a *Home Connection Handbook* in your *Classroom Resource Package* that contains articles, explanatory material about the *Everyday Mathematics* philosophy and program, and suggestions for parents regarding how to become involved in their children's mathematics education. Much of the information in the *Home Connection Handbook* can be copied and sent to families to provide information about and promote involvement in the *Everyday Mathematics* curriculum.

8.1 Home Links and Family Letters

Home Links activities serve two main purposes: They *promote follow-up* to classroom activities and *involve parents or guardians* in their children's mathematics education.

Home Links activities also:

- Encourage children to take initiative and responsibility;
- Reinforce newly learned skills and concepts;
- Relate what is learned in school to the children's lives outside of school, tying mathematics to their everyday world;
- Serve as informal assessment tools.

Home Links instruct children to complete activities with someone at home—a parent, guardian, older sibling, or other adult. At the beginning of the year, you are encouraged to send home the introductory Family Letter. Continue to involve families throughout the year by sending home unit-specific letters that explain the content that will be covered. *Everyday Mathematics* also provides some Family Letters to be sent home with particular Home Links. These letters explain an idea or an activity that parents might not be familiar with. All Family Letters and Home Links are included in the *Math Masters* book.

Number and Counting

Contents

Children already know a great deal of mathematics when they begin school. They are fluent in the practical geometry of everyday life; they enjoy patterns of sound, shape, and movement; they can reason a little. But probably their most important mathematical skill is counting. Counting provides a foundation for understanding our number system and the basic operations of arithmetic. Arithmetic operations with counting numbers lead, in turn, to other kinds of numbers such as positive rational numbers (fractions and decimals), negative numbers, and eventually to algebra and higher mathematics.

Numbers and counting are integral to most of the topics in this book. This chapter addresses noncomputational aspects of numbers, including number systems and uses of numbers. Numbers are also discussed at length in Chapter 10: Operations and Number Models; Chapter 16: Estimation, Mental Arithmetic, and Number Sense; and Chapter 17: Patterns, Sequences, Functions, and Algebra.

▸ 9.1 Number Uses

If you're looking for one phrase to capture the overall philosophy of *Everyday Mathematics*, it might be "Numbers All Around." In Kindergarten, children explore their surroundings and magazines and other media in search of numbers. In first grade, children create a "Numbers All Around Museum" and collect numbers about themselves. In second grade, children collect numbers about their worlds and curate another Numbers All Around Museum. Similar lessons using numbers and mathematics from children's everyday experiences continue through *Sixth Grade Everyday Mathematics.*

The numbers that surround us in today's world are not all the same. Some are counts, some are measures, and others are used for identification. The developers of *Everyday Mathematics* have identified five basic categories, or *use classes,* that cover 90% of number uses:

- Counts
- Measures
- Locations
- Ratio comparisons
- Codes

Counts and *measures* are straightforward: 6 eggs, 3 pounds, and so on. *Locations* are a bit trickier: 9:05 A.M. expresses a location in time; 72°C is a location on a temperature scale; pairs of numbers such as 42°N, 87°W mark a location on Earth's surface.

For more information on numbers as locations, see Chapter 15: Reference Frames.

A *ratio comparison* is a number such as *3 times as much* or $\frac{1}{2}$ *as many.* Ratio comparisons are less common in primary grade mathematics than are counts and measures, but they become increasingly important in later grades.

Codes are numbers used as identification tags, which often also include letters. Codes are used for credit cards, Social Security numbers, phone numbers, and so on. Often a code has several parts. For example, in the zip code 60637:

6 refers to Illinois, Missouri, Nebraska, or Kansas.

06 refers to Chicago.

37 refers to the neighborhood in Chicago that includes the University of Chicago.

Children are also interested in the way ancient people used numbers. In *Second Grade Everyday Mathematics,* they explore the Roman numeral system in which letters used alone and in combination to represent numbers are a sort of code when compared to our decimal system. Roman numerals are still found on clocks, building cornerstones, preliminary pages in books, and copyright dates in some movies.

Roman Numerals

I = 1	XX = 20 (2 tens)	CC = 200
II = 2	XXX = 30 (3 tens)	CCC = 300
III = 3	XL = 40 (50 less 10)	CD = 400
IV = 4	L = 50	D = 500
V = 5	LX = 60 (50 plus 10)	CM = 900
VI = 6	LXX = 70 (50 plus 20)	M = 1,000
VII = 7	LXXX = 80 (50 plus 30)	$\overline{X}$ = 10,000
VIII = 8	XC = 90 (100 less 10)	$\overline{C}$ = 100,000
IX = 9	C = 100	∞ = 100,000,000 or infinity
X = 10		

9.2 Whole Numbers

> **NOTE:** You may encounter the terms *natural numbers* and *counting numbers.* Usually these are synonymous and are defined to be the numbers 1, 2, 3, 4, . . . or sometimes 0, 1, 2, 3, ...

Thousands of years ago people managed without numbers or with only the numbers 1, 2, 3, 4, ... Eventually, however, these numbers were found to be inadequate for certain purposes, and other number systems were invented. The inventions of these new number systems were motivated either by the everyday needs of people or mathematical needs, or by both. In this and the following sections, we discuss various number systems, including whole numbers, positive and negative rational numbers, and real numbers.

The first numbers people used were for counting: 1, 2, 3, 4, ... These numbers were the beginning of mathematics. Zero was invented both to express "none" as a count and to make writing numbers easier. The numbers 0, 1, 2, 3, 4, . . . are known as the *whole numbers.*

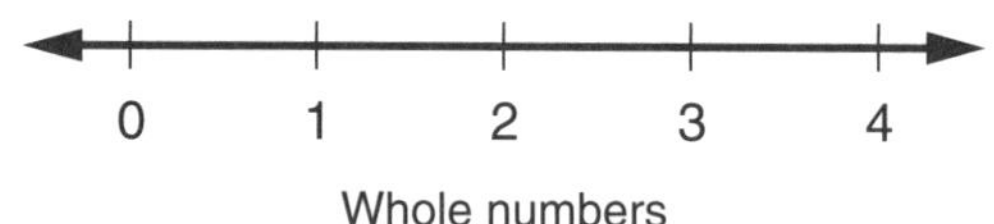

Whole numbers

9.2.1 Numeration and Place Value

> **NOTE:** In Arabic, the shapes of the digits differ from those used in most other languages, but the underlying system of numeration is the same.

Today, people everywhere write whole numbers in the same way. The system of numeration we all use was invented in India more than a thousand years ago and came to Western Europe via the Middle East and North Africa. This highly efficient system, known as *Hindu-Arabic numeration,* has contributed significantly to the tremendous advances in mathematics and science in the past 500 years.

Hindu-Arabic numeration uses 10 digits to represent whole numbers, called *base-ten numeration.* The digits are placed according to one basic rule: The value of a digit is 10 times the place to its right. Thus the 2 in 72 is worth just 2, but the 2 in 27 is worth 10 times as much, or 20; and the 2 in 275 is worth another 10 times as much, or 200. The system is called a *place-value* system because the value of a digit depends on its place in the number.

Mastering Hindu-Arabic numeration is a major goal of primary grade *Everyday Mathematics.* The process begins in Kindergarten when children count up to and beyond 100 by both 1s and 10s and observe what happens to the written numbers as the count passes landmarks like 100. Kindergarteners also work with number lines and number grids that include numbers beyond 100. At this stage, most children have no understanding of the place-value structure of numbers—writing the number 57 is more like spelling than mathematics—but these activities at least provide children a familiarity with 2- and 3-digit numbers that they can build on in later grades.

In first grade, children group objects by 10s and 100s and make exchanges across places. For example, they may trade 3 tens for 2 tens and 10 ones. First graders extend their counting beyond 1,000, including counts by 1s, 10s, and 100s, and continue to work with number lines and number grids. They also begin exploring ideas of place value and make connections between written numbers and manipulatives like base-10 blocks. First graders also do many activities that highlight the idea that numbers have equivalent names; for example, 100 = 10 tens. Realizing that numbers have equivalent forms is essential for understanding written procedures for whole-number computation and is an important building block for algebra.

Place value is presented more formally in second grade. Children rename 2- and 3-digit numbers in various ways and investigate place value to 10,000s. Much of this work is integrated with learning how to add and subtract multidigit numbers, because most computational algorithms depend heavily on place value. One of the main reasons Hindu-Arabic numeration has been so widely accepted is that it makes computation so much easier. (Imagine multiplying with Roman numerals!)

By third grade, children begin to extend their understanding of place value to numbers up to a million and to decimals. Again, much of the place-value work is integrated with learning various procedures for whole-number addition and subtraction. Indeed, one reason to study paper-and-pencil computation with multi-digit numbers is that the algorithms are an excellent context for learning about numeration and place value.

Through all of this number work in Kindergarten through Grade 3, children use a variety of manipulatives, such as base-10 blocks, counters, coins, straws, number lines, digit cards, and dominoes. Particular attention is paid to helping children make connections among various representations of numbers, including symbols, words, pictures, manipulatives, and real objects.

For more information, see Section 18.2: Problem Representations.

9.2.2 Plain and Fancy Counting

Research shows that very young children, as well as certain animals, have rudimentary nonverbal counting abilities. These counting foundations appear to be hard-wired into our being. Building on these fundamental nonverbal capabilities, verbal counting is one of the most useful ways to introduce young children to many important mathematical concepts. Just as one needs to be familiar with the progression of notes in a musical scale before one can play a piece of written music, children need a secure grasp of counting before they can understand the decimal number system and develop arithmetic competence. Throughout *Everyday Mathematics,* you are encouraged to incorporate many varied and playful rote-counting and rational-counting activities into your lesson plans.

Rote Counting

Children first learn to count aloud by reciting a string of number words by rote, without understanding the significance behind what they are saying. At first, they make mistakes like *one, two, three, six, nine, eleven, threeteen, . . .,* although they usually make the same mistakes every time. Eventually, they learn to recite the number sequence correctly to 10, 20, or beyond, but generally without full numerical understanding, especially for higher numbers.

Rote, oral counting is important for learning about our number system. As children count, they hear, and then later see, the order and number-word patterns of the decimal system. Types of rote counting include the following:

- Counting on from numbers other than 0 or 1;
- Counting backward from a number;
- Skip counting by 2s, 5s, 10s, and so on, from 0 at first and from other numbers later.

All these types of counting help children develop the skills and understandings that are used to solve problems. Counting on, for example, is a good way for Kindergarten or first-grade children to solve simple addition problems.

A variation on any of these rote-counting activities is called *interrupted oral counting.* This includes having one group of children count so far, stopping them, and then having another group continue. A more advanced version of interrupted counting is having children stop in the middle of a counting activity such as counting backward or skip counting by 2s and then giving them a new starting number from which they continue with the same activity.

NOTE: Number grids, scrolls, and lines are invaluable reference frames for helping children count and explore number patterns. See Section 9.7.2 for detailed descriptions of these tools.

Rational Counting

Reciting number words by rote is just the beginning. Children also need to learn to count collections of objects correctly. This involves coordinating the spoken number words with pointing to or touching the objects being counted. Children must also avoid skipping objects or counting some twice, and they must come to realize that the order in which objects are counted makes no difference. Such meaningful counting is called *rational counting* and is achieved only after a great deal of practice.

9.2.3 Ordinal Numbers

The counting numbers tell how many; for example, 5 apples, 3 books, or 2 birds. A different kind of number, called an *ordinal number,* tells the order of objects in a sequence, such as first, second, third, and so on.

Ordinal numbers are not as simple as they seem. Suppose you have an apple, a pear, a peach, a banana, and a plum. Counting these pieces of fruit is easy; there are 5 of them. But assigning ordinals is not so easy. The apple is listed first, but it could easily be listed third or fifth. Indeed, the apple might be first in alphabetical order and fifth in weight. Also, *5* refers to the entire

- Ask children, for example: *Who is first in line? Who is third from the end? Who is third from the beginning? What number is that person from the end? Who is eighth in line?*
- Identify children by their place in line; then ask them to perform some sort of action. For example, have the third child in line and the seventh child in line change places. Ask *Is the fourth child in line still the same one?*

Ordinal number exercises

chapter 9

collection of fruit, but *fifth* refers to only the last piece in a sequential ordering of the five fruits. Fortunately, children can learn to use ordinal numbers without having to bother about these rather abstract issues.

9.3 Fractions, Decimals, Percents, and Rational Numbers

The whole numbers are adequate for counting, but measurement requires numbers between the whole numbers. A pencil, for example, might be more than 5 inches long but less than 6 inches long. The *measure numbers,* or *positive rational numbers,* fill this need. The positive rational numbers include fractions, terminating or repeating decimals, and the numbers {1, 2, 3, . . .}. The efficient and convenient notations we have today for fractions and decimals evolved later, but the numbers themselves were invented thousands of years ago.

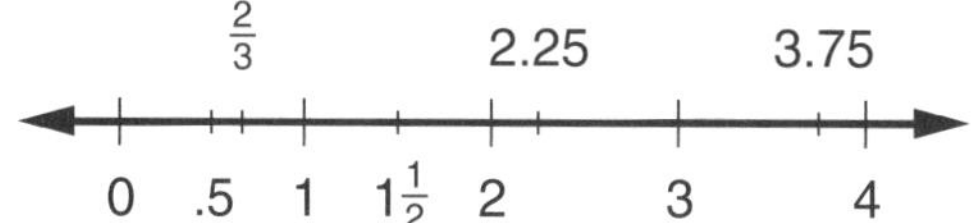

Zero and some positive rational numbers

The whole numbers are adequate for addition and multiplication of whole numbers in that the sum of any two whole numbers is a whole number and the product of any two whole numbers is a whole number. But not all differences and quotients of whole numbers are whole numbers. For example, $7 \div 2$ and $3 - 5$ do not have whole-number answers. With the positive rational numbers, however, all division problems with whole numbers have answers, except for division by zero.

Fractions are confusing to many people, perhaps because the procedures for adding, subtracting, multiplying, and dividing them seem arbitrary and unpredictable. For example, it is likely that few people really understand the "invert and multiply" rule for division by a fraction. It may be that these mysterious fraction manipulations, often taught without real-life problems or concrete embodiments to give them meaning, are what have convinced so many adults that mathematics is impossible to understand and that getting "correct" results is more a matter of good luck than good comprehension.

One reason many people experience difficulties with fractions may be that many school programs avoid fractions for several years while children work exclusively with whole numbers. When children are finally introduced to fractions, many find them confusing because the results often run counter to what they expect from having dealt only with whole numbers. For example, unlike whole numbers, fractions are generally harder to add than to multiply; a product may be smaller than its factors; a quotient may be larger than the number being divided; and "repeated addition" has little meaning in the multiplication of two fractions.

NOTE: The term *rational number* may be confusing. Rational numbers are no more "reasonable" than other numbers. Rational numbers are called *rational* because they can be written as *ratios* of integers. Every positive rational number can be expressed as a ratio or fraction in which the numerator is a whole number and the denominator is a nonzero whole number. For example, the rational number 7.5 can be expressed as the ratio $\frac{75}{10}$.

NOTE: Strictly speaking, only decimals that *terminate* or *repeat,* such as 1.5 and 0.123123 . . ., are rational numbers. Decimals that go on forever without repeating, such as 3.14159 . . . and 1.121221222 . . ., are not.

NOTE: The numbers used to handle whole-number differences without whole-number answers are the *integers,* which are discussed in Section 9.4: Positive and Negative Numbers.

For more information on division by zero, see Section 11.2.4: Division Algorithms.

NOTE: The *integers* are the whole numbers {0, 1, 2, 3, . . .} and their opposites {0, −1, −2, −3, . . .}. Note that zero is its own opposite. Zero is neither positive nor negative.

NOTE: Fractions may also be difficult for children simply because their symbols are more complicated than those of whole numbers.

 **perspective**

Early attention to fractions, decimals, and percents prepares students for learning about operations with numbers in these notations in Grades 4 through 6.

NOTE: You may sometimes encounter the terms *common fraction* and *decimal fraction*. While these terms emphasize that these are two different notations for the same numbers, *Everyday Mathematics* uses the simpler terms *fraction* and *decimal.*

NOTE: The development of decimal notation for rational numbers, which occurred many centuries after fraction notation was first used, has a similarly rich history. For more information, see *The Norton History of the Mathematical Sciences* by Gratten-Guiness (1997) and *Number Words and Number Symbols: A Cultural History of Numbers* by Menninger (1992). Complete references can be found on page 68.

So, while much of the content of traditional mathematics programs for the primary grades is concerned with whole numbers, including place-value notation, addition, subtraction, and multiplication, *Everyday Mathematics* extends traditional work with these numbers by introducing children to:

- Negative numbers, with temperatures, timelines, and number lines, in Kindergarten;
- Fractions, with measures and "part of" situations, and decimals, mainly with notation, in first grade;
- More fractions such as "1 tenth of . . ." in second grade.

Children can better understand these new numbers when they are presented as part of everyday experiences. For example, even before the authors began to develop *Everyday Mathematics,* they found, through interviews with 5- and 6-year-olds, that young children respond quickly and accurately when asked for "half of" something, probably as a result of sharing things equally with siblings and friends. Building on these observations, the primary grade program includes negative numbers, fractions, decimals, and percents. These are used mainly to convey information, without becoming involved in arithmetic operations. The authors found, in contrast to addition, subtraction, and division of fractions, that multiplication involving *half of . . .* or *1 tenth of . . .* is readily accepted by children, especially in contexts that pair *two of . . .* with *half of . . .* or *ten of . . .* with *1 tenth of . . ..*

9.3.1 Fraction and Decimal Notation

The importance of alternate notations for numbers is emphasized throughout *Everyday Mathematics.* All three notations for rational numbers—fractions, decimals, and percents—can help children see connections between rational numbers and whole numbers. Fractions build on ideas of equal sharing and whole-number operations, decimals extend the whole-number place-value system, and percents connect to the important ideas of ratio and proportion.

Fractions and decimals are technically interchangeable, but many common situations use one or the other as *standard* notation. For example, although fractions were once standard in stock-market reports, today decimals are used in most financial applications. Measures are commonly expressed as fractions in carpentry and other building trades, but decimals are used for virtually all measures in science and industry.

The history of the development of fractions is fascinating. Fractions were first used in ancient times, probably in response to the need for more precise measures in situations in which whole-number units were insufficient. The ancient Egyptians used *unit fractions*—fractions with a numerator of 1, such as $\frac{1}{2}$, $\frac{1}{3}$, and $\frac{1}{8}$—almost exclusively. More complicated fractions were then expressed as the sums of unit fractions, for example, $\frac{1}{2} + \frac{1}{4}$ for $\frac{3}{4}$. Even in modern times, unit fractions are sufficient for the everyday needs of many people.

Equivalent Names for Fractions

Like all numbers, fractions have many equivalent names. In fact, every fraction is just one of an infinite set of equivalent fractions. The fraction $\frac{2}{3}$, for example, is a member of the set $\{\frac{2}{3}, \frac{4}{6}, \frac{6}{9}, \frac{8}{12}, \frac{10}{15}, \ldots\}$. The fraction from such a set that has no common factors in the numerator and denominator is said to be in *simplest* or *standard* form, and this fraction is a convenient label for the entire set. But this simplest-form fraction is not always preferable to all other equivalent names. In fact, flexibility in arithmetic is gained by freely using whichever form is most convenient or appropriate for the purpose at hand. Truly numerate people artfully use one form for a number rather than another to express what they want or need to say. Also, "reducing" fractions to simplest form may result in the loss of important information. For example, saying that the fraction of people voting for a candidate was $\frac{7{,}500}{10{,}000}$ conveys more information than either $\frac{3}{4}$ or 75%.

Everyday Mathematics promotes flexibility in using numbers, including fractions. Standard or simplest forms have their place, but to demand their use as the only acceptable form is counterproductive to learning.

One goal of *Everyday Mathematics* is for students completing sixth grade to instantly recognize decimal and percent equivalents for many common fractions. These include halves, fourths, eighths, fifths, tenths, and thirds. In fourth grade, students explore strategies for finding equivalencies among fractions, decimals, and percents. In fifth grade, students use decimal division to convert fractions into decimals and percents. They also practice recognizing different forms by playing *Frac-Tac-Toe*. Throughout Grades 4 through 6, students practice operations with fractions, decimals, and percents in real-world contexts.

9.3.2 Uses of Fractions

One reason fractions may be confusing is that they have many different meanings. The fraction $\frac{1}{4}$, for example, can have any of the following meanings:

- A part of a whole: $\frac{1}{4}$ of a pizza;
- A part of a collection: $\frac{1}{4}$ of a group of children;
- A measurement: $\frac{1}{4}$ mile;
- A division: $1 \div 4$;
- A rate or ratio: 1 part vinegar to 4 parts oil;
- A probability: 1 chance in 4;
- A pure number: the number halfway between 0 and $\frac{1}{2}$.

The idea of a *unit whole* is essential in the first two of these meanings. How big $\frac{1}{4}$ of a pizza is, for example, depends on how big the whole pizza is. To know how many children are in $\frac{1}{4}$ of a group, one needs to know how big the whole group is. In order to understand such *part-whole* fractions, children must appreciate the role of the unit whole. They should also understand that the denominator tells how many parts are in the whole and that the numerator tells how many such parts are included in the fraction. In *Everyday Mathematics,* the unit whole is called the *ONE*. Part-whole fractions are perhaps the easiest to understand, and many primary grade activities in *Everyday Mathematics* involve them.

NOTE: The notation $a \div b$ is used primarily in elementary school textbooks and (÷) is a common division key on calculators. $\frac{a}{b}$ and *a/b*, which have identical meanings to $a \div b$, are used virtually everywhere else. Because of computers, the *a/b* notation is more important than ever. The link between fractions and division is the key to converting fractions to decimals and percents. Therefore, *Fourth* through *Sixth Grade Everyday Mathematics* uses the symbol / to indicate division.

In fractions and in measures, the unit is also vitally important: $\frac{1}{4}$ mile is quite different from $\frac{1}{4}$ inch. Using fractions makes it possible to measure with more precision. With a ruler marked only in whole inches, for example, it is possible to measure precisely to only the nearest inch. But if the spaces between the whole-number marks in perspective

Fractions as equal parts of unit wholes and fractions on measurement scales and number lines get a good deal of attention in Grades 1 through 3. These kinds of fractions, along with fractions for division and fractions for rates and ratios, appear often in Grades 4 through 6 in a variety of applications.

For more information, see Section 16.4: Number Sense and Mathematical Connections.

are subdivided into equal intervals, then more precise measurements become possible. Other measuring tools such as graduated cylinders, measuring cups, and kitchen scales also subdivide the spaces between whole numbers of units. A significant part of learning to use such tools is learning to interpret the marks on the scales correctly.

In most other uses of fractions, there is no clear unit whole. In a ratio, for example, there is no unit whole. A ratio like $\frac{1}{4}$, which can also be written "1:4" or "1 to 4," might mean "one tablespoon of vinegar to four tablespoons of oil in a salad dressing." There is no unit whole in such fractions, nor is there in fractions that indicate division.

9.3.3 Rates and Ratios

In both everyday situations and technical work, perhaps the most common use of fraction notation is to express *rates* and *ratios*. Rates, ratios, and what is sometimes called *proportional thinking* are very common in the everyday world, and people with good *number sense* and *measure sense* can handle such number relationships with ease. Unfortunately, everyday uses of rates seem to be difficult for many people. Much of the poor performance in mathematics reported in the professional literature and the popular press reflects failure with rate or ratio problems on inventory tests, or an inability to do proportional thinking in the workplace.

Rates

Rates are comparisons of pairs of quantities by division. The counts or measures in the numerator and denominator of a rate have *different* units, resulting in a compound unit for the rate.

A key to understanding rates is repeated exposure to the many uses of rates in everyday life. A rate of travel, or speed, can be expressed in miles per hour. For example, if a car travels 150 miles in 3 hours, its average speed is 150 miles/3 hours or 50 miles per hour (or 50 mi/hr, or 50 mph). Automobile fuel economy can be expressed in miles per gallon. For example, if a car travels 250 miles and uses 10 gallons of gasoline, its rate of fuel economy is 250 miles/10 gallons or 25 miles per gallon (or 25 mi/gal, or 25 mpg).

Ratios

Whereas rates compare quantities that have different units, *ratios* compare quantities that have the *same* unit. In effect, the units "cancel" each other, and the resulting number has no unit. For example, the fraction $\frac{2}{20}$ could mean that 2 people out of 20 people in a class got an A on a test or that 2 pears out of 20 pears are ripe. It may even be a simplified fraction that expresses the fact that 20,000 people out of 200,000 people voted for a certain candidate in an election. In part, percents were developed in order to express ratio comparisons in a standardized form that is easy to understand. For example, 10% of the class got an A, 10% of the pears are ripe, and 10% of the people voted for the candidate.

Another frequent use of ratios is to indicate relative size, or *scale.* For example, if a picture of an object is drawn to $\frac{1}{10}$ scale, every length in the picture is $\frac{1}{10}$ the corresponding length in the actual object. In the language of transformations, the picture is a *size-change* image of the object by a factor of $\frac{1}{10}$. Such ratios can be found in dictionaries as well as on maps and scale drawings.

For more information on size changes, see Section 13.7.2: Stretches and Shrinks.

Children begin making ratio comparisons informally in *Second Grade Everyday Mathematics* when they look at price data and investigate questions such as *Is the price of a bicycle now more than twice its price in 1897?*

A Note on *Rate* versus *Ratio*

In many mathematics books and in many dictionaries, rate and ratio are synonymous. But there is a growing tendency among technicians and scientists to use *rate* when the quantities have different units, resulting in a quantity with a compound unit, and *ratio* when the quantities have the same unit, resulting in a number that has no unit, also called a *scalar.*

The authors of *Everyday Mathematics* think this distinction is useful and have maintained it in the program. However, the use of rate and ratio as synonyms is so entrenched in school mathematics and in daily life that *Everyday Mathematics* student materials do not make an issue of it. Rate and ratio issues are entangled with the larger concern of how to handle units and units analysis in calculations with counts and measures. Keeping track of units is easy for sums and differences, as only counts or measures with exactly the same unit can be added or subtracted. Keeping track of units becomes more complicated with products, quotients, squares, cubes, and square roots, all of which are important in *Fourth* through *Sixth Grade Everyday Mathematics.*

9.3.4 Percents

> Landowner Jones has $\frac{3}{4}$ of an acre and landowner Smith has $\frac{4}{5}$ of an acre. Who has more land?

Answering the question above may be difficult because the denominators of the fractions are not the same. One represents fourths of an acre, while the other represents fifths of an acre. Several methods could be used to rewrite the data in comparable terms, that is, to *standardize* them. Three approaches to standardizing the landowners problem follow.

- *Draw pictures.*

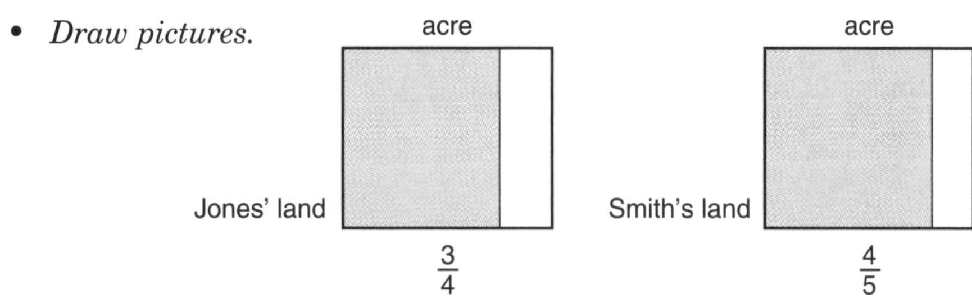

- *Rewrite the fractions with the same denominators.*

$\frac{3}{4} = \frac{15}{20}$ $\frac{4}{5} = \frac{16}{20}$

- *Rewrite the fractions as decimals or percents.*

$\frac{3}{4} = \frac{75}{100} = 0.75 = 75\%$ $\frac{4}{5} = \frac{80}{100} = 0.80 = 80\%$

Each approach shows that Smith owns more land than Jones does.

Because it is not always simple to draw a picture or find common denominators, as in the first two methods above, using the percent approach is probably the most convenient and efficient of the three. A *percent* is a ratio comparison based on 100ths. The word "percent" comes from the Latin *per centum,* meaning "for each 100."

The percent symbol % has three equivalent meanings:

Meaning	Example
times 0.01	$5\% = 5 \times 0.01 = 0.05$
times $\frac{1}{100}$	$5\% = 5 \times \frac{1}{100} = \frac{5}{100}$
divided by 100	$5\% = \frac{5}{100} = 0.05$

NOTE: Most calculators have a percent key [%]. Its purpose, however, is not the same from one machine to the next. If your calculators have percent keys, see the owner's manuals for instructions.

The payoff for repeated, early, and informal experiences with decimals, fractions, and percents comes later in the *Everyday Mathematics* program, when seeing relationships among the numbers allows children to use mental computation and estimation with a high degree of sophistication. For example, knowing that 10% is equal to $\frac{1}{10}$ or 0.1 makes the problem *How much is 10% of a $30 cab ride?* easy to solve mentally by taking $\frac{1}{10}$ or 0.1 of $30 to get $3.

9.4 Positive and Negative Numbers

The invention of negative numbers was prompted by both practical and mathematical considerations. From a mathematical point of view, negative numbers are needed:

- To make subtraction *closed.* When negative numbers are allowed, there is an answer to every subtraction problem, including differences such as $3 - 10$.
- To complete the number line. With negative numbers, the number line can extend below zero.
- To give every number an *additive inverse.* The sum of a number and its additive inverse is zero. The additive inverse of a positive number is negative.

In the everyday world, negative numbers answer the need for specifying locations in reference frames in relation to a *zero point* (starting point) and for naming measures that extend in both directions from the zero point.

Beginning in Kindergarten, children use positive and negative numbers to locate points in reference to a zero point, for example, on a temperature scale, and to represent the result of a change situation, such as using -3 to mean a loss of 3 pounds. Other situations in which positive and negative numbers are used are given in the table below.

Situation	Negative	Zero	Positive
bank account	withdrawal	no change	deposit
time	before	now	after
games	behind	tied	ahead
business	loss	break even	profit
elevation	below sea level	sea level	above sea level

Such situations are useful in helping children understand that negatives are opposites of positives. Positives and negatives come in pairs, and familiarity with negatives can be improved by comparing them with their positive opposites.

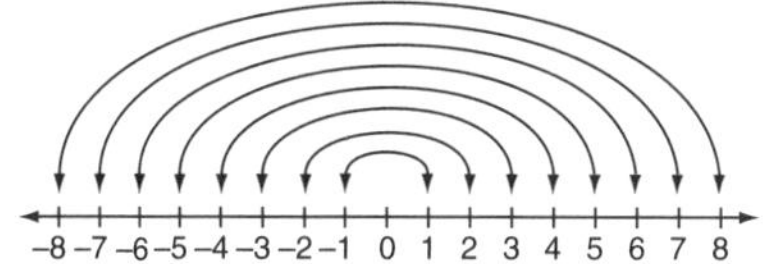

Negative numbers are opposites of positive numbers. Zero is its own opposite.

One way to represent negative numbers and their relationships to positive numbers is on a number line. The opposite relationship can be illustrated by folding a number line at zero and comparing where points coincide. This demonstration also shows that points on the negative side of zero are reflections of points on the positive side, and vice versa. Encourage children to draw number lines in their journals, on their slates, and on the board, that is, anywhere that may help them visualize the relative locations of positive and negative numbers while they solve problems.

For more about *reflections,* see Section 13.7.1: Flips, Turns, and Slides.

Positive and Negative Rational Numbers

Students in *Fourth* through *Sixth Grade Everyday Mathematics* learn about the opposites of all rational numbers and decimals. Together with zero, the positive and negative rational numbers form the *rational-number system,* which is sufficient for solving most everyday problems involving counting, measures, locations, and ratio comparisons. All rational numbers can be displayed on a number line such as the following one, but they do not account for every point on the number line. For this, we need both rational and irrational numbers together, forming the real-number system that is briefly described in Section 9.5 of this chapter.

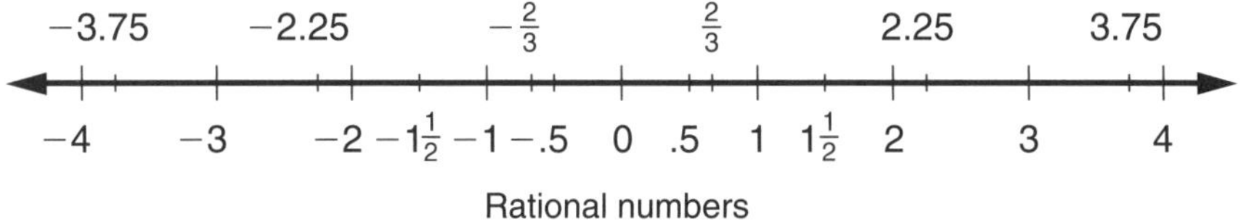

Rational numbers

9.4.1 Possibly Confusing Notation with Negative Numbers

Reading and writing expressions with positive and negative numbers has always been a difficult topic for children, and perhaps even for you. Notations with several distinct meanings can be confusing. This is certainly true of the symbol $-$.

- The symbol − immediately preceding a numeral, as in −3, −0.5, and −37, is read "negative" and is used in naming numbers on the number line (negative 3, negative 5 tenths, negative 37).
- The symbol − preceding parentheses, as in −(+3) and −(−17), is read "opposite of." The opposite of a negative number is a positive number; the opposite of a positive number is a negative number. So the "opposite of positive 3" is negative 3, and the "opposite of negative 17" is positive 17. The number zero is the only number that is its own opposite: −(0) = 0.
- The symbol − in 17 − 3 = 14 is read "minus," "subtract," or "take away" and indicates the operation of subtraction.

The meaning of the symbol − can get tangled in number sentences such as those in the table below.

In symbols	Read it like this
−17 − 3 = −20	"Negative 17 minus 3 is equal to negative 20."
12 − −(−4) = 8	"12 minus the opposite of negative 4 is equal to 8."

NOTE: A few calculators have a (−) key for entering the opposite of a number. This key looks like the key for subtraction, but it is not an operation symbol. Trying to use it for subtraction leads to an error message. To enter the opposite on these calculators, press (−) before entering the number. For example, to enter −3, press (−) 3.

Some mathematics programs attempt to reduce confusion by using − only for subtraction. Positive and negative numbers are represented with small raised symbols, for example, $^{-}3$, $^{-}17$, and $^{+}17$, and the opposite may be indicated by "OPP" or "op." But everyday usage and nearly all algebra books continue to use traditional notation, so children eventually have to reconcile the two notations.

The distinction between operation and sign may be clarified using a calculator with an *opposite* or *change-sign* key. The most common symbol for this key is [+/−]. It is the symbol on both the TI and Casio calculators the authors used to write this edition of *Everyday Mathematics.* The change-sign key can be used to change a number to its opposite.

On calculators with a [+/−] key, enter the number before pressing [+/−]. For example, to enter −8, press 8 [+/−]. The negative sign may appear in the margin of the display as in the left calculator, rather than next to the numeral as in the right calculator. Other than that, expressions are entered left to right as always.

NOTE: [+/−] is an example of a *toggle,* a key that switches the display back and forth between two numbers. In this case, it switches back and forth between a number and its opposite each time the key is pressed.

Third Grade Everyday Mathematics uses the traditional notation for "negative" and "minus" for activities in which children explore opposites of whole numbers. We urge you to help children learn the different meanings of these symbols by reading + as "plus" or "positive" and − as "minus," "negative," or "opposite," as required by the context. Eventually, students in Grades 4 through 6 do likewise when they read mathematical expressions.

9.5 Irrational and Real Numbers

Rational numbers suffice for addition, subtraction, multiplication, and division of any whole numbers except division by zero, but they are not enough for many other applications. For example, some whole numbers have whole-number square roots: a square root of 9 is 3 and a square root of 100 is 10. But the square roots of many whole numbers are not whole numbers. The square root of 2, for example, is more than 1 but less than 2; and −3 is another square root of 9.

One might hope that the square roots that "don't come out even" were rational numbers, but this is not the case. More than 2,000 years ago, the followers of the Greek philosopher Pythagoras proved that the square root of 2 is not rational. Numbers that are not rational are called *irrational.* When the irrationality of the square root of 2 was first proved, it caused a sensation among the Pythagoreans. It is said that the discoverer was thrown from a ship because Pythagorean dogma held that all numbers were rational.

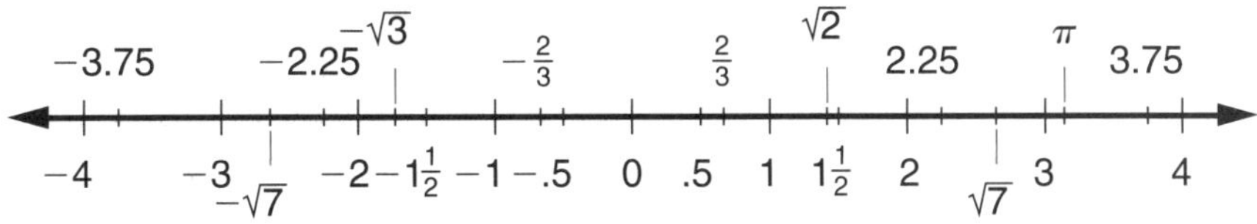

Real numbers

The name "irrational" for these numbers does not mean these numbers are unreasonable. It simply means that they cannot be written as ratios of two integers. The square root of 2, for example, cannot be written as a fraction in which the numerator and denominator are both whole numbers. Writing an irrational number in decimal notation would require an infinite number of digits. Instead, we use special symbols. For example, $\sqrt{2}$ for the square root of 2, or π (read "pi") for the irrational number shown to a few hundred decimal places in the margin.

The irrational numbers and the rational numbers together make up what mathematicians today call the *real numbers.* For practical purposes, we don't really need the real numbers; even scientists use rational-number approximations for real numbers to perform most calculations, as calculations with infinite decimals are not very convenient. In a mathematical system, however, real numbers are extremely important.

In many ways, the real numbers are the end of the number-system story. For example, every point on the number line corresponds with exactly one real number, and every real number matches exactly one point on the number line; there are no gaps. Real numbers are more than adequate for everything we do in *Everyday Mathematics.* One thing the real numbers cannot do, however, is name square roots of negative numbers. *Complex numbers* were invented for that purpose, but that's another story.

NOTE: A *square root* of a number is a number that multiplied by itself equals that number. A square root of 81, for example, is 9 because $9 \times 9 = 81$. Another square root of 81 is −9 because $-9 \times -9 = 81$. "The" square root of a number usually refers to the positive square root.

Some Digits of π

3.1415926535897932384626433832795
0288419716939937510582097494459
2307816406286208998628034825342
1170679821480865132823066470938
4460955058223172535940812848111
7450284102701938521105559644622
9489549303819644288109756659334
4612847564823378678316527120190
9145648566923460348610454326648
2133936072602491412737245870066
0631558817488152092096282925409
1715364367892590360011330530548
8204665213841469519415116094330
5727036575959195309218611738193
2611793105118548074462379962749
5673518857527248912279381830119
4912983367336244065664308602139
4946395224737190702179860943702
7705392171762931767523846748184
6766940513200056812714526356082
7785771342757789609173637178721
4684409012249534301465495853710
5079227968925892354201995611212
9021960864034418159813629774771
3099605187072113499999983729780
4995105973173281609631859502445
9455346908302642522308253344685
0352619311881710100031378387528
8658753320838142061717766914730
3598253490428755468731159562863
8823537875937519577818577805321
7122680661300192787661119590921
6420198938095257201065485863278
8659361533818279682303019520353
0185296899577362259941389124972
1775283479131515574857242454150
6959508295331168617278558890750
9838175463746493931925506040092
7701671139009848824012858361603
5637076601047101819429555961989
4676783744944825537977472684710
4047534646208046684259069491293
3136770289891521047521620569660
2405803815019351125338243003558
7640247496473263914199272604269
9227967823547816360093417216412
1992458631503028618297455570674
9838505494588586926995690927210
7975093029553211653449872027559
6023648066549911988183479775356
6369807426542527862551818417574
6728909777727938000816470600161
4524919217321721477235014144197
3568548161361157352552133475741
8494684385233239073941433345477
6241686251898356948556209921922
2184272550254256887671790494601
6534668049886272327917860857843
838279679766814541009538837 ...

References and Resources for Number and Counting

Gratten-Guinness, I. (1997). *The Norton History of the Mathematical Sciences.* New York: W. W. Norton.

Kline, M. (1977). *Mathematical Thought from Ancient to Modern Times.* New York: Oxford University Press.

Menninger, K. A. (1992). *Number Words and Number Symbols: A Cultural History of Numbers.* New York: Dover.

9.6 Numeric Relations

For more information, see Section 13.6: Geometric Relations.

In mathematics, a *relation* tells how one thing compares to another. This section discusses numeric relations, that is, relations between numbers and expressions. The most common numeric relations are equality (=) and inequality (< and >), but there are others.

Even preschool children have some idea of "more" and "less." They may be deceived by appearances but, under the right conditions, they can judge bigger/smaller, shorter/taller, heavier/lighter, and so on. This capacity for judging more/less is the basis for understanding numeric relations.

As children begin to count or measure objects, they learn to write symbols for relations between the counts or measures of different objects. The table below shows the most common symbols for expressing numeric relations.

Symbols for Numeric Relations

Symbol	Read it as	Examples
=	"equals" "is equal to" "is the same as"	$3 = \frac{6}{2}$ 3.0 seconds = 3 seconds $\frac{1}{2} = 50\%$
>	"is greater than"	12 > 4 1.23 > 1.2 6,000 ft > 1 mi
<	"is less than"	8 million < 12 million 0.1 < 1.1 $\frac{5}{2} < 4$
≥	"is greater than or equal to"	attendance ≥ 250 people 2 + 2 ≥ 4 area ≥ 2 acres
≤	"is less than or equal to"	2 + 2 ≤ 4 fee ≤ $25 time ≤ 2 hours
≠	"does not equal" "is not equal to" "is not the same as"	10 ≠ 100 $\frac{10}{120} \neq \frac{1}{2}$ 85% ≠ 85

NOTE: Some computer programming languages use "<>" for "not equal."

9.6.1 Equality

Although the concept of equality seems straightforward, children who have been through several years of schooling often have difficulty using the = symbol. Research studies show that many older children reject such number sentences as 5 = 5 (they say there is no problem), 4 = 2 + 2 (they say that the answer is on the wrong side), and 4 + 3 = 5 + 2 (they say there are two problems, but no answers).

The origin of these errors seems clear. Children in school usually see number sentences written only with a problem on the left-hand side of the equal sign and the answer on the right-hand side: 5 + 7 = 12. So, deliberately write 12 = 5 + 7 as often as 5 + 7 = 12, and encourage children to say *means the same as* or *looks different, but is really the same as* when reading the equal symbol.

In large part, arithmetic consists of simply replacing numbers or expressions with equivalent (equal) numbers or expressions. You can replace 7 + 8 with 15, or substitute 27 for 459 ÷ 17. When it suits you, you can use $\frac{1}{2}$ in place of $\frac{1}{3} + \frac{1}{6}$ and vice versa. Number sense and arithmetic skill consist largely of being aware of the many possibilities for equivalent names for numbers and being able to use them flexibly.

For most collections of equivalent names, one name is often recognized as the "simplest" and serves to identify the entire collection. But simplest doesn't necessarily mean best; for example, $\frac{50}{100}$ as in *50 per 100* may convey more information in a given situation than does $\frac{1}{2}$. It also serves as a better bridge to understanding that 50% is equivalent to $\frac{1}{2}$. Unfortunately, much of the traditional mathematics curriculum has made the "simplification" of numbers synonymous with mathematics itself. Children of *Everyday Mathematics* do not have this sterile experience.

NOTE: The French mathematician Henri Poincar (1865–1912) once remarked, "Mathematics is the art of giving the same name to different things." For example, mathematicians give the name "polygon" to many different shapes, including squares, triangles, and pentagons.

perspective

Students in Grades 4 through 6 learn that finding equivalent names for expressions is an important skill for solving algebraic equations.

NOTE: *Name-collection boxes* are important tools for managing children's work with equivalent names. For more information, see Section 9.7.3.

9.7 Number and Counting Tools and Techniques

Children in *Kindergarten* through *Third Grade Everyday Mathematics* use a variety of manipulatives including base-10 blocks, counters, coins, straws, number lines, digit cards, name-collection boxes, and dominoes. Some of the more important tools are discussed in the following sections.

9.7.1 Base-10 Blocks

In *Everyday Mathematics,* children use base-10 blocks starting in first grade. They build structures and count cubes to check estimates of height or length. They also make exchanges to investigate place value. In the *Money Exchange Game,* children work on exchanges up to 100 (100 pennies in a dollar). In the *Ones, Tens, Hundreds Game,* they use base-10 blocks to work on exchanges beyond 100.

A variety of names are used for base-10 blocks. The following names are used in *Everyday Mathematics: cube* for the smaller 1-cm cube, *long* for the block consisting of ten 1-cm cubes (1 × 10), *flat* for the block consisting of one hundred 1-cm cubes (10 × 10), and *big cube* for the larger cube consisting of one thousand 1-cm cubes (10 × 10 × 10).

First graders may also use base-10 blocks to solve number models. For example, to solve the number model 41 − 18 = *n,* children might match two sets of base-10 blocks one to one and then count the unmatched blocks; or they might count out 41 blocks, remove 18, and count the blocks left. The blocks also may be used on pan balances instead of weights to represent number sentences.

perspective

In fourth and fifth grades, the shaded grids are used to develop fraction sense and to represent percents.

In *Third Grade Everyday Mathematics,* base-10 blocks help children develop decimal-exchange concepts. A long may represent the ONE and 1-cm cubes represent tenths. If a flat is assumed to represent the ONE, then 1-cm cubes represent hundredths. Children make this last model pictorial when they color or shade hundredths of a 10-by-10 grid to represent decimals. Children work in the other direction as well, writing decimals for partially shaded grids.

In third grade, children also use base-10 blocks to model the partial-products algorithm for multiplication. First they work out 1-digit by 2-digit problems with arrays of the blocks and, eventually, 2-digit by 2-digit problems.

Sometimes you may want to make a written record of work with base-10 blocks. The shorthand shown below is handy for drawing quick pictures of base-10 blocks. Such pictures are often more convenient to use than are the actual blocks, especially the larger blocks, and can be useful for explaining and recording solutions.

Base-10-Block Shorthand

Name	Block	Shorthand
cube		▪
long		|
flat		□
big cube		

NOTE: Some readers of past editions of the *Teacher's Reference Manual* feel strongly that this section on number grids, scrolls, and lines belongs in this chapter on number and counting. Others feel just as strongly that the discussion belongs in Chapter 15: Reference Frames. Believing that teachers should find help wherever they look, it is now included in both chapters.

9.7.2 Number Grids, Scrolls, and Lines

Grid is short for *gridiron,* an old English word for a framework of metal bars or wires used to grill meat or fish. Generally, a grid is any set of equally spaced parallel lines, squares, or rectangles used to help establish locations of objects.

For more information, see Section 15.3.2: Coordinate Grids.

In *Everyday Mathematics,* children use many types of grids, including number grids, coordinate grids, grids for estimating area, and grids for interpreting maps. The tick marks on a number line form perhaps the most primitive grid structure. Lattices and arrays are organizations of objects into gridlike formations, a common example of which is a calendar.

Number Grids

A *number grid* consists of rows of boxes, usually ten in each row, containing consecutive integers (positive and negative whole numbers). In *First Grade Everyday Mathematics,* children are introduced to number grids early in the year.

−9	−8	−7	−6	−5	−4	−3	−2	−1	0
1	2	3	4	5	6	7	8	9	10
11	12	13	14	15	16	17	18	19	20
21	22	23	24	25	26	27	28	29	30
31	32	33	34	35	36	37	38	39	40
41	42	43	44	45	46	47	48	49	50
51	52	53	54	55	56	57	58	59	60
61	62	63	64	65	66	67	68	69	70
71	72	73	74	75	76	77	78	79	80
81	82	83	84	85	86	87	88	89	90
91	92	93	94	95	96	97	98	99	100
101	102	103	104	105	106	107	108	109	110

A number grid

Number grids have many wonderful features that can help children with pattern recognition and place value. However, their original use in *Everyday Mathematics* was simply to solve the problem of number lines being unmanageably long. Number lines can be cumbersome even when stretched along a classroom wall, and it is nearly impossible to print them in children's books without breaking them into chunks. Number grids may be considered number lines that fit nicely on a page or a classroom poster.

A number grid lends itself to many activities that reinforce understanding of numeration and place value. For example, by exploring the patterns in rows and columns, children discover that any number on the number grid is:

- *1 more* than the number to its left;
- *1 less* than the number to its right;
- *10 more* than the number above it;
- *10 less* than the number below it.

In other words, as you move from left to right, the ones digit increases by 1 and the tens digit is the same. As you move down, the tens digit increases by 1 and the ones digit is the same.

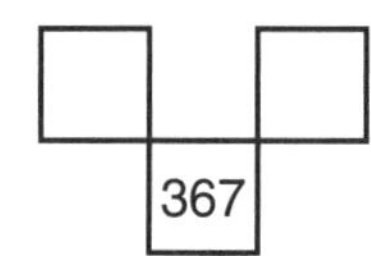

A number-grid puzzle

In the primary grades, *Everyday Mathematics* includes many counting activities that use number grids, for example, counting by 10s starting at 17 and counting backward by 10s starting at 84. Children also solve puzzles based on the number grid. These puzzles are pieces of a number grid in which some, but not all, of the numbers are missing. For example, in the puzzle at the left, the missing numbers are 356 and 358. Number-grid puzzles are used through third grade, where numbers are in the hundreds and thousands.

Identifying number patterns in grids can help children understand divisibility rules, prime numbers, and factoring in later grades.

Number grids can be used to explore number patterns. For example, children can color boxes as they count by 2s. If they start at zero and count by 2s, they will color the even numbers as shown below; if they start at 1, they will color the odd numbers. If they count by 5s, starting at zero, they will color numbers with 0 or 5 in the ones place.

−9	−8	−7	−6	−5	−4	−3	−2	−1	0
1	2	3	4	5	6	7	8	9	10
11	12	13	14	15	16	17	18	19	20
21	22	23	24	25	26	27	28	29	30
31	32	33	34	35	36	37	38	39	40
41	42	43	44	45	46	47	48	49	50
51	52	53	54	55	56	57	58	59	60
61	62	63	64	65	66	67	68	69	70
71	72	73	74	75	76	77	78	79	80
81	82	83	84	85	86	87	88	89	90
91	92	93	94	95	96	97	98	99	100
101	102	103	104	105	106	107	108	109	110

Number grids are also useful for addition and subtraction. For example, to find the difference 84 − 37 you can:

- Count the tens from 37 to 77 (*4 tens*) and then count the number of ones from 77 to 84 (*7 ones*) as shown on the next page. So 84 − 37 is 4 tens plus 7 ones, or 47. This difference corresponds to the *distance* between the points 37 and 84 on a number line.
- Start at 84 and count back to 37, noting as before how many numbers have been counted.
- Count back 37 from 84 by tens and ones: 74, 64, 54, 53, 52, 51, 50, 49, 48, 47.

−9	−8	−7	−6	−5	−4	−3	−2	−1	0
1	2	3	4	5	6	7	8	9	10
11	12	13	14	15	16	17	18	19	20
21	22	23	24	25	26	27	28	29	30
31	32	33	34	35	36	37	38	39	40
41	42	43	44	45	46	47	48	49	50
51	52	53	54	55	56	57	58	59	60
61	62	63	64	65	66	67	68	69	70
71	72	73	74	75	76	77	78	79	80
81	82	83	84	85	86	87	88	89	90
91	92	93	94	95	96	97	98	99	100
101	102	103	104	105	106	107	108	109	110

One way to find 84 − 37

Addition problems can also be solved on the number grid using similar methods. Clearly, the number grid simplifies "double counting," or counting the number of numbers counted, that is required in many addition and subtraction procedures.

From the time they are introduced, children see that number grids can be extended to negative numbers. This is especially useful as a tool for finding differences or to illustrate, for example, that −17 is less than −6.

−19	−18	−17	−16	−15	−14	−13	−12	−11	−10
−9	−8	−7	−6	−5	−4	−3	−2	−1	0
1	2	3	4	5	6	7	8	9	10
11	12	13	14	15	16	17	18	19	20

A grid extended to −19

Number Scrolls

Number scrolls are extended number grids. You can make them by adding single sheets of 100 numbers to existing sheets, either forward (positively) or backward (negatively). Among other things, scrolls give children the chance to experience the ongoing repetitive patterns of our base-ten number system beyond 100—*101, 102, 103, . . .*—so that they do not continue, as children often do, with *200, 300, 400, ...* Teachers have found that many children get excited when they discover these patterns and realize that they are capable of writing bigger and bigger numbers based on their discoveries. Meanwhile, they are practicing their handwriting as well as their counting skills.

Number Lines

A *number line* is a line on which points are indicated by *tick marks* that are usually at regularly spaced intervals from a starting point called the *origin,* the *zero point*, or simply "0." Numbers are associated with the tick marks, and the interval from 0 to 1 on the line is called the *unit interval.*

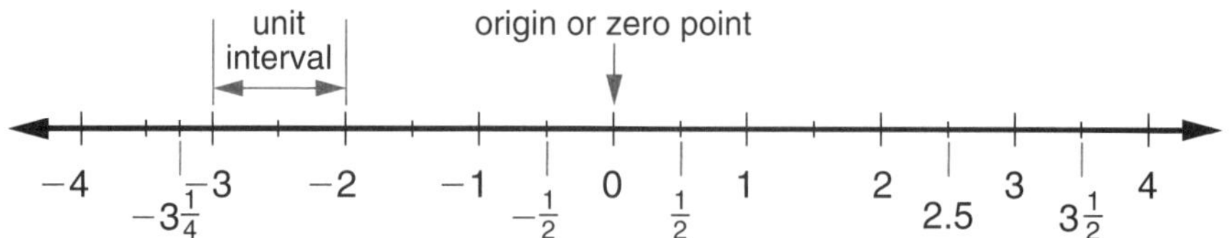

Like any line, a number line extends without end in both directions. Any drawing of a number line is a model of just part of the line. Where you place the zero point is arbitrary, and how you space the numbers depends on the situation you wish to illustrate. You might, for example, mark every other unit-interval point and label by 2s as in Figure 1 below; or you may mark every half-interval point and label by halves as in Figure 2. In *Everyday Mathematics,* children are often asked to solve incomplete-number-line problems that help them understand these concepts.

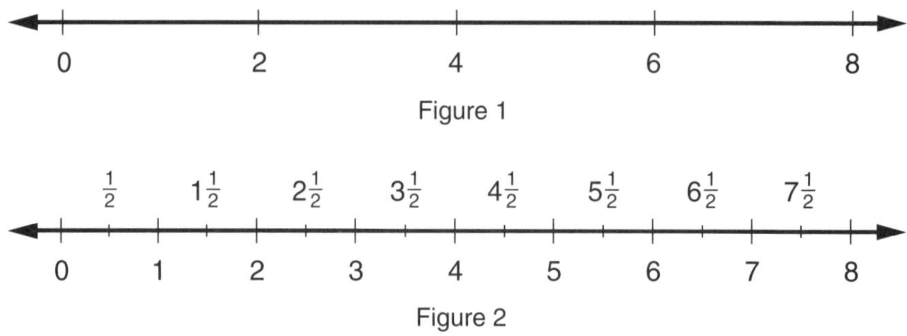

Figure 1

Figure 2

An ordinary ruler uses part of a number line for measuring length, with inch unit intervals, centimeter unit intervals, or other unit intervals. A ruler based on the number line in Figure 3, for example, can be used for measuring distances in inches and halves of inches.

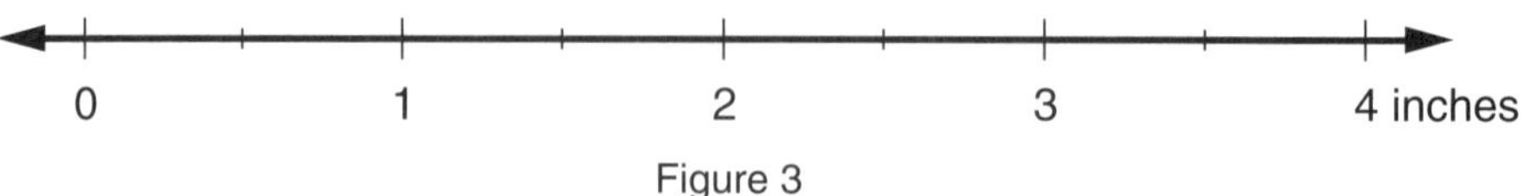

Figure 3

For more information, see Section 14.3: Length.

The number line in Figure 3 has tick marks at all unit and half-unit intervals. You may recognize the similarities between the scale on this line and the one on a U.S. customary foot ruler. This line has fewer fraction-of-unit intervals marked than most rulers. In contrast, foot rulers are usually marked every sixteenth of an inch.

You can assign any scale you wish to a number line. For example, a unit interval on a map scale might represent one mile on the map. Such a line would not be used to measure distances directly in the real world, but instead to convert distances on the map into distances in the real world.

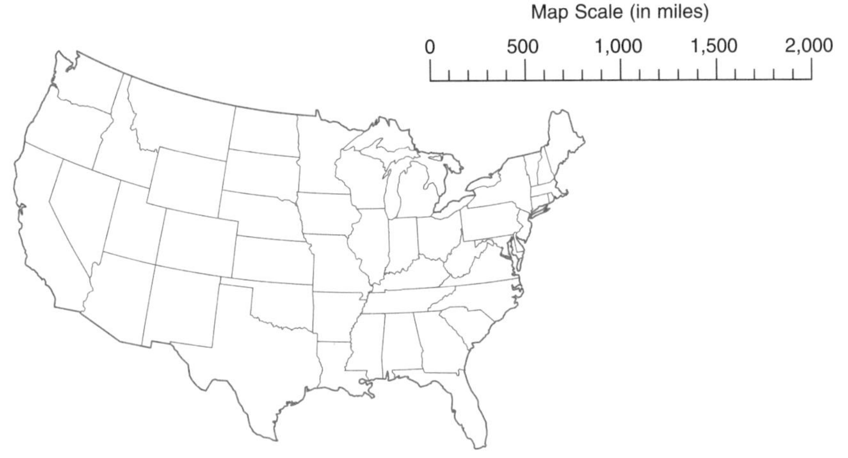

Number lines can also have nonlinear scales, meaning that the distances between the numbers are not proportional to the differences between the numbers. The distance between 10 and 20, for instance, might be the same as the distance between 1 and 2. Radio dials are based on logarithmic scales, one type of nonlinear scale. Nonlinear scales do not have unit intervals.

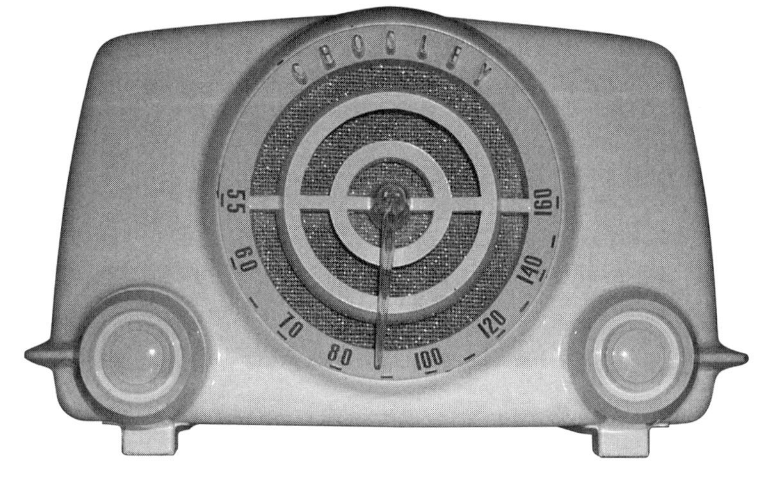

A number line always has a zero point, even when it doesn't show. On the number line in Figure 4, the zero point is understood to be off to the left. Sometimes you see a broken-line symbol as in the number line in Figure 5. This symbol indicates that a piece of the line between 0 and 330 has been omitted. The symbol, or another similar to it, is often used in technical drawings to show important details while still indicating that something is missing.

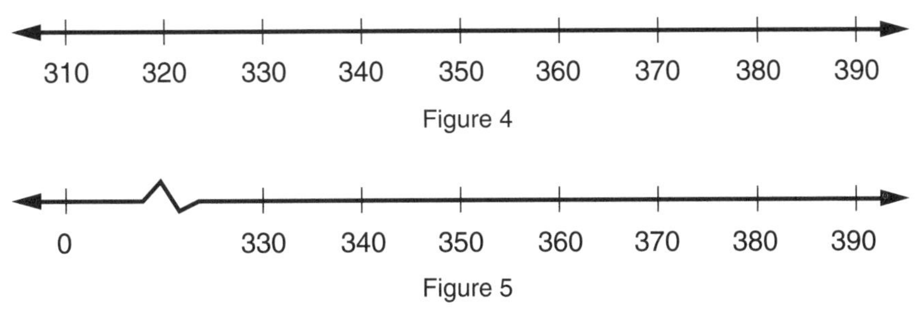

Figure 4

Figure 5

in perspective

Number-line ideas are expanded upon and treated more formally in Grades 4 through 6. Number lines continue to serve as one or more of the axes in data displays such as scatter plots, bar graphs, and line plots.

Beginning in *Kindergarten Everyday Mathematics,* children use number lines for counting and skip counting. They also create a Growing Number Line on the classroom wall by adding a new number every day.

In first and second grades, children use a number line to keep track of the number of school days in the school year. They also use number lines on thermometers (two different scales: Fahrenheit and Celsius) and on linear measuring tools. Incomplete-number-line problems begin in first grade. Number lines in coordinate graphing systems are introduced in third grade.

9.7.3 Name-Collection Boxes

Name-collection boxes give children the opportunity to experience the idea that numbers can be expressed in many different ways. In Kindergarten through third grade, a *name-collection box* is a box with a label identifying the number whose names are collected in the box. For example, the box shown below is a 16-box, a name-collection box for the number 16.

Names can include sums, differences, products, quotients, the results of combining several operations, words in English or other languages, tally marks, arrays, and Roman numerals.

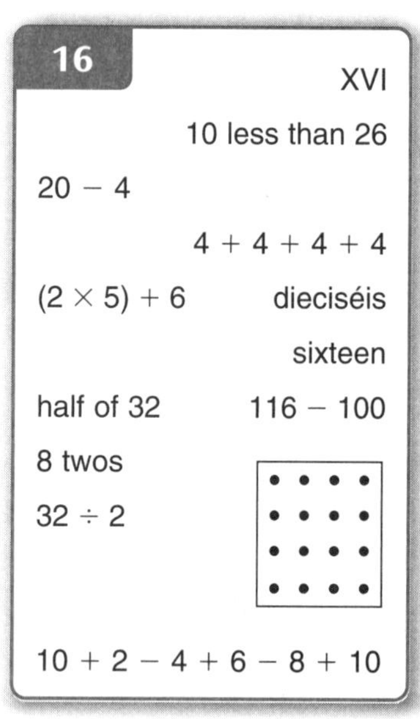

A 16-box

Beginning in fourth grade, *Everyday Mathematics* introduces a more compact name-collection box like the 14-box below.

14
1,400%
2 ∗ 7
$\frac{56}{4}$
20 − 6
1 + 13
700/50
$3^3 - 13$
0.028 ∗ 500
XIV
(3 ∗ 7) − 7

A simple 14-box

Operations and Number Models

Contents

For many adults, elementary school mathematics consisted of little more than learning to add, subtract, multiply, and divide whole numbers, fractions, and decimals. Unfortunately, this is still the experience of many children today. The authors of *Everyday Mathematics* hope that your acquaintance with our texts and your reading of this manual convince you that elementary school mathematics needs to be far more than arithmetic with the four basic operations.

Nevertheless, the importance of arithmetic in mathematics as well as in everyday life cannot be denied. *Everyday Mathematics* combines activities that focus on understanding the basic operations with activities that apply arithmetic in geometry, data exploration, measurement, and other contexts. This ensures that children receive ample practice with arithmetic skills and that they will be better able to use those skills to solve problems. Children in *Everyday Mathematics* see many uses of all the operations from the beginning of the program and build upon these uses year after year. Rather than having multiplication and division delayed until third grade or later, they see these operations as well as addition and subtraction in first and second grades.

Many adults who associate school mathematics with arithmetic also tend to think that an arithmetic operation is what you "do" to get the answer. For example, to these adults division means carrying out the traditional long-division algorithm. In *Everyday Mathematics,* how one "does" an operation is referred to as "applying an algorithm"

For descriptions of various algorithms, see Chapter 11: Algorithms.

or "carrying out a computation." Although *Everyday Mathematics* recognizes the importance of knowing algorithms and introduces a variety of algorithms for each operation, it also provides the activities that children need in order to understand the meaning behind each operation. Choosing the proper algorithm and interpreting the result correctly depends on understanding the operation itself. Children need to both understand the meanings of the operations and become proficient at carrying out algorithms to become successful problem solvers.

This chapter begins with discussions about arithmetic symbols, number expressions and sentences, and number models. It then turns to specific approaches to solving number stories using situation diagrams for the four basic arithmetic operations.

▶ 10.1 Number Sentences and Number Models

For information about managing children's use of number models, see Section 10.1.3: Teaching with Number Sentences and Number Models.

In *Everyday Mathematics,* number models are used to represent situations and to summarize relationships among quantities in problems. Although the first years of the program emphasize concrete, verbal (usually oral), and pictorial models, you are encouraged to write number models on the board or an overhead transparency, and to often include blank response lines for unknown numbers. Symbols for operations such as $+$, $-$, and $\times$ and for relations such as $=$, $>$, and $<$ are introduced informally. In second and third grades, children take on more responsibility for writing the number models.

Writing number models is in some ways similar to writing English sentences. Written English and written mathematics both have rules and conventions about grammar, syntax, punctuation, and usage. These rules clarify thinking and make communication easier. So before looking at a formal definition of number model, the authors discuss the arithmetic symbols themselves and how they are used in number sentences and numerical expressions.

10.1.1 Arithmetic Symbols

Many people feel that mathematics has too many symbols. Symbols, however, are vitally important to the subject. They make the language of mathematics more concise and, ultimately, easier to communicate and understand. Symbols can increase mathematical power by relieving the mind of unnecessary work and leaving it free to focus on problem solving.

Writers of school mathematics programs face a dilemma. On one hand, an efficient set of symbols is needed so that activities may progress smoothly in a classroom. But symbols, especially if they are introduced too early, may pose an unnecessary obstacle to the understanding of a concept. With this in mind, the authors of *Everyday Mathematics* have been careful to avoid the premature introduction of symbols, and mathematical vocabulary in general. Symbols are introduced only when they help children communicate more efficiently.

The curriculum must introduce both the symbols needed for classroom activities and the symbols required for real-world general knowledge. Symbols for classroom activities can be introduced on an *ad hoc* basis and could be restricted to a small and efficient set. But the need for children to understand mathematics within a broader social context means that *Everyday Mathematics* must include a more expansive list of symbols. Each group in society, for example, grocers, scientists, engineers, advertisers, and journalists, has a different set of symbols it considers necessary. Even the way we write numbers can spark debate: *Should it be .1 or 0.1? Is 1/2 better than $\frac{1}{2}$, or is ¹/₂ the best? Should we write -3, −3, or ⁻3?*

Calculators and computers, which might have been expected to help standardize notation, have actually increased the need for understanding that different symbols can mean the same thing. For example, there are several alternative symbols for multiplication, division, powers, and opposites (inverses). *Everyday Mathematics* provides activities to help children become aware of these alternative notations so that they can adapt to different situations as necessary. The program employs several notations for certain operations so students will become familiar with all common symbols.

Addition and Subtraction Symbols

The only symbols for addition and subtraction are + and −. Although the ideas behind the operations are thousands of years old, the symbols first appeared in print in 1498 in a book by the German mathematician Johann Widman. Widman's symbols gradually caught on and are now universally accepted. However, words for these symbols vary: *plus, add,* and *positive* all refer to +; *minus, take away,* and *negative* all refer to −.

Children in *Everyday Mathematics* see these symbols only after they have had informal experiences with the underlying operations. For example, Kindergarten children begin hearing the words *add* and *subtract* in the context of number stories based on their own experiences. Gradually, + and − are introduced in this context to help children link the spoken and symbolic representations. One of the first encounters that Kindergarteners have with the addition symbol occurs when they use [+] on their calculators in a counting-on activity. Establishing this informal connection between + and counting supports later use of + in paper-and-pencil representations of addition and the understanding of a rule such as "+ 3" in "What's My Rule?" and Frames-and-Arrows activities. Similar counting-back activities use [−].

For more on calculator skip counting, see Section 11.3: Algorithms on Calculators.

Multiplication and Division Symbols

Multiplication and division are each represented by several symbols in everyday life. All of the symbols are discussed in the *Everyday Mathematics Teacher's Lesson Guide;* but to standardize symbolic representation in the materials, the authors have made some choices that are clarified here.

Mathematics textbooks traditionally use the symbol × (read *times* or *multiplied by*) to indicate multiplication. The Englishman William Oughtred invented this symbol in 1631. The symbol × is used when multiplication models are introduced in *Second* and *Third Grade Everyday Mathematics.* There are at least three disadvantages to using × for multiplication:

- It can be confused with the addition symbol +.
- It does not appear on standard computer or typewriter keyboards, although it is standard on most calculator keypads.
- It can easily be mistaken for the letter *x,* presenting a problem when students use letter variables in Grades 4 through 6.

One solution to these problems is to use a raised dot for multiplication, that is, 5 • 6, rather than 5 × 6. Gottfried Leibniz, one of the inventors of calculus, introduced this dot notation in 1698. But an obvious difficulty with a raised dot is possible confusion with the decimal point. In fact, in some countries a raised dot *is* the decimal point.

After much consideration, the authors of *Everyday Mathematics* decided to use ∗ as the usual symbol for multiplication beginning in fourth grade. It is always the multiplication symbol on computer keyboards, and it is frequently used in print. It is also found on some calculators. The symbol is easy to write or type and is not likely to be confused with other symbols. Using ∗ for multiplication prepares students for the present as well as the future in a world of computers. A disadvantage is that ∗ is less familiar than × to teachers and parents.

Eventually, children learn to indicate multiplication by *juxtaposition,* that is, by writing symbols next to each other. For example, (15)(23) means 15 × 23, $2a$ means $2 \times a$, and ab means $a \times b$. Juxtaposition to indicate multiplication is common in formulas, which are among the earliest uses of letter variables that *Everyday Mathematics* students encounter. For example, the area A of a rectangle with width w and length l is written as $A = lw$. In fact, almost the only place where this formula is written as $A = l \times w$ is an elementary school mathematics textbook.

Historically, symbols for division have included ÷, $\overline{)\ }$, /, :, and the fraction bar. Their inventors were, respectively, the Swiss Johann Rahn in 1659; the German Michael Stifel in 1544; the Mexican Manuel A. Valdes in 1784; the German Gottfried Leibniz in 1684; and the Arab al-Ḥaṣṣâr in the twelfth century.

In second and third grades, *Everyday Mathematics* uses ÷. Unfortunately, ÷ shares two disadvantages with the multiplication symbol ×: it can easily be misread as +, and it does not appear on standard computer or typewriter keyboards. On the other hand, it is the symbol for division on almost all calculators.

in perspective

Beginning in fourth grade, *Everyday Mathematics* uses / and the fraction bar, along with ÷, to indicate division. The / has been used for centuries. It appears on some calculators, is easy to write, and is found on computer and typewriter keyboards. The use of / and the fraction bar for indicating division has an additional, most important advantage: the forms *a/b* and $\frac{a}{b}$ reinforce the relation between division and fractions. The fraction notation also prepares students for the division symbols they are likely to see in middle and high school mathematics and beyond.

Writing division with a remainder can be a bit of a problem. Consider what can happen if equal signs are used:

$$12 \div 5 = 2 \text{ R2}$$
$$102 \div 50 = 2 \text{ R2}$$

Because the right-hand sides of the two equations are the same, it appears that the left-hand sides should be equal too. Hence, we should be able to write:

$$12 \div 5 = 102 \div 50$$

But, if you do the division, it is apparent that the two sides are *not* equal:

$$12 \div 5 = 2.4$$
$$102 \div 50 = 2.04$$

That is, $2.4 \neq 2.04$. The problem is that 2 R2 is not really a number, so using it in equations can lead to trouble. Because $102 \div 50$ is a number, but 2 R2 is not, $102 \div 50$ cannot equal 2 R2. To eliminate this problem, *Everyday Mathematics* uses arrows in number models for divisions with remainders:

$$102 \div 50 \rightarrow 2 \text{ R2}$$

This notation, although nonstandard, will not mislead students as using = may. Later, when students learn to show remainders as fractions or decimals, the problem disappears altogether:

$$12 \div 5 = 2\tfrac{2}{5}$$
$$102 \div 50 = 2.04$$

The symbol $\overline{)\quad}$ is closely linked to the traditional long-division algorithm. Actually, it is really more like a template for carrying out a procedure than a mathematical symbol. Using it, therefore, may suggest the use of the long-division algorithm when another method is warranted. It can be useful, however, for recording answers to division problems with remainders.

NOTE: Some scientific and fraction calculators have a key for division with remainder. Some call it "integer division," which is a misnomer, as it implies that the operation is defined for negative numbers, which it is not. In general, how division with a remainder works varies widely across calculators, so please consult an owner's manual on how the function works and how to interpret the display.

Powers and Exponents

Although children do not see many exponents in *Kindergarten* through *Third Grade Everyday Mathematics,* in Grade 3 they receive an informal introduction to the *square numbers* {1, 4, 9, 16, 25, . . .} by observing how such numbers can be displayed in square arrays. Beginning in Grade 4, students use exponents to read and write large numbers using powers of 10. They are also introduced to scientific notation, which is used by both scientists and calculating machines.

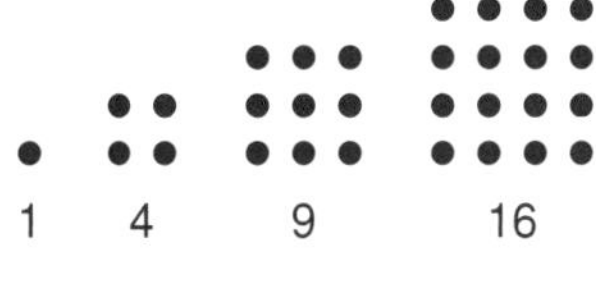

Square numbers

Next students see how the exponential notation can be used:

- For squaring, or *2 as a power:* $0^2 = 0$, $1^2 = 1$, $2^2 = 4$, $3^2 = 9$, $4^2 = 16$, $5^2 = 25$, . . .;
- For doubling, or *powers of 2:* $2^0 = 1$, $2^1 = 2$, $2^2 = 4$, $2^3 = 8$, $2^4 = 16$, $2^5 = 32$, ...

$$a^b = \underbrace{a \times a \times \ldots \times a}_{b \text{ factors}}$$

Finally, students generalize the use of exponential notation to represent the product of b factors of a base a as a^b where a is any number and b is a whole number.

Other Arithmetic Symbols

Along with the symbols discussed in previous sections, many other symbols are used in arithmetic. Several are discussed elsewhere in this manual: symbols for numbers are discussed in Section 9.3.1; symbols for relations such as =, <, and > are discussed in Section 9.6; and symbols for variables are discussed in Section 17.2.1.

Encourage children to create their own notations as well as learn the conventional symbols. While invented notations are not much good for formal mathematical communication, they can clarify complicated situations. It helps to remember that every standard notation we use today began as someone's creation.

10.1.2 Reading and Writing Number Sentences

Just as English words become meaningful when they are arranged into sentences, mathematical symbols become meaningful in sentences. And just as proper punctuation and grammar make written English easy to read, rules and conventions for writing number sentences ease mathematical communication.

A *number sentence* is an equation or inequality such as $10 = 7 + 3$, $12 \div n = 6$, or $14 > 3$. A number sentence has a left-hand side, a relation symbol, and a right-hand side. Symbols for numbers, unknowns, and operations can appear on each side of the relation symbol. Each side of a number sentence is a *numerical expression.* In the sentences above, 10, $7 + 3$, $12 \div n$, 6, 14, and 3 are expressions. In practice, however, single numbers are usually called just "numbers" or "constants" and expressions usually include one or more operations.

Number sentences can be true, false, or neither true nor false. A number sentence that is neither true nor false is called an *open sentence.* The sentence $5 + 3 = 8$ is true; the sentence $5 + 4 = 8$ is false; the sentence $5 + \_\_ = 8$ is open.

A *number model* is a numerical expression or number sentence that models (represents) some real or hypothetical situation. For example, consider this situation: *Rajiv had 7 pennies and got 3 more. Then he had 10 pennies.* The sentence $7 + 3 = 10$ is a number model of Rajiv's situation. Number models can be based on stories made up by children, on situations invented by you, or on information from everyday life.

An established order of operations eliminates ambiguity about the order in which additions, subtractions, and other operations are to be performed in number sentences. But before learning the formal order in later grades, children in *Kindergarten* through *Third Grade Everyday Mathematics* avoid ambiguity by using grouping symbols such as parentheses and brackets.

Grouping Symbols

The four basic operations of arithmetic—addition, subtraction, multiplication, and division—are called *binary operations* because each is carried out on two numbers at a time. Addition and multiplication can certainly involve more than two numbers, but repeatedly adding or multiplying *pairs* of numbers leads to final sums and products. When only two numbers and one operation are involved, there is no need for grouping symbols. Similarly, no grouping symbols are needed in adding several numbers or in multiplying several numbers because these operations may be performed in any order.

However, in situations involving more than two numbers with subtraction, division, or a combination of operations, you may obtain different results depending on the order in which the operations are performed. For example, the value of $4 + 3 \times 5$ is 35 if the addition is done first and 19 if the multiplication is done first. To avoid such ambiguity, you can insert parentheses to indicate the order in which operations are to be carried out. If the addition is to be done first in the expression above, write $(4 + 3) \times 5$; if the multiplication is to be done first, write $4 + (3 \times 5)$.

Brief exercises with parentheses are worth repeating throughout each year of the program. Most children find such exercises to have an appealing, game-like quality. Such exercises also provide children with practice with basic number facts and their extensions, reminders of the effect of multiplying by or adding zero, and practice with expressing solutions in games such as *Name That Number.*

In *Fourth* through *Sixth Grade Everyday Mathematics,* students expand their use of grouping symbols to a *horizontal fraction bar,* or *vinculum,* and to *nested grouping symbols* where parentheses may be within braces which may be within brackets, and so on. For example, $2 \times (3 + [2 - 1]) = 8$ because the $[2 - 1]$ group nested in the $(3 + [2 - 1])$ group is calculated first. Note that the square brackets aren't necessary, but they can make it easier to identify nested groupings than using all parentheses.

NOTE: Scientific and other advanced calculators have a formal order of operations built into them. Most 4-function calculators simply calculate with two numbers and an operation in the order that they are entered. If children in your classroom have different types of calculators, take the time to learn how each type handles the order of operations.

The Order of Operations

Beginning in Grade 2, children are encouraged to use grouping symbols, particularly parentheses, to make their number sentences clearer. However, once they begin to use variables and scientific calculators in Grade 4, students need to understand the mathematical convention called the *order of operations,* or more formally the *algebraic order of operations,* to distinguish it from other orders that are used in some calculators and computer applications. The order of operations specifies the sequence in which the operations in an expression are to be performed. Grouping symbols are used to specify an order different from the conventional order or simply for greater clarity.

The *algebraic order of operations* is:

1. Do the operations inside *grouping symbols.* Work from the innermost grouping symbols outward. Inside grouping symbols, follow Rules 2 through 4.
2. Calculate all expressions with *exponents.*
3. *Multiply* and *divide* in order, from left to right.
4. *Add* and *subtract* in order, from left to right.

According to this convention, $4 + 3 \times 5 = 19$ and $8 \div 2^2 - 12 \div 4 + 7 \times (9 - 3) = 41$.

NOTE: A mnemonic for the order of operations is ***P***lease ***E***xcuse ***M***y ***D***ear ***A***unt ***S***ally: Do work inside the *P*arentheses first, then *E*xponentiation, then *M*ultiplication and *D*ivision, and finally *A*ddition and *S*ubtraction.

NOTE: In each of Rules 3 and 4, neither operation has priority over the other.

chapter 10

In summary, the algebraic order of operations is used in most of the mathematics that students will encounter in middle school and beyond. The order of operations is formally introduced in *Fifth Grade Everyday Mathematics.* In *Kindergarten* through *Fourth Grade Everyday Mathematics,* grouping symbols such as parentheses and brackets are used primarily to increase clarity.

10.1.3 Teaching with Number Sentences and Number Models

In *Kindergarten* through *Third Grade Everyday Mathematics,* number models are not used to solve problems. Instead, they are used to represent and clarify the quantitative relationships in a problem. Although writing number models may help some children decide how to solve a problem, more importantly, it helps them learn the mathematical-symbol system. Translating a problem into a number model that is manipulated to find an answer comes later in the curriculum, when children begin to learn formal algebra.

When they are first introduced in *Everyday Mathematics,* number models usually appear after a problem has been solved. A typical instructional sequence might be as follows:

1. You pose a problem.
2. Children solve the problem.
3. Children share their solutions, and you record them on the board. During the discussion of solutions you write number models and draw situation diagrams on the board. There should be no blanks in the number models or situation diagrams.

For more information on situation diagrams, see Section 10.2: Use Classes and Situation Diagrams.

Later, the sequence might be as follows:

1. You pose a problem.
2. You and the children discuss the problem and write a number model or draw a situation diagram that corresponds to the problem. The number model or diagram includes a blank or a question mark for the unknown quantity.
3. Children solve the problem. They may use the number model or situation diagram to help them, or they may use another method entirely.
4. Children share their solutions, and you record them on the board. During the discussion of the solutions, you fill in the blanks in the number model or diagram.

10.2 Use Classes and Situation Diagrams

One way to understand something is to examine how it is used. A hammer is used for pounding nails. An umbrella is used for keeping dry in the rain. This is how *Everyday Mathematics* approaches the four basic operations of arithmetic—by examining how they are used. At a certain stage, formal definitions can be valuable, but in the elementary grades it is better to foster understanding of the operations indirectly by looking at how they are used.

Addition, subtraction, multiplication, and division can each be applied in many different situations, but most of those situations can be sorted into just a handful of categories, or *use classes.* In *Everyday Mathematics,* the three basic use classes for addition and subtraction are called *parts and total, change,* and *comparison.* Depending on what is known and what is unknown, each kind of situation can lead to either addition or subtraction problems. Multiplication and division situations are harder to sort out, but several basic use classes can be distinguished: *equal groups, arrays and area, rate and ratio, scaling,* and *Cartesian products.* Each type of situation can lead to either multiplication or division problems depending on what is unknown.

NOTE: A use class gets its name by asking *In what situation is this operation used?*

Everyday Mathematics uses *situation diagrams* to help sort out these various kinds of problem situations. These diagrams help children organize the information in simple 1-step number stories.

NOTE: The diagrams in *Everyday Mathematics* are adapted from work done by Karen Fuson at Northwestern University.

10.2.1 Addition and Subtraction Use Classes

Most situations that lead to addition and subtraction problems can be categorized into parts-and-total, change, or comparison use classes.

Parts-and-Total Diagrams

In a *parts-and-total* situation, there is a total quantity that can be separated into two or more parts. For example, the total number of children in a class can be separated into the number of girls and the number of boys. Or the total distance from Chicago to St. Louis can be separated into the distance from Chicago to Springfield and the distance from Springfield to St. Louis.

A parts-and-total diagram has a large rectangle on top for the Total and two or more smaller rectangles below for the Parts as shown below. The rectangles are filled with numbers for particular problems.

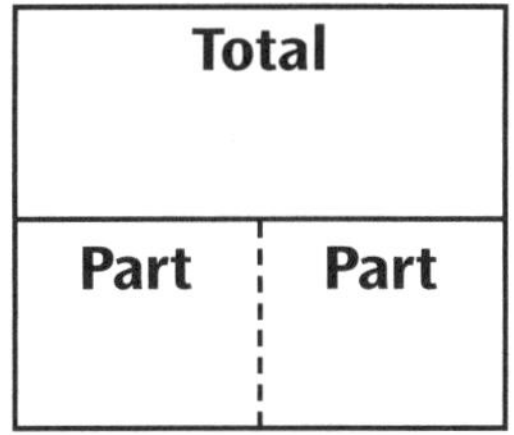

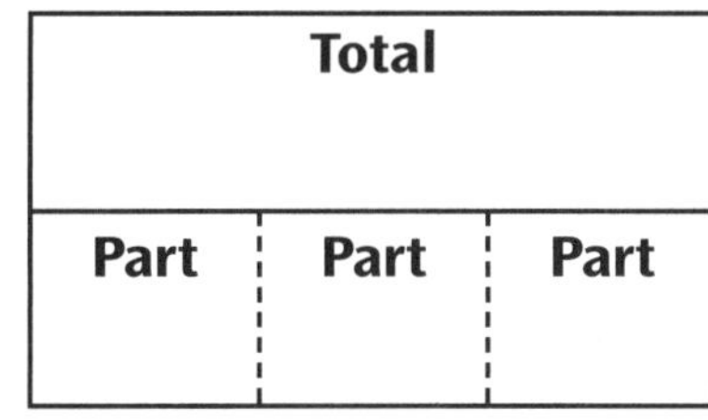

Parts-and-total diagrams

When you and your students draw your own diagrams, quick and easy freehand drawings are best. The words "Part" and "Total" can be omitted or replaced with words that better fit the problem situation as in the following examples.

In a situation where all the parts are known but the total is unknown, you can solve the problem by adding the parts.

Example 1: Twelve fourth graders and 15 first graders are on a bus. How many children in all are on the bus?

The parts are known. You are looking for the total.

Possible number model: 12 + 15 = __

total number of children on bus ?	
4th graders 12	1st graders 15

?	
12	15

For a situation in which the total is known but one of the parts is unknown, you can use subtraction to find the unknown part.

Example 2: Thirty-five children are riding on the bus. Twenty of them are boys. How many girls are riding on the bus?

One part and the total are known. You are looking for the other part.

Possible number models:

20 + __ = 35

35 − 20 = __

Total 35	
Part 20	Part ?

Change Diagrams

A second kind of addition/subtraction situation is *change.* In a change situation there is a starting quantity, a change in quantity, and an ending quantity. For example, a 15-cm-tall plant might grow 5 cm in a week and end up 20 cm tall. Or, you might start with a certain amount of money, spend some, and then have less money at the end. Change situations can lead to either addition or subtraction problems depending on the direction of the change *(change to more* or *change to less)* and what is known or unknown.

A change diagram has a rectangle on the left for the Start quantity, then an arrow above a blank for the Change, and finally a rectangle on the right for the End quantity.

Example 3: Twenty-five children are riding on the bus. At the next stop, 5 more children get on. How many children are on the bus now?

This is a change-to-more situation, or an increase, with the ending quantity unknown.

Possible number model: 25 + 5 = __

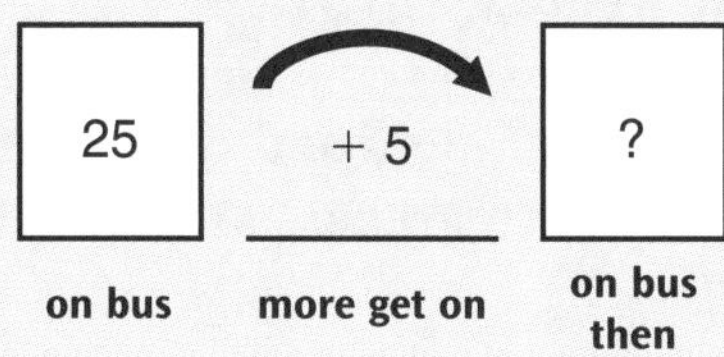

NOTE: You can simplify change diagrams by omitting words or changing to words that fit the problem as in Example 3.

Example 4: A bus leaves school with 35 children. At the first stop, 6 children get off. How many children are left on the bus?

This is a change-to-less situation, or a decrease, with the ending quantity unknown.

Possible number models:

35 − 6 = __

6 + __ = 35

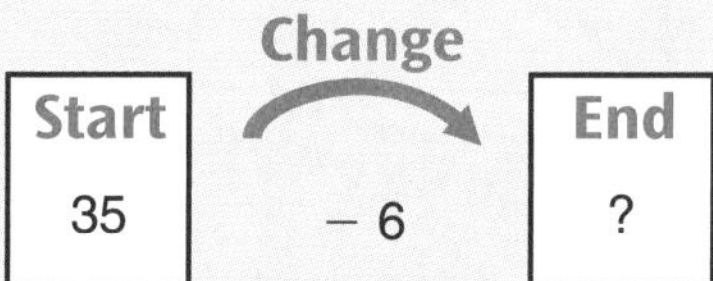

Example 5: Tom had some money. He bought a magazine for \$1.50. Then he had \$6.50. How much money did Tom have to start with?

This is a change-to-less situation with the starting quantity unknown.

Possible number models:

____ − \$1.50 = \$6.50

\$1.50 + \$6.50 = ____

Change

Start ? | − \$1.50 | End \$6.50

Comparison Diagrams

Comparison situations involve two separate quantities and the difference between them. For example, one person might be 60 inches tall and another 70 inches tall; the difference in heights is 10 inches. Or one person might be 25 years old, another 6 years old, and the difference in ages 19 years. As with change and parts-and-total situations, comparison situations can lead to addition or subtraction depending on what is known and what kind of comparison is being made.

A comparison diagram has a large rectangle on top for the larger Quantity being compared and smaller rectangles below for the smaller Quantity and the Difference.

Example 6: There are 12 fourth graders and 8 third graders. How many more fourth graders are there than third graders?

Here both quantities being compared are known and the difference is unknown.

Possible number models:

12 − 8 = _

8 + _ = 12

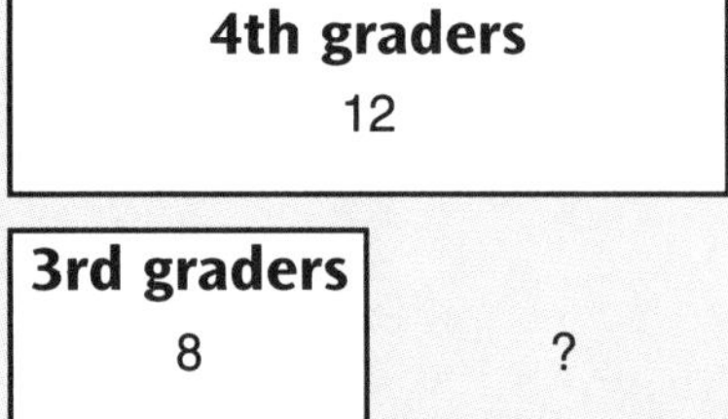

Example 7: Vicky is 40 inches tall. Amelia is 4 inches shorter. How tall is Amelia?

Here one of the quantities being compared and the difference are known. The other quantity being compared is unknown.

Possible number models:

40 − _ = 4

40 − 4 = _

_ + 4 = 40

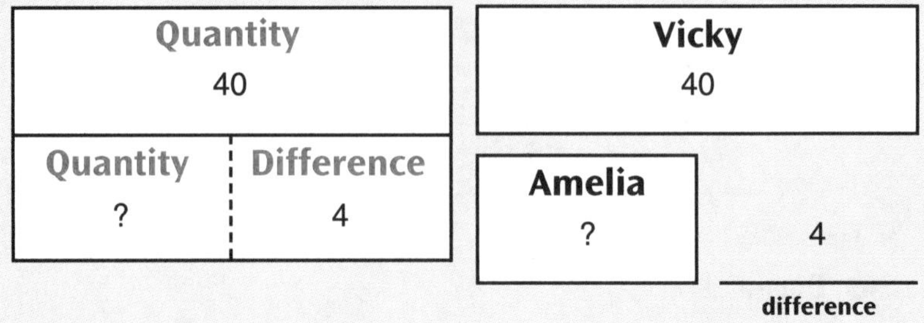

chapter 10

Teaching with Addition/Subtraction Diagrams

It is important to remember that situation diagrams are simply devices to help organize problem solving; they are not ends in themselves. Some children do not need to organize their thinking on paper, and to require them to do so would not be constructive.

For those children who find diagrams useful, *Everyday Mathematics* suggests that they follow these steps, although not necessarily in this order:

- Choose a diagram that fits the problem situation, but keep in mind that more than one diagram may fit. One person might think of a problem as a parts-and-total situation, while another person sees it as a change situation. Don't be too inflexible about which diagram is the most appropriate for a given situation, and remember that many situations are not suitable for any diagram. Multistep problems, for example, do not easily fit into these diagrams.
- Write the known quantities and a question mark for the unknown quantity in the appropriate parts of the diagram.
- Use the diagram to help decide how to solve the problem. Most problems can be solved in more than one way. A change-to-more problem, for example, might be solved by addition, by counting up mentally or on a number grid, by acting out with counters, or by drawing pictures.
- Calculate an answer.
- Write a number model that fits the problem. The number model does not need to reflect how the problem was solved. For example, a child might write "8 + 3 = 11" for a change-to-more problem that she solved using counters. Often, several number models can fit a single situation. Connecting number models to situations can help children understand both the arithmetic operations and the symbols for those operations.
- Write an answer. Be sure to include a measurement unit or other label.
- Check to see if the answer makes sense.

Unit Boxes

The importance of including a unit or other label in an answer cannot be over-emphasized. Numbers and operations make the most sense to children when they are thought of in real-world contexts. Encourage children to attach appropriate units of measure or other labels, such as cents, lions, or feet, to the numbers they are using.

Because labeling each number in a situation diagram can be tedious, *Everyday Mathematics* suggests that you and the children use *unit boxes* for addition and subtraction problems. These rectangular boxes can be displayed beside the problem or at the top of a page of problems. Unit boxes contain the labels or units of measure used in the problem(s). Unit boxes help children organize their mathematics while keeping a particular context in mind.

Unit
cents ¢

A unit box

For more information on facts practice, see Section 16.3.2: Basic Facts and Fact Power.

Some teachers post a unit box for the day on the board so that children will have a context in which to think about all the abstract numbers used in the day's activities, such as facts practice. Or children can supply the context themselves; they can choose topics of current interest or, if they prefer, fanciful or silly labels.

10.2.2 Multiplication and Division Use Classes

Multiplication and division arise in many different situations, but most of these situations can be sorted into just a few use classes: *equal groups, arrays and area, rate and ratio, scaling,* and *Cartesian products.*

For more information on alternative approaches, see Chapter 18: Problem Solving.

Everyday Mathematics uses diagrams to organize the information in many of these situations. The diagrams have two rows of rectangles. The top row is for the units; the bottom row is for the numbers. As with the diagrams for addition and subtraction situations, these diagrams are meant as problem-solving tools, not as ends in themselves. If using a diagram is not helpful, try some other approach, such as making a table or acting the problem out with objects.

Equal Groups

Much of the multiplication and division work in *Kindergarten* through *Third Grade Everyday Mathematics* involves equal groups. In an equal-groups situation, there are several groups of objects with the same number of objects in each group. Depending on what is unknown, equal-groups situations can lead to either multiplication or division problems.

In an equal-groups situation where the total is unknown but the number of groups and the number of objects in each group are known, you can solve the problem by multiplication.

Example 1: A vase holds 5 flowers with 6 petals on each flower. How many petals are there in all?

Possible number model: $5 \times 6 = \_$

flowers	petals per flower	total number of petals
5	6	?

In situations where the number of groups and the total number of objects are known, the problem is to find the number in each group. In *Everyday Mathematics,* these are called *equal-sharing* problems. Equal sharing is also known as *partitive division.*

Many children solve equal-sharing problems by "dealing out" the objects to be shared.

Example 2: Twenty-eight baseball cards are to be shared equally by 4 children. How many cards does each child get?

Possible number models:

$4 \times \_ = 28$

$28/4 = \_$

$28 \div 4 = \_$

children	baseball cards per child	total number of cards
4	?	28

In situations where the number in each group and the total number of objects are known, the problem is to find the number of groups. In *Everyday Mathematics,* these are called *equal-grouping* problems.

Many children solve equal-grouping problems by making as many groups of the correct size as possible and then counting the number of groups.

Example 3: Twenty-four Girl Scouts are going on a canoe trip. Each canoe can hold 3 scouts. How many canoes are needed?

Possible number models:

$3 \times \_ = 24$

$24/3 = \_$

$24 \div 3 = \_$

canoes	scouts per canoe	total number of scouts
?	3	24

Equal-grouping problems are also called *measurement division* or *quotitive division.* The term measurement division comes from thinking about using the divisor to "measure" the dividend. For example, consider 26 ÷ 6. Think *How many 6s would it take to make 26?* Then imagine measuring off 6-unit lengths on a number line:

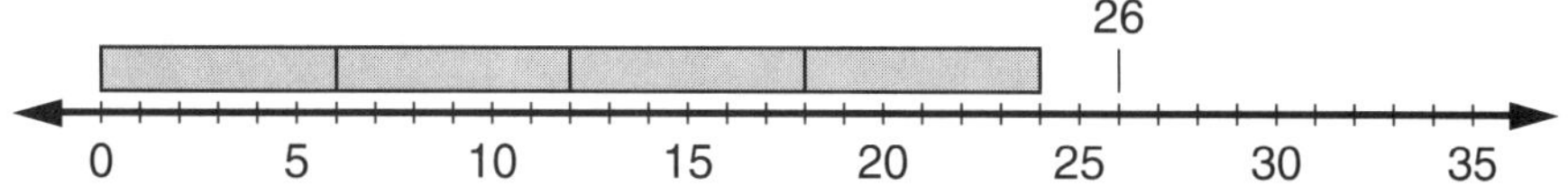

The figure above shows that there are four 6-unit lengths in 26, with 2 units left over. Thus 26 ÷ 6 is 4 with remainder 2.

chapter 10

An array of chairs

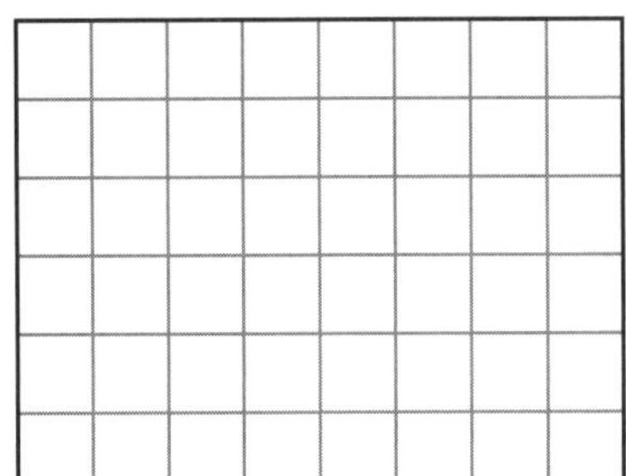

Arrays and Area

Arrays are closely related to equal-groups situations. If the equal groups are arranged in rows and columns, then a rectangular *array* is formed. As with equal-groups situations, arrays can lead to either multiplication or division problems.

Example 4: There are 6 rows with 15 chairs in each row. How many chairs are there in all?

Possible number model: $6 \times 15 = \_$

rows	chairs per row	total chairs
6	15	?

Arrays are closely related to *area.* An array of square-centimeter tiles with no gaps between the tiles will have an area in square centimeters equal to the number of tiles.

Example 5: The area of a rectangle is 48 cm^2. The rectangle's length is 8 cm. What is its width?

Possible number models:

$8 \times \_ = 48$

$48 \div 8 = \_$

length (cm)	width (cm)	area (cm^2)
8	?	48

Note that because of the Commutative Property of Multiplication, the factors in array and area situations can be interchanged without affecting the value of the product. The total number of chairs in Example 4 would not change if there were 15 rows with 6 chairs in each row. And if the rectangle in Example 5 had a width of 8 cm, its length would be 6 cm to give an area of 48 cm^2.

However, the difference between a 6-by-15 array and a 15-by-6 array is important not only in the context of some problems, for example, the direction the chairs have to face determines which number represents a row, but in mathematics that students may study later in school. A *matrix* is a mathematical name for an array, and to perform arithmetic with matrices requires keeping track of rows and columns. For these reasons, it is a good idea to always talk about the dimensions of an array as meaning "rows" by "columns," in that order.

This does not mean that children should be penalized for getting rows and columns switched, especially when they correctly answer problems in array situations. If a child has them backward, simply point out *Oh, your array is turned.*

Rates and Ratios

Rate and *ratio* situations are common in higher mathematics and in real-life applications. A *rate* compares two quantities with *different* units. A common situation involving a rate is speed, which is the rate of distance per time, but many other situations can also be thought of as rates as well. When you buy apples, for example, the total cost depends on the amount you purchase and the price per pound, a rate.

Example 6: The 8 people on the pep squad worked a total of 20 hours preparing for the school assembly. What was the average number of hours per person?

Possible number models:

$20/8 = \_$

$20 \div 8 = \_$

$8 \times \_ = 20$

people	hours per person	total person-hours
8	?	20

For more information, see Section 9.3.3: Rates and Ratios.

Ratio situations are modeled just like rate situations, but in a ratio, the quantities have the *same* unit.

Scaling

Scaling is another situation that leads to multiplication or division. A *scale factor* tells how much larger or smaller something becomes. For example, when you double a recipe you are scaling by 2. If the scale factor is less than 1, then scaling makes something smaller, such as halving a recipe by the factor $\frac{1}{2}$.

Example 7: Hector weighed 6 lb at birth. At 1 year, he weighed 3 times his birth weight. What was his weight at 1 year?

Possible number model: $3 \times 6 = \_$

scale factor	birth weight (lb)	1-year weight (lb)
3	6	?

Scale factors, also known as *scalars,* can be fractions or percents. Scaling problems can involve either multiplication or division, depending on what is known and what is to be found.

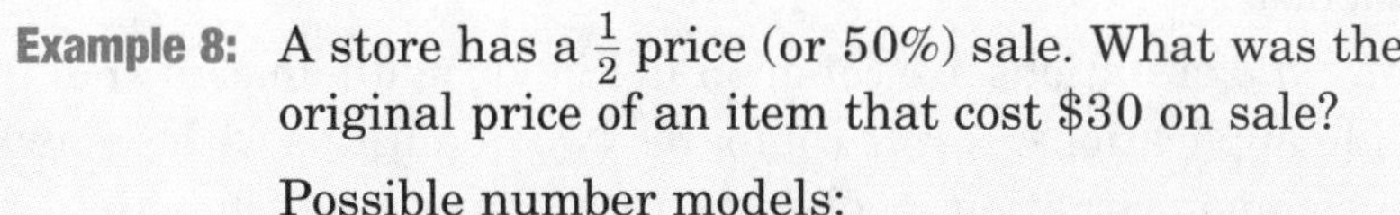

Example 8: A store has a $\frac{1}{2}$ price (or 50%) sale. What was the original price of an item that cost \$30 on sale?

Possible number models:

$\frac{1}{2} \times \_ = 30$

$30 \div \frac{1}{2} = \_$

scale factor	original price	sale price
$\frac{1}{2}$	?	\$30

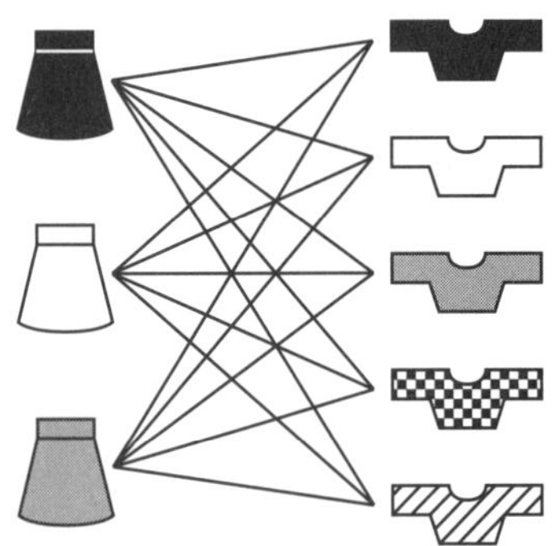

A Cartesian product:
3 × 5 = 15 outfits

Cartesian Products

The last kind of multiplication and division situation in *Everyday Mathematics* involves Cartesian products. Despite the imposing name, the idea is not difficult. A *Cartesian product* is the number of pairings of each item from one set to each item of another set. For example, suppose someone has 3 skirts (black, white, gray) and 5 blouses (black, white, gray, checked, striped). The Cartesian product 3 × 5 tells how many outfits that person has: black skirt and black blouse, black skirt and white blouse, and so on. If the two sets are not too large, this can be shown in a drawing like the one in the margin.

Teaching with Multiplication/Division Diagrams

See "Teaching with Addition/Subtraction Diagrams" on page 89 for suggestions on how students might use these diagrams. Keep in mind that the diagrams are devices to help organize problem solving, not ends in themselves. Some students simply do not need to organize their thinking on paper, and to oblige them to do so is not advisable.

▸ 10.3 Operations and Number-Models Tools and Techniques

Tools and techniques to help children learn operations and facts include the following:

- Situation diagrams described in Section 10.2: Use Classes and Situation Diagrams;
- Computational algorithms, both traditional and invented, discussed at length in Chapter 11: Algorithms;
- Calculators, discussed in Section 3.1.1: Calculators.

11 Algorithms

Contents

An *algorithm* is a well-defined procedure or set of rules used to solve a problem. Algorithms are often used in everyday life. A recipe, for example, is an algorithm. Having children become comfortable with algorithmic and procedural thinking is essential to their growth and development as solvers of everyday problems.

Skillful use of algorithms can help children:

- Use a single method to solve an entire class of related problems;
- Improve their use of mental arithmetic skills;
- Develop sound number sense, including a good understanding of place value;
- Strengthen their mathematical power.

This chapter begins with an explanation of how *Everyday Mathematics* approaches computational algorithms, including the role of invented algorithms in developing understanding of operations, place value, and computational procedures.

Then algorithms are described for the four basic arithmetic operations with whole numbers. For each operation, one algorithm has been designated as a *focus* algorithm. The focus algorithms are not identical to the computational algorithms that are traditionally taught, but they are similar. In addition to being easier to learn and use than are traditional algorithms, the focus algorithms reveal more about underlying concepts such as place value and are less likely to lead to wrong answers.

The chapter ends with a brief discussion of calculator key sequences as algorithms and how to "program" calculators to skip count.

▶ 11.1 Algorithms and Procedures

As a teacher, you establish many procedures and routines to help your classroom run smoothly. For example, in the beginning of the year, you probably discuss the proper procedures for hanging up coats, lining up, and using materials. *Everyday Mathematics* encourages you to establish similar, but more mathematical, routines such as keeping a weather record or class calendar.

NOTE: The term *algorithm* comes from the name *al-Khwarizmi.* Muhammad ibn Musa al-Khwarizmi (c. 780–850) was one of the greatest mathematicians of the Arab-Islamic world. We also have al-Khwarizmi to thank for the word *algebra*, which comes from *Hisab Aljabr w'al-muqabalah,* the title of one of his books.

An *algorithm* is a well-defined, step-by-step procedure guaranteed to achieve a certain objective, often with several steps that "loop" as many times as necessary. For example, an algorithm for multiplication will produce the correct product no matter what the factors are.

A good algorithm is efficient, unambiguous, and reliable. Although you may be most familiar with the traditional elementary school procedures for adding, subtracting, multiplying, and dividing, there are many other algorithms both in mathematics and in real life. A computer program is an algorithm that specifies what a computer is to do at each step. The instructions for operating calculators or complicated equipment, such as FAX machines and VCRs, are forms of algorithms.

Everyday Mathematics includes a variety of both traditional computational algorithms and children's invented procedures. Inventing procedures is valuable because it:

For more information, see Section 11.1.2: Algorithm Invention.

- Promotes conceptual understanding and mental flexibility, both of which are essential for effective problem solving;
- Helps students learn about our base-ten place-value (decimal) system of numeration;
- Involves solving problems that the solver does not already know how to solve. Thus, asking children to devise their own computational methods provides valuable experience in solving nonroutine problems.

For more information, see Section 11.2: Traditional and Alternative Algorithms.

Traditional algorithms have advantages, too. They are generally efficient and can help children understand both the decimal number system and the underlying operations. Traditional algorithms also provide a common vocabulary for further development of mathematical ideas.

In addition to studying specific algorithms in *Everyday Mathematics,* children engage in activities to help them understand algorithms in a more general sense. Included are:

- Understanding specific algorithms or procedures provided by other people;
- Applying known algorithms to everyday problems;
- Developing algorithms and procedures when necessary;
- Realizing the limitations of algorithms and their procedures so that they are not used inappropriately;
- Adapting known algorithms to fit new situations.

Mathematics advances in part through the development of efficient procedures that reduce difficult tasks to routine exercises. An effective algorithm will solve an entire class of problems, thus increasing the user's mathematical power. The authors of *Everyday Mathematics* have found that the study of paper-and-pencil computational algorithms can be valuable for developing algorithmic thinking in general.

11.1.1 Computational Algorithms

Several teachers have asked the *Everyday Mathematics* authors about the role of computational algorithms in elementary school mathematics. *Should traditional paper-and-pencil algorithms be taught? Should children be expected to use these algorithms to solve complex computational problems? Should calculators be used in the classroom? If so, in which circumstances and under what conditions?*

Before we attempt to answer these questions, consider the following stories told by Professor Zalman Usiskin of the University of Chicago:

Scene 1: An Office Hal is preparing an end-of-the-month sales report. This involves doing many calculations, which he does, churning out each computation on paper. In walks the boss, horrified, saying, "Hal, why aren't you using a calculator? You're wasting valuable time!"

Scene 2: A Fourth-Grade Classroom The class is working on a page of difficult computational problems. Susie gets out her calculator and starts completing the assignment. The teacher walks over to Susie, horrified, saying, "Susie, put that calculator away or you'll get done too quickly!"

These two scenarios highlight the need to rethink the school mathematics curriculum in light of the widespread availability of calculators and computers outside of school. Children certainly still need:

- To know the meanings and uses of all the arithmetic operations in order to function in the practical world and to succeed in mathematics in high school and beyond;
- To know the basic addition and multiplication facts automatically, especially to help solve mental-arithmetic problems in our technological society;
- To understand and be able to apply paper-and-pencil algorithms for addition, subtraction, multiplication, and division of whole numbers, decimals, and fractions, especially in an environment of standardized testing.

Today's elementary school children also need to be prepared to be productive workers in the second half of the 21st century. Among other things, this means they need a conception of computation that takes into account advances in technology. For example, skill at judging the reasonableness of results is especially important for anyone using technology, whether sophisticated computer spreadsheets and modeling programs or simple four-function calculators. Estimation and approximation skills are also important both because many

NOTE: Algorithmic thinking has its place in geometry, too. The axiomatic method used by Euclid to prove theorems relies on clear definitions and logical, deductive steps. Although having students understand geometric proof is not a goal in *Everyday Mathematics*, students in Grades 4 through 6 perform compass-and-straightedge constructions that are step-by-step algorithms proving geometric theorems.

For more information on these articles, see "Resources on Algorithms in Schools" on page 99.

NOTE: In *Mind Bugs: The Origins of Procedural Misconceptions,* cognitive scientist Kurt Van Lehn said this about using the traditional subtraction algorithm in some of his research:

> [O]rdinary multidigit subtraction . . . is a virtually meaningless procedure [for] most elementary school children. . . . When compared to procedures they use to operate vending machines or play games, subtraction is as dry, formal, and as disconnected from everyday interests as the nonsense syllables used in early psychological investigations were different from real words. This isolation is the bane of teachers. . . .

everyday applications of mathematics require quick, approximate answers and because one good way to judge whether a result is reasonable is to compare it to a sensible estimate. For all these purposes, mental arithmetic, both exact and approximate, is more useful than ever.

Along with increased attention to estimation and approximation, the broader approach to computation in *Everyday Mathematics* also includes paper-and-pencil algorithms taught with both efficiency and understandability in mind. That is, children are expected to know both *how* to add, subtract, multiply, and divide using paper and pencil methods and also *why* the methods they are using work. Research carried out in the past 30 years by Kurt Van Lehn and others has shown that many children develop "buggy" algorithms that resemble standard procedures but do not work properly. In subtraction, for example, some children always subtract the smaller digit from the larger digit. Van Lehn has shown that bugs such as this develop because children are trying to carry out procedures they don't understand and can't remember well enough to reproduce accurately. Procedures that are well understood, on the other hand, are more easily recalled, are more easily "repaired" when they are not recalled accurately, and are more easily modified to fit new situations.

Children who solve mathematics problems using methods that they understand come to believe that mathematics is logical, that if they work at mathematics they can figure it out, and that doing mathematics can be enjoyable.

Because there are many paper-and-pencil methods that are both efficient and understandable, the authors of *Everyday Mathematics* believe that children should be exposed to paper-and-pencil algorithms for these reasons:

- Exploring different algorithms builds estimation skills and number sense and helps children see mathematics as a meaningful and creative subject.
- There are situations in which the most efficient or convenient way to carry out a computation is with paper and pencil.
- If taught properly for understanding, but without demands for "mastery" by all children by some fixed time, paper-and-pencil algorithms can reinforce children's understanding of our number system and of the operations themselves.

In the debate about algorithms, *Everyday Mathematics* takes a moderate position, combining elements from both the child-centered, invented-algorithms approach and the subject-matter-centered, traditional-algorithms approach. During the early phases of learning an operation, *Everyday Mathematics* encourages children to invent their own procedures. Children are asked to solve arithmetic problems from first principles about situations in which operations are used, before they develop or learn systematic procedures for solving such problems. This helps them to understand the operations better and also gives them valuable experience solving nonroutine problems.

Later, when children thoroughly understand the concept of the operation, several alternative algorithms are introduced. Some of these algorithms are based on approaches that many children devise on their own. Others are less likely to be discovered by children but have a variety of desirable characteristics. Children are urged to experiment with various algorithms in order to become proficient at using at least one alternative.

You may find it useful to examine the issues involved with teaching and learning paper-and-pencil algorithms by reading the following:

Resources on Algorithms in Schools

Brownell, W. A. (1986). The revolution in arithmetic. *Arithmetic Teacher, 34 (2)*, pp. 38–42. (Original work published in 1954.)

Coburn, T. G. (1989). The role of computation in the changing mathematics curriculum. In P. R. Trafton (Ed.), New directions for elementary school mathematics. Reston, VA: National Council of Teachers of Mathematics.

Morrow, J. J., and Kenney, M. J. (Eds.) (1998). *The Teaching and Learning of Algorithms in School Mathematics: 1998 Yearbook.* Reston, VA: National Council of Teachers of Mathematics.

Pollak, H. O. (1983). The mathematical sciences curriculum K-12: What is still fundamental and what is not. Reprinted in T. A. Romberg and D. M. Stewart (Eds.), The monitoring of school mathematics: Background papers (Vol. 1). Madison, WI: Wisconsin Center for Education Research. (Originally published as a report from The Conference Board of the Mathematical Sciences, 1983.)

Randolph, T. D., and Sherman, H. J. (2001). "Alternative Algorithms: Increasing Options, Reducing Errors." *Teaching Children Mathematics 7(8),* p. 480.

Van Lehn, K. (1990). *Mind Bugs: The Origins of Procedural Misconceptions.* Cambridge, MA: MIT Press.

11.1.2 Algorithm Invention

Because the authors of *Everyday Mathematics* view computational algorithms as more than rote procedures, the program aims to make children active participants in the development of algorithms. Such participation requires a good background in the following three areas:

- *The decimal system for number writing* In particular, children need to understand place value.
- *Basic facts* To be successful at carrying out multistep computational procedures, children need to know basic facts automatically.
- *The meanings of the operations and the relationships among operations* To solve 37 – 25, for example, a student might reason *What number must I add to 25 to get 37?*

The authors of *Everyday Mathematics* believe that children should be encouraged to invent their own procedures. As children devise their own methods, they use their prior mathematical knowledge and their common sense, along with new skills and knowledge. They also learn to manage their resources by asking *How long will this take? Is there a better way?* Such resource management is important in problem solving. As children devise their own methods, they also develop persistence and confidence in dealing with difficult problems. Children who invent their own methods learn that their intuitive methods are valid and that mathematics makes sense.

For more information, see Section 16.3: Mental Arithmetic.

Inventing procedures also promotes proficiency with mental arithmetic. Many techniques that children invent are much more effective for mental arithmetic than standard paper-and-pencil algorithms are. *Everyday Mathematics* wants all children to develop a broad repertoire of computational methods and the flexibility to choose whichever procedure is the most appropriate in any particular situation.

Learning a single traditional algorithm for each operation, especially at an early stage, may inhibit the development of children's mathematical understanding and is likely to cause them to miss out on the rich experiences that come from developing their own methods. Although prematurely teaching traditional paper-and-pencil algorithms can foster persistent errors and "buggy" algorithms, the main problem with teaching traditional algorithms too early is that children may use the algorithms as substitutes for thinking and common sense.

$$\begin{array}{r} 300 \\ -\ 1 \\ \hline \end{array}$$

Many children resort to the traditional algorithm to solve this subtraction problem.

For example, the authors of *Everyday Mathematics* presented the problem in the margin to a large number of children. Most traditionally taught second and third graders immediately resorted to the traditional algorithm, often failing to get the correct answer. Only a handful of these children interpreted the problem as asking *What is 1 less than 300?* or *What number plus 1 gives 300?* or *What is the number just before 300?* and answered "299" without performing any computations.

In the modern world, most adults reach for calculators when faced with any moderately complicated arithmetic computation. This behavior is sensible and should be an option for children, too. Nevertheless, children benefit in the following ways from developing their own noncalculator procedures:

- Children are more motivated when they do not have to memorize traditional paper-and-pencil algorithms without understanding why they work. In fact, most people are more interested in things that they can understand, and children generally understand their own methods, as obscure as they may be to others.
- Children are better at maneuvering among different mathematical models. They readily translate among manipulatives, oral and written words, pictures, and symbols. The ability to represent a problem in more than one way is important in problem solving.
- Children are more able to transform any given problem into an equivalent, easier problem. For example, 32 − 17 can be transformed to the easier 35 − 20, because adding 3 to both numbers in a subtraction problem does not change the answer.

NOTE: Working on a grid of small squares such as a piece of graph paper can help many children to organize the placement of digits as they use paper-and-pencil algorithms. The grid lines help children keep digits with the same place value in a vertical orientation. Often, such a grid is provided in *Everyday Mathematics* when children are expected to calculate using paper and pencil.

- Children gain experience in nonroutine problem solving by devising creative problem-solving strategies and in refining those strategies for use on a more permanent basis. They learn to manage their resources efficiently and build on what they already know. They also develop persistence and confidence in dealing with difficult problems.

Algorithm invention develops best when:

- It is allowed to flourish in an accepting and supportive classroom environment;
- You allow time for experimentation;
- Computational tasks are embedded in real-life contexts;
- Children share their solution strategies with you and with one another.

Through classroom discussion of solution methods, you will gain valuable insight into children's progress, while they become more skilled at communicating mathematics and at understanding and critiquing others' ideas. Such communication skills will be especially important in the collaborative workplaces where children are likely to find themselves when they enter the workforce.

11.1.3 Alternative and Focus Algorithms

After children have had plenty of opportunities to experiment with computational strategies of their own, *Everyday Mathematics* introduces several algorithms for each operation. Some of these algorithms closely resemble methods that children are likely to have devised on their own. Others are traditional algorithms, both those that have been customarily taught in U.S. classrooms and other algorithms that have been traditional in other times and places. Still others are simplifications of traditional algorithms or wholly new algorithms that have significant advantages in today's technological world. Many of the algorithms presented are highly efficient, and most are easier to understand and learn than are traditional algorithms.

Everyday Mathematics also designates one of the alternative algorithms for each operation as a *focus algorithm*. Focus algorithms are powerful, relatively efficient, and easy to understand and learn. All children are expected to learn the focus algorithm for each operation. In solving problems, however, children may use either the focus algorithm or any other methods they choose. The aim of this approach is to promote flexibility while ensuring that all children know at least one reliable method for each operation.

The authors of *Everyday Mathematics* believe that the focus algorithms are superior to the U.S. traditional algorithms for today's children and tomorrow's working adults. Nevertheless, parents and others may value the traditional algorithms highly for various reasons and may therefore believe they should be included in the school curriculum. This may also be your own preference.

In any case, *Everyday Mathematics* hopes you will do what is best suited to your situation. The program's aim is to help teachers, not to impose ideas or demands on them.

Everyday Mathematics encourages you to observe children's algorithmic and procedural thinking when they are engaged in activities dealing with topics other than computation. For example, one child may have an algorithmic approach to drawing geometric figures or patterns, and another may invent ways to convert metric measures by "moving" decimal points. If a procedure warrants it, have a student share it with the class and point out the use of the "idea of an algorithm." A really good procedure might even be named after the student and entered into a class database of algorithms.

11.2 Traditional and Alternative Algorithms

Decimal, or base-ten place-value, numeration spread from India to the Middle East and eventually all over the world, in part because it is easier to calculate with it than with other bases. In the thousand years or so that Hindu-Arabic numeration has been in use, many algorithms have been devised for each of the fundamental arithmetic operations. In some sense, all of these algorithms are traditional, or standard, in that at some time and in some place a group of people used each of them. The traditional addition algorithm that many of us learned in school is only one of many alternatives. The same can be said for algorithms for each of the other arithmetic operations.

Students in *Fourth* through *Sixth Grade Everyday Mathematics* extend whole-number algorithms to decimals and learn several new algorithms for operating with fractions.

Over a dozen algorithms for adding, subtracting, multiplying, and dividing whole numbers are presented in the following sections. Some of them are easier to understand than the U.S. traditional algorithms, although they may seem more complicated at first because they are unfamiliar. Several of the algorithms presented are well suited for mental arithmetic or for very large numbers. Some are easier to learn, if perhaps a bit less efficient than others. If efficiency is the goal, however, note that in many situations any paper-and-pencil algorithm will be inferior to mental arithmetic or technology. Several of these algorithms are based on children's mental arithmetic efforts and search for procedures. All are procedures that you may suggest to children who need some help getting started.

11.2.1 Addition Algorithms

This section discusses several algorithms for whole-number addition: *partial-sums addition, column addition, the opposite-change rule,* and *U.S. traditional addition.*

Focus Algorithm: Partial-Sums Addition

As the name suggests, the *partial-sums-addition algorithm* calculates partial sums, working one place-value column at a time, and then adds all the partial sums to find the total.

		6,802
		+ 453
Add the thousands.	6,000 + 0	6,000
Add the hundreds.	800 + 400	1,200
Add the tens.	0 + 50	50
Add the ones.	2 + 3	+ 5
Add the partial sums.	6,000 + 1,200 + 50 + 5	**7,255**

The partial sums can be found in any order, but working from left to right is the usual procedure. This order seems natural because we read from left to right, and it also focuses on the most important digits in the addends first (thousands before hundreds, hundreds before tens, and so on). A variation on this algorithm can be used to estimate sums quickly: The sum is estimated from only the partial sum(s) for the addends' left-most digits. This is known as *leading-digit estimation.* The partial-sums algorithm can be readily adapted for mental arithmetic.

Partial-sums addition is the algorithm most similar to addition with base-10 blocks. Finding each partial sum corresponds to combining all of one kind of base-10 block. Adding the partial sums corresponds to exchanging blocks as necessary and then combining like blocks.

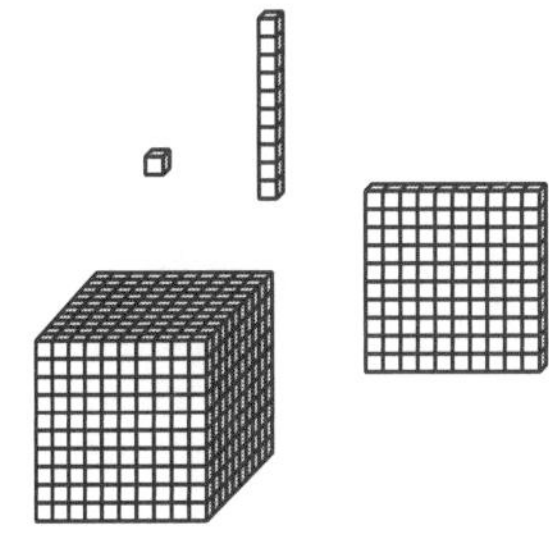

For more information, see Section 9.7.1: Base-10 Blocks.

Column Addition

In the *column-addition algorithm,* vertical lines are drawn to separate ones, tens, hundreds, and so on. Once columns have been created, the usual place-value convention that each place must have only one digit can be broken without confusion. If you wish, you can label the columns "ones," "tens," and so on. The digits in each column are then added, beginning in any column. Finally, any necessary trades are made, again starting in any column. For example, to calculate 967 + 495:

	9	**6**	**7**
	+ **4**	**9**	**5**
Add each column separately, working in any order.	13	15	12
If necessary, adjust, working in any order.	14	5	12
If necessary, adjust, working in any order.	**14**	**6**	**2**

So 967 + 495 = 1,462. Many students find this algorithm natural and instructive. For some, the process becomes so natural they start at the left and write the answer column by column, adjusting as they go without writing any of the intermediate steps. If asked to explain, they might say something like the following about the sum in the margin:

> *200 plus 400 is 600, but* (looking at the next column) *I need to fix that, so I write 7. Then 60 and 80 is 140, but that needs fixing, so I write 5. The 8 and 3 is 11. With no more to do, I can just write 1.*

$$\begin{array}{r} 268 \\ +\ 483 \\ \hline 751 \end{array}$$

The column-addition algorithm was shown and explained to the *Everyday Mathematics* authors by a first grader. It has become a favorite. The algorithm occurs naturally to many children, and it also has the advantage of quickly producing a rough estimate of the sum. It is also better suited to mental arithmetic than the U.S. traditional algorithm.

The Opposite-Change Rule for Addition

In the *opposite-change rule,* a number is added to one addend and the same number is subtracted from the other addend. So the sum remains the same. For example, consider:

$$8 + 7 = 15$$

If 2 is added to the 8 and subtracted from the 7, you have:

$$(8 + 2) + (7 - 2) = 10 + 5 = 15$$

The idea behind this method is to rename the addends so that one ends in one or more zeros. This may take several steps, but eventually the addition becomes trivial.

Example 1: Rename so that the first addend ends in zeros.

268	$\xrightarrow{+2}$	270	$\xrightarrow{+30}$	300
+ 483	$\xrightarrow{-2}$	+ 481	$\xrightarrow{-30}$	+ 451
			Add:	751

Example 2: Rename so that the second addend ends in zeros.

268	$\xrightarrow{-7}$	261	$\xrightarrow{-10}$	251
+ 483	$\xrightarrow{+7}$	+ 490	$\xrightarrow{+10}$	+ 500
			Add:	751

The opposite-change rule is also well suited to mental arithmetic. With a little practice, children can become quite proficient.

U.S. Traditional Addition

The *U.S. traditional addition algorithm* has many strengths. It is widely known, relatively efficient, and fairly easy to learn. Many children learn how to use this algorithm from their parents or siblings because it is as much a cultural tradition as a mathematical procedure. Therefore, it is likely to be mentioned when you ask children to explain their solutions to multidigit addition problems.

The U.S. traditional addition algorithm is similar to column addition shown above, but it requires the user to proceed column by column from right to left and to observe place values at all times. These requirements make the algorithm more efficient but harder to learn than some of the others.

The user begins with the right-most column, mentally finds the sum of all the digits in that column, writes the ones digit of the sum below the line, and "carries" the tens digit of the sum to the top of the next column to the left. The process is repeated for each column to the left. The "carry" digits can be mysterious to children, so be sure to explain them in terms of place value and renaming when you discuss this algorithm.

	588 + **143**
Add the ones. *(8 ones + 3 ones = 11 ones)* Regroup. *(11 ones = 1 ten and 1 one)* →	1 588 + 143 1
Add the tens. *(1 ten + 8 tens + 4 tens = 13 tens)* Regroup. *(13 tens = 1 hundred and 3 tens)* →	11 588 + 143 31
Add the hundreds. *(1 hundred + 5 hundreds + 1 hundred = 7 hundreds)* → **731** is the total.	1 588 + 143 **731**

588 + 143 using the U.S. traditional algorithm

In whole-number addition, the starting column is the ones place. In decimal addition, the starting column is the right-most decimal place.

The addition algorithm is probably the best of the U.S. traditional computation algorithms. While *Everyday Mathematics* does not focus on it, it is a viable alternative. If you decide to teach this algorithm, be sure to treat it as one of several possibilities and, as with any algorithm, be sure that children understand how it works.

11.2.2 Subtraction Algorithms

There are even more algorithms for subtraction than for addition, probably because subtraction is more difficult. This section discusses five algorithms for whole-number subtraction: *trade-first, counting-up, European, left-to-right,* and *partial-differences.*

Focus Algorithm: Trade-First Subtraction

The *trade-first subtraction algorithm* resembles the U.S. traditional subtraction algorithm, except that all the trading is done before all the subtraction, allowing the user to concentrate on one thing at a time. The following steps are involved:

1. Examine all columns and trade as necessary so that the top number in each place is as large or larger than the bottom number. The trades can be done in any order. Working left to right is perhaps more natural, as with partial-sums addition; but working right to left is a bit more efficient.

```
 8 10 5 12
 9,0 6 2
- 4,7 3 8
```

2. Check that the top number in each place is at least as large as the bottom number. If necessary, make more trades.
3. Subtract column by column in any order.

```
 8 10 5 12
 9,0 6 2
- 4,7 3 8
  4,3 2 4
```

Trade-first subtraction is highly efficient, similar to the traditional algorithm, and relatively easy to learn. It is an effective algorithm for paper-and-pencil calculation.

Many teachers find that drawing vertical lines between the places is helpful for children when first learning this algorithm. The vertical

chapter 11

lines allow children to focus on one column at a time. They also help children avoid mistakes if unnecessary trades have been made.

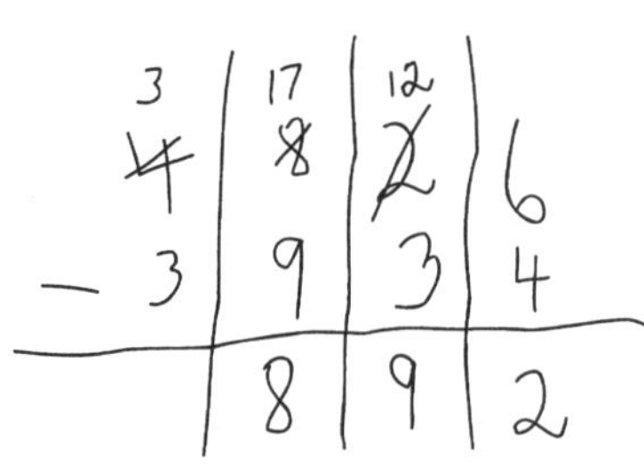

Trade-first subtraction with columns

Trade-first subtraction with an unnecessary trade

Counting-Up Subtraction

The *counting-up subtraction algorithm* is similar to what cashiers do when they give change. In both procedures, the user begins at the smaller number and counts up to the larger number. In giving change, the cashier tenders bills or coins to the purchaser. In counting-up subtraction, the user keeps a running total of the amounts counted up and then totals all of the count-up amounts to find the difference.

The counting-up technique that is the basis for this algorithm is useful in mental computation, although mentally keeping a correct running total requires practice. When the procedure is carried out mentally, it helps to start with the larger places.

Solve 932 − 356 by counting up.

356	
(+ 4)	Count to the nearest 10.
360	
(+ 40)	Count to the nearest 100.
400	
(+ 500)	Count to the largest possible 100.
900	
(+ 32)	Count to the larger number.
932	

Then add the numbers you circled.

$$\begin{array}{r} 4 \\ 40 \\ 500 \\ +\ 32 \\ \hline 576 \end{array}$$

So, 932 − 356 = 576.

European Subtraction

The U.S. traditional subtraction algorithm involves regrouping, or "borrowing," from the next place to the left. That is, in the problem 623 − 345, one of the 2 tens in 623 is traded for 10 ones. This is written:

$$\begin{array}{r} {\scriptstyle 1\ 13} \\ 6\not{2}\not{3} \\ -\ 345 \\ \hline \end{array}$$

A variation on this procedure called the *European subtraction algorithm* increases the bottom number in the next column to the left:

$$\begin{array}{r} {\scriptstyle 13} \\ 62\not{3} \\ -\ 3{\scriptstyle 1}45 \\ \hline 8 \end{array}$$

The small mark next to the 4 in 345 is a ten that compensates for adding 10 to the 3 on top. The next step is to subtract 50 instead of 40. Because you can't take away 5 tens from the 2 tens in 623, use the same strategy again, this time increasing the hundreds digit in the bottom number. Then subtract 1 + 4 = 5 tens from 12 tens to get 7 tens.

$$\begin{array}{r} 6\,\overset{12}{\not 2}\,\overset{13}{\not 3} \\ -\ {}_{1}3\,{}_{1}4\,5 \\ \hline 7\,8 \end{array}$$

The mark next to the 3 on the bottom is a hundred that compensates for adding 10 tens to the top. The final step is to subtract 1 + 3 = 4 hundreds from 6 hundreds to get 2 hundreds.

$$\begin{array}{r} 6\,\overset{12}{\not 2}\,\overset{13}{\not 3} \\ -\ {}_{1}3\,{}_{1}4\,5 \\ \hline 2\,7\,8 \end{array}$$

You may find the European algorithm confusing, but it is the traditional algorithm used in many other countries in the world today. You might want to spend a few minutes thinking about how increasing the number on the bottom has the same effect as decreasing the number on the top. If you want to experience what it might be like for a child to learn the U.S. traditional subtraction algorithm, you might try learning this European subtraction algorithm.

Left-to-Right Subtraction

With the *left-to-right subtraction algorithm,* the user starts at the left and subtracts column by column. For the problem 932 − 356:

	932
Subtract the 100s.	− 300
	632
Subtract the 10s.	− 50
	582
Subtract the 1s.	− 6
	576

Like left-to-right addition, the left-to-right subtraction algorithm can be used to find a rough estimate of a difference.

Partial-Differences Subtraction

The *partial-differences subtraction algorithm* is a fairly unusual method, but one that appeals to some children.

The procedure is fairly simple: Write partial differences for each place, record them, and then add them to find the total difference. A complication is that some of the partial differences may be negative.

		932
		− 356
Subtract 100s.	*900 − 300*	600
Subtract 10s.	*30 − 50*	−20
Subtract 1s.	*2 − 6*	−4
Add the partial differences.		576

11.2.3 Multiplication Algorithms

Adults usually reach for calculators when they have to multiply "difficult" numbers. Similarly, calculators should be available to children when they deal with problems that they understand but that involve calculations beyond their current skills. This allows the curriculum to include more realistic, interesting, and instructive problems. Nevertheless, for the reasons discussed in Section 11.1.1, *Everyday Mathematics* includes a significant amount of work with paper-and-pencil multiplication.

As always, *Everyday Mathematics* suggests that children share their strategies and discuss how they created their computational procedures. Inventing procedures for multiplication and division is more difficult than for addition and subtraction, but children who have experience with the latter two will be well prepared to attempt the former two. When doing mental arithmetic, for example, many children begin to compute partial products: *Ten of these would be . . ., so 30 of them would be . . ., and then we need 5 more, so . . .*. Beginning in *Third Grade Everyday Mathematics,* this approach is formalized as the partial-products algorithm, the focus algorithm for multiplication.

There are many multiplication algorithms besides the partial-products algorithm and traditional right-to-left long multiplication. Former University of Chicago graduate student Raven Deerwater (formerly known as Dan Hirschhorn), after only a few hours' search of old schoolbooks and mathematics education articles, found more than 40 different multiplication algorithms. About 25 of them were special "tricks" for quick mental multiplication of numbers with special characteristics or procedures you may remember from high school algebra. Some were very efficient but difficult to explain. More than 15 of the 40 were general algorithms for multiplying any two whole numbers. Several of these algorithms are discussed below.

Focus Algorithm: Partial-Products Multiplication

In the *partial-products multiplication algorithm,* think of each factor as a sum of ones, tens, hundreds, and so on. For example, think of 67 × 53, 67 as 60 + 7 and 53 as 50 + 3. Then multiply each part of one factor by each part of the other factor. Finally, add all the resulting partial products.

	67
	× 53
50 × 60	3000
50 × 7	350
3 × 60	180
3 × 7	+ 21
	3551

You don't have to work from left to right; any order will do as long as all possible partial products are found. Working from left to right, however, does help keep the procedure orderly and also, as with left-to-right procedures for addition and subtraction, produces a quick estimate of the product.

In order to use the partial-products algorithm efficiently, children must be adept at multiplying multiples of 10, 100, and 1,000, such as 60×50 in the example above. These skills also help children to make ballpark estimates of products and quotients.

The partial-products algorithm can be demonstrated visually using arrays. The diagram below shows how a 23-by-14 array represents all of the partial products in 23×14.

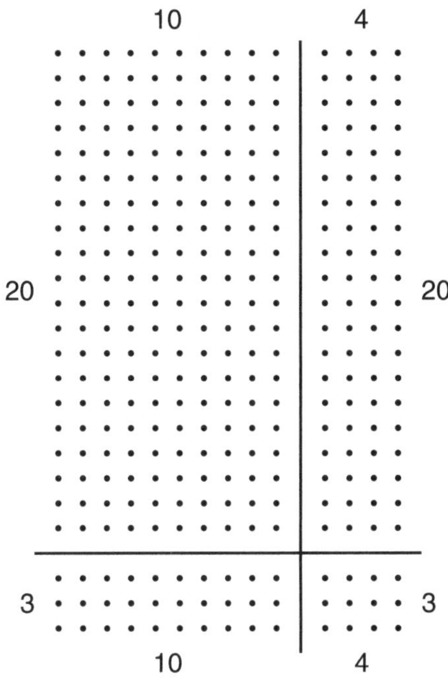

$$
\begin{aligned}
23 \times 14 &= (20 + 3) \times (10 + 4) \\
&= (20 \times 10) + (20 \times 4) + (3 \times 10) + (3 \times 4) \\
&= 200 + 80 + 30 + 12 \\
&= 322
\end{aligned}
$$

NOTE: The partial-products algorithm uses the Distributive Property of Multiplication over Addition repeatedly.

First, $20 \times (10 + 4) = (20 \times 10) + (20 \times 4)$.
Second, $3 \times (10 + 4) = (3 \times 10) + (3 \times 4)$.

Lattice Multiplication

Everyday Mathematics initially included *lattice multiplication* for its recreational value and historical interest and because it provided practice with multiplication facts and adding strings of single-digit numbers. To our surprise, lattice multiplication has become a favorite of many children.

chapter 11

Why the lattice method works is not immediately obvious, but it is very efficient and powerful. The authors have found that with practice, it is more efficient than standard long multiplication for problems involving more than two digits in each factor. And problems that are too large for long multiplication or for most calculators can be solved using lattice multiplication.

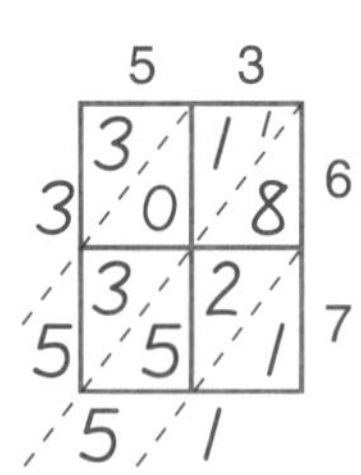

67 × 53 = 3,551 by lattice multiplication

NOTE: In 1478, in Treviso, Italy, lattice multiplication appeared in what is said to be the first printed arithmetic book. Amazingly, it was in use long before that, with historians tracing it to Hindu origins in India before A.D. 1100.

To multiply 67 by 53:

1. Draw a 2-by-2 lattice as in the margin.
2. Write one factor along the top of the lattice and the other along the right, one digit for each row or column.
3. Multiply each digit in one factor by each digit in the other factor. Write the products in the cells where the corresponding rows and columns meet. Write the tens digit of these products above the diagonal and the ones digit below the diagonal.
4. Starting at the bottom-right corner, add the numbers inside the lattice along each diagonal. Write these sums along the bottom and left of the lattice. If the sum on a diagonal exceeds 9, carry the tens digit to the next diagonal to the left.

Multiplying larger numbers requires a larger lattice.

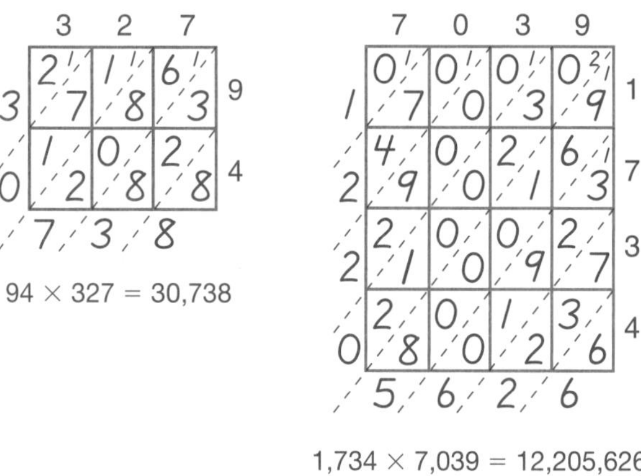

94 × 327 = 30,738

1,734 × 7,039 = 12,205,626

To understand why lattice multiplication works, note that the diagonals in the lattice correspond to place-value columns. The far right-hand diagonal is the ones place, the next diagonal to the left is the tens place, and so on.

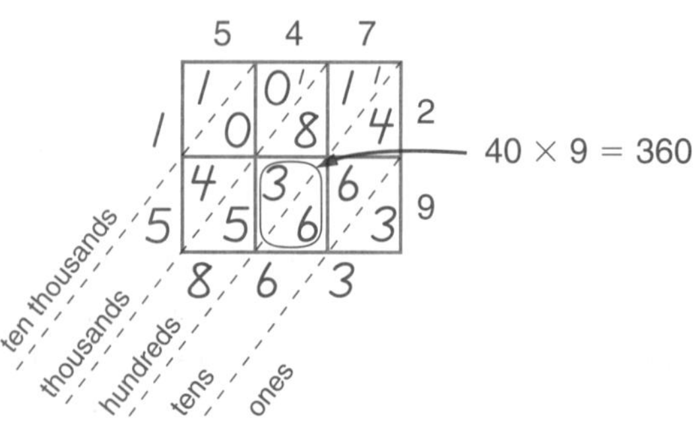

Modified Repeated Addition

Contrary to what is often taught, multiplication is not merely repeated addition, even for whole numbers and certainly not for decimals and fractions. Moreover, as a computational method for multiplying, repeated addition is inefficient for anything but small numbers. For example, it would be unbearably tedious to add fifty-three 67s in order to compute 67 × 53.

If you think of ten 67s as 670, however, you can first add the 670s (there are five of them) and then add the three 67s, as shown in the margin. This *modified repeated-addition algorithm* is a good "broken calculator" exercise to find a product without using the [×] key.

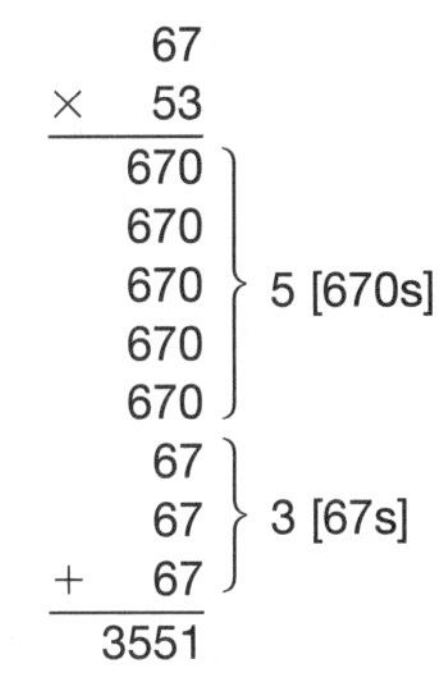

Modified repeated addition

Modified U.S. Traditional Multiplication

Example 1 in the margin shows the U.S. traditional multiplication algorithm for calculating 67 × 53. Although this algorithm does indeed work and is moderately efficient, many people who use it cannot explain the shifting to the left in successive partial products. Even harder to explain is why the 3 in the 35 from 5 × 7 is written above the 6 in 67. When asked why the 3 is written in the tens place, many adults say that the 3 stands for 3 tens, which is incorrect. The 3 actually stands for 300 because it comes from 50 × 7 = 350.

When many adults say they "understand" this algorithm, what they really mean is simply that they can carry it out correctly. The authors believe that real understanding includes both knowing what to do and knowing why it works. By these criteria, many adults' "understanding" of the traditional long multiplication algorithm is incomplete.

Example 2 solves the shift-over-a-place mystery by inserting a zero in the blank. This makes clear that for the second partial product, we are multiplying by 50 (five 10s) and not by 5. The reason for putting the 3 above the 6 is still unresolved; it's actually there for convenience in mentally adding to the product of 5 times 6, which is really 50 times 60. This version is a bit easier to understand than the traditional form.

Example 3 uses a left-to-right approach. Though it has its advantages, it is otherwise no different from the standard algorithm with 0s in place of the blanks.

Examples

1.	2.	3.
3	3	2
2	2	3
67	67	67
× 53	× 53	× 53
201	201	3350
335	3350	201
3551	3551	3551

Modified U.S. traditional algorithms

11.2.4 Division Algorithms

Children can benefit from mastering a paper-and-pencil division algorithm for several reasons. It supports their understanding of the concept of division, can be practically useful, meets societal expectations, and completes a set of paper-and-pencil algorithms that enables them to solve problems involving all the fundamental operations of arithmetic.

For more information, see Section 10.2.2: Multiplication and Division Use Classes.

The practical needs of children to succeed on standardized tests may also require the teaching of paper-and-pencil division algorithms. Moreover, as discussed above and in Section 11.1.1, there are good reasons for teaching certain paper-and-pencil methods for division.

$37 \div 5$

$$\begin{array}{r} 37 \\ -\ 5 \\ \hline 32 \\ -\ 5 \\ \hline 27 \\ -\ 5 \\ \hline 22 \\ -\ 5 \\ \hline 17 \\ -\ 5 \\ \hline 12 \\ -\ 5 \\ \hline 7 \\ -\ 5 \\ \hline 2 \end{array}$$

7 [5s] in 37

Repeated subtraction

In *Fourth Grade Everyday Mathematics, partial-quotients division,* an efficient whole-number division algorithm, is developed from the straightforward repeated subtraction approach outlined above. *Fifth Grade Everyday Mathematics* integrates mental-math techniques with this paper-and-pencil algorithm.

Equal-size grouping is the basis for many division algorithms. For example, $a \div b$ can be interpreted as *How many* b*s are in* a? One approach is simply to subtract b from a as many times as possible and then to count the number of subtractions. To calculate $37 \div 5$ using this repeated subtraction method is feasible (see margin), but for larger numbers this straightforward approach becomes impractical.

Although a formal introduction to division algorithms is not included in *Kindergarten* through *Third Grade Everyday Mathematics,* children do solve many division problems using conceptual methods like repeated subtraction, "dealing out" items to be shared, or looking for missing factors. Rather than a goal of computational efficiency, the goals are to develop children's conceptual understanding of division and to build proficiency in the many skills that are required in multidigit division.

A Note on Division by Zero

One often hears that dividing by zero is not defined or allowed. The reason for this is that dividing by zero does not produce a proper answer. Here are several ways to see why this is so:

- Any division problem can be rewritten as a missing-factor multiplication problem. For example, the problem $56 \div 7 = n$ can be rewritten as $7 \times n = 56$. The task then becomes to find the missing factor. In $7 \times n = 56$, the missing factor is 8, which is the answer to the original division problem.

  When a division by zero is rewritten as a missing-factor multiplication problem, it becomes apparent that no answer will work. Consider, for example, $24 \div 0 = n$. When the problem is rewritten as $0 \times n = 24$, it is clear that no number can be multiplied by zero to get an answer of 24.
- When a series of division problems using the same dividend but smaller and smaller divisors is graphed, it becomes apparent that the closer the divisor is to zero, the larger the quotient becomes. For example, consider dividing 12 by a series of divisors: $12 \div 6 = \mathbf{2}$, $12 \div 4 = \mathbf{3}$, $12 \div 3 = \mathbf{4}$, $12 \div 2 = \mathbf{6}$, $12 \div 1 = \mathbf{12}$. The quotient is clearly larger each time the divisor gets closer to zero. The effect becomes even more striking with divisors less than 1: $12 \div \frac{3}{4} = \mathbf{16}$, $12 \div \frac{1}{2} = \mathbf{24}$, $12 \div \frac{1}{4} = \mathbf{48}$, $12 \div \frac{1}{8} = \mathbf{96}$, $12 \div \frac{1}{16} = \mathbf{192}$. The graph on the next page illustrates this situation. As the divisor approaches zero, the quotient "approaches infinity," that is, becomes large without limit. Because infinitely large quotients make no sense, division by zero is not allowed.

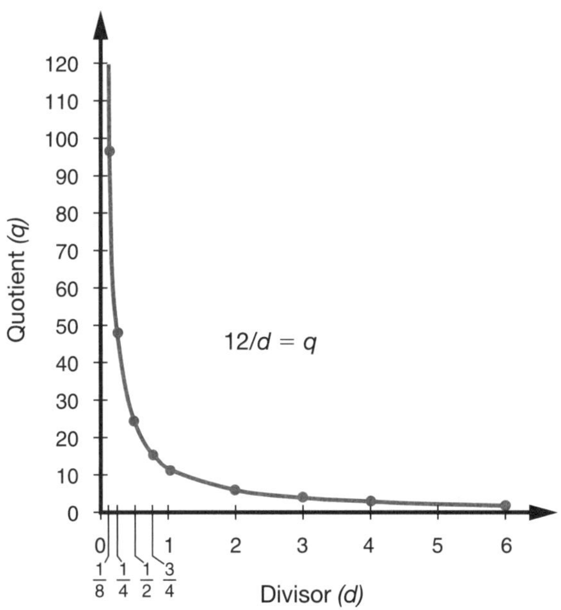

As the divisor approaches zero,
the quotient approches infinity.

- Just as multiplication can be seen as repeated addition of equal groups, division can be seen as repeated subtraction of equal groups. For example, $15 \div 5 = n$ can be solved by finding out how many times 5 can be subtracted from 15. However, if the divisor is zero, the question becomes how many times zero can be subtracted from a given number. Clearly, there is no sensible answer.
- Division problems can also be written as fractions. For example, $8 \div 4 = 2$ can be written as $\frac{8}{4} = 2$ and $3 \div 4 = 0.75$ can be written $\frac{3}{4} = 0.75$. Just as division by zero is not allowed, having zero as the denominator of a fraction is not allowed.

  The denominator of a fraction represents the number of parts into which a whole has been divided, but a whole cannot be divided into zero parts. For example, a pizza can be cut into fourths, or four equal parts; it can also be cut into halves, or two equal parts; or it could be left uncut, which means it has one part. But, there is no way to cut it so that it has zero parts. One whole pizza is one part before you start cutting it.

$$\left.\begin{array}{r} 15 \\ -\;\;5 \\ \hline 10 \\ -\;\;5 \\ \hline 5 \\ -\;\;5 \\ \hline 0 \end{array}\right\} 15 \div 5 = 3$$

$$\left.\begin{array}{r} 15 \\ -\;\;0 \\ \hline 15 \\ -\;\;0 \\ \hline 15 \\ -\;\;0 \\ \hline 15 \\ . \\ . \\ . \end{array}\right\} 15 \div 0 = ???$$

Repeated subtraction
of 0 makes no sense.

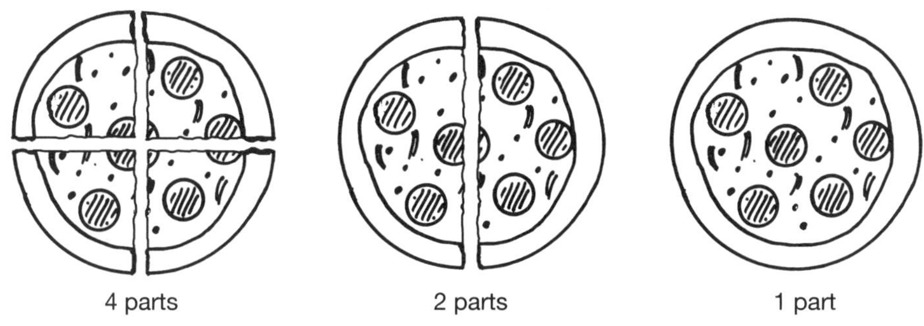

There is no way to cut a pizza so it has 0 parts.

chapter 11

11.3 Algorithms on Calculators

In a sense, using a calculator requires learning new algorithms, namely the *key sequences,* to get an anticipated result. Learning a new key sequence should be a topic of instruction, not something left for children to figure out for themselves. Therefore, when children encounter new keys and key sequences, spend a few minutes talking about the correct procedures for the model of calculator they have. Write the proper key sequences on the board and have students work through several sample problems.

For more information, see Section 3.1.1: Calculators.

Although the authors used the Texas Instruments TI-108 and Casio SL-450 calculators while writing *Kindergarten* through *Third Grade Everyday Mathematics,* many other calculators work just as well. Whatever the model, if all children have the same one, then the same key sequences work on every child's calculator, making it easier for you to manage activities. In particular, having one model of calculator ensures that they will all follow the same algorithm for the order of operations. Both of the 4-function calculators above simply calculate expressions from left to right, unlike scientific calculators that follow the algebraic order of operations.

For more information on the order of operations, see Section 10.1.2: Reading and Writing Number Sentences.

Key sequences in the *Teacher's Lesson Guide* and in the student materials are for both TI-108s and Casio SL-450s. In most cases, one or both of the key sequences also work with other calculators. If you have different calculators, you should check that the given sequences work with your machines. In some cases, you may need to consult the owner's manual that came with your calculators.

Without specifically identifying the brands and models, the basic operations of the TI-108 and Casio SL-450 are described in the *Student Reference Book.* The TI is Calculator A; the Casio is Calculator B. The authors have consciously limited ourselves to discussing features, or functions, that are common to both calculators and that are appropriate for each grade level. If you wish to explore other functions with your children, please consult the owner's manual for ideas.

One important kind of algorithmic thinking in the world of computers and calculators is *programming.* Every program is an algorithm, whether it be as simple as the one that a calculator uses to add two numbers or as complicated as the ones in a word processor. Programming computers is not a goal of *Everyday Mathematics,* but children do program their calculators to skip count.

Skip Counting

Many calculators have a repeat function that can be used to skip count on or back by some number from any starting number. The function is actually a sequence of two or more steps, depending on the calculator. Have children learn to "program" their calculator to skip count using the following activity.

You can program your calculator to skip count up or back. The program needs to tell the calculator four things.

- What number to *count by;*
- Whether to *count up or back;*
- What number to *start* at;
- *When* to count.

The order of the steps in the program depends on your calculator. Here's how to program the TI and Casio calculators.

Starting at 1, count by 2s on your calculator.

TI-108

Purpose	Key Sequence	Display
Clear the calculator short-term memory and display.	ON/C ON/C	0.
Tell the calculator to start at 1 and count up.	1 +	1.
Tell the calculator to count by 2s and do the first count.	2 =	3.
Tell the calculator to count again.	=	5.
Keep counting by pressing =.	=	7.

To count back by 2s on a TI-108, enter 1 − in the second step.

Casio SL-450

Purpose	Key Sequence	Display
Clear the calculator short-term memory and display.	AC	0.
Tell the calculator to count up by 2. The "K" on the display means "constant." It means the calculator knows the count-by number and direction.	2 + +	K 2.
Tell the calculator to start at 1 and do the first count.	1 =	K 3.
Tell the calculator to count again.	=	K 5.
Keep counting by pressing =.	=	K 7.

To count back by 2s on a Casio SL-450, enter 2 − − in the second step.

NOTE: On more advanced calculators, a "K" (constant) key is sometimes used for repetitive operations. See your owner's manual for details.

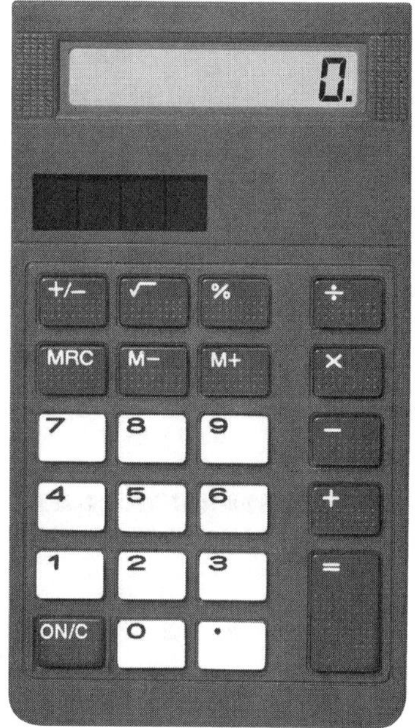

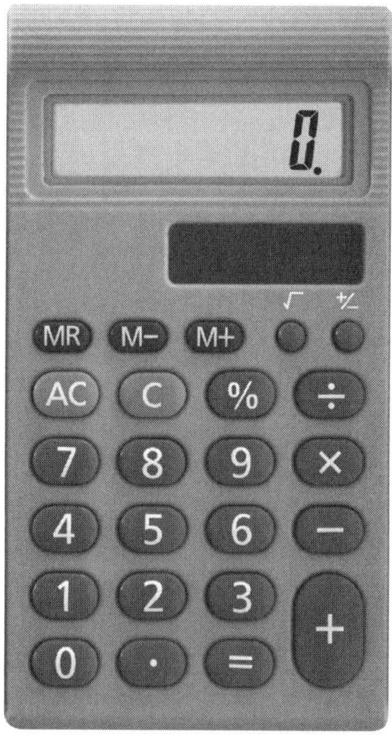

chapter 11

Data and Chance

Contents

Understanding statistics and probability is more important now than ever before. In a world inundated with numbers, citizens and consumers need to understand claims about data and probabilities in journalism and advertising. Workers need to know how to gather, display, and analyze data in order to work efficiently and effectively. Even many recreational activities such as fantasy sports leagues involve data and chance. Statistics and probability have become prominent in the elementary school curriculum, both because of their current importance and as a source of contexts for practicing arithmetic and other skills.

12.1 Probability

Everyday Mathematics authors believe that most children need to be exposed to concepts and skills many times in many different ways, often only briefly, before they are able to master them. The treatment of probability in the curriculum is a good example of this approach. Children play informal games and engage in activities involving the idea of fairness and the use of random-number generators such as cards, number cubes, and spinners. The first step toward a more formal treatment occurs in *Third Grade Everyday Mathematics.*

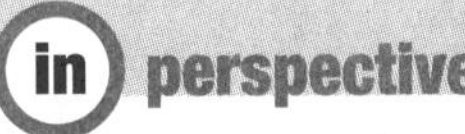

Probability ideas are extended and made more precise throughout the rest of *Everyday Mathematics.* The *Probability Meter,* a number-line device for recording probabilities, is introduced in Grade 5.

12.1.1 Why Study Probability?

Most people are aware that our world is filled with uncertainties. Although there are some things that we can be sure of, for example, that the sun will rise tomorrow or that it will be hot this summer in Florida, we also know that there are degrees of uncertainty and that some things are more likely to happen than others. We know that there are also uncertain occurrences, such as weather patterns, that can be predicted with increasing accuracy. These qualitative ideas of probability—*impossible, possible, likely, certain,* and so on—are the basis for the mathematical treatment of probability in *Everyday Mathematics.*

Few people understand how to calculate the chance that something will take place. Yet many decisions in our personal lives, from the relatively trivial *Should I take an umbrella with me?* to the vitally important *Should I undergo surgery?* are based on probabilities. Probability is more useful in daily life than are most other branches of mathematics and fully deserves the greater prominence given to it in most contemporary elementary school mathematics curricula.

12.1.2 The Language of Chance

Because children should become comfortable talking about chance events as early as possible, *Everyday Mathematics* begins by focusing on vocabulary development. Some of the many terms introduced are *sure, certain, probably, 50-50, unlikely,* and *impossible.* These terms should not be taught formally. Through repeated use, children will gradually make them part of their vocabularies. Many children are familiar with terms like *forecast* and *predict,* but not with the term *probability.* Probability is a difficult word and need not be used at first.

All children have had experience comparing the chances of various outcomes of a random process. They understand everyday statements like *Rain is more likely than snow today.* They may also understand that getting a sum of 7 is more likely than getting a sum of 3 when two dice are rolled. Such informal comparisons are a good place to begin, because they provide a context in which the language of chance can be intuitively introduced. Discuss the fact that some things are certain to happen and other things are certain to not happen. The most interesting things are in between, neither certain nor impossible. Point out that if we think hard enough, we can often say which of these uncertain things are more likely to occur than others.

Randomness

Throughout *Everyday Mathematics,* many activities rely on spinning spinners, drawing from card decks, rolling dice, and flipping coins. All of these are procedures for generating random results, but randomness is not formally defined until fifth grade. This is because randomness is simple to describe with words such as *haphazard, unpredictable, without pattern,* and *chaotic,* but difficult to define formally and hard to verify in practice. Technically, a *random outcome* is an event selected from a set of outcomes, all of which have an equal probability of being selected. There are several reasons why randomness is hard to verify in practice.

First, there is the problem of assuring truly equal probabilities. Many variables affect this, such as position of a spinner, weight distribution

For more information, see Section 12.4.1: Random-Number Generators.

in a die, and thoroughness of the shuffle of a card deck. These problems affect classroom activities that rely on randomly generated numbers, but they are essentially beyond control. In *Everyday Mathematics,* random-number generators are trusted to provide numbers that are random enough to serve their purpose.

The second problem in verifying random results is an individual's perception of what such results should look like. Imagine a list of 1,000 randomly generated single-digit numbers. Somewhere in the list there are six consecutive 3s. Is this a problem? Most people would think so; it is counter to the notion that random means "all shook up." Six 3s in a row seems to be a pattern, and therefore the list is suspect. Similarly, if you flip a coin 8 times and get 8 HEADS, the coin seems suspect.

Results like these lead people to believe that previous outcomes can affect the next outcome. For example, one might think *After 8 HEADS in a row, it seems that I should expect TAILS on the next toss, because I believe that on average, a fair coin will land TAILS half the time. TAILS are now overdue.* The belief that a fair coin will land TAILS half the time is correct *on average, in the long run*. However, it is incorrect to think that the previous eight HEADS affect the ninth toss, for which there is still a 50-50 chance of getting HEADS (or TAILS). If you see children acting as though past results affect the probability of future outcomes, you might ask them about their thoughts on the matter.

Two 6-sided dice

For more information on rolling two dice, see Section 12.4.1: Random-Number Generators.

12.1.3 Making Predictions

In most of the probability activities in *Everyday Mathematics,* children make a prediction about the likelihood of a particular outcome of some random process such as rolling a die or flipping a coin. Then they check their predictions by performing an experiment that involves collecting, organizing, and interpreting data. Some activities call for students to compare the likelihood of several possible outcomes. Other activities ask students to estimate the chance that something will happen by assigning it a numerical value. For example, when a coin is tossed, the chance of it landing HEADS up is 1 out of 2 or $\frac{1}{2}$ because there are two ways the coin could land, one of which is HEADS up. When a single die is rolled, the chance of getting an even number is 3 out of 6, or $\frac{3}{6}$, because there are three even numbers {2, 4, 6} out of the six ways the die can land {1, 2, 3, 4, 5, 6}.

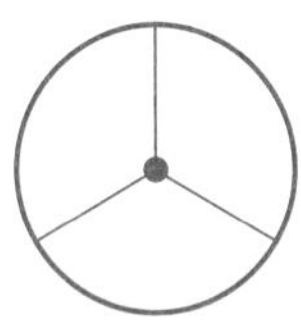

A *fair* spinner: The probability that a spin will land in any one of the three regions is $\frac{1}{3}$.

All outcomes are equally likely for some situations such as flipping a fair coin, rolling a fair die, and spinning a spinner that is divided into equal-size parts, and so on. In other situations, the outcomes are not equally likely. For example, when two 6-sided dice are rolled, a sum of 7 on the top faces is more likely than a sum of 4. In experiments with unequally divided spinners, most children will probably conclude quickly that the spinner is more likely to land on the larger regions than on the smaller ones. Spinners are extremely useful for helping students to visualize the idea of chance.

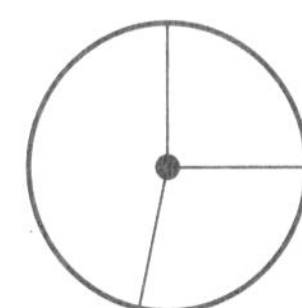

An *unfair* spinner: The probability that a spin will land in any one of the three regions is not $\frac{1}{3}$.

Many random processes lend themselves to intuitive predictions because their outcomes follow very definite laws of chance. Coin tosses and spinner experiments are good examples of these. Other processes do not lend themselves to such precise analysis. Predicting the weather is much harder than predicting the outcome of a coin toss.

The Law of Large Numbers

In the long run, *Everyday Mathematics* aims to help children understand that the more often they repeat an experiment, the more reliable their predictions will be. For example, if a coin is tossed 10 times, it is possible, but not certain, that it will land HEADS up about half the time. If you try it, you may be surprised at how often you obtain a 7-3 or 8-2 split. But if the coin is tossed 100 times, it is more likely to land nearer to a 50-50 split, as the occurrences of HEADS and TAILS tend to "even out" with more tosses.

Children have a variety of experiences throughout *Everyday Mathematics* that illustrate this important idea, known to mathematicians as the *law of large numbers.* For example, in *Third Grade Everyday Mathematics,* children participate in a block-drawing experiment. Children are asked to figure out how many blocks of different colors are hidden in a bag by examining the results of repeatedly drawing a block from the bag. The more times they draw a block, the more likely it is that they will make the correct guess.

In *Fifth Grade Everyday Mathematics,* pairs of students each take small samples from a bowl of multicolored candy and count how many of each color they have. The class then pools the results from each pair to form one large sample, thereby concluding that a large sample produces a better estimate of the color distribution than does a small sample.

12.2 Data Collection, Organization, and Analysis

Children's initial data explorations should be informal, allowing them to collaborate with you and with one another to decide on methods of collecting, representing, and explaining their data. As children gain experience using common displays such as bar and line graphs and appropriate statistical landmarks such as median and range, they can answer questions and communicate their findings to others.

For more information on landmarks, see Section 12.2.4: Data Analysis.

12.2.1 Formulating a Question

Ordinarily, data are collected and analyzed to describe a situation and/or to make predictions. The process almost always begins with a question. When we want to know something, a good strategy is to gather information. Then we look at the information—the *data*—in various ways to determine whether we found what we wanted to know.

There are two important reasons to take time to formulate a question for data exploration. The first is motivational. Data-collection activities are usually more meaningful to children if they are connected to a real-life problem or involve situations that children really care about. *Everyday Mathematics* presents many problem situations that require data collection and analysis. You are encouraged to personalize them and to add your own.

An example of personalization comes from a Kindergarten class. A number of children didn't know how to tie their shoes, always relying on the teacher to do this for them. The children decided it would be much more efficient to find out who among them could tie shoes so that they could help those that could not. This led to a survey, a tally, and a display of the collated data, as well as a solution to a problem meaningful to the children in the class.

A second reason to take time to formulate a question for data exploration is to clarify the essential information that can lead to an answer. In the shoe-tying survey, for example, is it important to know what color the shoes are or how long the laces are? If you want to know who runs the fastest, does hair color matter? Does distance matter? What about footwear or clothing? Even if the questions sometimes seem silly, it is important to ask them to help children develop habits of thinking about the possible effects various factors may have on the data they collect.

12.2.2 Collecting and Recording Data

Everyday Mathematics uses many sources of data and a variety of collection procedures, such as the following:

- Counting and measuring in the classroom;
- Observing and measuring at home;
- Taking surveys at school, including surveys of other classes;
- Collecting data from such sources as TV, newspapers, magazines, encyclopedias, and the Internet.

In *Kindergarten* through *Third Grade Everyday Mathematics,* the most common data are counts, and the usual goal is to examine the frequency of various occurrences. *How many . . . ?* is the classic beginning to the questions that are formulated by children: *How many of each kind of Halloween candy did you get? How many brothers and sisters do you have? How many pets are in your family?* Investigations of this sort genuinely interest children and can be used to build a foundation for later, more sophisticated work in statistics and probability.

Data activities include games such as *Dice Roll and Tally,* in which results are kept with tally marks. Other investigations are formatted as Projects and Explorations, such as the second grade's "How Far Can I Run in 10 Seconds?" activity. Many opportunities arise naturally in the course of classroom life.

Data analysis begins as the data are collected. If the information is not recorded in an organized table or chart, children will likely end up with an indecipherable heap of numbers instead of useful information. *Everyday Mathematics* provides various tools to help with the initial collection and organization of data, including journal pages, masters, and suggestions for the Class Data Pad and bulletin-board displays.

Sampling

Beginning in *Third Grade Everyday Mathematics,* children explore sampling when collecting and analyzing data. A *sample* is a relatively small part of a group chosen to represent the larger group being studied. The larger group is the *population.* The population might be all of the children in a school, all of the people in a state, all adults of voting age in a country, or any other large group that has been designated for study. Often, the collection of data from every member of the population is impossible; therefore, a representative sample of the population is surveyed.

An important aspect of certain samples is that they are random. A *random sample* is taken from a population in a way that gives all members of the population the same chance of being selected. Large samples give more precise estimates of the population's characteristics than do small samples.

For more information about randomness, see Section 12.1.2: The Language of Chance.

12.2.3 Organizing and Displaying Data

The tools in *Everyday Mathematics* provide some organization during data collection, but it is also important for children to design their own ways of recording and displaying data. Organization can help you "see the data *better,*" while reorganizing it can help you "see the data *differently*" in a way that may better suit your needs. Children are encouraged to make and observe a wide variety of data displays.

Two simple methods for organizing data are:

- To arrange the data in order from the smallest value to the largest;
- To sort the data by one or more characteristics.

When the data come from children's characteristics, this can be done concretely in the classroom. For example, you could order children's age data by having them line up by age. Or you could organize children by gender and then handedness. Direct all boys to move to the north wall of the room and all girls to the south wall; then have all right-handers move to the east wall and all left-handers to the west wall.

Several types of data displays are described in the following sections. Do not insist that all displays be neat and nicely labeled, especially tally tables or line plots. If children sketch many plots quickly, they can "see" the data in several different ways. After they analyze the data, ask children to report on their findings in some way. You may then require that tables and graphs in a report be neat and nicely labeled.

Data Tables

Tables are one of the most basic formats for the display of data. Newspapers, reference books, scientific articles, Web sites, and some publications are filled with data tables. Tables have specific uses, such as tally tables, lists, and the in/out tables used in "What's My Rule?" activities. Tables of numbers, arithmetic facts, and statistics such as the ones on the next page are also used extensively to help children improve their mental-arithmetic skills.

World's Largest Urban Agglomerations Projected 2015 Populations	
City, Country	**Population**
Tokyo, Japan	36,214,000
Bombay (Mumbai), India	22,645,000
Delhi, India	20,946,000
Mexico City, Mexico	20,647,000
Sao Paulo, Brazil	19,963,000
New York City, U.S.	19,717,000
Jakarta, Indonesia	17,498,000

Source: World Almanac, 2005

NBA Eastern Conference Standings				
7 March, 2005	**W**	**L**	**PCT**	**GB**
Miami	45	16	0.738	0.0
Detroit	36	22	0.621	7.5
Boston	31	29	0.517	13.5
Washington	33	25	0.569	10.5
Cleveland	31	27	0.534	12.5
Orlando	31	27	0.534	12.5
Chicago	29	27	0.518	13.5
Philadelphia	29	30	0.492	15.0
Indiana	29	30	0.492	15.0
New Jersey	26	34	0.433	18.5
Toronto	25	34	0.424	19.0
New York	25	34	0.424	19.0
Milwaukee	24	33	0.421	19.0
Charlotte	12	45	0.211	31.0
Atlanta	10	48	0.172	33.5

Source: www.nba.com

Number of Children

X X X X X X X X X X X X

0 1 2 3 4

Number of Siblings

A line plot

NOTE: Line plots are also called *sketch graphs, dot plots,* or *pictographs* when the tally marks are pictures. Bar graphs are sometimes called *bar charts.*

Line Plots and Bar Graphs

Line plots are used extensively to organize and display data. A *line plot* is a sketch of data in which checks, Xs, stick-on notes, or other marks above a labeled line show the frequency of each value. A line plot can be thought of as a rough sketch of a bar graph.

Bar graphs are introduced in second grade and are used throughout the rest of *Everyday Mathematics.* Bar graphs are excellent for displaying *how much* or *how many* and can be drawn vertically or horizontally like the ones below. Children need to be aware of the important parts of a graph, including the title, labels for axes, and the scales for numbering the axes.

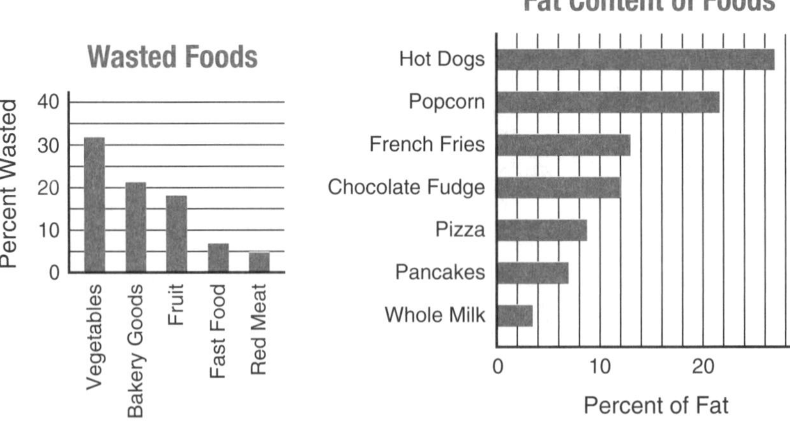

Source: The Garbage Product

A vertical bar graph

Source: The New York Public Library Desk Reference

A horizontal bar graph

Several teachers have expressed concern that *Everyday Mathematics* does not distinguish between *bar graphs* and *histograms.* This is because the authors view a histogram as a specific kind of bar graph and do not believe that children benefit from such fine distinctions. However, we briefly describe the differences here because some state objectives and tests distinguish between the two, as do some spreadsheets and data analysis applications for computers.

Bar graphs are useful for comparing counts, or frequencies, of data. Sometimes the data are *categorical,* such as the food types in the "Wasted Foods" graph on page 122. Usually, each category is assigned its own bar in a graph so frequencies or other information about the categories can be compared. But you could combine categories to get a different picture of the data. For example, you could make a new category called "probably healthy foods" that combines vegetables, fruit, and red meat, and another category called "questionably healthy foods" that combines bakery goods and fast food. A graph with two bars could then compare waste based on healthiness of foods.

For *noncategorical* data, such as measurements, there are likely to be so many distinct data values that they need to be collected into intervals or else there would be too many bars on the graph. A *histogram* is a fancy name for a bar graph of noncategorical data. To make a histogram, you decide on a fixed interval, or scale, on the horizontal axis and count all of the values in each interval. For example, to display a histogram of the heights of all the children in your school, you might decide to group them by 4-inch intervals: 30–33 inches, 34–37 inches, and so on. In *Everyday Mathematics*, this histogram is still called a bar graph.

NOTE: Categorical data are also called *qualitative* or *discrete* data; noncategorical data are *quantitative* or *continuous* data.

NOTE: Sometimes the interval in a bar graph of quantitative data is called a *bin* or *bin width.* This fits with a view of the graph as a collection of equal-width bins into which the data are sorted.

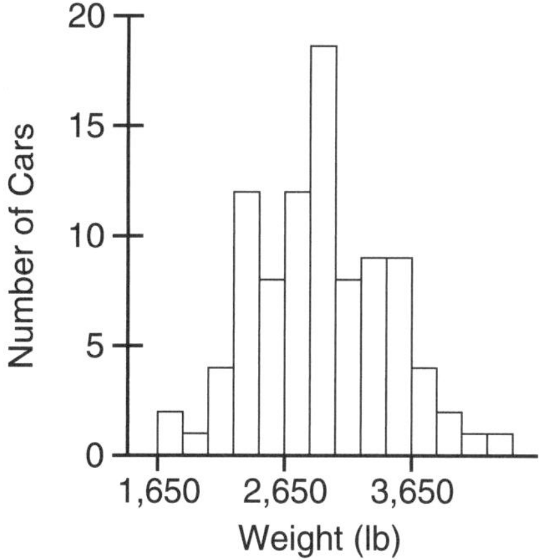

A histogram of car weights: Scale 200 pounds. Eighteen cars weighed between 2,850 and 3,050 pounds.

In any bar graph, if the scale used on the axis displaying the counts or frequencies is too small or too large, the "look" of the data can be distorted, as in the "Favorite Flavors of Ice Cream" bar graphs below.

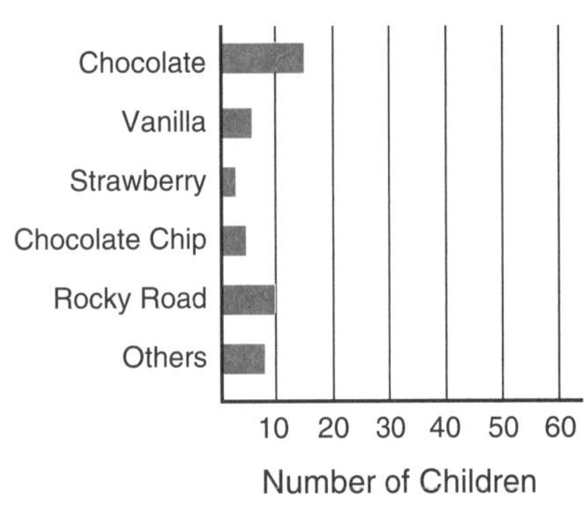

A bar graph with too large a scale

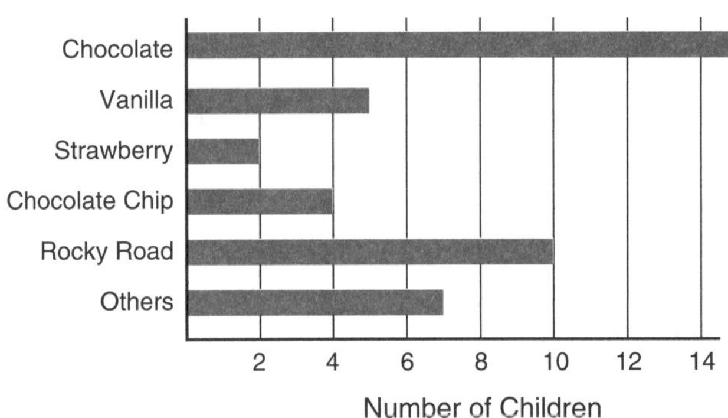

A bar graph with too small a scale

NOTE: In bar graphs of categorical data, it does not matter if the bars touch each other. In bar graphs of quantitative data, adjacent bars share a common endpoint, so they touch.

perspective

Students in *Fourth* through *Sixth Grade Everyday Mathematics* learn how to read and construct several other types of graphs, including circle graphs, stem-and-leaf plots, step graphs, and both stacked and side-by-side bar graphs.

Computer or graphic-calculator programs may distinguish between bar graphs and histograms. The main reason is that before you enter the data, you usually need to tell the program whether it is categorical or noncategorical. Better programs then let you manipulate the scales of both the frequency counts and the bar widths of histograms. If you have access to such a program it is a wonderful way to show children how easily the "look" of a graph can affect the way the data are perceived.

Line Graphs

Line graphs are good applications of ordered pairs, which are introduced in *Third Grade Everyday Mathematics.* These graphs are particularly good for showing how data change over time, and time is often one of the variables used and labeled. Drawing and analyzing line graphs gives students good practice in working with the coordinate plane.

Median Number of Years of School Completed by Peoples Age 25 or Over in the United States

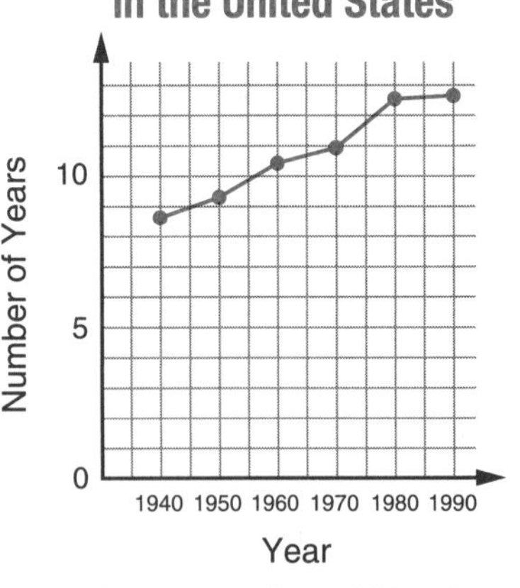

Source: 1995 Digest of Education

A line graph

12.2.4 Data Analysis

To many people, data analysis is synonymous with statistics. In *Everyday Mathematics,* however, this is not the case. For our purposes, *data analysis* means the examination and explanation of data. A good data analysis for a first grader can be summed up in a single well-phrased comment, such as *More than half the people in class are girls.* Statistics may be completely irrelevant in such an analysis. A *statistic* is simply a number used to describe some characteristic of one or more data sets and may not necessarily shed any particular light on the situation being examined.

One of the most common statistics is the *average,* or *mean,* of a set of data. Finding the mean requires adding a set of numbers and then dividing, tasks too difficult for most young children. Yet a lack of arithmetic skills should not bar students from data analysis of a more general nature. *Everyday Mathematics* provides activities for children to study two general attributes of data at increasingly sophisticated levels: useful *landmarks* within a data set and the *spread and pattern* of the set as a whole.

Landmarks of Data Sets

Once data have been organized, take every opportunity to have children discuss things they notice about the data. The following terms are commonly used to describe features of *ordered,* or *sorted,* data. These statistics are called *landmarks* in a data set because they show important features of the data.

- *Maximum* – the *largest* data value observed;
- *Minimum* – the *smallest* data value observed;
- *Range* – the *difference* between the maximum and minimum values;
- *Mode* – the *values observed most often;* the most popular or frequent data value or values;
- *Median* – the *middle data value* or, if there is an even number of values, the number halfway between the two middle data values.

Children can use landmarks as reference points when they discuss other features of the data, just as cartographers use landmarks as reference points when they discuss the lay of the land on maps.

Note that finding a median may require averaging the two values nearest the middle. This is probably the first use of average that children encounter other than as a descriptive term for data found in newspapers, TV, and other media. Children often develop the idea of an average in the context of finding a median. The question *What do we do if there is no single middle value?* leads to an important discussion about what is a fair value between two others. One approach to finding that fair value is to point to a spot on a number line. Another is to guess a value and check if its differences from the two nearest values are equal. Some children may develop the common algorithm of averaging on their own.

Some data sets may have no landmarks other than the mode. For example, a survey of favorite hair color would not lead to a largest or average color but just the most popular color among the people who are surveyed.

Spread and Pattern of Data Sets

Encourage children to talk about the spread and pattern, or distribution, of the data in tables or graphs. Terms such as *clump, hole, bump, way-out number,* and *all-alone number* are fine for describing how data values are arranged in a table or along a number line. Sometimes these characteristics can spark interesting explorations. Data that are clumped too closely together may suggest the need to ask a more discriminating question or to change the scale in a display.

The range of a data set can be useful in comparing the spreads of different sets of similar data. However, taken by itself it can hide the clumps or holes or singularities that make a data set really interesting.

In *Kindergarten* through *Third Grade Everyday Mathematics,* children discuss landmarks, spread, and patterns of *raw* data, that is, data as they are recorded, and of *ordered* data, or data that are numerically ordered or grouped by categories. Children also discuss their data qualitatively without using landmarks such as median or range, noting where the data bunch together or spread out. Exploring reasons for the "shape of the data" can lead to a better understanding of the data set in question and the data analysis process in general. Formal treatment of averages and other statistics begins in Grades 4 through 6.

Remember that a typical reason for analyzing data is to solve a problem, make a prediction, or arrive at a decision. Never finish a data lesson before children have had an opportunity to summarize, discuss, report, or reach some sort of conclusion. Think of data analysis as a process with several stages: gathering the data, displaying the data, analyzing the data, and looking back. In some ways, the last step—to achieve closure—is most important.

▸ 12.3 Using Data and Probability

Everyday Mathematics is committed to developing mathematics through applications, and virtually any number drawn from an application is a piece of data. In Kindergarten through Grade 3, each year of the program has at least one routine centered around uses of data and/or probability:

- The *Weather Chart* (in Kindergarten);
- Explorations (*Group Tally of Penny Dates* in Grade 1);
- Projects (the *Collections Project* in Grade 2);
- Games (the *Block-Drawing Game* in Grade 3).

In *First* and *Second Grade Everyday Mathematics,* children also have special Data Days on which they collect data and work with data sets. They put data in order; observe the spread or range from minimum to maximum; make graphs; estimate representative, typical, or middle measurements; and count to the middle to find the median of each data set.

You probably do not need specific suggestions for data sets as much as you may need suggestions for applications in other subjects. Children are naturally interested in surveying topics like favorite

in perspective

In *Fourth* through *Sixth Grade Everyday Mathematics*, students continue to collect, organize, and analyze data, as well as explore probability. In Grades 4 and 5, most of the data analysis occurs within the context of the World Tour and American Tour, respectively. In Grade 6, data analysis and probability are explored in individual lessons.

colors, favorite foods, pets, and handedness. You know better than anyone else what interests the children, so use your best ideas and theirs. The goal is to have children understand data exploration as a *sensible process.* Can they ask sensible questions? Can they make sense of graphs? Can they make sensible graphs? If so, then they are intelligent users of data and probability.

12.4 Data and Chance Tools and Techniques

Along with measurement tools for collecting data discussed in Section 14.10 and the tables and graphs for representing data described in Section 12.2.3, random-number generators play an important role in *Everyday Mathematics,* especially in the context of games.

12.4.1 Random-Number Generators

Everyday Mathematics uses a variety of devices to generate random outcomes. These tools are integral to the success of many games. Often these devices do not generate perfectly random outcomes, but they are good enough for most purposes. Several tools for helping children generate random outcomes are listed below.

Dice

Use a regular die to generate the numbers 1 through 6. Use a polyhedral die (with 12 or 20 sides) to extend the range of numbers to be generated. Note that rolling more than one die and adding the resulting numbers of dots produces a nonuniform distribution of possible outcomes. For example, if you roll two standard dice, the 36 possible ways for them to land are shown below. Only one of the 36 has a sum of 2 (two 1s), but six of the 36 have a sum of 7 {[1,6], [2,5], [3,4], [4,3], [5,2] and [6,1]}. Therefore, the chance of rolling a sum of 7 is much greater than the chance of rolling a sum of 2. This is what is meant by a *nonuniform distribution.* Shaking a die in a cup may lead to slightly more random results than throwing the die by hand.

					6+1					
				5+1	5+2	6+2				
			4+1	4+2	4+3	5+3	6+3			
		3+1	3+2	3+3	3+4	4+4	5+4	6+4		
	2+1	2+2	2+3	2+4	2+5	3+5	4+5	5+5	6+5	
1+1	1+2	1+3	1+4	1+5	1+6	2+6	3+6	4+6	5+6	6+6
2	3	4	5	6	7	8	9	10	11	12

Sums of two dice

Egg Cartons

Label each egg-carton cup with a number. For example, you might label the cups 0 through 11. Place one or more pennies, beans, or centimeter cubes inside the carton, close the lid, shake the carton, and then open it to see in which cups the objects have landed. Randomness depends on how thoroughly the carton is shaken. This is probably the least random method of the list.

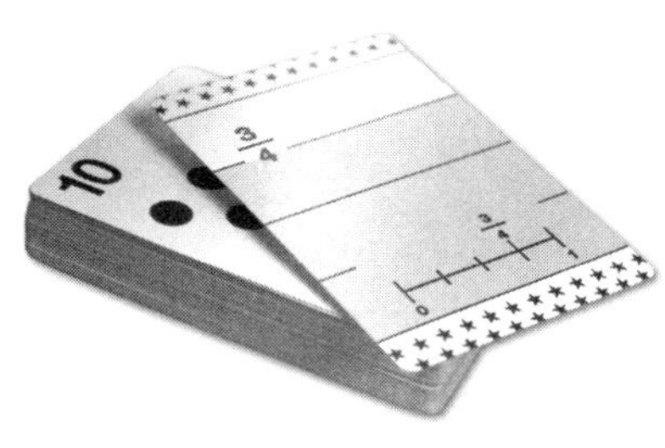

The Everything Math Deck

This deck of cards consists of four sets of number cards 0 through 10 and one set of number cards 11 through 20. Fractions are on the reverse side of the 0 through 10 cards. You can limit the range of numbers to be generated simply by removing some of the cards from the deck. For a uniform distribution of numbers 0 through 20, for example, use only one set of 0 through 10 cards and the set of 11 through 20 cards. To use the cards, simply shuffle and draw. The better the shuffle, the more unpredictable the draw will be.

Spinners

Spinners are used throughout *Everyday Mathematics,* usually in games. They are extremely useful for helping children visualize the idea of chance. There are many commercially available spinners, though it is not necessary to purchase them. Children can use a pencil and paper clip with a spinner mat as shown in the margin. Use either a large (about 2-inch) or standard (about 1-inch) paper clip for the part that spins. The larger size is preferred because it spins more easily. Make a mark, as a pointer, at one end of the paper clip using a permanent felt-tip marker.

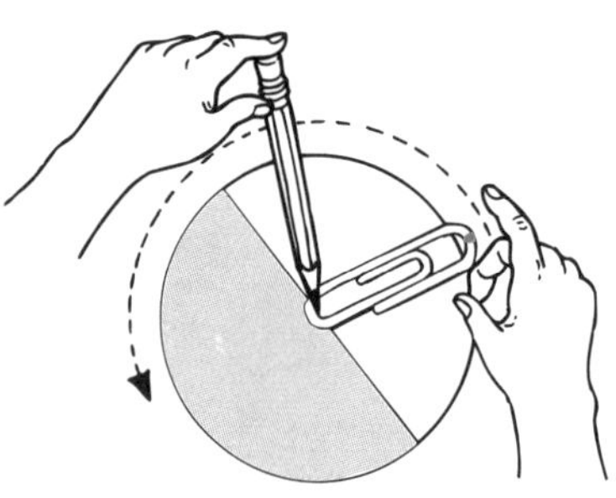

The spinning mat may be drawn on cardstock or paper. Sometimes a mat is supplied as a master or journal page. If you make your own mat, start with a circle or square large enough to accomodate the paper clip. Mark the center of the circle, choose the number and sizes of the regions, and then measure and draw the appropriate angles. For example, six equal regions would each measure $360° \div 6 = 60°$. You can use shapes other than circles for the spinner, and the regions do not have to be the same size, as in the square mat in the margin.

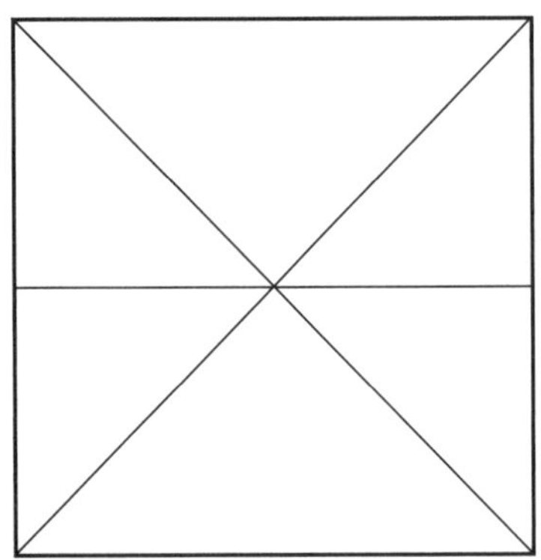

Before spinning, tape the mat to a level surface. You need only two small pieces of tape, one at the top and one at the bottom. To spin, place the tip of a pen or pencil on the center of the circle and within the paper clip as shown in the diagram. Flick the paper clip about halfway between the center of the circle and the tip of the paper clip, as flicking the paper clip near the pointer end generates less of a spin.

Standard Playing Cards

Use the 2 through 9 cards, the aces for 1s, and the queens for 0s. Draw one card to get a 1 in 10 chance for each one of the digits 0 through 9. Draw two cards to make 2-digit numbers, three cards for 3-digit numbers, and so on. If more than one card is drawn, you need to decide whether to replace it before another card is drawn. If the first card is replaced in the deck and the deck is reshuffled, the probability will remain the same for each draw. If the card is not replaced, the chance of drawing that digit decreases.

13 Geometry

Contents

Geometry, the study of visual patterns of objects in space, is a natural and deeply intuitive part of mathematics for children. From birth, children need to make sense of forms and shapes, such as a mother's face, their own bodies, shapes that move, shapes that don't, curved things, and sharp things. Then, with a wealth of informal knowledge about spatial objects, they come to school. The teacher's role is first to acknowledge and value what children already know and then to help them "notice" what they see and to organize their perceptions into a meaningful system.

The word *geometry* derives from Greek words for "earth" and "measure," which gives a clue about the first geometric activity of humans. The earliest records of geometric thinking, from the Egyptians, Babylonians, and Chinese, confirm that it centered on solving practical problems, such as laying out fields, finding areas and volumes, and constructing houses and temples.

The Greeks are credited with formalizing geometry. In high school, most of us encountered the geometry of Euclid with its axioms and theorems. And, for many, this was a mystifying experience. This was due in part to the inappropriate structure and content of many of these geometry courses—a situation that is slowly changing as new approaches to secondary school geometry instruction are being developed. But, an equally compelling reason is that many students have little or no formal experience with geometry prior to their high school courses. The *Everyday Mathematics* curriculum places significant emphasis on this part of mathematics beginning in Kindergarten.

Students investigate geometry through many hands-on experiences, including manipulating pattern blocks; building shapes with straws; tracing, cutting out, and folding shapes; forming figures on geoboards; and constructing figures with compasses, straightedges, and protractors.

–Adapted from *Everyday Teaching for Everyday Mathematics*™ by Sheila Sconiers

This chapter first describes common 1-, 2-, and 3-dimensional objects. Next, it discusses some operations on these objects and some relationships that the objects have with one another. Then it briefly discusses tessellations, topology, and geometric constructions. The chapter concludes with an outline of the approach used in *Everyday Mathematics* for teaching geometry.

13.1 Dimension

NOTE: Both *3-D* and *3D* are widely used shorthand for 3-dimensional. If you ever search the Web for information about 3-D objects, try both.

Dimension is a tricky word. One meaning refers to the size of an object, as in the dimensions of a room or of a piece of paper; another meaning, the one implicit in terms like *3-dimensional,* refers to how much information is required to specify an exact location. For example, a checkerboard is *2-dimensional* because two pieces of information can specify a particular square: its row and its column. A line is *1-dimensional* because a point on it can be located using one number—its distance from an origin. An opera house is *3-dimensional* because a seat in it can be determined using a row number, a seat number, and a floor level.

NOTE: Although the objects of geometry are presented here from less complicated to more complicated, children encounter them in the opposite order in *Everyday Mathematics,* a more developmentally appropriate order in which 1- and 2-dimensional objects are introduced informally as parts of 3-D objects. For example, a line segment is modeled by an edge of a box and a rectangle by four adjoining edges of a box. For more information on developmental stages in the learning of geometry, see Section 13.9.1: The van Hiele Levels.

We live in 3-dimensional space, *3-D space.* The objects that constitute our physical experience are all 3-dimensional. Objects in other dimensions, such as lines, triangles, and circles, are abstractions that do not physically exist in the way dogs, cellular telephones, and pencils exist. Even the checkerboard, which was called 2-dimensional a moment ago, is really 3-dimensional; it has length, width, and depth. The 2-dimensional surface of the checkerboard is an abstraction.

Many 1- and 2-dimensional abstractions are so useful in the 3-dimensional world that we name them and study their properties. You can model them with wood or plastic, with drawings, and with special manipulatives. But the models are always 3-dimensional, not the "real" thing. Even a drawing made with ink has length, width, and depth.

The following sections discuss objects in dimensions 0 through 3 and describe how children examine them in *Everyday Mathematics* activities.

13.2 Points

Point is an undefined term in geometry, so no one can say exactly what it is. Nevertheless, most people have some idea of what a point is and what it is not. A point cannot be broken into pieces; it is one indivisible thing and so it has 0 dimensions. Because a point has no parts, no information is needed to specify which part of a point is being referred to; it cannot be measured.

You can model a point by drawing a *dot* on a piece of paper. If you get a finer pen and draw a smaller dot, then you have a better model of a point. But no matter how small you make your dot and no matter how fine your pen's tip, you still cannot draw a true point. Even the smallest dot of ink has length, width, and depth, and therefore it is not a point.

Models of points

Another way to think about a point is as a *location,* or an exact position. On a map or other reference frame, a point marks where something is. For example, there is a point on a number line that is exactly 3 units from the origin. In fact, there are two such points, one at +3 and one at −3. In *Kindergarten Everyday Mathematics,* children use points as locations when they follow maps and count steps to get from one classroom to another. Children also locate points on number lines beginning in Kindergarten. *Length* is the distance between two points, so children imagine points as locations on objects every time they measure a height, width, or depth. Points on maps are used to estimate distances, and children learn about map scale beginning in Grade 3.

NOTE: *Synthetic* geometry is the study of geometric objects without concern for their position on a line, in a plane, or in space. *Analytic* geometry is the study of geometric objects on a number line, coordinate plane, or 3-D coordinate grid.

Sometimes a location is considered a point, but its position is not important. For example, the vertices (corners) of a polygon are the points where two sides meet, but unless the polygon is on a coordinate system, the position of a vertex is of little interest. Yet the fact that the point is a vertex *is* interesting, because the vertex often receives a name and that name contributes to a name for the whole polygon. On geometric objects, points are usually named with capital letters, such as point *A,* point *B,* and so on. Naming geometric figures using the names of points begins in Grade 2, for example, "triangle *ABC.*"

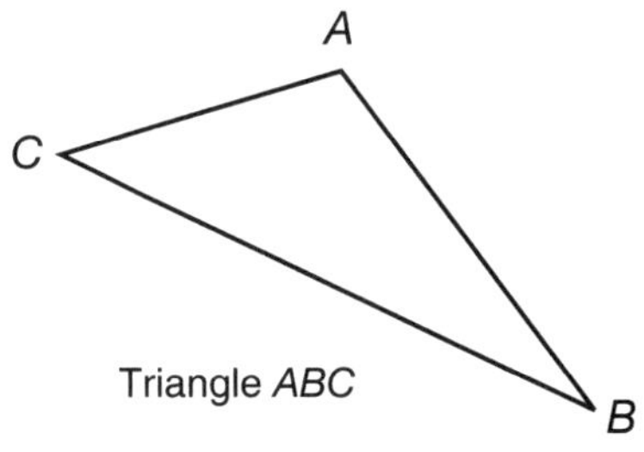

Triangle *ABC*

In analytic geometry, points correspond to numbers on a number line, ordered pairs of numbers on a coordinate plane, and ordered triples of numbers in coordinate space. Graphing ordered pairs begins in third grade. Applications of ordered pairs, such as latitude and longitude, appear in Grades 4 through 6. The idea of a function as a set of ordered pairs can be visualized by plotting the pairs on a coordinate graph.

For more information on coordinate geometry, see Section 15.3: Coordinate Systems.

There are other uses and models of points not discussed here. The aim is simply to give you some ways to think about points and to help you realize how often they are used in the 3-dimensional world.

> **NOTE:** In formal Euclidean geometry, *line* is an undefined term. The informal definition used in *Everyday Mathematics* builds on a common intuition that lines go on forever in a fixed direction. In that spirit, the shortest segment between any two points on a line determines the line's direction, or the way it is oriented in a plane or space.

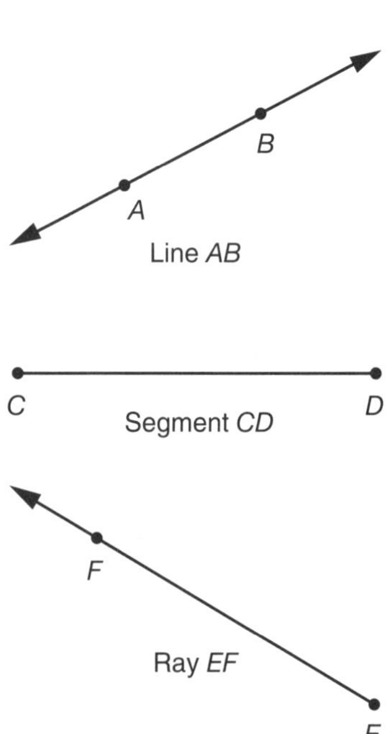

> **NOTE:** Computer geometry packages such as the *Geometer's Sketchpad®* and *Cabri Geometry™* do not place arrowheads on lines. It is not practical to draw arrowheads in these packages because you can "grab" lines and rays with a cursor and move them around. What you see, then, are models for rays and lines that extend to the edge of the screen and, in your mind's eye, beyond.

▸ 13.3 Lines, Segments, and Rays

Line is another undefined term, but, again, one for which most people have good intuition. You can model a line with pen and ink, by folding a piece of paper, or by pulling a piece of string taut.

A *line* is made up of infinitely many points extending forever in opposite directions. "Forever" is an important word here; it means that a line has no ends. If you started marking off unit intervals on a line, you would never finish, no matter how many intervals you marked. One-dimensional figures on a line are called *linear figures.* Zero-dimensional points make up 1-dimensional figures.

A line is 1-dimensional in that one number is enough to specify any point on a line relative to an origin. One-dimensional objects on a line have length, but no width or depth.

A drawing of a line has arrowheads on its "ends" to indicate that it does not stop. A line is named using any two points on it, as in line *AB* in the margin. Shorthand for "line *AB*" is $\overleftrightarrow{AB}$.

Now think about any two points on a line. No matter how close together they are, there are infinitely many points on the line between them. Mathematicians say lines are *dense,* meaning that between any two points on a line there is always another point. The fact that each point on a line can be associated with a number is a key to understanding why our real-number system does not run dry. Just as there is always a point between any two points on a line, there is always a number between any two numbers.

A *line segment,* or *segment* for short, is a part of a line between and including two different endpoints. Although you cannot measure the length of a line, a segment has a finite length that you can approximate. A segment is labeled using any two points on it, as in line segment *CD* in the margin. Shorthand for "line segment *CD*" is $\overline{CD}$.

A *ray* is a part of a line with only one endpoint and all the points on the line to one side of the point. For this reason, rays are sometimes called *half-lines.* Like a line, a ray has no measure. A drawing of a ray has an arrowhead at the "end" opposite its endpoint. A ray is labeled using the name of the endpoint and another point on it, as in ray *EF* in the margin. Shorthand for "ray *EF*" is $\overrightarrow{EF}$.

Everyday Mathematics is consistent about using arrowheads in drawings of lines and rays. Encourage children to use them as well. However, it is not important for them to use the shorthand names for lines, segments, and rays.

▸ 13.4 Planes and Plane Figures

Plane is yet another undefined geometric term for which most people have some intuition. A tabletop, a smooth floor, and the surface of a calm body of water all suggest planes.

A *plane* extends forever in every direction in two dimensions. There are infinitely many points and infinitely many lines in a plane.

Two-dimensional objects that are entirely contained in a plane are called *plane figures* or *planar figures.* And just as 0-dimensional points make up 1-dimensional objects like lines, both 0-dimensional and 1-dimensional objects make up plane figures.

A plane is 2-dimensional in that two numbers can specify any point in a plane relative to an origin. Two-dimensional objects in a plane have length and width, but no depth. Like a line, a plane cannot be measured.

The next three sections discuss some of the common planar figures that children explore in *Everyday Mathematics:* angles, polygons, and circles.

NOTE: In formal Euclidean geometry, *plane* is an undefined term. The informal definition used in *Everyday Mathematics* builds on a common intuition that planes go on forever in a fixed direction. In that spirit, any three points in a plane determine the plane's direction, or the way it is oriented in space.

13.4.1 Angles and Rotations

In mathematics, an *angle* consists of two rays that have the same endpoint, called the *vertex* of the angle. The rays are called the *sides* of the angle. An angle usually takes the name of its vertex, as in angle A in the margin. Sometimes the name of an angle contains three points—a point on one ray, the vertex, and a point on the other ray—as in angle BAC in the margin. And sometimes an angle is named with a number in the region between the rays, as in angles 1 and 2 in the margin. Shorthand for "angle A" is $\angle A$.

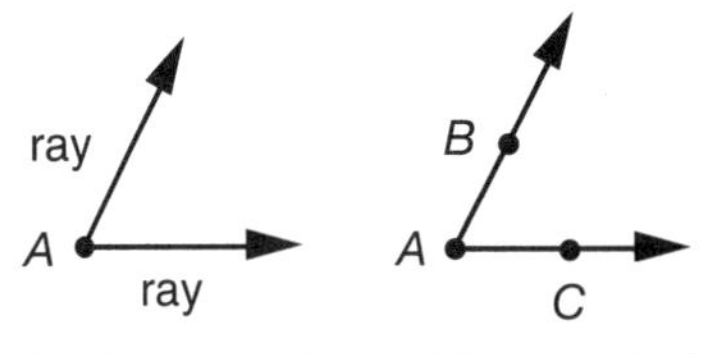

Angle A or $\angle A$ $\angle BAC$ or $\angle CAB$

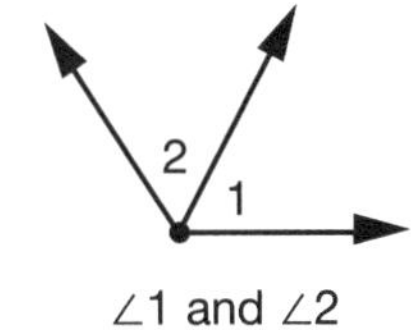

$\angle 1$ and $\angle 2$

Sometimes it is convenient to think of the sides of an angle as line segments, for example, "the angles of a square," but strictly speaking, the sides of an angle are rays, each continuing without end. In *Everyday Mathematics,* angles are often modeled using segments because they are introduced in Grade 1 as features of solids and in Grades 2 and 3 as features of polygons. In Grades 4 through 6, angles are studied as features of polygons and polyhedrons.

It is often useful to think of an angle as being formed by starting with the two rays or segments pointing in the same direction and then rotating one ray or segment around the common endpoint. In first grade, children model angles in this manner by bending a straw and rotating one of the sides around the bend.

Angles are most commonly measured in *degrees.* One complete rotation, a full circle, measures 360 degrees. Shorthand for "360 degrees" is 360°. If a child begins with both parts of a bent straw together and then rotates one of the parts 1 quarter of the way around the bend, the resulting figure models an angle of $360° \div 4 = 90°$. If the rotation continues another 1 quarter of the way around the bend, the straw is straight and models an angle of 180°. A further 1-quarter rotation models an angle of 270°. A final 1-quarter rotation returns the straw to its starting position, an angle of 360°, which looks like an angle of 0°.

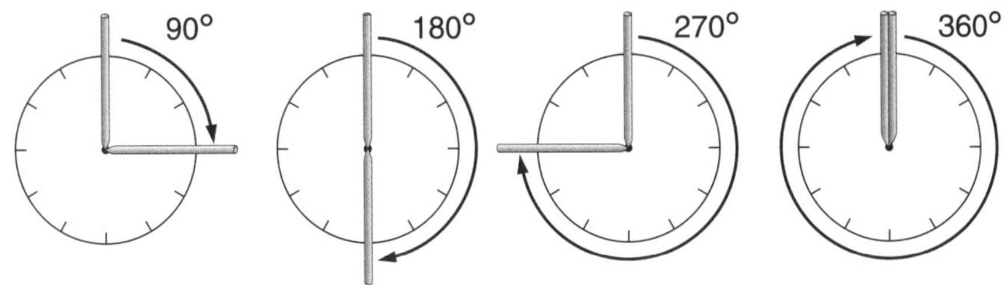

chapter 13

An analog clock also shows angles. At 12 o'clock, the overlapping hands model an angle of 0° or 360°; at 3 o'clock, an angle of 90° or 270°; at 6 o'clock, an angle of 180°; and at 9 o'clock an angle of 270° or 90°.

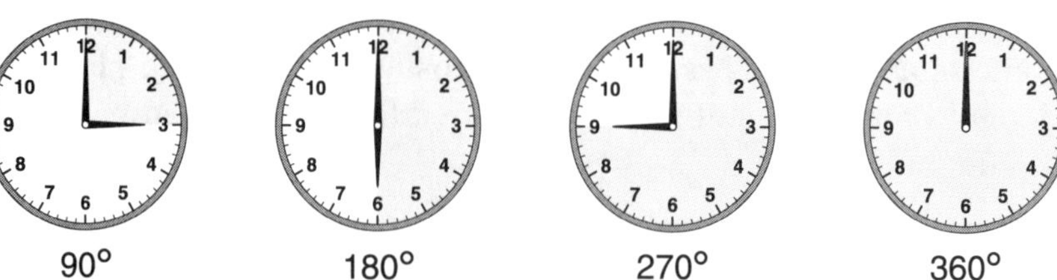

Angles are categorized according to their measures as follows:

- An *acute* angle measures less than 90°.
- A *right* angle measures 90°.
- An *obtuse* angle measures between 90° and 180°.
- A *straight* angle measures 180°.
- A *reflex* angle measures between 180° and 360°.

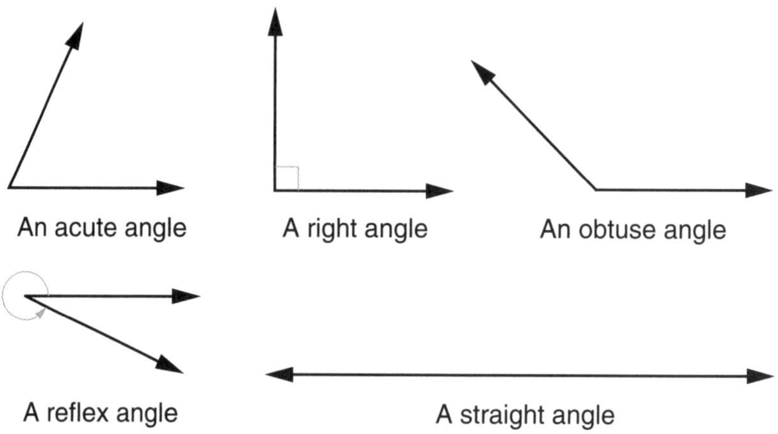

NOTE: The region between the rays of an angle is not part of the angle. If the angle measures between 0° and 180°, the region is called the *interior of the angle.* However, people commonly refer to both the angle proper and its interior as "the angle," and you should not hold children responsible for knowing the difference.

Children in Grades 1 through 3 are not expected to learn the categories of angles, but they manipulate angles of each category. Students in Grades 4 through 6 examine angles more closely as they measure angles with protractors, construct angles with a compass and straightedge, and learn about categories and relationships of angles.

NOTE: The region inside a polygon is not part of the polygon. The polygon is just the line segments. *Polygonal region* is a name for both the polygon and the region inside. However, people commonly ignore the difference, saying, for example, that a cracker is a square or that a piece of paper is a rectangle. Do not hold children responsible for knowing the difference.

13.4.2 Polygons (*n*-gons)

A *polygon* is a 2-dimensional figure formed by three or more line segments that meet only at their endpoints to make a closed path. The sides may not cross one another. The segments are the *sides* of the polygon. The endpoints are *vertices,* or *corners.* Each pair of adjacent sides defines an interior *angle of the polygon.*

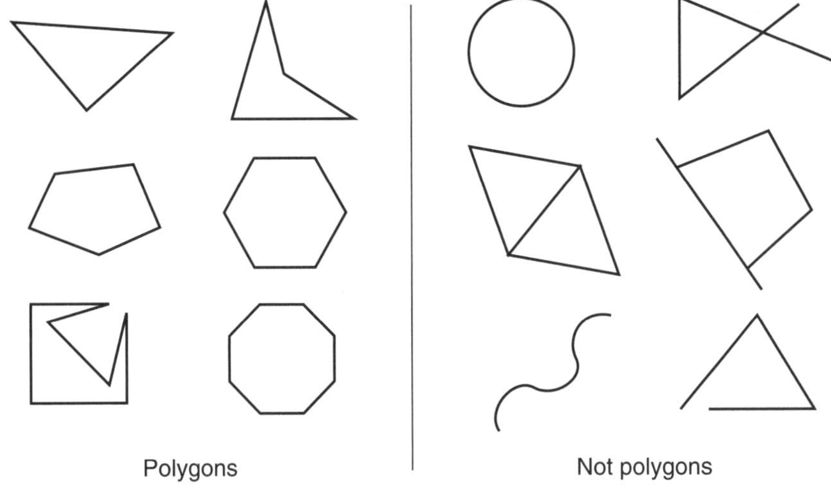

Number of Angles	Name
3	triangle
4	quadrangle or quadrilateral
5	pentagon
6	hexagon
7	heptagon
8	octagon
9	nonagon
10	decagon
12	dodecagon

The term *polygon* comes from the Greek *polu-,* "many," and *-gonon,* "angled." Polygons are named according to the number of angles (or sides or vertices) they have. A 12-gon is a polygon with 12 sides. In general, an n-*gon* is a polygon with *n* sides.

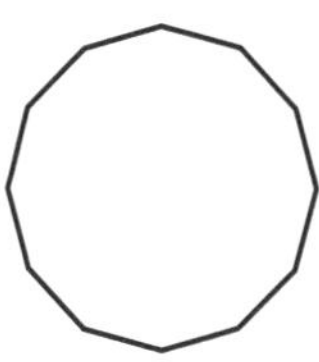
A dodecagon, or 12-gon

A few *n*-gons have their own names, as shown in the table in the margin. Children in Grade 3 classify triangles and quadrilaterals by special features such as parallel sides, right angles, and sides or angles of equal measure. Triangles and quadrilaterals are discussed in more detail in the next two sections.

in perspective

In *Fourth* through *Sixth Grade Everyday Mathematics,* the exploration of polygons is extended to include transformations of polygons by slides, flips, and turns (translations, reflections, and rotations), and classifications of polygons as regular, concave, and convex. Polygons are also studied in the coordinate plane as part of analytic, or coordinate, geometry.

Triangles

A *triangle* is a 3-sided polygon. A triangle is usually named for its three vertices as in triangle *ABC*. Shorthand for "triangle *ABC*" is ΔABC.

Triangles may be classified in three ways according to side lengths:

- A *scalene triangle* has no two sides with the same length.
- An *isosceles triangle* has two sides of equal length. This makes two of the angles equal in measure.
- An *equilateral triangle* has all three sides of equal length. This makes all the angles equal in measure (60° each), so an equilateral triangle is also an *equiangular triangle*. Every equilateral triangle is also an isosceles triangle.

NOTE: Unlike quadrangles, which are also called quadrilaterals, triangles are not usually called "trilaterals."

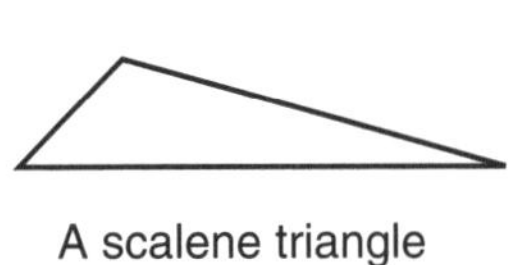
A scalene triangle

An isosceles triangle

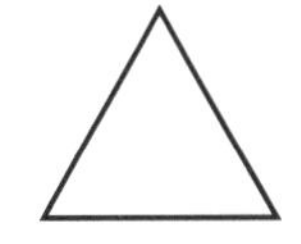
An equilateral triangle

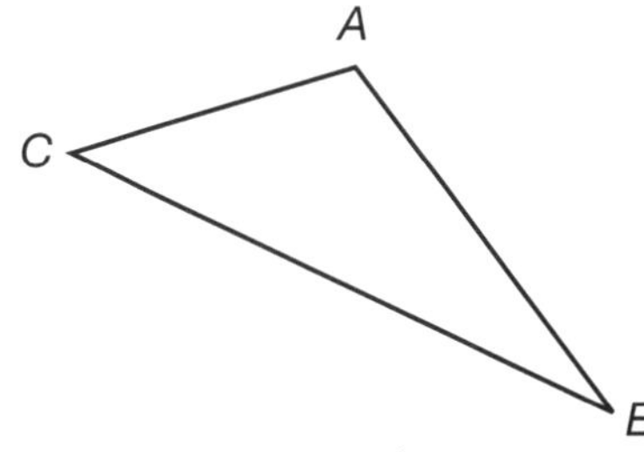

Triangle *ABC* or $\triangle ABC$

in perspective

In Grades 4 through 6, students find areas of triangles, use triangles in tessellations, and represent triangles analytically by graphing them in the coordinate plane. In Grade 6, they learn about one of the most profound discoveries in the history of mathematics, the Pythagorean theorem.

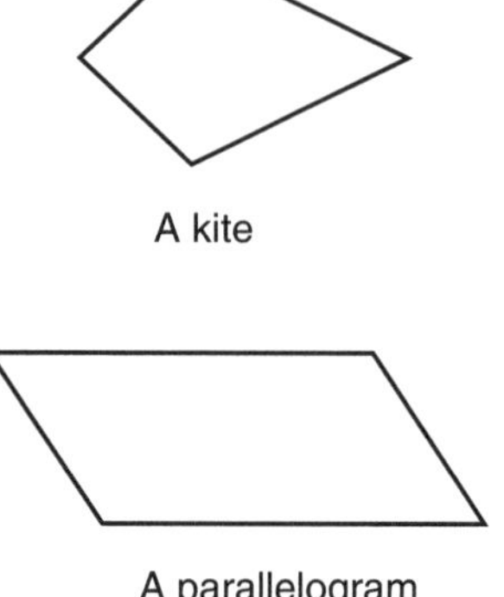

A kite

A parallelogram

chapter 13

A triangle may also be classified according to its angles:

- An *acute triangle* has every angle measure less than 90°.
- A *right triangle* has a right angle.
- An *obtuse triangle* has an angle with measure greater than 90°.

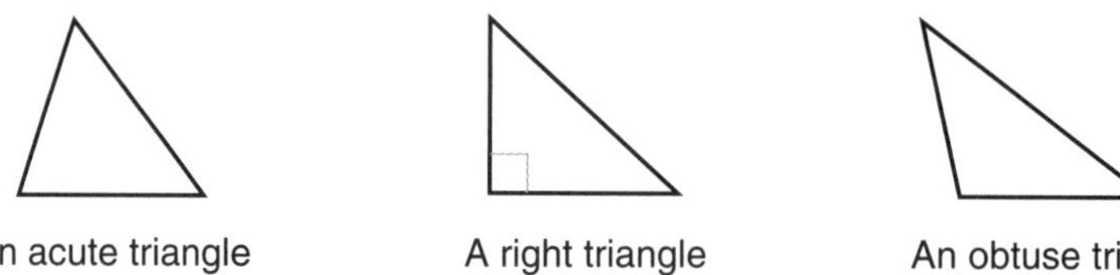

An acute triangle | A right triangle | An obtuse triangle

Any triangle can be given two names, one for its sides and the other for its angles. Some examples are shown below.

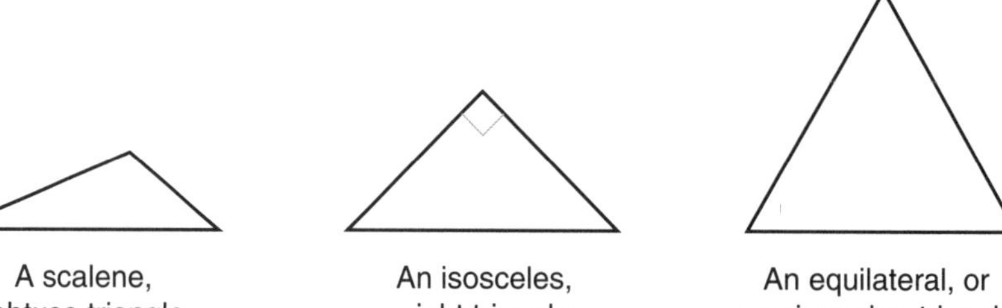

A scalene, obtuse triangle | An isosceles, right triangle | An equilateral, or equiangular, triangle

Over the course of Kindergarten through Grade 3, children learn some of the triangle categories, label vertices, write and read names for triangles, and write and read names for their sides.

Quadrangles (Quadrilaterals)

A *quadrangle,* or *quadrilateral,* is a 4-sided polygon. *Diagonals* of a quadrangle are line segments connecting opposite vertices. Some quadrangles have special features and names:

- A *trapezoid* is a quadrangle with exactly one pair of parallel sides. In an *isosceles trapezoid,* the two nonparallel sides are the same length.

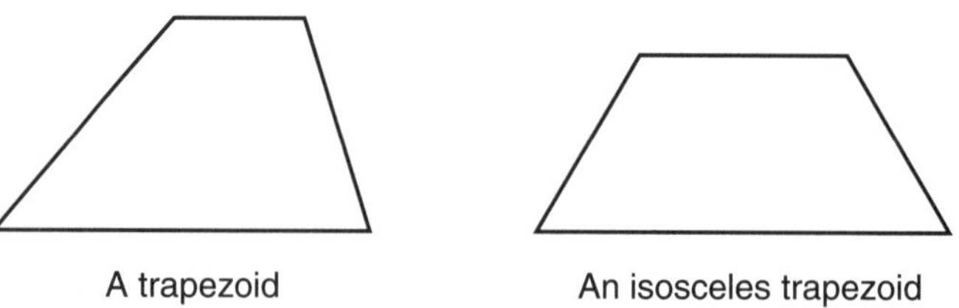

A trapezoid | An isosceles trapezoid

- A *kite* is a quadrilateral with two adjacent sides of one length and two other sides of a different length. The diagonals of a kite are perpendicular.
- A *parallelogram* is a quadrangle with two pairs of parallel sides. Both parallelograms and kites have pairs of equal-length sides, but in kites the equal-length sides are adjacent, not opposite. The diagonals of a parallelogram intersect at their midpoints, or *bisect* each other.

- A *rhombus* is a parallelogram with all sides the same length. The diagonals of a rhombus bisect each other and are perpendicular.

Rhombuses

- A *rectangle* is a parallelogram in which all angles are right angles. Diagonals of a rectangle are equal in length.
- A *square* is a rectangle with all sides the same length. It is also a rhombus with four right angles. Diagonals of a square are equal in length, bisect each other, and intersect at right angles.

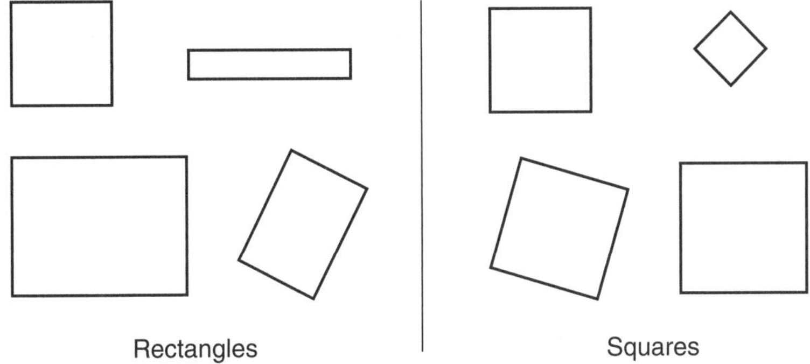

Rectangles   Squares

Some definitions depend on previously defined quadrangles. For example, a rectangle is first a parallelogram, then a parallelogram with right angles. This means that all the features and properties of parallelograms are also features and properties of rectangles, along with new ones specific to rectangles.

This diagram shows the *Everyday Mathematics hierarchy of quadrangles.* Pick any quadrangle in the hierarchy. It has all the properties of any quadrangle on a path leading to it. For example, a square is a rectangle, a rhombus, a parallelogram, and a quadrangle.

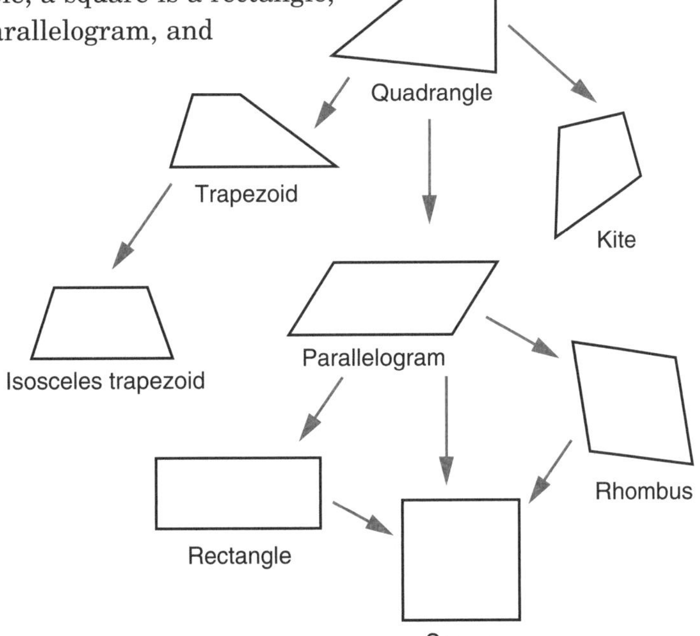

NOTE: If children have trouble identifying equal-length sides in polygons, you and they can mark the sides with hash marks as shown below. Equal-length sides have equal numbers of hash marks.

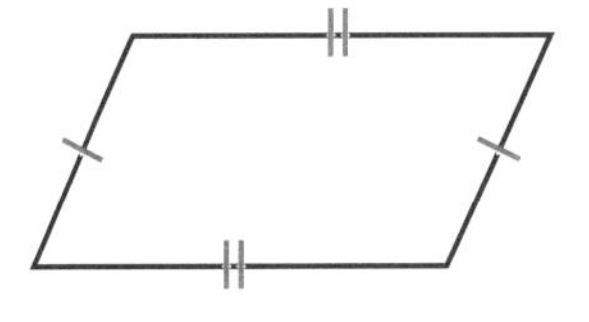

NOTE: Definitions of geometric objects are not carved in stone. For example, some people define a *trapezoid* as a quadrilateral with *at least* one pair of parallel sides. So a parallelogram is also a trapezoid under this definition. Similarly a kite is sometimes defined as a quadrilateral with two different pairs of adjacent sides having the same length. So a rhombus is also a kite under this definition. *Everyday Mathematics* uses the narrower definitions to help children focus on unique properties of the figures.

For more information on the stages of geometric understanding, see Section 13.9.1: The van Hiele Levels.

The authors hope the hierarchy of quadrilaterals may be useful to you, but you are not expected to use it with children unless you think they can understand it. In fact, many children in any grade of elementary school may not have reached the stage of geometric understanding necessary to make sense of the hierarchy.

Other Features of Polygons

Although children in Kindergarten through Grade 3 explore polygons with the following features, defining them at that time is not especially helpful. In Grades 4 through 6, the terminology becomes more useful, especially in compass-and-straightedge constructions and when talking about tessellations.

- A *regular polygon* is a polygon in which all sides are the same length and all angles have the same measure. If a polygon is regular, then it is possible to draw a circle that passes through all its vertices. Equilateral triangles and squares are regular polygons.
- A *convex polygon* is a polygon on which no two points can be connected with a line segment that passes outside the polygon. Each angle of a convex polygon measures less than 180°.
- A *concave,* or *nonconvex, polygon* is a polygon that is not convex. At least one line segment drawn to connect points on two different sides contains at least one point that is outside the polygon. At least one angle of a concave polygon has a measure greater than 180°.

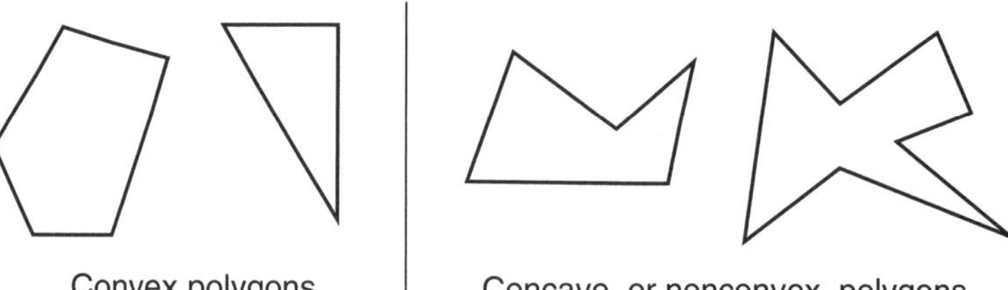

Convex polygons | Concave, or nonconvex, polygons

Most children have little difficulty distinguishing convex and nonconvex polygons, but they may often give crude explanations, such as *The hexagon is not convex because these two sides bend in.* Try to use more precise definitions yourself, but do not insist that students master them.

13.4.3 Circles and Pi (π)

A *circle* consists of all the points in a plane that are the same distance from a given point in the plane called the *center* of the circle. Many physical objects have circular shapes, although none are likely to be perfectly circular. Features of a circle include the following:

- A *radius* is a segment connecting the center of a circle and any point on the circle. The radius is also the length of that segment.
- A *chord* is a segment with endpoints on a circle.
- A *diameter* is a chord through the center of a circle. The diameter is also the name of the length of such a chord. The diameter of a circle is twice its radius.

NOTE: As with angles and polygons, the interior of a circle is not part of the circle itself. Sometimes the circle and its interior are together called a *disk,* or simply a *circular region.* As with the other figures, do not expect children to make this distinction.

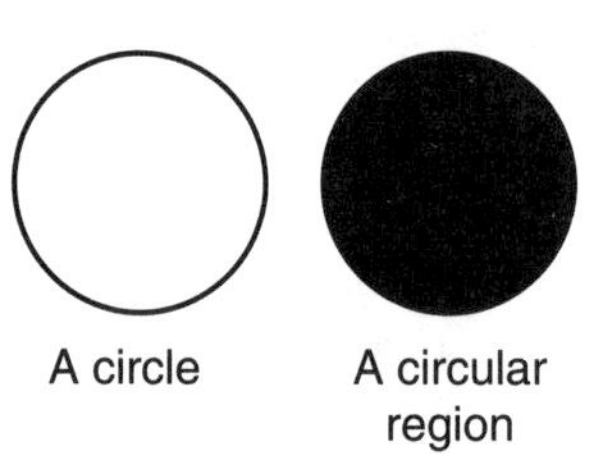

A circle | A circular region

- The *circumference* is the distance around a circle, or its perimeter.

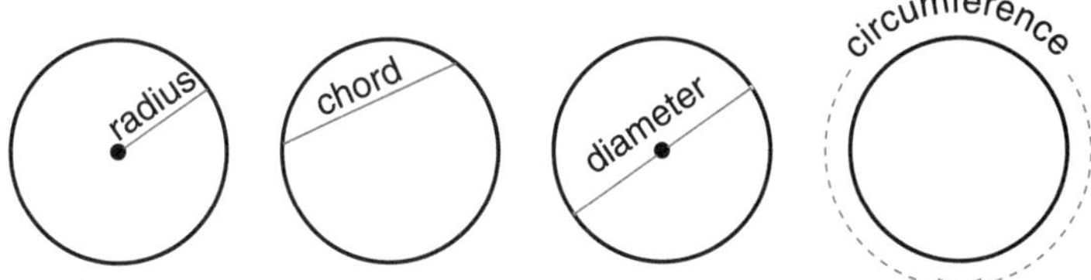

Another way to think of a circle is as a regular n-gon where n is infinitely large. For example, start with a square, not a very good approximation of a circle, but a start. Next, double the number of sides of the square to obtain a regular octagon; this is closer to a circle. Next, double the number of sides again to obtain a regular 16-gon; this is closer still. Doubling a few more times would give a figure that could be distinguished from a circle only with a magnifying glass. Double infinitely many times and the result would actually be a circle.

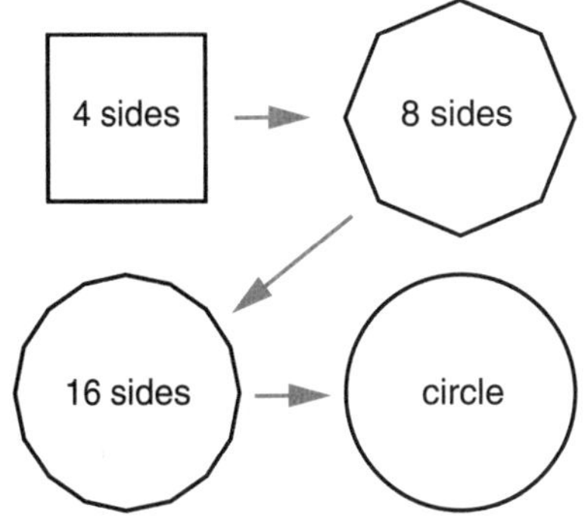

Pi is the ratio of the circumference of a circle to its diameter. This ratio, represented by the Greek letter π, is the same for all circles. If C is the circumference and d is the diameter of a circle, then:

$$\frac{C}{d} = \pi \qquad \text{or} \qquad C = \pi d$$

NOTE: Another definition of the *circumference* of a circle is the limit of the perimeter of a regular n-gon as n gets infinitely large.

In third grade, children begin an inquiry into the relationship between the diameter and the circumference of a circle. They roll food cans to find circumferences, measure across the tops of the cans to find diameters, and display the results in a table. From these results, they discover that the circumference of a circle is consistently about 3 times its diameter. This is a first approximation of π, and a pretty good approximation at that.

Pi is also the ratio of the area A of a circle to the square of its radius r:

$$\frac{A}{r^2} = \pi \qquad \text{or} \qquad A = \pi r^2$$

Pi is an irrational number; its decimal does not repeat and never ends. Two common approximations for pi are 3.14 and $\frac{22}{7}$.

For more information, see Section 9.5: Irrational and Real Numbers.

Mountains of Pi

The earliest known reference to π occurs in an Egyptian papyrus scroll written around 1650 B.C. by a scribe named Ahmes. He found the area of a circle using a rough approximation of π. Around 200 B.C., Archimedes of Syracuse (in Sicily, then a Greek colony) found that π is between $3\frac{10}{71}$ and $3\frac{1}{7}$. Little more was learned about π until the 17th century, when new formulas were discovered. Ludolph van Ceulen, a German mathematician, spent most of his life calculating π to 35 decimal places. Now most inexpensive calculators display π to 7 or 9 decimal places.

Today, investigations of π often involve powerful computers. Such calculations have been a standard task for each new generation of computers. In 1949, π was calculated to 37,000 places on ENIAC, one of the first computers. Later, π was computed to 100,000 digits on an IBM 7090 computer and in 1981 to 2 million digits on an NEC supercomputer. In the next few years, these calculations were extended to 17.5 million digits, then 34 million, then past 200 million, and then in 1989 to more than 1 billion digits. As of December 2002, the laboratory of Dr. Yasumasa Kanada of the University of Tokyo held the world record of 1.2411 *trillion* digits.

NOTE: Pi to 1,832 digits is shown on page 67.

The article "The Mountains of Pi" by Richard Preston relates the fascinating history of π and why it has captivated mathematicians for thousands of years. According to the article:

NOTE: Preston, R. (1992). "The Mountains of Pi." *The New Yorker, March 2, 1995*, pp. 36–67.

> The decimal for pi goes on forever, so the number cannot be written with complete accuracy: 3.14159265358979323846 2643383279502884197 . . . is only an approximation . . .. No apparent pattern emerges in the succession of digits . . .. They do not repeat periodically, seeming to pop up by blind chance, lacking any perceivable order, rule, reason, or design . . ..

"The Mountains of Pi" tells the story of two mathematicians, David and Gregory Chudnovsky, who calculated π to more than 2 billion digits on a computer of their own design, which they built in Gregory's apartment using mail-order parts. Calculating π to so many digits not only tests the power of new supercomputers, but also continues the search for patterns in the digits, a search that, so far, has yielded no results. As the article states:

> [The Chudnovskys] wonder whether the digits contain a hidden rule, as yet unseen architecture, close to the mind of God . . .. If we were to explore the digits of π far enough, they might resolve into a breathtaking numerical pattern . . . and it might mean something . . .. On the other hand, the digits of π may ramble forever . . ..

13.5 Space and 3-D Figures

Space is one more undefined geometric term about which people have plenty of intuition. Space is the 3-dimensional, or 3-D, world we live in. Everything around us is space.

Space extends forever in three dimensions. There are infinitely many points, infinitely many lines, and infinitely many planes in space. *Spatial figures* are objects in space, and they come in infinitely many shapes, sizes, and orientations.

Having good *spatial* sense means you can mentally manipulate 1-, 2-, and 3-dimensional objects in space and describe their orientations. Spatial sense is important in constructing 3-D objects, in representing 3-D objects in two dimensions by drawing on paper or on a computer screen, and in interpreting drawings of 3-D objects. Video games often demand a well-developed spatial sense of the latter kind, at least if you want to win.

13.5.1 "Solid" Figures

The items listed below are models for familiar 3-D mathematical shapes. The items in the left column are "hollow." The items in the right column are "filled up."

empty box with lid	brick
basketball	baseball
empty ice-cream cone	filled ice-cream cone
empty food can	rolling pin

All these objects are solid in the sense that they can be felt when touched. All concrete models of 3-dimensional figures are solid in this sense. For example, a cube can be modeled by a construction made of drinking straws, by an empty box, or by a die. All three models are solid, but each highlights a different mathematical aspect of cubes. The drinking-straw model emphasizes a cube's edges, the box emphasizes the surfaces of a cube, and the die emphasizes a cube and its interior.

To be consistent with definitions in 0-, 1-, and 2-dimensions, *Everyday Mathematics* defines a *geometric solid* as all the points on the surface of a 3-dimensional figure. According to this definition, a geometric solid is actually just the "skin" of 3-D objects. Common 3-dimensional figures such as cones, pyramids, spheres, cubes, cylinders, and prisms do not include the points in their interior. That's why the objects listed in the left column above are better models for a prism, sphere, cone, and cylinder, respectively, than the objects in the right column.

Yet perhaps even more so than for plane figures, people commonly think of solids as solid through and through. So, just as with the difference between a polygon and a polygonal region, do not expect children to distinguish between the proper definition of a cone versus the solid and its interior. When the distinction eventually becomes mathematically relevant, it can be made and understood easily enough.

13.5.2 Polyhedrons

A *polyhedron* is a 3-dimensional shape formed by *polygons* and their interiors and having no holes. The word polyhedron comes from Greek words meaning "many bases" or "many seats." Polyhedrons include cubes, pyramids, prisms, and many other shapes. Features of polyhedrons include the following:

- *Faces* are the polygonal regions that make up a polyhedron. Although faces are always regions, they are often called by the name of the polygon defining the region. For example, it's common for a face that is a triangular region to be simply called a triangle.
- An *edge* of a polyhedron is a line segment where two faces meet.
- A *vertex,* or *corner,* of a polyhedron is a point where three or more edges meet.

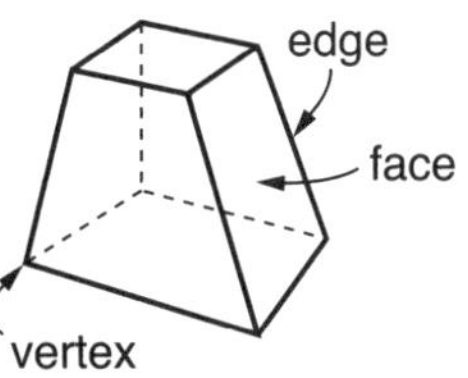

An irregular polyhedron

For more information, see Section 13.6.2: Congruence and Similarity.

In a *regular polyhedron*, all the faces are congruent, that is, the same shape and the same size; and the same number of faces join at the same angles at each vertex. Although there are infinitely many regular polygons, there are only five regular polyhedrons, which are illustrated here. The regular polyhedrons are also known as the *Platonic solids*.

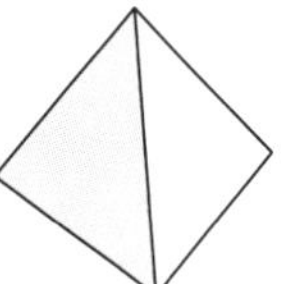

A tetrahedron (4 equilateral triangles)

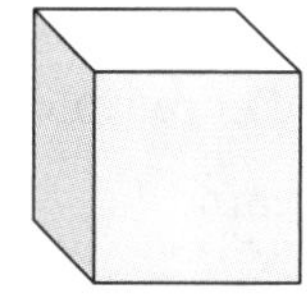

A cube (6 squares)

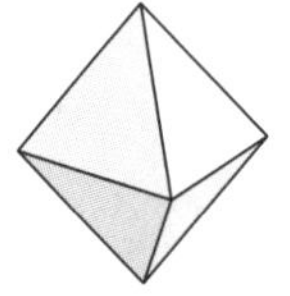

An octahedron (8 equilateral triangles)

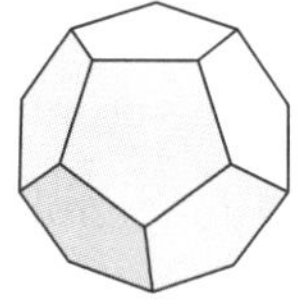

A dodecahedron (12 regular pentagons)

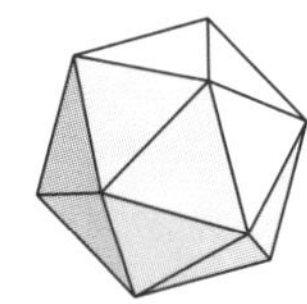

An icosahedron (20 equilateral triangles)

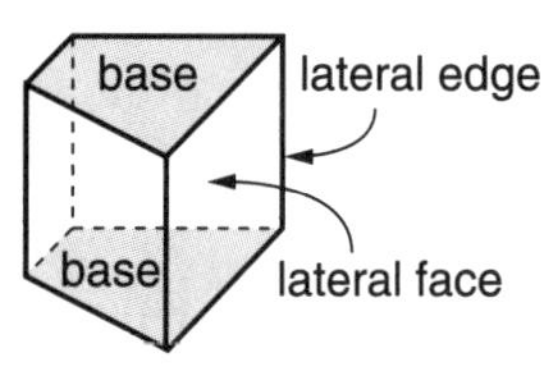

A prism

For more information, see Section 13.7.1: Flips, Turns, and Slides.

Prisms

A *prism* is a polyhedron with two congruent and parallel polygonal regions for *bases.* The bases are connected by line segments with endpoints on corresponding edges of the bases. These segments form parallelograms and their interiors called *lateral faces*. Lateral faces intersect at *lateral edges*.

A prism can also be defined using transformations. Start with a polygonal base in one plane and translate (slide) this preimage to a parallel plane to get its image (the other base). The line segments that are the sides of the preimage generate lateral faces of the solid as they slide to the image, and the vertices of the preimage generate the lateral edges.

A crystal

Prisms are usually named according to the shape of their bases. If a prism has a triangular region for a base, it is called a *triangular prism*. If a prism has a pentagonal region for a base, it is called a *pentagonal prism*. Emerald crystals often take the form of *hexagonal prisms*.

In a *right prism,* all the lateral faces are rectangles. This means that the lateral edges are perpendicular to the bases. If a prism is not a right prism, it is a *slanted* or *oblique prism*.

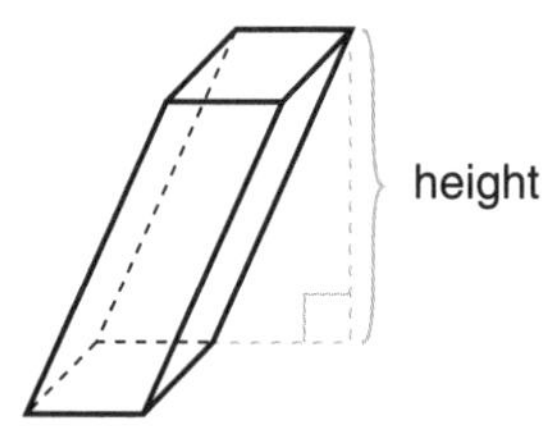

A slanted or oblique prism

NOTE: Slanted figures are sometimes called *oblique.*

The *height,* or *altitude,* of a prism is the perpendicular distance between the planes containing the bases.

Pyramids

A *pyramid* is a polyhedron consisting of a polygonal region for a *base*, a point *(apex)* not in the plane of the base, and all of the line segments with one endpoint at the apex and the other on an edge of the base. The *lateral edges* of a pyramid are the segments from the vertices of the base to the apex. The lateral edges form triangles, and the triangular regions are the *lateral faces* of the pyramid.

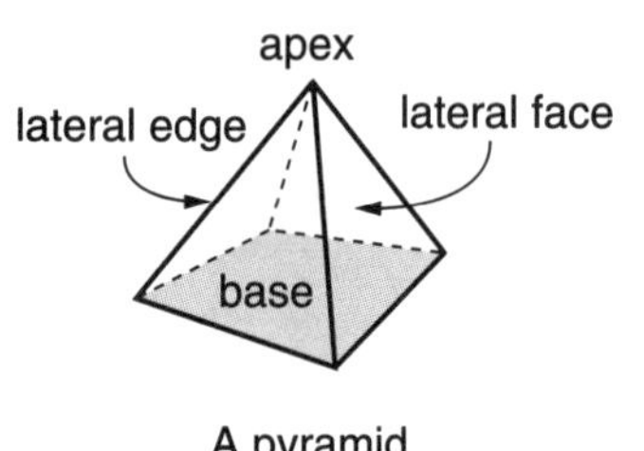

A pyramid

A pyramid can also be defined by transformations. Start with a polygonal base, an apex not in the plane of the base, and a line segment with one endpoint at the apex and the other endpoint on an edge the base. Keep the endpoint at the apex fixed and slide the other endpoint around the edges of the base until it returns to the starting point. The line segments generate the lateral faces of the pyramid.

In a *right pyramid,* a line segment with endpoints at the apex and the center of the base is perpendicular to the base. If it is not a right pyramid, it is a *slanted* or *oblique pyramid.*

Like a prism, a pyramid is usually named according to the shape of its base. The famous Pyramids at Giza, Egypt, are square, right pyramids. A triangular-based pyramid is also known as a *tetrahedron.*

All prisms and pyramids are polyhedrons, but not all polyhedrons are prisms or pyramids. For example, three of the five regular polyhedrons shown on page 142 are neither pyramids nor prisms.

13.5.3 Solids with Curved Surfaces

All the faces of a polyhedron are flat. Three interesting geometric solids with curved surfaces are spheres (entirely curved), cylinders (two flat surfaces and one curved surface), and cones (one flat surface and one curved surface).

Spheres

A *sphere* consists of all the points in space at an equal distance, the *radius,* from a given point at its *center.* A sphere is modeled by a basketball.

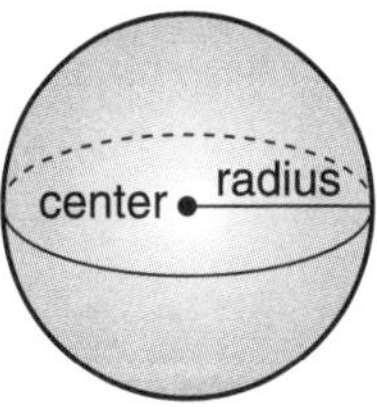

A sphere

Cylinders

A *cylinder* is a geometric solid with two congruent, parallel, circular regions for bases and a face formed by all the segments with an endpoint on each circle. These segments are parallel to a segment with endpoints at the centers of the circles. Food cans with top and bottom on, but no food inside, are models of cylinders.

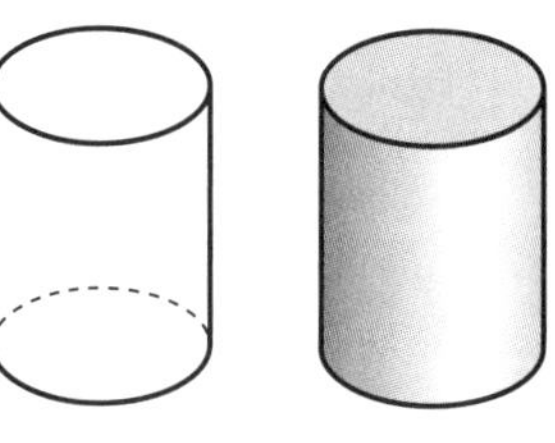

Cylinders

A cylinder may be defined in terms of transformations. Start with a circular base in one plane and generate a translation, or slide, image in a parallel plane to form the other base. All the segments with endpoints on the edges of the bases form the curved face of the cylinder.

NOTE: A cylinder resembles a prism in every way except that the former has circular bases and the latter has polygonal bases.

In a *right cylinder,* a line segment with endpoints at the centers of the bases is perpendicular to the bases. If it is not a right cylinder, it is a *slanted* or *oblique cylinder.* Most cylinders in everyday life are right rather than slanted.

The *height,* or *altitude,* of a cylinder is the perpendicular distance between the planes containing its bases.

Cones

A *cone* is a geometric solid with a circular base, a point *(apex)* not in the plane of the base, and all of the line segments with one endpoint at the apex and the other endpoint on the edge of the base. Together, these line segments form the *lateral face* of the cone.

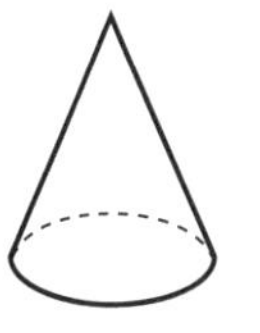

Cones

In a *right cone,* a line segment with endpoints at the apex and the center of the base is perpendicular to the base. If it is not a right cone, it is a *slanted* or *oblique cone.*

NOTE: A cone resembles a pyramid in every way except that the former has a circular base and the latter has a polygonal base.

The *height,* or *altitude,* of a cone is the perpendicular distance from the apex to the plane of its base.

In *Kindergarten* through *Fourth Grade Everyday Mathematics,* children explore geometric solids by manipulating blocks available in most classrooms, paper models constructed from blackline masters, and a variety of real-life materials such as shoe boxes and tin cans. More formal definitions such as those on the previous page are introduced in Grades 5 and 6.

13.5.4 Connecting 2-D and 3-D

A goal of the geometry strand at all levels of *Everyday Mathematics* is to help students see connections between 2-dimensional figures, such as polygons and curves, and the corresponding polyhedrons and curved surfaces in three dimensions. Children work toward this goal by building 3-dimensional models using materials such as straws, twist-ties, paper, and clay. Beginning in first grade, these constructions help children develop good connections between 1-dimensional line segments, 2-dimensional polygons, and 3-dimensional figures having polygonal regions as faces.

A Note about 2-Dimensional Drawings of 3-Dimensional Figures

This section briefly explains the conventions used for most of the geometric drawings in *Everyday Mathematics.* It is not intended to be a drawing tutorial, but rather a summary of various approaches, highlighting the one used in most geometry textbooks.

An artist needs to pick a point of view when drawing a 3-D object on paper or any other 2-D surface such as a computer monitor. The three main points of view, or *projections,* are *orthogonal, nonorthogonal,* and *perspective.*

Orthogonal Views

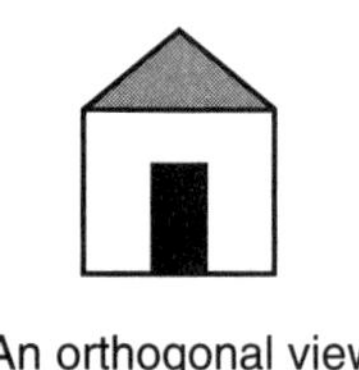
An orthogonal view

An *orthogonal* point of view looks at a 3-dimensional object head on. It generally ignores depth and simply draws the 2-dimensional part of the object that is in full view. Children's drawings are typically orthogonal; a drawing of a house is only face-on with no perspective or angles, as in the margin. A drawing of a die would be a square or rectangle showing the top face because that's the one that counts.

chapter 13

Orthogonal views are useful in engineering and architecture. Blueprints often have three orthogonal views; a front, top, and side view all drawn to the same scale so that a builder can get accurate measurements of the object to be built.

Semioblique orthogonal views show both front and side views as if seen head on, but attached to each other to indicate the "wrap-around." Many artists in the middle ages used this technique, along with "primitive " artists such as Warren Kimble, who painted the house on page 144.

A semioblique orthogonal view

Nonorthogonal Views

Nonorthogonal views of 3-dimensional objects attempt to show the third dimension, depth, that may be hidden in a head-on view of an object. The depth of the object is shown using lines drawn at an angle to the front of the object, and all these depth lines are parallel. These views are common in mathematics, science, engineering, and other textbooks that aim to show the technical aspects of 3-dimensional objects. Three types of nonorthogonal views briefly described below are *oblique, axonometric,* and *isometric.*

Oblique 2-dimensional views of 3-D objects show a life-size or similar view of the front of the object, with the sides angled away from the front to show the object's depth. Sometimes the lengths of the sides are proportional to the front, but more often they are shorter to mimic the depth perception of the human eye.

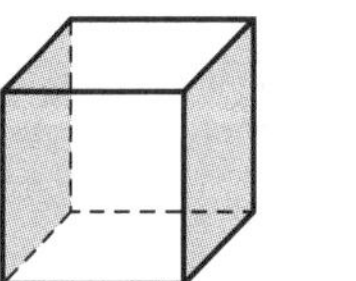

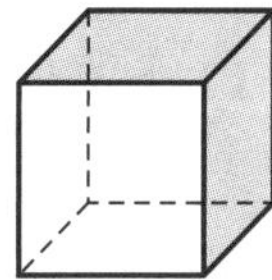

Oblique views of a cube

Oblique views are the most common views in geometry textbooks and in *Everyday Mathematics*. For example, the oblique drawings in the margin highlight parallel and perpendicular sides of a cube. Note that shading of faces and the inclusion or omission of dashed lines to indicate hidden edges can reveal more or less about the 3-dimensional features of the object being drawn. The dashed edges are always parallel to corresponding visible edges.

NOTE: In computer applications, oblique views are commonly called *dimetric* views.

Axonometric 2-dimensional views of 3-D objects show a life-size or similar view of the top of an object, usually rotated 45°, with the sides angled away to show the object's height. As in oblique views, lengths of the vertical edges are at the discretion of the artist; shorter ones mimic human perception better than proportional ones.

Axonometric views are used in architectural drawings showing the insides of buildings with the roofs removed. People want the true dimensions of the floor plan, and shorter walls make it easier to see objects placed in rooms.

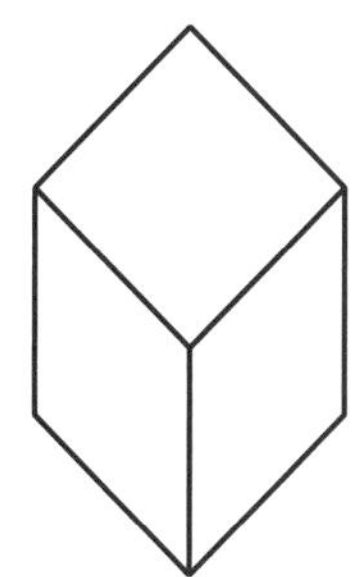

An axonometric view

Isometric 2-dimensional views of 3-D objects preserve all distances in the object. For example, each edge of the isometric drawing of a cube at the right measures 1.5 cm. The view is also symmetric so that all the faces are rhombuses.

Isometric means "equal distance," and isometric drawings are common in technical manuals for machine parts, car manuals, and so on. The drawing orients the sides to each other so an observer can picture the whole object, while the actual measures, or similar ones, can help an observer determine if a replacement part might actually fit into a space.

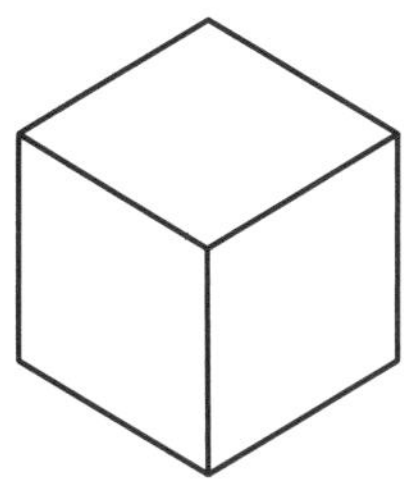

An isometric view

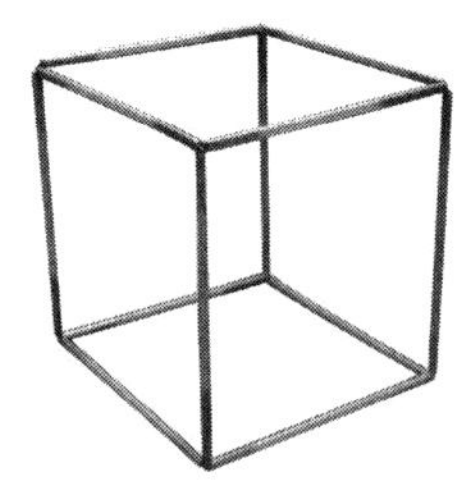

Perspective Views

A 2-dimensional view of a 3-D object in *perspective* does not attempt to display actual or similar measurements of the object. Instead, perspective views are intended to mimic how objects look to a human eye. Although there is much geometry to be found in perspective views, along with other advanced mathematics such as trigonometry, such views are not as useful as orthogonal and nonorthogonal views in showing the features of abstract geometric objects. This is not to say that perspective views have no purpose in *Everyday Mathematics.* The photograph at left of a straw-and-twist-tie cube does a nice job of showing what a finished model would look like. In this context, it does not matter too much that none of the parallel edges appear to be parallel in the 2-dimensional image.

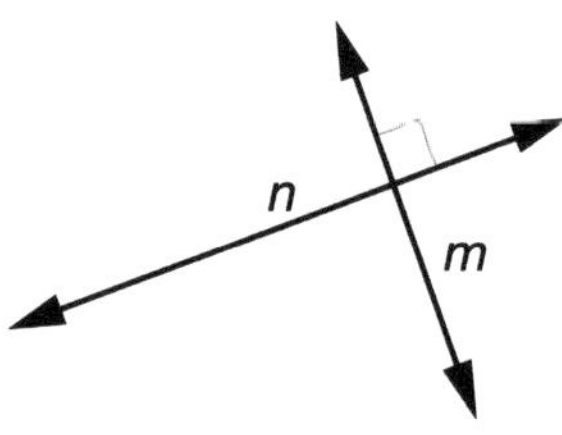

Line *n* is perpendicular to line *m*, or $n \perp m$.

NOTE: The ⌉ symbol is also used in right triangles, rectangles, and other polygons to indicate which angles are right angles.

13.6 Geometric Relations

Just as numbers can be related to one another in various ways, for example, $5 > 2$, $\frac{6}{2} = 3$, and $5 \neq 3$, geometric objects can likewise be related to one another. For example, if two figures are exactly the same size and shape, we say they are *congruent.* In the following sections, we discuss several interesting geometric relations.

13.6.1 Perpendicular and Parallel

Two lines in a plane either cross or do not cross. Lines that cross each other are said to *intersect.* When two lines intersect, they form several angles. When the angles formed are right angles, the lines are *perpendicular.* The symbol ⌉ is often included in a drawing of perpendicular lines to indicate a right angle. The symbol $\perp$ means *is perpendicular to.*

Lines in a plane that never cross are *parallel.* Parallel lines are always the same perpendicular distance apart, as shown below for parallel lines *AC* and *DF.* Many objects in our everyday world suggest parallel lines: window gratings, highway lane markings, and lines on notebook paper. The symbol $\parallel$ means *is parallel to.*

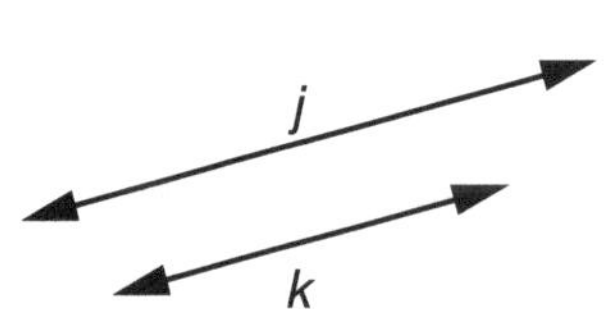

Line *j* is parallel to line *k*, or $j \parallel k$.

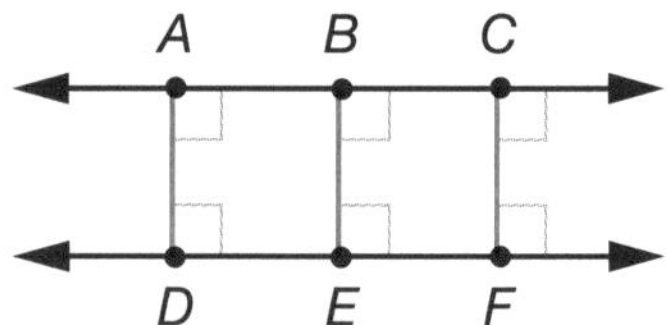

$\overline{AD}$, $\overline{BE}$, and $\overline{CF}$ have equal measure.

Skew lines can be modeled with two pencils.

Skew lines are neither intersecting nor parallel. For example, an east-west line on the floor of a room and a north-south line on the ceiling are skew. Skew lines cannot be in the same plane.

Planes, or figures in planes, such as line segments and squares, can also be parallel or intersecting. If two planes intersect at right angles, they are perpendicular, and two squares, one in each of those planes, are also perpendicular. Opposite faces of a cube are parallel, and adjacent faces are perpendicular.

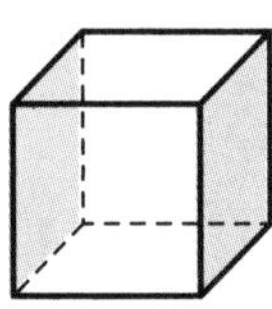
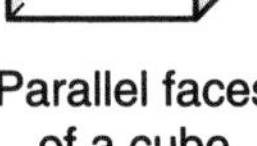

Parallel faces of a cube

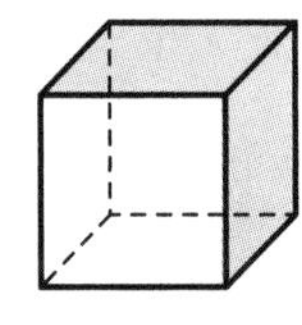

Perpendicular faces of a cube

Beginning in first grade, children are introduced to the ideas of parallel and perpendicular through the exploration of solids, their faces, and their edges. Drawing and naming parallel and perpendicular line segments begins in second grade. You can also point out the vast array of perpendicular and parallel objects throughout your classroom and school.

13.6.2 Congruence and Similarity

Congruent figures are exactly the same size and shape. They can be as simple as line segments or as complicated as polyhedrons. The symbol ≅ means *is congruent to.*

Congruent figures do not have to be oriented the same way to be congruent. They may be rotated, flipped, or otherwise arranged, as shown in these drawings. Isometric transformation images are congruent.

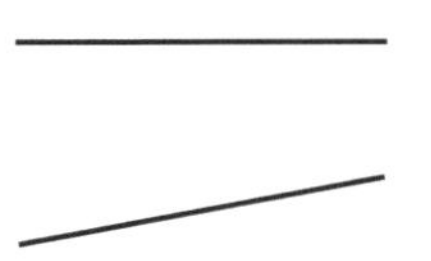

Congruent segments

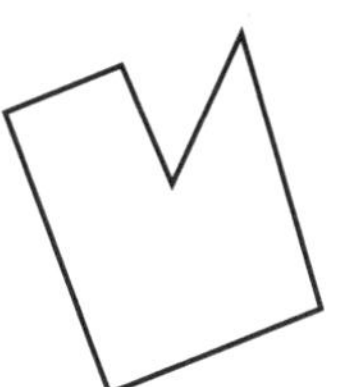

Congruent polygons

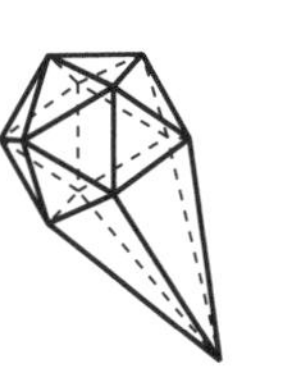

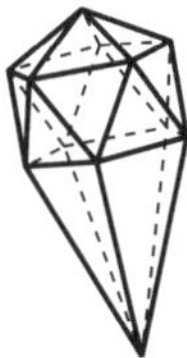

Congruent polyhedrons

NOTE: In theory, even two rocket motors could be congruent; the same blueprints could be used to build both. But as in most real-life applications of geometry, the motors could not be exactly the same, as each would have nicks and marks the other would not. Only abstract geometric objects can be congruent.

For more information on isometric transformations, see Section 13.7.1: Flips, Turns, and Slides.

Similar figures are the same shape but not necessarily the same size. For example, any two squares are similar, as are any two equilateral triangles, or the two polyhedrons in the drawing below.

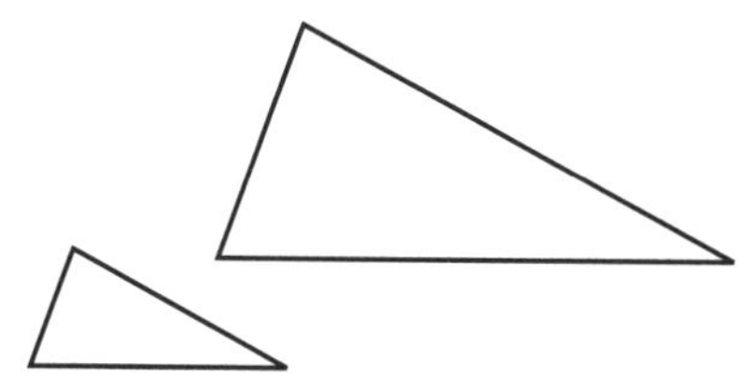

Similar triangles

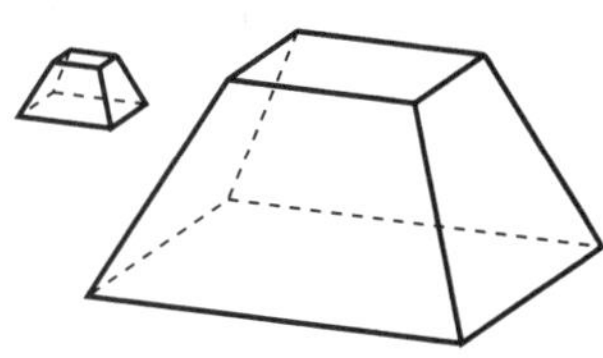

Similar polyhedrons

NOTE: In theory, two copies of Michelangelo's statue of David could be similar. But in reality, they are likely to have minor differences in shape. Like congruence, similarity is possible for only abstract geometric objects.

13.7 Transformations

A *transformation* is an operation on a figure that produces a new figure. The original figure is called the *preimage;* the figure produced by the transformation is called the *image.* The transformations usually studied in elementary school mathematics produce images that have either the same shape as the preimages or both the same size and the same shape as the preimages.

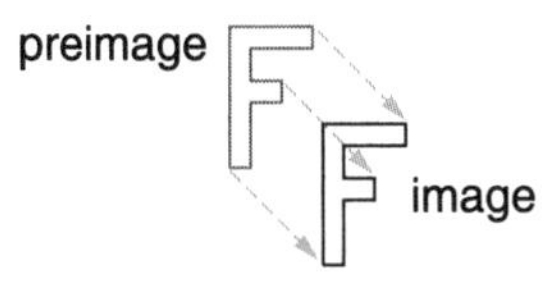

A transformation

In *Kindergarten* through *Third Grade Everyday Mathematics,* children explore reflection images. Students in Grades 4 through 6 explore the other isometries and size changes. For your information, we include brief descriptions of all four in the following sections.

13.7.1 Flips, Turns, and Slides

An *isometry* is a transformation in which a preimage and image are congruent. In *Everyday Mathematics,* children investigate three isometries: reflections (flips), rotations (turns), and translations (slides).

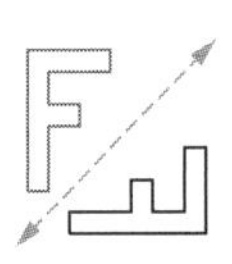

A reflection (flip)

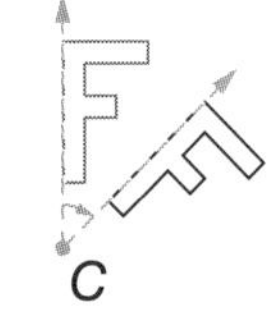

A rotation (turn)

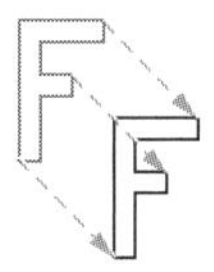

A translation (slide)

Reflections (Flips)

Two points A and A' are *reflection* images of each other over a line of *reflection* if line segment AA' is perpendicular to the *line of reflection* and is bisected (cut in half) by the line of reflection. If all the points in one figure are reflection images of all the points in another figure, the figures are reflection images. The images are congruent, but their orientation is reversed or flipped.

NOTE: Sometimes the line of reflection is called a *mirror,* or *mirror line.*

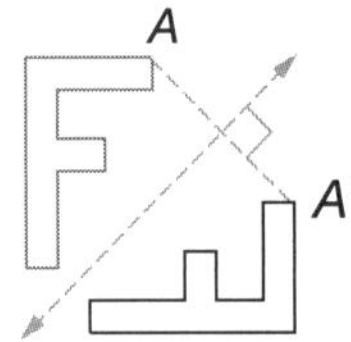

A reflection

For more information, see Section 13.8.1: Line Symmetry.

In Kindergarten through Grade 3, children explore reflections of objects through lines of symmetry.

Rotations (Turns)

A point P' is a *rotation* image of a point P around a *center of rotation* C if P' is on the circle with center C and radius CP. For a specific rotation, you would pick both the center of rotation and an angle of rotation. If all the points in one figure are rotation images of all the points in another figure around the same center of rotation and with the same angle of rotation, the figures are rotation images. The images are congruent, but their orientation is turned.

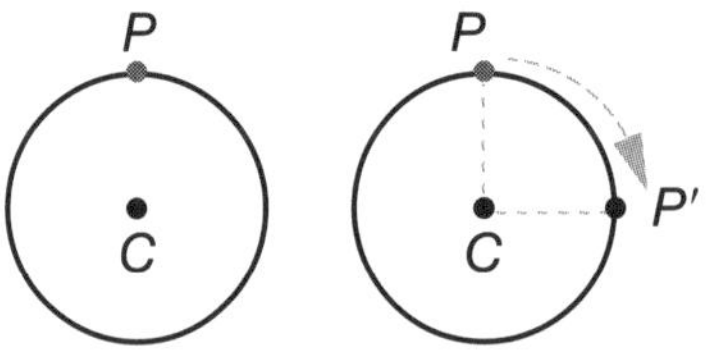

A rotation image of *P* around center of rotation *C*

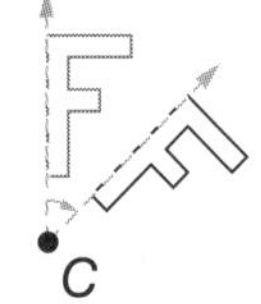

A rotation by 45° clockwise around point *C*

In *Kindergarten* through *Third Grade Everyday Mathematics,* children informally explore rotations when they model angles with drinking straws. Children form angles by bending a straw in half and rotating one half away from the other half. In the language of transformations, the final position of the rotated half is the image of its original position, or preimage. So an angle is a preimage ray together with its image after a rotation.

NOTE: A point T' is a *translation* image of a point T if it is the reflection image of T through two parallel lines. This definition of a translation is not very intuitive to most people, even adults. Because of this difficulty, *Everyday Mathematics* expects students to give informal descriptions of translations as slides of objects in a plane or through space.

Translations (Slides)

A figure is a *translation* image of another figure if every point in the image is at the same distance in the same direction from its corresponding point in the preimage. A ray can be drawn to indicate the direction of the translation.

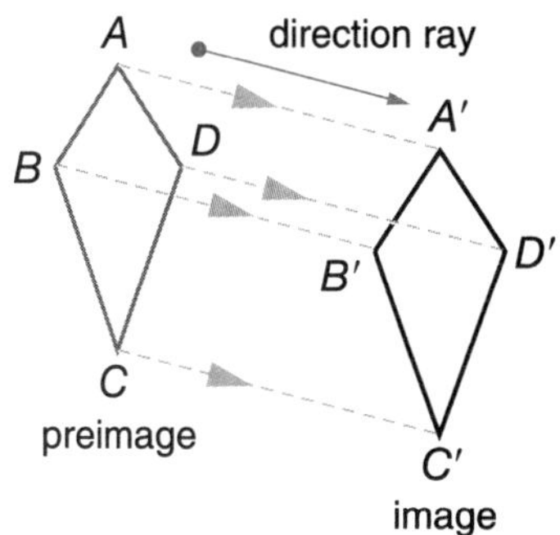

A translation of quadrilateral *ABCD*

13.7.2 Stretches and Shrinks

In a *similarity transformation,* the image of a figure stays the same shape but changes size. The name comes from the fact that the image is *similar* to the preimage. In *Kindergarten* through *Third Grade Everyday Mathematics,* children do not encounter similarity transformations, so this section is just a brief summary of what they will see in later grades.

A *size-change transformation* is defined by a *center of similarity P* and a *size-change factor k*. For example, if $k = 2$, then the image will be 2 times as large as the preimage. A point A' is a size-change image of A if it is on ray PA and the length of segment PA' is k times the length of segment PA.

If all the points on one figure are *size-change images* of all the points on another figure through the same center of similarity and with the same size-change factor, then the figures are size-change images.

For more information, see Section 13.6.2: Congruence and Similarity.

NOTE: A *size-change factor* is sometimes called a *scale factor* because the image is at a different scale than the preimage.

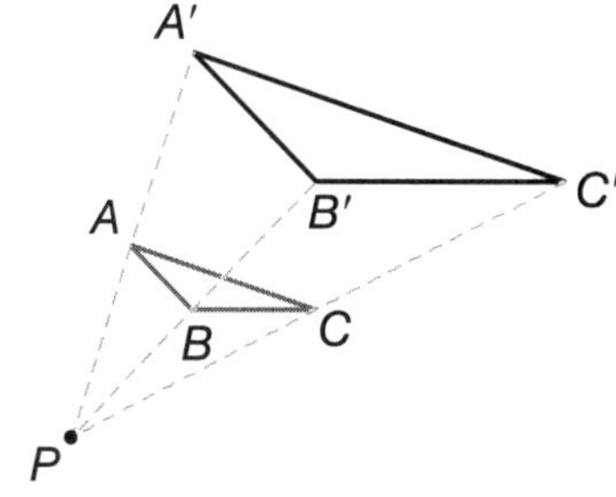

A size-change through P by a factor of 2 (length of $\overline{PA'} = 2$ times length of $\overline{PA}$)

13.8 Symmetry

A figure is *symmetric* if you can transform it and the image looks exactly like the original. For example, a butterfly has reflection symmetry, or line symmetry, because you can fold it and the two halves (wings) align perfectly. A starfish has rotation symmetry because you can turn one arm to where the next one was and it looks the same. A strip of wallpaper border has translation symmetry if a tracing of one part slides over and exactly matches another part of the pattern.

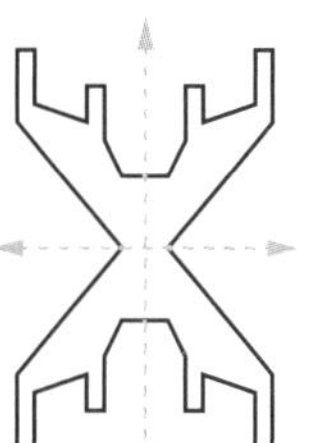

Line symmetry

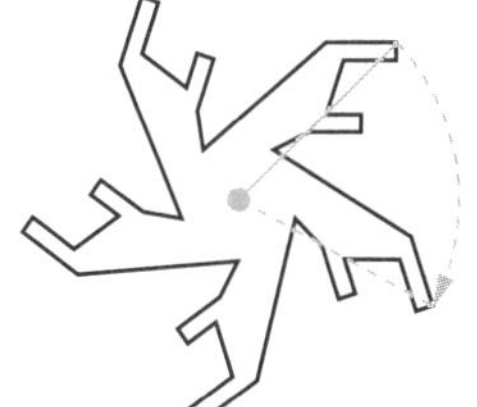

Rotation symmetry

Translation symmetry

13.8.1 Line Symmetry

A figure has *line symmetry* if there is a line that divides it into two halves that are reflection images of each other. They are the exact size and shape, but have opposite orientation. The line is called a *line of symmetry* of the figure, but no part of it is necessarily part of the figure. The two halves look exactly the same but face in opposite directions.

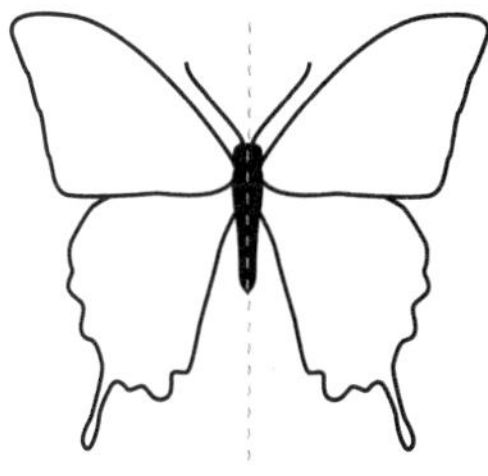

For more information, see Section 13.7.1: Flips, Turns, and Slides.

To check a figure for line symmetry, fold, or imagine folding, the figure on a line. If the halves match, the fold is a line of symmetry. An isosceles trapezoid has one line of symmetry. Figures may have more than one line of symmetry. A square has four lines of symmetry. A circle has infinitely many lines of symmetry through its center.

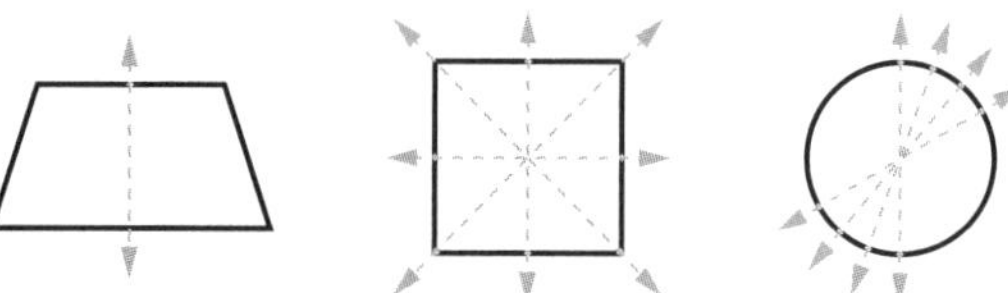

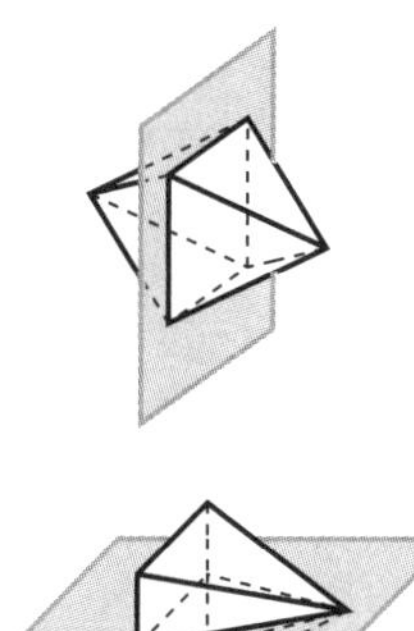

A solid figure has *bilateral symmetry* if there is a *plane* that divides it into two haves that are reflection images of each other in space. For example, each half of a human face is the mirror image of the other half, more or less. Other living things have this sort of bilateral symmetry, as do many human-made objects such as car grilles and traffic lights. Verifying bilateral symmetry is trickier than verifying line symmetry because it's very difficult to fold solid figures.

13.8.2 Other Symmetries

Sometimes people think a figure has line symmetry when it doesn't. They may think, for example, that there is a way to fold the parallelogram at left so that the two halves match.

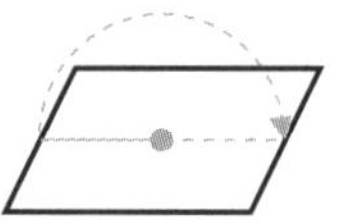

Parallelograms that are not rectangles do not have line symmetry, but they do have *rotation symmetry.* If a parallelogram is given a half-turn around its center (where the diagonals bisect), it will look unchanged. Other figures take less turning to show rotation symmetry. For example, a regular pentagon looks the same after 1 fifth of a full turn around its center.

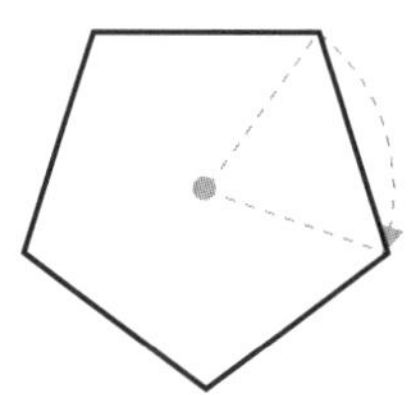

To test for rotation symmetry, turn, or imagine turning, a figure around a point. If it coincides with itself before a full rotation of 360°, then it has rotation symmetry. The number of times a figure coincides with its preimage during one full rotation is called its *order of rotation symmetry.* The pentagon at left has order-5 rotation symmetry.

For more information, see Section 13.7.1: Flips, Turns, and Slides.

Line symmetry and rotation symmetry are not the only kinds of symmetry. Some tessellations, or tilings of a plane, involve symmetry based on translation (slide) symmetry. In general, *tessellations* can be simple or complicated combinations of several isometries.

In *Kindergarten* through *Third Grade Everyday Mathematics,* children focus on line symmetry, but they may notice other symmetries when they are working with pattern blocks or looking for mathematics in their world. Many corporate logos, for example, have line symmetry or rotation symmetry. Some figures have both, as do the star and pentagon below.

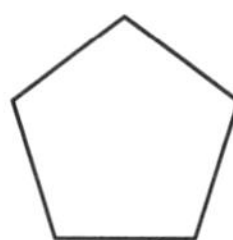

13.9 Teaching Geometry

Children in *Kindergarten Everyday Mathematics* play with models of shapes, manipulate pattern blocks, cut shapes out of paper, and look for shapes in their everyday environment. This informal approach is intended to let children's curiosity lead them toward recognizing features of polygons and other geometric figures. Vocabulary is introduced as necessary in order to identify groups of shapes by name. Informally, many common shapes that young children recognize are embedded in solids. For example, a square is a face on a cube, a rectangle is a face on a box, and a circle is the rim of a can.

The approach of using concrete manipulations leading to the recognition of key features and the naming of objects continues throughout the grades. Children in Grade 3 reach a point when they know the names of most common polygons. They are also able to informally classify triangles and quadrilaterals by describing such characteristics as parallel sides, equal sides, right angles, and equal angles.

13.9.1 The van Hiele Levels

The *Everyday Mathematics* curriculum is based on research that has been carried out by the authors and others over several decades. In geometry, some of the most important research was done in the late 1950s by two Dutch researchers, Dina and Pierre van Hiele.

The van Hieles identified five stages in the development of geometric understanding. During the first stage, children approach shapes holistically. A triangle is a triangle because its overall shape is like other objects that are also called triangles. At this stage, shapes are not broken down into parts; line segments, vertices, and angles of the triangle are not considered separately. Instead, the child grasps the whole figure at once. At this visualization stage, children can benefit from hands-on work with pattern blocks, geometric solids, geoboards, straws and connectors, and real objects from their everyday environment.

During the second stage of geometric understanding, children begin to notice the individual elements that make up geometric figures. They see that a triangle has three sides and three corners and that a square has four sides all the same length and four right angles. At this stage, children continue hands-on work and begin to compare, measure, sort, and describe shapes. They can also begin to learn the names for the parts of geometric figures: side, angle, face, edge, and so on.

In the third stage of geometric understanding, children begin to move beyond the analysis of single shapes and start thinking about relationships among different shapes. They can, for example, understand that squares are rectangles because they meet the minimal requirements of four sides and four right angles. Children also begin to understand hierarchical classification schemes like the one for quadrilaterals in Section 13.4.2. They also begin formulating simple chains of reasoning. If the context is not too abstract, children at this

In Grade 4, students explore properties of angles, polygons, and solids; classify quadrilaterals using a hierarchical scheme similar to the one in Section 13.4.2; and begin to work with compass-and-straightedge constructions and transformations. Work with classification and definition continues in *Fifth Grade Everyday Mathematics*. Students also explore tessellations, the effects of similarity transformations on area, perimeter, and angles, and transformations on the coordinate grid. In sixth grade, students classify tessellations, explore cross sections of geometric solids, and investigate the relationships among the angles formed when parallel lines are crossed by a transversal.

stage can work with definitions of geometric objects and properties. This is also the stage of informal proof, which is the highest level expected of children in elementary school geometry.

Beyond the informal proof stage, the van Hieles identified two further levels. One is the level of deductive reasoning, the level at which high school geometry is traditionally taught. The highest level is the formal axiomatic geometry of professional mathematicians, a level most of us would not even recognize as geometry.

13.9.2 Solid versus Plane Geometry

Which is less abstract, a cube or a square? In a purely mathematical sense, both are equally abstract. But in a practical sense, a cube is less abstract than a square. Good, concrete models for cubes are commonplace; a sugar cube, a die, or a lump of clay pressed into shape are all excellent representations of a cube. A square, on the other hand, is not so easily modeled. The face of a cube is a model for a square region, not a square. You can use straws to build a model of the square, but everyday objects that are good models of squares, circles, triangles, and other plane figures are hard to find.

So, odd as it may sound, solid geometry is more concrete than plane geometry. For this reason, *Everyday Mathematics* includes work with spheres, prisms, cylinders, and other 3-dimensional figures much sooner than in a traditional curriculum.

Beginning in fourth grade, students do detailed explorations of categories of triangles and quadrangles using a Geometry Template that contains more varied shapes than Pattern-Block Templates. The Geometry Template also includes inch and centimeter scales, a percent circle for making circle graphs, and two protractors.

13.10 Geometry Tools and Techniques

The study of geometry in *Everyday Mathematics* involves many hands-on experiences, such as manipulating pattern blocks and attribute blocks, tracing shapes from templates, working with geoboards, cutting out shapes, folding shapes, drawing shapes with straightedges or compasses, constructing shapes out of straws, and constructing 3-dimensional figures from 2-dimensional nets (flat figures that can be folded to form closed, 3-dimensional solids). The following sections highlight some of the most widely used tools.

13.10.1 Pattern-Block Template

Pattern-Block Templates are used for exploring plane figures. Children are encouraged to use the templates to make designs in Explorations, Projects, and some lessons. For example, in first grade, children are asked to estimate how many triangles, squares, or other figures it will take to "fill up" a piece of paper. They check their guesses by drawing the shapes using the templates. This informal introduction to area develops valuable background for formal definitions later. Children in Kindergarten through third grade also use their Pattern-Block Templates, rather than compasses, to draw circles.

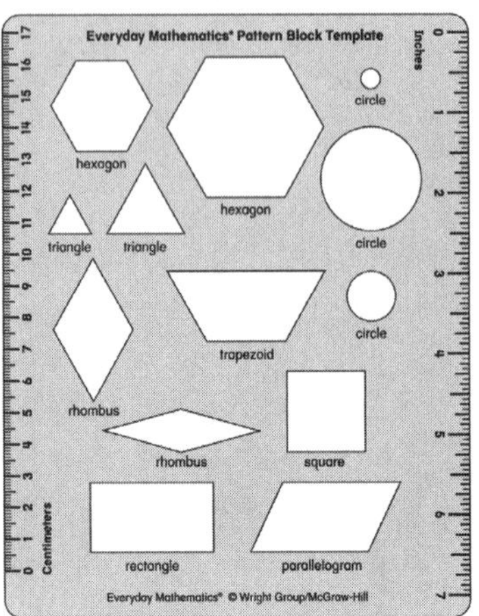

13.10.2 Pattern Blocks and Geometric Solids

Pattern blocks help children learn the names and features of geometric objects. In Kindergarten and first grade, children identify categories of shapes, colors, and weights of pattern blocks. Beginning in first grade, children are encouraged to find different ways of categorizing blocks on their own, that is, to create multiple perspectives of a given set of blocks. This ability to think about the same things in different ways is important for many problem-solving activities. Science educators also identify classification as one of the most important processes of science.

Kindergarten Everyday Mathematics introduces children to measurement, in part, through the use of geometric solids and building blocks. In later grades, children use both metric and U.S. customary rulers to measure the lengths of block edges and the heights and lengths of structures they build using several blocks. Such uses of models of geometric solids continue as a basis for the study of 1- and 2-dimensional geometry through third grade.

13.10.3 Straws and Twist-Ties

Constructing 2- and 3-dimensional objects with straws and twist-ties is a popular activity beginning in *First Grade Everyday Mathematics*. Suggestions for managing the activities are given in Section 3.2.4 of the Management Guide. Because these activities result in representations of geometric shapes, we include a few words here about the true nature of the shapes compared to the actual straw and twist-tie models of them.

Two-dimensional shapes such as polygons and circles are defined as boundaries of flat regions without the interiors. For example, a polygon is made up of line segments; the region inside a polygon is not part of the polygon. Straws and twist-ties make good models of polygons because the straws actually represent the sides of the figures and don't suggest including the interiors. In contrast, straw and twist-tie models for 3-D figures such as prisms and pyramids accurately show the edges, but not the interiors of the faces. So while straws and twist-ties can suggest 3-D shapes, a model such as an empty cereal box is truer to an actual rectangular prism.

Measurement

Contents

Measurement is one of the most widespread uses of mathematics in daily life. Even very young children show considerable interest in measurement. Questions such as *How tall is my block building? How long can we make this block train? How much water until the sink overflows?* and *How long until lunchtime?* are spontaneously pursued by preschool and primary-grade children. Older children continue to be curious about how much, how long, how far, and the like. Many become fascinated with measures and ways of determining them, whether it is the height of a tall building or the amount of water in a swimming pool. *Everyday Mathematics* recognizes and capitalizes on children's natural curiosity about measurement and measures. Throughout the grades, children engage in interesting and purposeful tasks as they learn how to measure and how to interpret other people's measures. Measurement tasks become more complicated as children gain experience.

Measurement is the source of many of the numbers that we use in everyday life. Measures, along with their units, tell "how much" of something there is. Arithmetic operations performed with measures lead to results that make sense in real-life contexts. For example, a 6-pound cabbage weighs twice as much as a 3-pound cabbage, and someone who spends 30 minutes on homework spends twice as much time as someone who spends 15 minutes on homework. Quantifying and comparing are common quests of childhood as well as adulthood, and both are important when exploring measurement. Furthermore, because all measures are approximate, knowing how to measure means knowing how to deal with error.

For more information, see Section 14.10.1: Measurement and Estimation.

This chapter begins with a discussion of measurement systems and units, including personal measures, the metric system, and U.S. customary measures. Then it turns to specific uses of measurement in one, two, and three dimensions (length, area, and volume), followed by discussions of weight and mass, angle measures, elapsed time, and money.

 **perspective**

Measures in geography are a focus throughout *Fourth* through *Sixth Grade Everyday Mathematics.*

14.1 Personal Measures

Units for measures of length appeared relatively early in human history and were based on things familiar to people, namely, their bodies. Just as many early number systems were based on *ten,* probably because humans have 10 fingers, many early linear measures were based on the lengths of certain body parts. This is the origin of such measures as *foot, digit, span,* and *hand,* each of which was, or still is, a commonly used unit for measuring length.

The problem with a measurement system based on body parts is that bodies differ. Who is to say whose *cubit,* a measure based on the distance between the elbow and fingertips, is the cubit to measure by? Without agreement, how do buyers know that they are getting their money's worth when someone sells them 56 cubits of cloth? In ancient Egypt, this problem led to the creation of a *royal master cubit* made of black granite. The royal master cubit was the *standard* against which every cubit stick in the land was periodically matched for building projects. For example, the length of any side of the Great Pyramid of Cheops at Giza differs only 0.05% from the mean length of all four sides. This precision is evidence of the consistency of the thousands of cubit sticks used to build the monument. Eventually, individual nations established their measures by agreeing on standards against which all measurement implements were compared.

Another problem arose when members of two or more groups that had been isolated because of distance, geography, or politics came into contact with one another. In the medieval trade fairs of Europe, for example, merchants from many nations gathered to sell their wool cloth. Most agreed to measure cloth in *ells,* but the length of an ell differed among the various nations' merchants. Therefore, an *iron standard ell* of 2 feet, 6 inches was made and left with the Keeper of the Fair. Each participating merchant was required to use this ell in all business dealings at the fair.

In England, cheating and abuse of measures became so common that a few years after the Magna Carta was signed in 1215, the *Assize of Weights and Measures* was drawn up. For almost 600 years, the Assize defined and standardized a broad list of units. One of these units, *The Iron Yard of Our Lord the King,* was divided into 3 feet of 12 inches each. Eventually, all kinds of measures became standardized in some way, and many national systems of measures came into being. Nearly all of these systems were replaced in Europe by the metric system during the 19th century. Britain and its former colonies in America kept to their old ways until well into the 20th century. The United States still uses the old system.

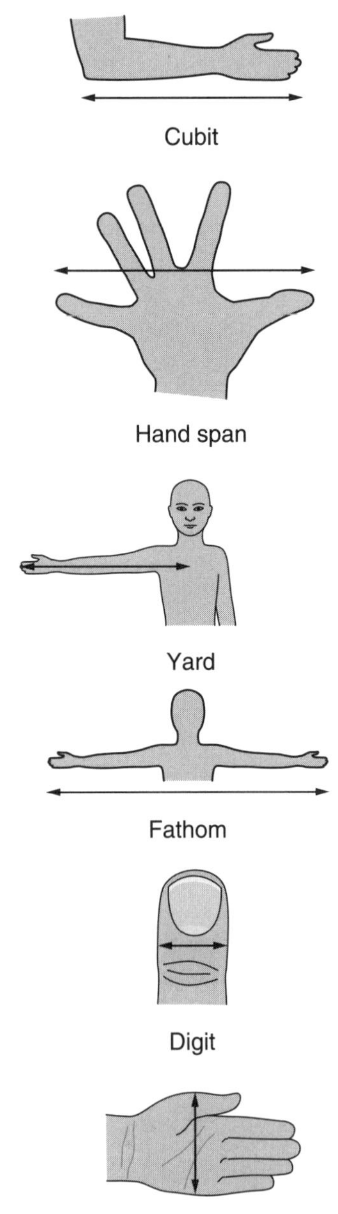

Cubit

Hand span

Yard

Fathom

Digit

Hand

Several of the original common measures are still good for approximating lengths today. Some measures based on dimensions of an adult human body are listed below. For children, of course, these personal measurements are likely to be smaller than the standards.

- *Cubit* A very old unit of measure, based on the distance between the elbow and the extended fingertips. The Egyptians used the cubit as early as 3000 B.C. to build pyramids. The cubit has been standardized at various times at values between 18 and 22 inches.
- *Hand span* The distance from the end of the thumb to the end of the little finger in an outstretched hand; used to measure things smaller than a cubit. The span has been standardized at 9 inches.
- *Yard* The distance from the center of the chest to the tips of the fingers of an arm held out to the side of the body; often used to measure cloth. A yard has been standardized at 3 feet (36 inches).
- *Fathom* The distance from fingertip to fingertip of the outstretched arms; said to be derived from an Anglo-Saxon word meaning "embrace." Fathoms are often used to measure the depth of water. Perhaps this is because the "leadsman" on a boat or ship in the days before electronic depth finders would drop a lead weight on the end of a rope until it hit bottom and then count the number of fingertip-to-fingertip measures as he gathered in his line. A fathom has been standardized at 6 feet (2 yards).
- *Digit* The width of a finger. One twenty-fourth of the royal master cubit in ancient Egypt.
- *Hand* The width of a hand laid flat. Horses are said to be so many "hands" high. The hand has been standardized at 4 inches.

Units of length too long to be measured conveniently with body parts tended to vary widely from country to country before the adoption of the metric system. For example, for distances for which the United States used a *mile* (5,280 feet), the Russians used a *verst* (about 3,500 feet or about 1 kilometer).

Beginning in Kindergarten, children measure various items or parts of their classrooms with parts of themselves and discuss which body parts are more appropriate for which objects. This is a predecessor to choosing measurement tools and units that fit a given measuring task. These activities are expanded in first grade as children learn techniques for measuring with their body-part units, such as putting the measuring device end to end to measure larger objects. They are also asked to make a habit of labeling their measures with appropriate "units." This practice is important not only for the act of measuring itself but as an important part of learning to solve number stories.

NOTE: Originally, 4 *fingers* made a *palm,* 3 palms a *span,* and 2 spans a *cubit.* Later, a thumb was included with a palm to make a *hand,* presumably because it is easier to lay a hand flat than to tuck the thumb under.

From second grade on, children continue to use personal reference measures, but the focus shifts to finding body parts that approximate customary or metric units. These parts can then be used to estimate measures without using a ruler, tape measure, or other standardized measuring device. For example, the width of a finger may be about 1 centimeter or a child's foot may be about 8 inches long.

Body-part estimation activities continue in Grades 4 through 6; as children grow, they need to adjust their personal reference measures.

14.2 Measurement Systems

This section discusses the two standardized measurement systems most commonly used today, the *U.S. customary system* and the *metric system*. By "customary" measures, we mean the ones commonly used in the United States. If you have children from other countries in your class, the metric system may be customary to them, so be sure the meaning of "customary" is clear in discussions.

There are also several commonly used measures that are neither metric nor U.S. customary: measures of angles, elapsed time, and monetary values, to name a few. *Everyday Mathematics* activities that engage children in understanding these measures are discussed later in this chapter.

14.2.1 U.S. Customary System

The *U.S. customary system* of measures is adapted from the English system, which was developed around the 13th century. Although most people in the United States are relatively comfortable with the U.S. customary system, it has definite drawbacks compared to the metric system. For one thing, because they evolved gradually out of specific, often local, needs, customary units of length, weight, and capacity are largely independent of one another. Another drawback is that the relationships among units are somewhat cumbersome. For example, a foot is $\frac{1}{3}$ of a yard, but an inch (the next-smaller standard unit) is $\frac{1}{12}$ of a foot. A quart is $\frac{1}{4}$ of a gallon, but a pint (the next-smaller standard unit) is $\frac{1}{2}$ of a quart.

NOTE: The relationships among inches, feet, yards, and miles are based on a *duodecimal* (base-12) number system. An advantage to this is that many different whole numbers divide 12, including 2, 3, 4, and 6. In this way, the U.S. customary system is much like the ancient Egyptian system.

14.2.2 Metric System

Scientifically minded people in France deliberately developed the metric system at the end of the 18th century. The basic unit of length in this system is the *meter*. Originally, the meter was defined as 1 ten-millionth of the distance from the North Pole to the equator along the global meridian through Paris. These days, the meter is defined as the distance light will travel in a vacuum in $\frac{1}{299{,}792{,}458}$ second.

In the metric system, many units are defined relative to the meter. Next-smaller or next-larger units are ratio comparisons by a power of 10, so they are easily converted from one to another. For example, a *decimeter* is 1 tenth (0.1) of a meter, and a *centimeter* is 1 tenth (0.1) of a decimeter.

Metric units of length, area, volume, capacity, and weight are interrelated. For example, a *liter* is a measure of volume or capacity equal to 1 cubic decimeter, and a cubic decimeter is equal to the volume of 1 kilogram of distilled water at 4°C.

14.2.3 Converting between Measures

Because the United States uses both metric and customary measures, being able to convert between these systems can sometimes be important. For example, Minnesota, a neighbor of metric-using Canada, has posted road signs proclaiming that 55 miles per hour is 88 kilometers per hour. It is also important to be able to convert from one unit to another within a system. Knowing how many inches are in a foot, feet in a yard, yards in a mile, and so on, provides the power to convert measures from one unit to another, which can be handy in many situations.

In the early grades of *Everyday Mathematics,* children learn what U.S. customary and metric measures are, how to estimate them generally, and how to approximate them using measuring tools. Children in *Kindergarten* through *Third Grade Everyday Mathematics* do not convert units from one system to the other but only within a given system.

in perspective

Converting between measurement systems is first addressed in *Fourth Grade Everyday Mathematics,* and students in Grades 5 and 6 continue to practice and apply this skill.

▶ 14.3 Length

Distances along 1-dimensional objects or along paths are measured with *linear* measures. Like all measures, a linear measure consists of a value and a *unit*. For example, *The edge of my desk is about 3.5 long* makes no sense. However, *The edge of my desk is about 3.5 feet long* provides both the approximate length and a unit of measure.

Two common linear measures are *length,* the distance between two points on a line or arc, and *perimeter,* the distance around an object. The perimeter of a circle is called the *circumference* of the circle.

2 inches

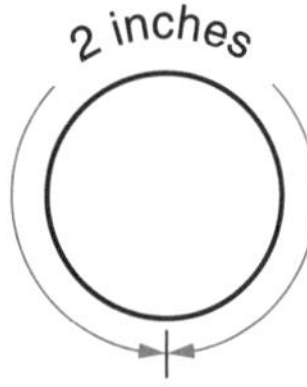

For information on tools to measure length, see Section 14.10.2: Rulers and Tape Measures.

▶ 14.4 Area

While length and perimeter are measures of a finite distance along a path, *area* is a measure of a finite amount of a 2-dimensional surface. This surface may lie in a single plane such as the interior of a rectangle; or it may exist in 3-dimensional space, such as the curved surface of a cylinder or cone. This latter type of area is called *surface area.*

interior of a rectangle

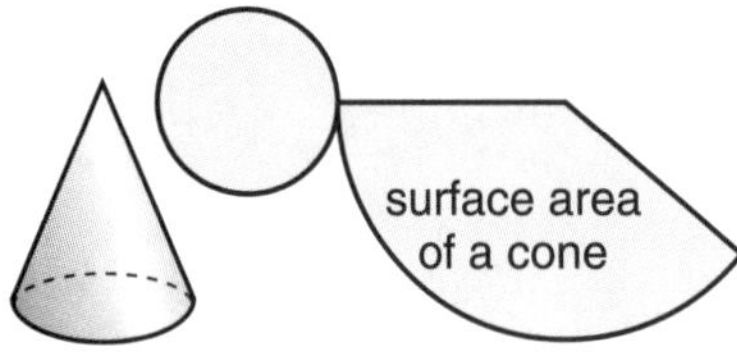

Like other numerical measures, a measure of area always includes both a value and a unit. Units of area are typically square units based on linear units such as square inches, square centimeters, square yards, and square meters. Some traditional units of area are not square units. For example, it is said that long ago an acre of land was the amount of land a farmer could plow in one day.

14.4.1 Discrete and Continuous Models of Area

This section discusses two different models for thinking about area. Each model has its strengths and weaknesses in helping children understand a concept that many people find difficult.

Discrete Model of Area

In most schoolbooks, the definition of area is based on the idea of *tiling,* or covering a surface with identical unit squares without gaps or overlaps and then counting those squares. This is a *discrete model of area* because it involves separate, countable parts. If the surface is bounded by a rectangle, you can arrange the tiles in an array and multiply the number of tiles per row by the number of rows. The formula $A = l \times w$ is then easily linked to array multiplication: area A is the number of square-unit tiles in one row (the length l of one side of the rectangle in some linear unit) times the number of rows (the width w of the rectangle in the same unit).

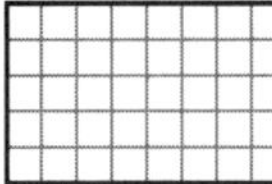

40 square units

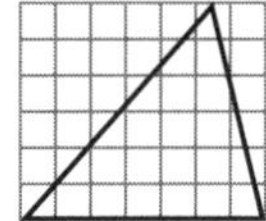

About 21 square units

For other surfaces, defined by regular or irregular boundaries, the tiling with square units can be thought of as, or actually done by, laying a grid of appropriate square units on the region and counting, estimating, or otherwise calculating how many squares or partial squares it takes to cover the region.

Continuous Model of Area

Tiling activities develop a discrete model of area, as described above. In later grades, students touch on a *continuous model of area*. Imagine rolling a paint roller 1 foot wide on the floor of a rectangular room. For every foot the roller travels, a square foot of the floor is painted.

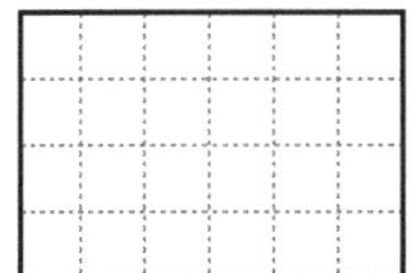

A discrete model of area

Now imagine that the room is 20 feet wide and that you use a roller the width of the room (a 20-foot-wide roller). Then, for every foot the roller travels, 20 square feet of floor will be painted. When the roller reaches the other side of the room, the entire floor will be painted.

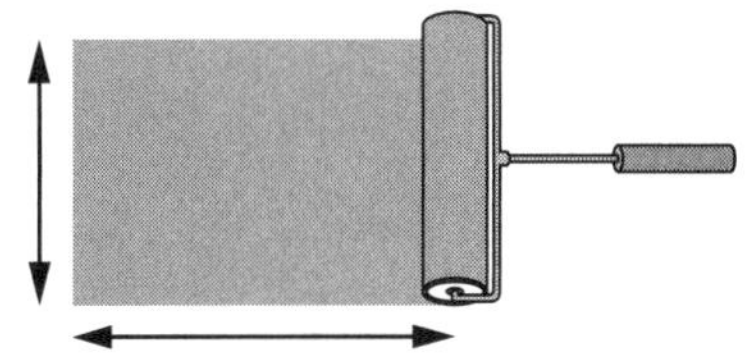

A continuous model of area

If you think of the floor as the interior of a rectangle, then the area of the rectangle is obtained not by counting squares (a discrete model) but by *sweeping* the width of the rectangle across the interior of the rectangle, parallel to its base (a continuous model). The area is simply the product of the length of the base and the width of the rectangle. This can be shown by rubbing the long part of a piece of chalk on the chalkboard to mark a rectangular region; the farther it is swept along, the larger the rectangle and the greater the area.

Beginning in Grade 4, students use formulas to model area symbolically. In Grades 4 and 5, students estimate areas of land and research areas of states, countries, and continents in the World Tour and American Tour, respectively.

Children have experience with area throughout *Everyday Mathematics*. Younger children focus on manipulating discrete conceptions of area through tiling activities. Beginning in third grade, children are asked to estimate area measures, and sometimes they check them by actually measuring.

14.5 Volume (Capacity)

Volume, or *capacity,* is the measure of a finite amount of 3-dimensional space. As with measures in one and two dimensions, all measures of volume require a unit, and all are approximate. Volume units are often cubic units based on linear measures, such as cubic inches, cubic centimeters, cubic yards, and cubic meters. Other units for volume, such as milliliters, teaspoons, pints, quarts, and liters, are used to measure liquids or fine-grained materials such as sand and sugar.

NOTE: Dry ingredients such as sugar are sometimes measured by weight.

As with all measures, it is possible to convert from one unit to another. For example, a *fluid ounce* is 1.804 cubic inches, and a *liter* is 1,000 cubic centimeters. You can see why the U.S. customary system is not as popular as the metric system when it comes to conversions.

14.5.1 Discrete and Continuous Models of Volume

Discrete and continuous models of volume are analogous to the corresponding models of area.

Discrete Model of Volume

In a *discrete model of volume,* imagine building 3-dimensional shapes with identical cubes, or filling shapes completely with such cubes, and then counting the cubes. If the shape is a rectangular prism, you can build one layer of cubes, count the cubes in that layer, and then multiply that number by the number of layers needed to fill the prism. Because the number of cubes in one layer corresponds to the area of the base, often represented by the formula $A = l \times w$, this process of counting cubes can be linked to two standard formulas for the volume V of rectangular prisms: $V = B \times h$ (the product of the area B of the rectangular base and the height h perpendicular to that base) and $V = l \times w \times h$ (the product of the length l and width w of the rectangular base and the height h perpendicular to that base).

NOTE: The formula $V = l \times w \times h$ is commonly used in elementary textbooks and on standardized tests. $V = B \times h$ is used in many mathematics courses and technical applications.

Continuous Model of Volume

The formula $V = B \times h$ for volume of a rectangular prism captures a *continuous model of volume* similar to the "sweeping out" of area. For example, imagine the base of a box as a rectangular region. Then imagine sweeping this rectangular region through the height of the box, and so filling the space. Or imagine gradually filling the box with water. The surface of the water is rectangular, like the base of the box, so the higher the water level, the more space the water occupies and the greater is its volume.

This model for a rectangular prism leads to a general formula for the volume of prisms and cylinders—the area of the base multiplied by the height. Unlike $V = l \times w \times h$, the formula $V = B \times h$ works for any shape base.

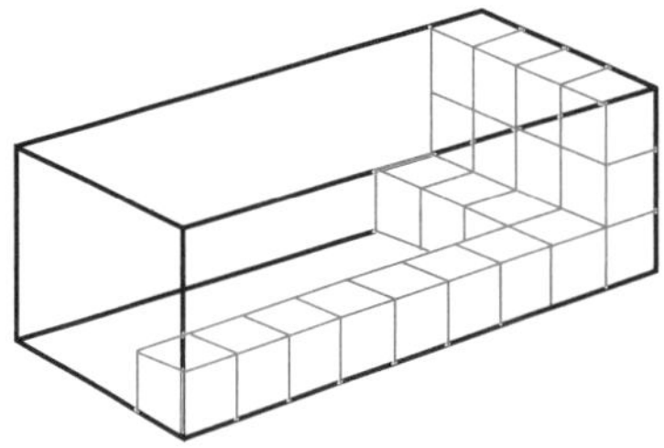

Filling a box with cubes is a discrete model of volume.

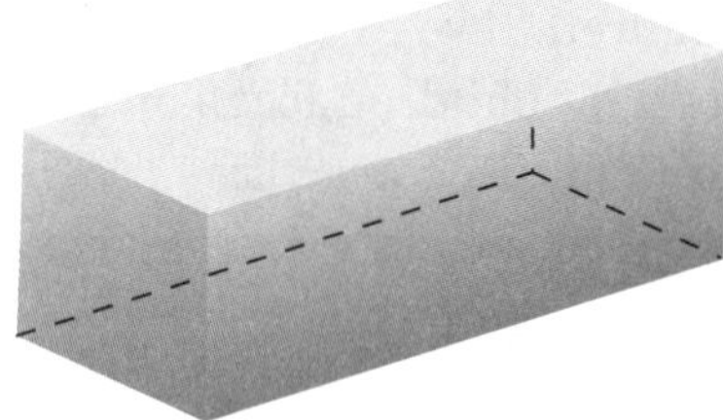

A continuous model of volume

Both models of volume are used throughout *Everyday Mathematics,* with a discrete approach dominating first and second grade as young children fill objects with cubes. In Grades 3 and 4, they experiment with a continuous approach by filling objects with water or sand.

in perspective

In Grades 5 and 6, students focus on the use of variables in formulas to model volume symbolically.

chapter 14

14.5.2 Linking Area and Volume

The idea of dimension is at the heart of area and volume, and understanding dimension requires plenty of experience with 1-, 2-, and 3-dimensional figures, both individually and in relation to one another. This is one reason why measuring actual objects for their 1-dimensional attributes such as length or perimeter, 2-dimensional attributes such as area and surface area, and 3-dimensional attributes such as volume is such an integral component of *Everyday Mathematics* beginning in Kindergarten.

perspective

By fourth grade, students should be comfortable identifying attributes of 1-, 2-, and 3-dimensional figures and their measures. They will also have had many informal experiences relating objects in different dimensions. In *Fourth* through *Sixth Grade Everyday Mathematics,* students explore relationships between the dimensions based on the continuous models of area and volume.

14.6 Weight and Mass

Mass is a measure of the amount of matter in an object. *Weight* is the force of gravity on an object. If you weighed yourself on different planets on a trip around the solar system, your weight would vary drastically depending on the size of the planet. You would weigh more on large planets because their gravitational pull is stronger. You would weigh less on small planets because they don't exert as much pull. Your mass, however, would be the same regardless of the planet you were on because the amount of matter in your body is not affected by gravity.

NOTE: Your weight even varies slightly at different altitudes above sea level on Earth. Yet your mass remains the same.

In *Everyday Mathematics,* children focus on measuring weight, not mass. It can be measured with a variety of scales. For example, a *balance scale* compares an object's weight to a standard set of weights, or it can simply compare relative weights of any two objects to see which is heavier without measuring. A *spring scale* measures the pull of gravity as evidenced by an object's push or pull on a spring.

For more information, see Section 14.10.3: Scales and Balances.

The units of measure most common to your classroom will depend on the units defined by your scales. Some scales measure with U.S. customary units such as ounces and pounds, while others measure with metric units such as grams and kilograms.

14.7 Angle Measure

For more information, see Section 13.4.1: Angles and Rotations.

Angular measures quantify turns or rotations. In Kindergarten through third grade, children measure angles as fractions of a circle; for example, a right angle is a quarter turn and a straight angle is a half turn.

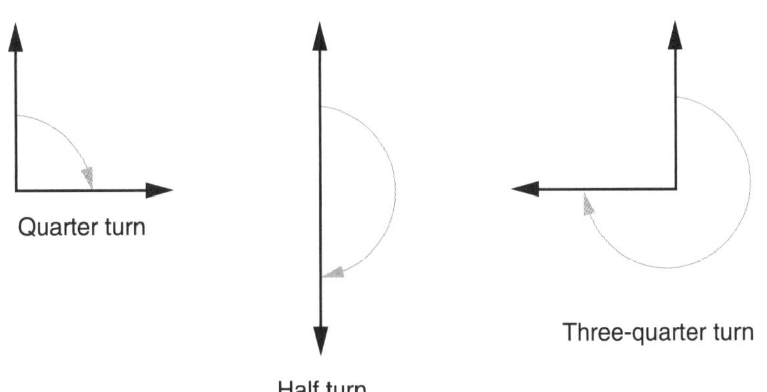

perspective

Students in *Fourth Grade Everyday Mathematics* start using protractors to measure angles in degrees. A degree is $\frac{1}{360}$ of a full rotation and is the angle measure used in most practical situations. In Grades 5 and 6, angle measurement is often a part of contexts for problem-solving activities. In later mathematics courses, students will learn about other angle measures, especially the *radian* (2π radians = 360°).

▸ 14.8 Elapsed Time

For more information, see Section 15.2: Time.

Numbers are used both to mark time and to measure it. We mark time by establishing reference frames, such as a calendar year and the number of days in a month. Events are then described by locations on one or more of these frames, such as *She was born August 15, 1989, at 2:00 A.M.* These numbers are not measures because they cannot be added or subtracted with any meaning. For example, 2:00 P.M. plus 3:00 P.M. is not 5:00 P.M., nor is April 12 plus April 15 equal to April 27. The reference labels *P.M.* and *April* are not units of measure.

Once reference frames have been established, however, there are reference units that can be used as measures. For example, *The play lasted 68 minutes. He finished the race in 3.9 seconds. The past 4 years have been warm.* The use of time units to measure the duration of an event or the time between events is called *elapsed time.*

 **perspective**

In Grades 4 through 6, time measurements are important parts of rate problems. For example, students figure out gallons per minute of water flow, an animal's speed in feet per second, or calculations per millisecond by a computer. Students also answer ratio-comparison questions about time, such as *What fraction of a year is 9 months?*

Our units of time have the longest-known history of any measuring units. The 24-hour day comes from the ancient Egyptians, who divided the period from sunrise to sunset into 12 equal parts and the period from sunset to sunrise into 12 equal parts as well. Because the times of sunrise and sunset vary, the lengths of these two kinds of "hours" changed daily. The 7-day week is credited to the Babylonians, who observed seven moving celestial bodies: the sun, the moon, and five planets. The Babylonians also used a numeration system based on 60, probably because 60 is divisible by many whole numbers. This led to the 60-second minute and the 60-minute hour.

Children use time measures frequently throughout *Everyday Mathematics,* most often in the context of number stories. As children learn new arithmetic skills, elapsed-time applications of these skills are developed. For example, in first and second grades, children use addition and subtraction to figure out elapsed times: *What time was it 2 hours ago? What time will it be in 3 hours?*

▸ 14.9 Money

Money may be viewed as a reference frame because it is an arbitrary scale used to establish the values of goods and services. Like the variations in the linear measure *foot* before standardization, however, different people place different values on the same goods or services. To make matters even more complicated, the differences are not just physical but emotional, spiritual, and intellectual in nature. Even an individual's perceived value of something changes with time and experience.

However, in everyday life, money is more a *measure of relative value* than a reference frame. We measure the value of one thing versus another or of one thing now versus that thing yesterday or last year. Statements such as *This TV costs $50 more now than it did three months ago* and *Bananas are up 17% this season* are examples of how we use arithmetic to compare monetary values. This is a sign that money behaves like a measure, so it is categorized as such in *Everyday Mathematics.*

Young children are exposed to money, prices, buying, and selling on a daily basis, but few have experience with money details. That is, children observe money transactions, are given an exact amount to spend, or hand over coins and accept change without checking. Although there are exceptions, many first-grade children are unable to distinguish among coins; for example, nickels and quarters are often confused. Also, relatively few beginning first graders know the exchanges among coins or their links to the basic dollar unit.

Experience with money is important because of its inherent usefulness and, like most measures, because of the context it provides for number stories. Additionally, our base-ten monetary system is an excellent vehicle for the study of place value, fractions, and decimal notation. *Everyday Mathematics* provides children with early experiences to develop their knowledge about the details of money. Then the familiar context of money makes it easier for children to become acquainted with fractions and decimals at earlier ages than they would in a traditional mathematics curriculum.

NOTE: In the wizard world of Harry Potter®, there are 29 copper *knuts* in a silver *sickle* and 17 sickles in a gold *galleon.* This is certainly a context in which a calculator can help with conversions.

In *Kindergarten* through *Third Grade Everyday Mathematics,* money is a focus of instruction. By fourth grade, it is assumed that most students have a good understanding of money and can use it in number stories without explicit coverage or review.

14.9.1 Money Facts

Talking about coins and bills also provides a unique opportunity to bridge various curriculum subjects. Money lore contains interesting facts about the history of our country, about the science of metals, and about symbols in our heritage. Use these facts liberally in your teaching about coins and bills in the *Everyday Mathematics* money lessons and at other times during the year. Selected definitions follow.

- *Alloy* A mixture of two or more chemical elements, at least one of which is a metal.
- *Denomination* The official value of a coin.
- *E Pluribus Unum* The original motto of the United States; translated from Latin as "From many, one." This motto is required by an 1873 law to appear on any coin that contains an eagle. In fact, it appears on all U.S. coins.
- *In God We Trust* A motto that was permitted, but not required, on coins by the 1873 law; a 1955 law required that the motto be placed on all coins and bills. In 1956, President Dwight D. Eisenhower signed a law making "In God We Trust" the official motto of the United States.
- *Intrinsic value* The actual worth of the metal in a coin.
- *Obverse* The face, or "front," of a coin; "HEADS."
- *Reverse* The back, or "rear," of a coin; "TAILS."
- *Rim* The edge of a coin, which is quite functional because it allows coins to be stacked and protects the design from damage. Most U.S. coins worth more than 5 cents have always had rims that are ornate, lettered, or *reeded,* that is, with parallel grooves

NOTE: To make it easier to distinguish from a quarter, which is about the same size, the Sacagawea dollar coin is *not* reeded.

that are perpendicular to the face of the coin, as in our dime and quarter. This is intended to discourage the scraping of the coin edges to steal some of its metal; it also makes it easier to identify coins by touch, which is necessary for people with visual impairments and useful for pulling a specific amount of change out of your pocket without looking.

New designs for coins and bills are adopted periodically, putting currency in the United States in a constant, albeit slow, state of flux. Recently, the U.S. Treasury Department has been producing a quarter commemorating each state and has minted a new American-bison nickel. A rewarding cross-curricular activity is to explore individual coins and their designs while touching upon history, metallurgy, and architecture. For example, some interesting facts about nickels are given below.

Nickels

Until 1866, 5-cent pieces were called "half-dimes." The word *nickel* comes from the metal in the coin. Currently, nickels are made of an alloy of 75% copper and 25% nickel.

Obverse

Obverse The Jefferson bust was designed by Felix O. Schlag, whose initials, FS, appear between the rim and the bottom of the bust on nickels produced after 1965.

Information about Thomas Jefferson	
Born	April 13, 1743; Shadwell (now Albemarle County), Virginia
Died	July 4, 1826; at Monticello, his estate in Albemarle County, Virginia. Jefferson died on the 50th anniversary of the signing of the Declaration of Independence. The second President of the United States, John Adams, died on the same day.
Occupations	Lawyer; delegate to the Continental Congress; author of the Declaration of Independence; Governor of Virginia; ambassador to France; Vice President; President; founder of the University of Virginia; farmer; architect
Important Dates	1797 elected Vice President under President John Adams 1801 inaugurated as third President 1803 Louisiana Purchase 1804 reelected President

Reverse

Reverse Monticello appears on the reverse, along with its name. President Franklin D. Roosevelt suggested this coinage design in 1938.

Information about Monticello	
Location	Albemarle County, Virginia
Architect	Thomas Jefferson
Built	First version, 1769–1793 Second version, 1793–1809

14.9.2 Money History

The history of money in our country is also quite interesting. The first coin used extensively in the American colonies was the *Spanish milled dollar,* a silver coin referred to as a *piece of eight* because it was worth 8 reales, pronounced "ray-al-ays." The coin was also called a peso. Even today, our $ symbol is the same as that for the Mexican peso. The milled dollar was often cut into eight pieces to allow for smaller denominations. Each of the eight pieces was called a *real* or a *bit.* Thus, for many years, a dollar was referred to as eight bits, a half-dollar as four bits, and a quarter as two bits.

When the United States began to produce its own coins, it used the Spanish milled dollar as its model. The first U.S. dollars, which weighed exactly as much as the Spanish coins, were made of an alloy composed of 15 parts silver to one part gold. In 1792, Congress passed the first coinage act for the new country and authorized the production of coins in various denominations: an *eagle* ($10), a *half-eagle* ($5), coins with the modern values, and a *half-cent.* With the exception of the cent and the half-cent, these early coins did not show their denominations. An Act of Congress corrected this oversight in 1837. Until 1909, the heads, or busts, of all people represented on U.S. coins were abstractions, such as Liberty, or generic figures, such as an Indian. In 1909, Abraham Lincoln appeared on the first coin picturing a real person.

The American eagle, which appears by law on all coins with a value of more than 10 cents, is the likeness of an actual eagle, "Peter the Mint Bird," the mascot of the Philadelphia Mint in the 1840s and 1850s. After his death, Peter was stuffed and is to this day preserved in a glass case in the Philadelphia Mint.

NOTE: Cheers like "Two bits, four bits, six bits, a dollar! All for Springfield, stand up and holler!" continue to carry the early terms for coins into the present. "Shave and a haircut, two bits" may be dying out, but the rhythm behind the saying lives on.

Resources on Money

Information about U.S. coins and bills and the history of money can be found in these books and Web site:

Barabas, K. (1997). *Let's Find Out About Money.* New York: Scholastic.

Doty, R. (1988). *America's Money, America's Story.* Iola, WI: Krause.

U.S. Treasury Web site: www.ustreas.gov/topics/currency/

Yeoman, R. S. (Yearly). *Guide Book of United States Coins.* New York: Golden Books Adult.

14.10 Measurement Tools and Techniques

No matter which system or unit is being used, measuring tools provide ways to attach numbers to many common and uncommon things in everyone's life. There are measuring tools to measure in any unit or system; some tools even provide help with conversions. The history of science is intertwined with the development of improved measuring instruments. New scientific discoveries often hinge on new and more precise measuring tools, and verification or rejection of theories often depends on increasingly precise measurements. Much of modern industry and technology depends on using very precise measures that are standardized throughout the world. Children learn that the measuring tools that we all use are based on mutually agreed-upon standards and that our own measurements are mere approximations, as the following section explains.

14.10.1 Measurement and Estimation

All measurements are approximate. Even measures that seem exact are actually estimates that are "close enough" for practical considerations. We can never line up the precise edge of an object with a precise point on a measuring tool. For example, this page is not exactly 11 inches long. If you look at its edge under a microscope you will see that it is not even straight. So, is the actual measure the straight-line path from one corner to the other, or is it the path following all the dips and curves of the paper's edge? No matter how careful the measurer, no physical measurement can be exact.

The measuring tool also affects how good a measurement can be. A ruler marked only with inches can be used only to give measures to the nearest inch. And no matter how small the subdivisions on a ruler, there are always unmarked spaces between the marked lines. In general, the *precision* of a measuring tool is the smallest interval on its scale.

For more on precision, see Section 16.2: Approximation and Rounding.

So when children learn to measure, whether it be with inexact body measures in Kindergarten or to the nearest half-inch, quarter-inch, or centimeter in later grades, they also are learning to approximate and deal with error.

14.10.2 Rulers and Tape Measures

Along with weighing scales and balances, *rulers* and *tape measures* are among the first tools used for practical everyday measurements, both in human history and in the lives of children. In the early grades, children learn to give ballpark estimates of heights and lengths; then, over the years, they get progressively more sophisticated in their use of measuring instruments to find approximate lengths. In later grades, *carpenters' rules* are important tools for applying the "half" fractions—$\frac{1}{2}$, $\frac{1}{4}$, $\frac{1}{8}$, and so on, each fraction being half the previous one. Metersticks and centimeter rulers are instructive when teaching about decimals.

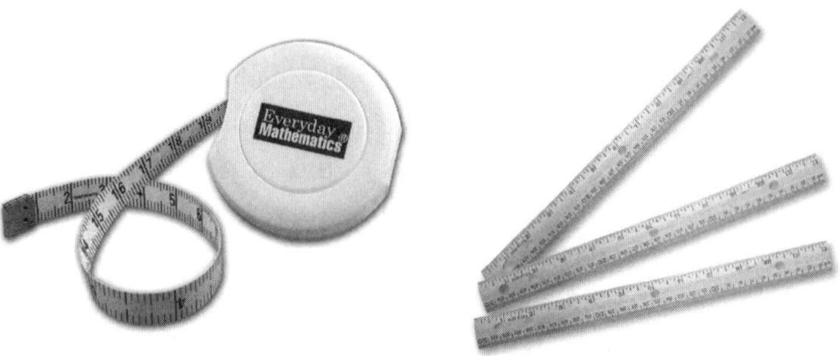

If the children are using retractable tape measures, teach and enforce the "2-inch, 5-centimeter no-zap rule": Do not "zap" the tape measure until no more than 2 inches or 5 centimeters show. This will extend the life of these tools, as well as make your own life quieter and easier.

14.10.3 Scales and Balances

A scale is another historically old measuring tool. *Scales* are used to measure how heavy things are according to a standard weight. There are many different kinds of scales. Some of the scales that *Everyday Mathematics* children will become most familiar with are highlighted here.

For more information, see Section 14.6: Weight and Mass.

A *balance scale* is the first known device for weighing. It was used in Egypt about 3500 B.C. and made use of a simple lever. In ancient Egypt, gold dust was used as currency and needed to be weighed very precisely in order to determine its value.

A balance scale

Balances with the *fulcrum,* the support on which a lever moves, at the center of a horizontal bar are called *equal-arm* balances. The material being weighed is placed in a pan at one end, and known weights are placed in a pan at the other end until a pointer at the fulcrum indicates that the pans are balanced. The ancient Romans developed balances with unequal arms, known as *steelyards*. The object to be weighed is placed on the shorter arm, and a weight is moved along the longer arm until it balances the load.

NOTE: The balance scales most widely used in *Everyday Mathematics* are pan balance scales, or *pan balances* for short.

Beam scales use a counterweight that is moved along the beam until the load is balanced. Calibrations on the beam give the weight. Many health-care providers use this type of scale to weigh patients. Similarly, platform scales use a system of levers, so that a heavy object can be balanced by a relatively small counterweight on the beam. Truck and railroad scales are often of this type.

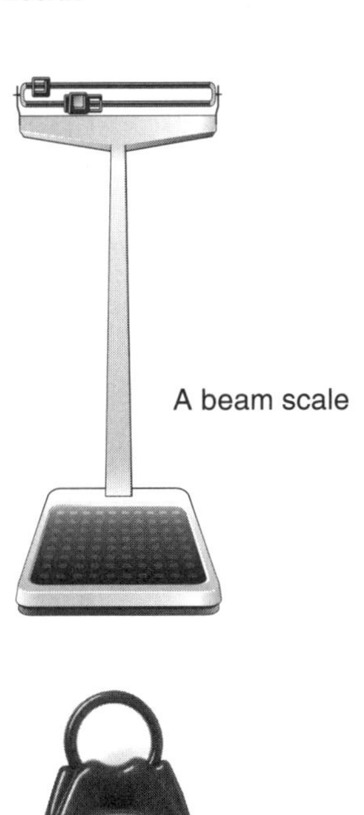

A beam scale

Spring scales, such as bathroom scales, use linkages to stretch or compress one or more springs. One spring causes the weight indicator to move and automatically give the weight. With simple spring scales, a pan or hook at the bottom of the spring holds the object to be weighed. This type is often seen hanging from ceilings in the produce sections of supermarkets.

A spring scale

chapter 14

An electronic scale

Electronic scales were first commercially used in the 1950s and are now seen everywhere, notably in grocery stores and markets. They use a device called a "strain-gauge load cell," which measures the stress an object puts on a mechanical element. The measurement is converted into an electrical signal and transferred to an electronic weight indicator, which gives the weight reading. Some high-precision scales determine weight by measuring the magnetic force needed to counter the downward pull of gravity and support the load on the scales.

Different scales are designed to measure different amounts of weight. There are scales with a variety of capacities and a variety of increments. High-precision scales can measure the weight of a piece of hair or a dose of medicine in increments as small as 0.001 gram or 0.000001 pound. Some platform scales can accommodate trucks weighing as much as 100 tons or railroad cars weighing 825 tons.

Scales have a variety of uses. In the kitchen, they are used to weigh food for cooking and for monitoring diets. Bathroom, nursery, and doctor's scales help monitor personal health. All kinds of scales are used by businesses that sell produce, meat, fish, and bakery items. The post office and other delivery services determine shipping prices based on package weight. Scales are used to weigh trucks to determine the amount of tax that drivers must pay for using the roads. Scales are also used to count pieces, such as the number of nails in a box or pennies in a bag. Scales may give the weight on a dial or digital display in U.S. customary units, metric units, or both.

Reference Frames

Contents

Reference frames are something of an oddity in mathematics. Unlike measurements or counts, numbers in reference frames locate things only within definite systems or contexts. Examples include dates, times, Celsius and Fahrenheit temperatures, and coordinates on maps. The numbers in reference frames are set to meet the needs of their creators. For example, the year 2000 in our calendar system is not the same as the year 2000 in the traditional Chinese calendar system, and the Celsius temperature scale is quite different from the Fahrenheit scale.

Most reference frames have a *zero point,* or *origin.* Positive and negative numbers may describe locations on one side of zero or the other. Zero in a reference frame means something different from zero as a count or a measure. A measure or count of zero means that there is none of whatever is being measured or counted. In contrast, the zero point in a reference frame is simply a starting point; it does not necessarily correspond with nothingness or a lowest bound for positive numbers. As a result, numbers in reference frames are not necessarily governed by the same mathematical rules as other numbers.

Doing arithmetic with numbers in reference frames often makes no sense. For example, adding the year 1950 to the year 2010 gives no meaningful result; 30°C is not 3 times as warm as 10°C; and 3:00 P.M. plus 2:00 P.M. does not equal 5:00 P.M. On the other hand, the numbers in reference frames can be used to find the distance from one point to another in the same reference frame. For example, 1950 was 60 years earlier than 2010, 30°C is 20 degrees warmer than 10°C, and 5:00 P.M. is 2 hours later than 3:00 P.M.

Frank and Ernest

With permission of Bob Thaves.

In *Everyday Mathematics,* children learn about a variety of contemporary and historical reference frames. This chapter discusses reference frames for temperature and time, along with coordinate systems and maps, which are often based on coordinate grids.

15.1 Temperature

Temperature is the amount of heat something has relative to a reference frame usually called a *temperature scale.*

15.1.1 Temperature Scales

The two *temperature scales* with which most people are familiar are the Fahrenheit and Celsius scales. Each scale has a zero point based on when water freezes (but not the same kind of water) and each has a unit interval called a *degree* (but Fahrenheit degrees are smaller than Celsius degrees).

> **NOTE:** Both the Fahrenheit and Celsius scales are examples of a reference frame that first defines where two points are on the scale and then arbitrarily divides the distance between the points into unit intervals, in this case, called *degrees.*

The Fahrenheit Scale

German physicist D. G. Fahrenheit developed the *Fahrenheit scale* in the early 1700s, although it may have been based on a similar scale invented by Danish astronomer Ole Christensen Romer. The zero point of this scale (0°F) was originally the freezing point of a saturated salt and water solution *(brine)* at sea level. The point at which pure water freezes at sea level was set at 32°F for reasons that are not clear. After Fahrenheit's death, the scale was recalibrated to the temperatures that pure water freezes (32°F) and boils (212°F), and brine was left out of it. The normal temperature for the human body is 98.6°F. The Fahrenheit scale is used primarily in the United States.

> **NOTE:** A Fahrenheit degree is $\frac{1}{180}$ of the difference between the boiling and freezing temperatures of pure water, and a Celsius degree is $\frac{1}{100}$ of that difference. Once again, U.S. customary units are much more difficult to calculate with than metric units.

The Celsius Scale

Swedish astronomer Anders Celsius developed the *Celsius scale* in 1742. The zero point for this scale (0°C) is the freezing point of pure water at sea level. The boiling point of pure water at sea level was set at 100°C in order to divide the span of temperatures into a convenient 100 parts. For this reason, the Celsius scale is also called the *centigrade scale.* The normal temperature for the human body is 37°C. The Celsius scale is standard for most people living outside of the United States and for most scientists everywhere.

15.1.2 Thermometers

Thermometers have been evolving since the late 16th century. Galileo built the first known thermometer, an inaccurate device called a *thermoscope,* in about 1592. In 1709, D. G. Fahrenheit made an accurate thermometer using alcohol. In 1714, he built a mercury thermometer like those still in use today. In 1954, U.S. Army Colonel George T. Perkins invented an electronic thermometer.

The designs of thermometers depend on the temperature scale(s) they intend to display and the range of temperatures of interest. Common thermometers include those used to measure cooking temperatures, (candy; deep-frying; oven), machine temperatures (automobile engine; climate control), body temperatures, and air temperatures. Some thermometers have circular scales, others are straight, and still others have digital readouts. The zero point and scale intervals are often not evident on the third type, making them less desirable as learning tools than the circular and straight-line designs.

The form of the display is perhaps less interesting than how thermometers are constructed. Three common types of thermometers are described below. Each of them can be calibrated to quantify temperature in degrees Celsius or degrees Fahrenheit.

Mercury or Colored-Alcohol Thermometers

When their temperature rises, most liquids increase in volume. So if a liquid is contained in a little bulb attached to a thin, straight tube with a sealed end, the liquid rises in the tube as the temperature increases. Both *alcohol* and *mercury* are commonly used in thermometers. Mercury freezes at a little above −40°F or −40°C. Alcohol thermometers are used to display temperatures lower than that. These liquid-in-glass-type thermometers are the least expensive and are quite popular. They are the kind often used in homes to determine if someone has a fever or to measure how warm or cold it is inside or outside.

Bimetallic Thermometers

When their temperature rises, most solids expand, but different solids expand by different amounts. For example, brass expands about twice as much as iron when heated. If a *bimetallic* bar is made by fastening a strip of brass next to a strip of iron, the bar will bend as the temperature rises. The bend will be toward the iron side, which expands less. If one end of the bar is fixed in place, the other end can act as a pointer on a scale. Most home thermostats contain bimetallic thermometers.

NOTE: The *Kelvin scale,* suggested in 1848 by British physicist Lord Kelvin, is used in science and engineering. Its zero point is a temperature at which the atoms and molecules in any substance have minimum energy. Thus there are no negative temperatures on the Kelvin scale. Pure water at sea level freezes at 273.15 K and boils at 373.15 K. The zero point of this scale (0 Kelvins or 0 K) is called *absolute zero*. The Kelvin unit interval is the same as the Celsius degree.

A thermometer with a circular scale

NOTE: The Celsius and Fahrenheit scales are equal at −40°.

An alcohol thermometer

A bimetallic thermometer

chapter 15

NOTE: In 2001, the National Institutes of Health (NIH) recommended that the public switch to nonmercury-based thermometers because mercury is classified as a hazardous toxin. This classification means not only that mercury is poisonous to humans, but that it is not even legal for them to clean it up if their thermometer breaks and it spills. However, mercury thermometers are much more accurate than other forms, so in science applications the NIH recommends using Teflon-coated ones.

Thermocouple Thermometers

A *thermocouple* contains a loop made by joining end to end two wires of different materials, such as copper and iron. If the temperatures at the two joints are different, a voltage proportional to that difference is created. One joint is placed where the temperature is to be taken, while the other is kept at a constant lower temperature. The voltage is read by a measuring device and translated into a temperature reading.

In *Kindergarten Everyday Mathematics,* children keep daily temperature charts that are color-coded by temperature range for easier reading. Most air-temperature thermometers use mercury or colored alcohol and are based on straight-line, vertical, or circular number-line scales. In first grade, the Fahrenheit temperature scale is emphasized. In second and third grades, both Fahrenheit and Celsius scales should be available.

In all grades of *Everyday Mathematics,* temperature is the context for number stories, data exploration, and graphical displays.

Be careful about doing arithmetic with temperatures. Temperature changes can be calculated within one scale but not across different scales. For example, if it was 58°F this morning and the temperature rose 30°F to the high for the day, then the high was 58 + 30 = 88°F. Differences in Fahrenheit and Celsius temperatures are not meaningful; for example, 30°F minus 20°C does not equal 10° of anything.

The limitations of doing arithmetic with reference-frame numbers can be a difficult concept. Although some children will grasp it intuitively, others will need to work with many examples over time before they understand when reference frame numbers cannot be manipulated like other numbers and when they can be meaningfully added and subtracted.

15.2 Time

As with many reference frames, locating an event or a point in time requires a zero, or starting, point and a unit interval. Both of these depend on the context in which time is being examined. This section begins with discussions of clocks to keep track of short-term time passage and calendars and timelines to keep track of broad expanses of time, from days to millennia.

As with units in other reference frames, it does not always make sense to compute with numbers pertaining to time. For example, June 8 plus June 13 is not June 21, and 8:30 P.M. minus 1:20 P.M. is not 7:10 P.M. Within one reference frame, however, you can calculate elapsed time as a difference, or distance, between two times.

In *Kindergarten* through *Third Grade Everyday Mathematics,* children engage in many everyday activities with clocks and calendars that help them develop a *time sense* and become familiar with the language of time. Older children are expected to be comfortable with clocks and calendar reference frames; they use them as a context for number stories, investigations, and other problem-solving situations.

15.2.1 Clocks

Clock time is a reference frame with second, minute, and hour intervals that, although logical to most adults, can seem quite arbitrary and confusing to children. Learning to tell time accurately on an analog clock is one of the objectives of *Kindergarten* through *Second Grade Everyday Mathematics.* For older children, elapsed time is a common context for number stories.

Clocks have been important in the development of many human enterprises, such as navigation, business, and science. Three important types of clocks are analog, digital, and atomic. In *Kindergarten* through *Third Grade Everyday Mathematics,* children practice telling time using both digital and analog clocks.

Analog Clocks

Analog clocks, which used to be called simply "clocks" before the invention of digital clocks, are clocks with hands. In general, *analog* refers to any system that measures a *continuously* changing quantity, such as time, with continuously varying markers of some kind. The first analog clocks may have been trees with markers showing where their shadows fell at different times during the day. These were precursors to sundials, which work on the same principle. For thousands of years, water clocks have been a standard for telling time. They work even when the sun is down or behind a cloud. In a water clock, the water flows from one vessel to another, the flow being the analog for the time. The first successful mechanical clocks were constructed late in the Middle Ages, a development that thoroughly transformed the world.

An analog clock

Nowadays, most people who say "analog clock" mean the type with hands on a round face. The first of these, with only an hour hand on it, is credited to the German inventor Henry de Vick in the 1300s. More advanced features came along in the 1700s, including minute and second hands and a pendulum. Electric analog clocks use an alternating current that vibrates 60 times per second to keep the clock on time.

Digital Clocks

Digital clocks are not analog because time is displayed in *discrete* units, not in a continuous manner. Every digital clock has a smallest unit of time that it displays without changing until an interval of that unit has gone by. Commonly, the smallest unit is a minute. For example, a display of 10:10 on a digital clock does not change until a minute has passed.

A digital clock

On some digital clocks, the colon in the time display blinks on and off once per second to indicate that time is still passing or perhaps just to let you know the clock is still working. Yet even the seconds are discrete. A "hand" does not sweep from one second to the next. Instead, the time displayed on a digital clock jumps discretely from one minute or second to the next. Most digital clocks work on alternating current.

Atomic Clocks

Atomic clocks keep time according to the vibrations of atoms or molecules. The vibrations are so reliable that an atomic clock may lose or gain only a few seconds in 100,000 years. There are both analog and digital versions of atomic clocks.

15.2.2 Calendars

There are many different calendric systems, each one its own reference frame for marking the passage of time. The word *calendar* has roots in the Latin word *kalendae,* meaning "first of the month." *Kalendae,* in turn, is rooted in the word *calare,* which means "to call out solemnly." This etymology points to the importance that people have always placed on keeping track of months and marking their beginning and passing.

In the earliest times, the lunar month of 29.5 days was an important measure because of its close association with seasonal planting and harvesting schedules. Unfortunately, no whole number of lunar months coincides with a solar year of 365 days, 5 hours, 48 minutes, and 46 seconds (about 365 and 1 fourth days). Twelve lunar months are 354 days; 13 lunar months are 383.5 days. The fact that these important, naturally occurring cycles can't easily be reconciled has led to the peculiar natures of the calendar systems used throughout history. According to *The World Book Encyclopedia,* some noteworthy calendars include the following:

- *Babylonian Calendar* This ancient Middle-Eastern calendar was based on a now-unknown zero point and a lunar month interval. The calendar had alternating 29- and 30-day months, with an extra month added three times every 8 years to make up for error.
- *Egyptian Calendar* This ancient calendar had a zero point at the annual flooding of the Nile when the Dog Star, Sirius, first appeared. The year was broken into twelve 30-day months, with 5 days added at the end of the year. Because the extra 1 fourth of a day per year wasn't accounted for, the calendar slowly became inaccurate over the years. It has been calculated that the earliest recorded date on this calendar corresponds to 4236 B.C. on our current Gregorian calendar.
- *Roman Calendar* According to legend, Romulus, the founder of Rome, introduced the earliest Roman calendar in the eighth century B.C. It came from the Greeks and was made up of 10 months and a 304-day year. The zero point was March 1 by our current calendar. It is not clear how the other 61-odd days were accounted for.

  The names of eight of our current months came from the names for the ten Roman months: *Martius, Aprilis, Maius, Junius, Quintilis, Sextilis, September, October, November,* and *December.* Quintilis through December came from the numbers 5 through 10. The name *Martius* came from Mars, a Roman god; *Junius* from Juno, a Roman goddess; and *Maius* from Maia, a Greek goddess. It is thought that *Aprilis* may derive from the Latin word *aperire,* "to open," referring to the unfolding of buds and blossoms during this month. Another possibility is that it may derive from Aphrodite, the Greek goddess of love and beauty.

Every two years, a 22- or 23-day month was added to account for error with the solar year. Later, two more months, *Januarius* and *Februarius,* were added to the end of the year. *Januarius* was likely named after Janus, the Roman god of gates and doorways, and *Februarius* took its name from Februa, a Roman festival of purification held on the 15th day of this month.

- *Julian Calendar* In 46 B.C., Julius Caesar acted on suggestions from his astronomer Sosigenes to upgrade the Roman calendar. A system close to our own was implemented, including what we now know as a *leap day* in February every fourth year. To accommodate the fact that the Roman calendar was three months out of line with the seasons, Caesar made the year 46 B.C. 445 days long. Later, *Quintilis* was renamed July for Julius Caesar and *Sextilis* was named August to honor Emperor Augustus Caesar.

  The Christian version of the Julian calendar was invented in A.D. 532 by an abbot named Dionysius Exiguus, or Dennis the Short. In his plan, the Christian era began January 1 of the year after Christ was born. He called the beginning year the Year of Our Lord, or Anno Domini (A.D.) 1. The Christian version of the calendar was not taken up immediately by church authorities but became widely used in Western Europe beginning in the 11th century. The abbreviation B.C. for "Before Christ" was introduced later. However, Dennis got the year of Christ's birth wrong. It now seems likely that Christ was born in 4 B.C., if not earlier. The abbreviations C.E. (Common Era) and B.C.E. (Before the Common Era) are sometimes used instead of A.D. and B.C.

- *Gregorian Calendar* By 1582, the Julian calendar was off by about 10 days because of the slight difference between $365\frac{1}{4}$ days and 365 days, 5 hours, 48 minutes, and 46 seconds. So Pope Gregory XIII dropped 10 days from October. He then decreed that February should continue to get an extra day every four years, as in the Julian calendar, except in century years that were not divisible by 400. This calendar is so accurate that, more than 400 years later, the time is only about 26 seconds off. Most of the Western World uses the Gregorian calendar.
- *Hebrew Calendar* The zero point for the Hebrew calendar is Creation, which has been calculated at 3,760 years and 3 months before the Christian era began. To find a year on the Hebrew calendar, add 3,760 or 3,761 to the year in the Gregorian calendar. The Hebrew year is based on the phases of the moon and usually has 12 months, each 29 or 30 days long. Seven times every 19 years, an extra 29-day month is added.
- *Islamic Calendar* The zero point for the Islamic calendar is Muhammad's flight from Mecca to Medina in A.D. 622 on the Gregorian calendar. This calendar is also lunar, with 12 months alternating between 29 and 30 days long. The months do not keep to the same seasons relative to the sun each year, and

NOTE: 46 B.C. is known as the "year of confusion" because of calendar reform.

NOTE: There is no year 0 in the Christian versions of the Julian and Gregorian calendars, but just a "zero moment" at which Christ was born, that was labeled as year "1". So this is a reference frame without a real zero point; that is, from 1 B.C. to A.D. 1 is only 1 year, not 2.

so the Islamic New Year moves backward through the seasons. Nineteen of every 30 years have 354 days each, and the other 11 years have an extra day each.

There are groups that advocate standardizing all calendars around the world. Three such calendars have been proposed: the Thirteen-Month calendar, with 13 months each 4 weeks long; the World calendar; and the Perpetual calendar. The latter two propose variations on a 12-month, 30- or 31-day-per-month design. And, according to *Star Trek*® creator Gene Roddenberry, the calendar will be metric by the 24th century.

15.2.3 Timelines

For more information, see Section 15.3.1: Number Grids, Scrolls, and Lines.

Timelines, which are number lines labeled with time units, are also reference frames. As with all reference frames, a timeline's zero point and unit interval vary according to its intended use. For example, a timeline designed to track the development of Earth may have "The Big Bang" as its zero point and use a large interval (millions or perhaps billions of years) to allow for a display over billions of years. A family-history timeline might use generational intervals and mark its zero point with the most distant, known relative.

A timeline of someone's life might use the person's birth date as its zero point and a 1-year unit interval corresponding to the person's age. For example, a timeline of a young child's landmarks might include such events as rolling over at about $\frac{1}{2}$ year, learning to walk at age 1, having a sibling when she was 3, and going to Kindergarten shortly after her fifth birthday. A timeline such as this could also include numbers that refer to the Gregorian dates for the above events, for example, birth (1999), walking (2000), sibling (2002), and Kindergarten (2004), but it would not need to include these dates if birth were established as the zero point and age intervals were the specified unit. Keep in mind that in each instance above, times before the chosen zero point exist. This is true with most reference frames.

You may have timelines associated with social studies or science units, or your colleagues teaching different grades may have them. If they are available and appropriate, it would be instructive to review them with children from a reference-frame point of view. Ask *What is the zero point? What is the unit interval? Why did they choose this zero point and these intervals for this timeline?* Children can make their own timelines to demonstrate or reinforce knowledge in other content areas, especially social studies. Because timelines are visual, they are very useful tools for many children as they learn about history.

▸ 15.3 Coordinate Systems

Coordinate systems are reference frames in which one or more numbers, called *coordinates*, are used to locate points. The simplest coordinate system is a number line, a 1-dimensional reference frame on which one number corresponds to one point. Coordinate planes and coordinate space are 2- and 3-dimensional reference frames in which to locate points.

15.3.1 Number Grids, Scrolls, and Lines

Grid is short for *gridiron,* an old English word for a framework of metal bars or wires used to grill meat or fish. Generally, a grid is any set of equally spaced parallel lines, squares, or rectangles used to help establish locations of objects.

In *Everyday Mathematics,* children use many types of grids, including number grids, coordinate grids, grids for estimating area, and grids for interpreting maps. The tick marks on a number line form perhaps the most primitive grid structure. Lattices and arrays are organizations of objects into gridlike formations, a common example of which is a calendar.

NOTE: Some readers of past editions of the *Teacher's Reference Manual* feel strongly that this section on number grids, scrolls, and lines belongs in this chapter on reference frames. Others feel just as strongly that the discussion belongs in Chapter 9: Number and Counting. Believing that teachers should find help wherever they look, it is now included in both chapters.

Number Grids

A *number grid* consists of rows of boxes, usually ten in each row, containing consecutive integers (positive and negative whole numbers). In *First Grade Everyday Mathematics,* children are introduced to number grids early in the year.

For more information, see Section 15.3.2: Coordinate Grids.

−9	−8	−7	−6	−5	−4	−3	−2	−1	0
1	2	3	4	5	6	7	8	9	10
11	12	13	14	15	16	17	18	19	20
21	22	23	24	25	26	27	28	29	30
31	32	33	34	35	36	37	38	39	40
41	42	43	44	45	46	47	48	49	50
51	52	53	54	55	56	57	58	59	60
61	62	63	64	65	66	67	68	69	70
71	72	73	74	75	76	77	78	79	80
81	82	83	84	85	86	87	88	89	90
91	92	93	94	95	96	97	98	99	100
101	102	103	104	105	106	107	108	109	110

A number grid

Number grids have many wonderful features that can help children with pattern recognition and place value. However, their original use in *Everyday Mathematics* was simply to solve the problem of number lines being unmanageably long. Number lines can be cumbersome even when stretched along a classroom wall, and it is nearly impossible to print them in children's books without breaking them into chunks. Number grids may be considered number lines that fit nicely on a page or a classroom poster.

A number grid lends itself to many activities that reinforce understanding of numeration and place value. For example, by exploring the patterns in rows and columns, children discover that any number on the number grid is:

- *1 more* than the number to its left;
- *1 less* than the number to its right;
- *10 more* than the number above it;
- *10 less* than the number below it.

In other words, as you move from left to right, the ones digit increases by 1 and the tens digit is the same. As you move down, the tens digit increases by 1 and the ones digit is the same.

In the primary grades, *Everyday Mathematics* includes many counting activities that use number grids, for example, counting by 10s starting at 17 and counting backward by 10s starting at 84. Children also solve puzzles based on the number grid. These puzzles are pieces of a number grid in which some, but not all, of the numbers are missing. For example, in the puzzle at the left, the missing numbers are 356 and 358. Number-grid puzzles are used through third grade, where numbers are in the hundreds and thousands.

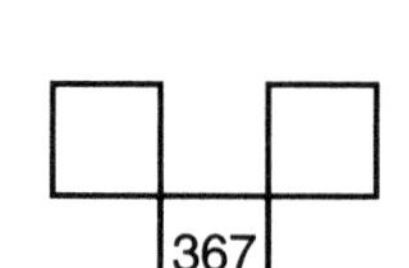

A number-grid puzzle

Number grids can be used to explore number patterns. For example, children can color boxes as they count by 2s. If they start at zero and count by 2s, they will color the even numbers as shown below; if they start at 1, they will color the odd numbers. If they count by 5s, starting at zero, they will color numbers with 0 or 5 in the ones place.

Identifying number patterns in grids can help children understand divisibility rules, prime numbers, and factoring in later grades.

−9	−8	−7	−6	−5	−4	−3	−2	−1	0
1	2	3	4	5	6	7	8	9	10
11	12	13	14	15	16	17	18	19	20
21	22	23	24	25	26	27	28	29	30
31	32	33	34	35	36	37	38	39	40
41	42	43	44	45	46	47	48	49	50
51	52	53	54	55	56	57	58	59	60
61	62	63	64	65	66	67	68	69	70
71	72	73	74	75	76	77	78	79	80
81	82	83	84	85	86	87	88	89	90
91	92	93	94	95	96	97	98	99	100
101	102	103	104	105	106	107	108	109	110

Number grids are also useful for addition and subtraction. For example, to find the difference 84 − 37 you can:

- Count the tens from 37 to 77 *(4 tens)* and then count the number of ones from 77 to 84 *(7 ones)* as shown below. So 84 − 37 is 4 tens plus 7 ones, or 47. This difference corresponds to the *distance* between the points 37 and 84 on a number line.

−9	−8	−7	−6	−5	−4	−3	−2	−1	0
1	2	3	4	5	6	7	8	9	10
11	12	13	14	15	16	17	18	19	20
21	22	23	24	25	26	27	28	29	30
31	32	33	34	35	36	37	38	39	40
41	42	43	44	45	46	47	48	49	50
51	52	53	54	55	56	57	58	59	60
61	62	63	64	65	66	67	68	69	70
71	72	73	74	75	76	77	78	79	80
81	82	83	84	85	86	87	88	89	90
91	92	93	94	95	96	97	98	99	100
101	102	103	104	105	106	107	108	109	110

One way to find 84 − 37

- Start at 84 and count back to 37, noting as before how many numbers have been counted.
- Count back 37 from 84 by tens and ones: 74, 64, 54, 53, 52, 51, 50, 49, 48, 47.

Addition problems can also be solved on the number grid using similar methods. Clearly, the number grid simplifies "double counting," or counting the number of numbers counted, that is required in many addition and subtraction procedures.

From the time they are introduced, children see that number grids can be extended to negative numbers. This is especially useful as a tool for finding differences or to illustrate, for example, that −17 is less than −6.

−19	−18	−17	−16	−15	−14	−13	−12	−11	−10
−9	−8	−7	−6	−5	−4	−3	−2	−1	0
1	2	3	4	5	6	7	8	9	10
11	12	13	14	15	16	17	18	19	20

A grid extended to −19

chapter 15

Number Scrolls

Number scrolls are extended number grids. You can make them by adding single sheets of 100 numbers to existing sheets, either forward (positively) or backward (negatively). Among other things, scrolls give children the chance to experience the ongoing repetitive patterns of our base-ten number system beyond 100—*101, 102, 103,* . . .—so that they do not continue, as children often do, with *200, 300, 400,* . . .. Teachers have found that many children get excited when they discover these patterns and realize that they are capable of writing bigger and bigger numbers based on their discoveries. Meanwhile, they are practicing their handwriting as well as their counting skills.

Number Lines

> **NOTE:** Mathematically, number grids and scrolls are simply number-line reference frames with a different format. They are presented in the order here because this is the order that children encounter them in *Everyday Mathematics.*

A number line is a line on which points are indicated by *tick marks* that are usually at regularly spaced intervals from a starting point called the *origin,* the *zero point,* or simply "0." Numbers are associated with the tick marks, and the interval from 0 to 1 on the line is called the *unit interval.*

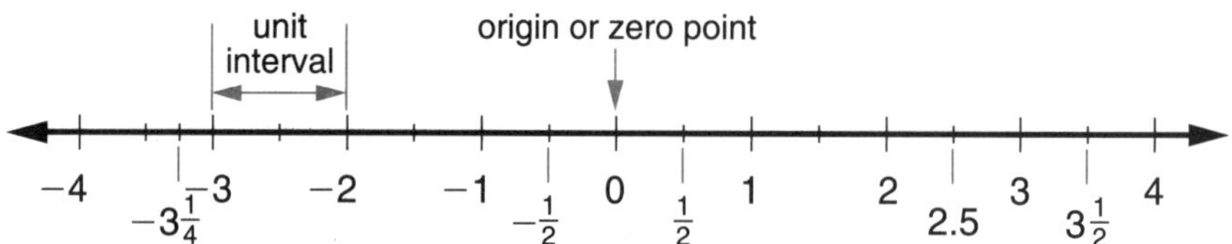

Like any line, a number line extends without end in both directions. Any drawing of a number line is a model of just part of the line. Where you place the zero point is arbitrary, and how you space the numbers depends on the situation you wish to illustrate. You might, for example, mark every other unit-interval point and label by 2s as in Figure 1, or you may mark every half-interval point and label by halves as in Figure 2. In *Everyday Mathematics*, children are often asked to solve incomplete-number-line problems that help them understand these concepts.

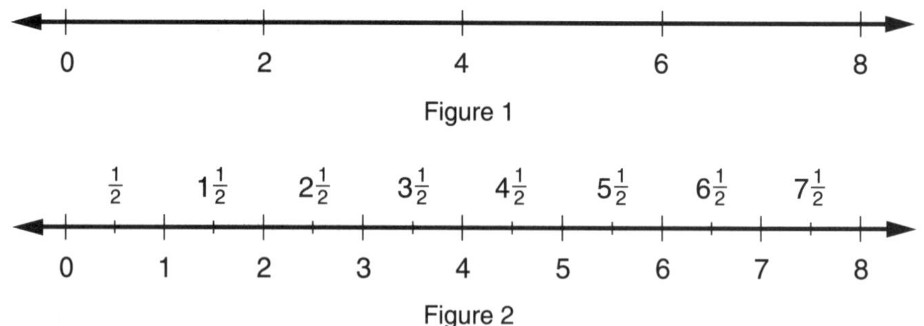

Figure 1

Figure 2

An ordinary ruler uses part of a number line for measuring length, with inch unit intervals, centimeter unit intervals, or other unit intervals. A ruler based on the number line in Figure 3, for example, can be used for measuring distances in inches and halves of inches.

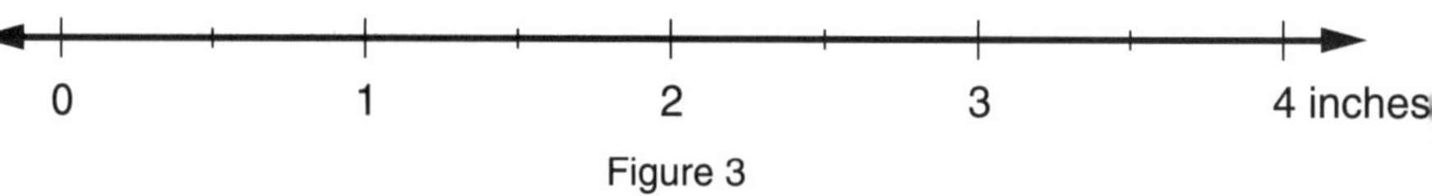

Figure 3

The number line in Figure 3 has tick marks at all unit and half-unit intervals. You may recognize the similarities between the scale on this line and the one on a U.S. customary foot ruler. This line has fewer fraction-of-unit intervals marked than most rulers. In contrast, foot rulers are usually marked every sixteenth of an inch.

For more information, see Section 14.3: Length.

You can assign any scale you wish to a number line. For example, a unit interval on a map scale might represent one mile on the map. Such a line would not be used to measure distances directly in the real world but instead to convert distances on the map into distances in the real world.

Map Scale (in miles)

0 500 1,000 1,500 2,000

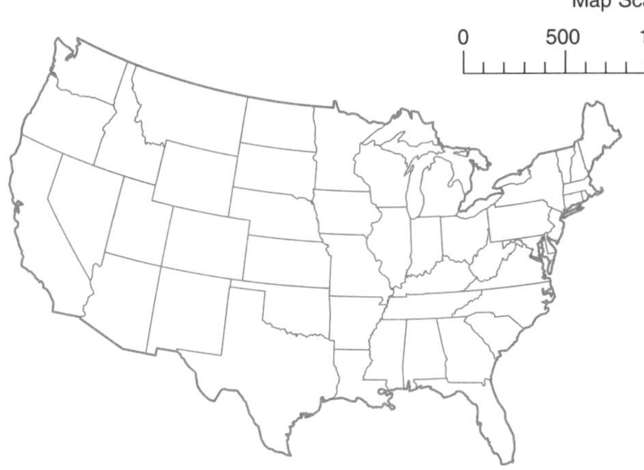

Number lines can also have nonlinear scales, meaning that the distances between the numbers are not proportional to the differences between the numbers. For example, the distance between 10 and 20 might be the same as the distance between 1 and 2. Radio dials are based on logarithmic scales, one type of nonlinear scale. Nonlinear scales do not have unit intervals.

Photograph courtesy of Bill Lettow, 1999

A number line always has a zero point, even when it doesn't show. On the number line in Figure 4, the zero point is understood to be off to the left. Sometimes you see a broken-line symbol as in the number line in Figure 5. This symbol indicates that a piece of the line between 0 and 330 has been omitted. The symbol, or another similar to it, is often used in technical drawings to show important details while still indicating that something is missing.

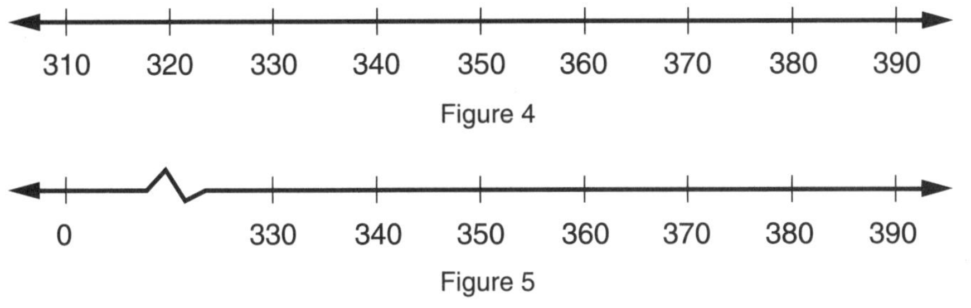

Figure 4

Figure 5

in perspective

Number-line ideas are expanded upon and treated more formally in Grades 4 through 6. Number lines continue to serve as one or more of the axes in data displays such as scatter plots, bar graphs, and line plots.

NOTE: A 3-dimensional coordinate grid in space begins with a coordinate grid in a plane, to which is added a third axis perpendicular to the other two through the origin.

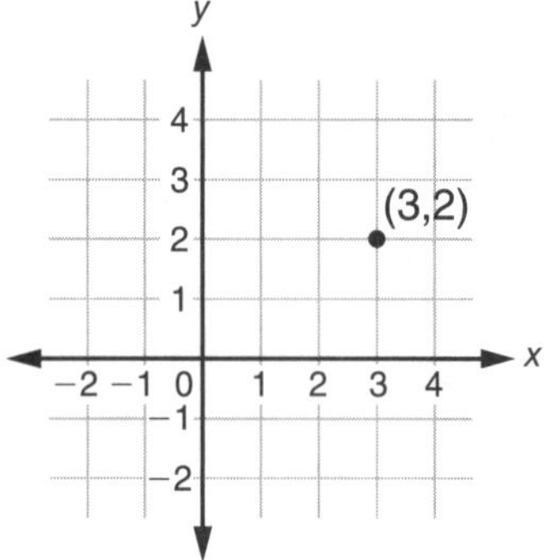

Point (3,2) plotted on a coordinate plane

Beginning in *Kindergarten Everyday Mathematics*, children use number lines for counting and skip counting. They also create a "Growing Number Line" on the classroom wall by adding a new number every day.

In first and second grades, children use a number line to keep track of the number of school days in the school year. They also use number lines on thermometers (two different scales: Fahrenheit and Celsius) and on linear measuring tools. Incomplete-number-line problems begin in first grade. Number lines in coordinate graphing systems are introduced in third grade.

15.3.2 Coordinate Grids

A *coordinate grid,* or *coordinate system,* is a reference frame defined by two or more number lines called *axes*. Axes are usually, but not always, perpendicular to each other and intersect at a common point called the *origin* where the zero points of the axes coincide. In a 2-dimensional coordinate grid in a plane, one axis is usually horizontal, the other vertical; and the axes usually have the same scale. A grid with perpendicular axes is called a *rectangular coordinate grid*.

In *analytic geometry,* or *coordinate geometry,* points on geometric objects are located using coordinates. On a number line, the coordinate is a single number. In a 2-dimensional *coordinate plane,* points are located using *ordered pairs* of numbers. In *Everyday Mathematics,* they are called *rectangular coordinate planes* because the axes are always perpendicular. By convention, the first number in a pair locates the position of a point relative to a horizontal axis. This axis is often called the *x-axis,* and the number is called the *x-coordinate*. The second number locates a position relative to a vertical axis. This axis is often called the *y-axis,* and the number is called the *y-coordinate.* The point (3,2) is plotted and labeled in the drawing in the margin.

Coordinate planes have many practical uses. For example, the streets in many cities and towns are laid out in a grid pattern and are sometimes numbered accordingly. Many maps are based on coordinate planes, as discussed in the next section.

Coordinate planes have been used for centuries. The ancient Egyptians and Romans used them to survey fields. Coordinate planes received a big boost in the early 17th century when the French philosopher and mathematician René Descartes (1596–1650) made significant advances in coordinate geometry. Today, rectangular coordinates are often called Cartesian coordinates in honor of his work.

Since Descartes, coordinate geometry has been a powerful tool for advances in many areas of mathematics. In *Everyday Mathematics,* the serious study of coordinate geometry begins in fourth grade. Before that, work with coordinate geometry is restricted mostly to number lines and graphing data.

15.4 Maps

A common use of reference frames in *Everyday Mathematics* is with maps, where coordinate grids help locate geographic points within a given region. In Kindergarten through Grade 6, mapping activities range from using maps to track steps from classroom to classroom, to estimating distances between cities and towns, to interpreting temperature contour maps. Maps also serve as rich supplies of ideas children can use to invent number stories.

15.4.1 Map Coordinates

Often, the reference frame for a map is a 2-dimensional, rectangular coordinate grid. One axis is usually horizontal, the other vertical; and they usually have the same scale. Often, the full grid is not drawn on the map. Rather, points along each axis are labeled at the outer edges of the map. You can envision drawing horizontal and vertical lines across the page and through or between these points to complete the coordinate grid upon which the map is built. We have included the grid lines in the map below.

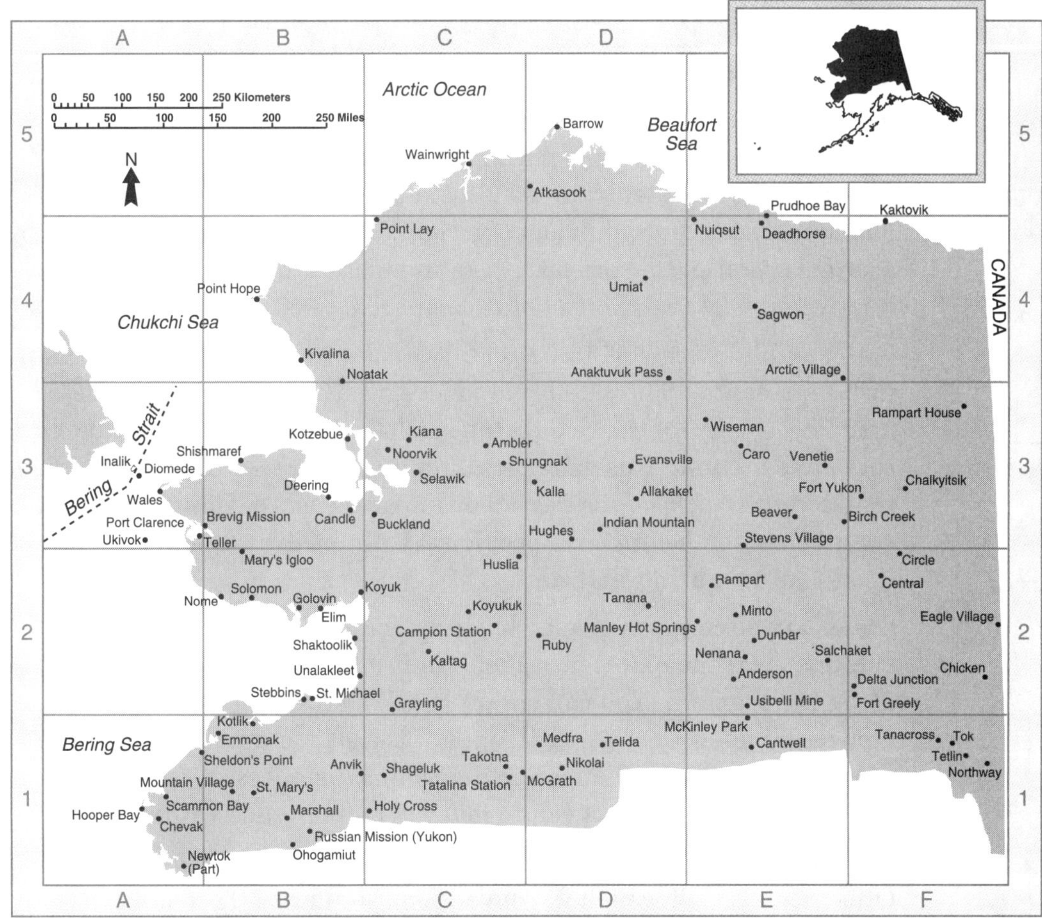

A map with a coordinate grid

Unlike mathematical coordinate grids, an ordered pair on a map grid refers to more than just a single point. Rather, it refers to a rectangular region centered at the point located by the ordered pair. For example, in the map of Alaska above, Indian Mountain is in the region centered

chapter 15

at (D,3), or "D3." But several other towns are located "at" D3, such as Allakaket and Hughes. An index of towns on the map would locate all three of these towns, and others as well, as being "at" D3. Note that the gridlines on the map are not centered on the coordinates in the margins, but rather halfway between coordinates. This approach highlights the rectangular regions that the coordinates such as D3 define.

Different maps label their coordinates differently, some with all numbers, some with letters and numbers (but not always in the same order as on the Alaska map), and some with other markings. However, in each case, ordered pairs identify points or regions within the coordinate grid.

Many cities and towns use a 2-dimensional coordinate grid to determine the address of each building in town. For example, 200 Third Avenue NE may locate a house two blocks north and three blocks east of the intersection (the zero point) of two central roads in that town. The map scale is a block. Assuming that north is "up" on the vertical axis, east is to the right of the zero point, and the position of the house is given by the ordered pair (3,2).

For more information on scale, see Section 13.7.2: Stretches and Shrinks and Section 10.2.2: Multiplication and Division Use Classes.

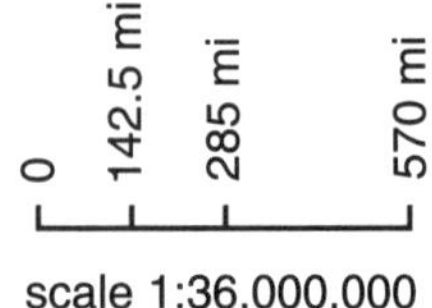

scale 1:36,000,000

One inch represents 570 miles.

15.4.2 Map and Model Scales

A *map scale* is an application of a *size-change factor,* usually in which one of the figures is from real life and the other is a model. For example, a model train is a scaled-down version of a real train; a map is a scaled-down model of a real landscape. More precisely, a *scale* is a ratio comparison. It is a number used to quantify the relative sizes of two things being compared.

For example, a scale of 1:36,000,000 (inches) on a map means 1 map inch represents 36,000,000 real inches; that is, a distance on the map is $\frac{1}{36{,}000{,}000}$ of the real distance. Note that a scale, as with any ratio, has no unit. This example could be rewritten with the word *inch* replaced by *centimeter* or any other linear measure. However, a unit must be chosen before any specific map can be drawn, and the map itself is drawn using that unit.

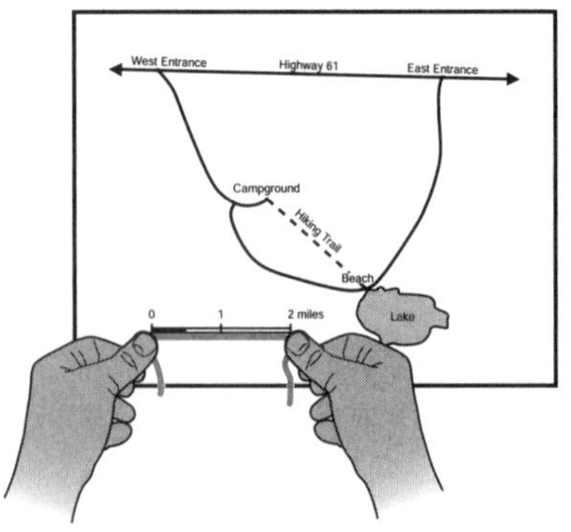

Using string to read map distances

Scales are often given graphically on a map, where the overall length of a line segment represents a map unit and real units are marked along the segment. You can simply mark a string (or the edge of a piece of paper) to show the length of the segment and then lay the string repeatedly on the map to determine distances in real units. Using string even allows you to follow winding roads with greater accuracy than is possible with a ruler.

Woodpecker (8 in.) at $\frac{1}{4}$ scale

Other scale drawings follow conventions similar to those used in maps. For example, in architectural drawings, $\frac{1}{4}$ inch often represents 1 foot, so the scale is 1:48. A drawing of an insect might have the notation "2 times actual size," meaning that every linear measure in the drawing is twice the actual measure of a part of the insect.

Map scales are introduced in *Third Grade Everyday Mathematics,* when children use them to estimate mileage between cities on a U.S. map.

16 Estimation, Mental Arithmetic, and Number Sense

Contents

If you list everyday situations that involve arithmetic and identify the kind of answer and method of calculation that is likely in each situation, you may end up with something like the table below.

Situation	Kind of Answer	Likely Method
doubling a recipe	exact	mental arithmetic
making change	exact	mental arithmetic
deciding if you have enough money for a purchase	estimated	mental arithmetic
planning a daily schedule	estimated	mental arithmetic
balancing a checkbook	exact	calculator
computing gas mileage	estimated	mental arithmetic
comparing prices	estimated	mental arithmetic
calculating a discount percent	estimated	mental arithmetic
figuring income tax	exact	calculator
tipping	estimated	mental arithmetic

Of course, in certain situations you may seek a different kind of answer or use a method different from that listed above; but, in any case, your list is likely to reveal how common and valuable estimates and mental arithmetic are in everyday life. The practical importance of paper-and-pencil computation for daily living, which was never very great, is even further diminished in today's highly technological society. Sensible use of calculators and proficiency at mental arithmetic are more important than ever.

This diagram displays six ways to find answers to arithmetic problems. The traditional school mathematics curriculum focuses almost exclusively on just one of these—obtaining exact answers with paper-and-pencil algorithms. The authors of *Everyday Mathematics* believe that children deserve to be proficient in all six.

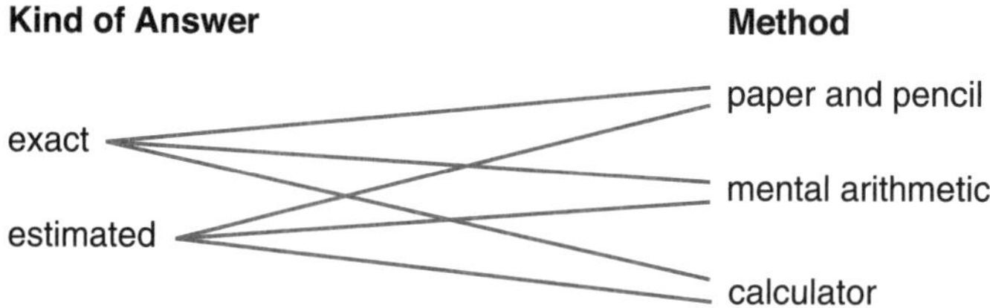

Paper-and-pencil and calculator algorithms for finding exact answers are discussed in Chapter 11. This chapter examines the other varieties of computation shown in the diagram above. The first part discusses why estimates may be necessary or desirable and how estimates may be obtained. The second part describes the *Everyday Mathematics* approach to mental arithmetic for exact and estimated answers. The last part is about basic facts, which must be mastered if facility at mental arithmetic and paper-and-pencil algorithms is to be achieved.

▸ 16.1 Estimation

Estimation is a major thread in *Everyday Mathematics* because of its importance in mathematics and everyday life. We estimate counts, measures, and results of calculations. In practical matters, ballpark estimates are often as important as exact answers.

Despite its utility, many children and some adults feel that estimation is like cheating or lying. In reality, estimation is not a shoddy alternative to doing things right. Estimation requires good intuition about numbers, good understanding of problem situations, and a flexible repertoire of techniques. Good estimation skills take years to develop but are worth striving for. Focusing on estimation can help children develop mental flexibility, good number sense, and confidence that mathematics makes sense.

The next section of this chapter outlines the principal reasons for estimating. Later sections address "extreme" numbers, estimates in calculations, rounding, number sense, and mathematical connections.

NOTE: Many ideas and examples in this chapter come from "Reasons for Estimating and Approximating" in *Applying Arithmetic* by Max Bell and Zalman Usiskin. A full reference is available on page 201.

16.1.1 Why Estimate?

Sometimes we use estimates because we have no choice; other times, because they are easier to understand than exact quantities; and still other times to help us solve problems or to check answers given by machines.

Estimates May Be Necessary

Estimates are necessary in many situations because exact values are unobtainable for a variety of reasons:

- *A number may simply be unknown.* Predictions about the future, guesses about the past, measurements of economic conditions, and even educated guesses about what groceries will cost are all examples of estimates necessitated by lack of precise knowledge.

- *A quantity may be different each time it is measured.* Temperatures, populations, air pressures, and keyboarding speeds are examples of this type of estimate, as are situations involving random processes such as the number of HEADS to come up in 100 tosses of a coin.
- *Physical measurements are never exact.* Even measures that seem exact are approximate, although they may be close enough to exact for all practical purposes. For example, no sheet of paper is exactly 11 inches long; if you look at the edge under a microscope, it will appear quite rough and uneven.
- *Getting an exact value may be too expensive.* In many situations, the numbers are so large that exact counts cannot be easily obtained. More often than not, large counts are estimated by taking samples and using statistics. To estimate how many people saw a particular TV program, pollsters interview just a sample of the viewing public, not the entire viewing public.
- *Decimal or fractional results may not make sense.* For example, if the price of items is 3 for \$1, you do not pay $33\frac{1}{3}$¢ for each item because there are no longer coins for fractions of pennies. Instead, you pay 34¢ for the first item and 33¢ for each of the other two items.
- *Some situations require a built-in margin of error, so quantities are overestimated.* For example, you overestimate the costs of items you are buying to make sure you have enough money to pay the cashier. Safety factors in new buildings are overestimated to more than meet minimal requirements.
- *Numbers may not be in a form suitable for computation.* For example, to compute with irrational numbers like $\sqrt{2}$ or π, you need to replace them with rational approximations.

In the situations above, there is no choice about whether to estimate. People who believe that estimates are inferior to exact answers are thus ignoring many situations in which it is necessary to estimate.

Estimates Are Easy to Understand

Estimates help us communicate by making numbers easier to understand.

- *Estimates may be clearer than exact values.* A school budget of \$148,309,563 for a school population of 62,772 children might be reported as "about \$150 million for 63,000 children." A house on a lot with a surveyed width of 40.13 feet is likely to be described as being on a 40-foot lot. In such cases, estimates are easier to understand than more precise numbers are.

  Sometimes estimates themselves are approximated to make them easier to understand. For example, an almanac estimates the area of Canada to be 3,849,674 square miles. Approximating this estimate to 3.8 million or 4 million square miles makes the measure easier to understand and communicate.

Children in *Everyday Mathematics* encounter many examples of estimates made for clarity. Many are found in data-analysis activities throughout the program.

- *Estimates provide consistency.* Estimates for consistency are often prompted by a desire to show data uniformly in tables, charts, and graphs. For example, government unemployment reports often give a percent rounded to the nearest tenth. So, if 8.5 million of 99 million potential workers are unemployed, the government reports 8.6% unemployed rather than 8.59% or any closer approximation to 8.5858 . . .%. Here an estimate is necessary because the original data are inexact, but the particular choice to report in tenths is done both to be consistent from month to month and to reflect the 2-digit precision of the original data.

  Sometimes the desire for consistency comes from tradition. For example, the batting average of a baseball player is found by dividing the number of hits by the number of times at bat. The answer is rounded to the nearest thousandth and is usually referred to as a percent in tables, even though it is shown as a 3-place decimal. A batting average is usually cited as if the decimal point were not there. For example, in 1941 Ted Williams made a hit in over 40 percent of his times at bat when he hit *406,* usually pronounced "four-oh-six."

For more information on precision, see Section 16.2: Approximation and Rounding.

Everyday Mathematics does not emphasize the need for children to make their estimates consistent. All around them, however, children see numbers that are written with just this goal in mind, so point out such instances when they arise.

Estimates Can Help in Problem Solving

Estimation can be useful in solving problems both before and after an answer is obtained. During the early phases of the problem-solving process, estimating may help you better understand the problem. Estimating helps clarify what is known and what is unknown and helps guide your search for a solution. Even if an estimate made early in the problem-solving process turns out to be very inaccurate, simply having made one may help you get insight into a particularly difficult problem.

Once an answer is obtained, an estimate can be used to check its reasonableness. Looking back over the problem-solving process is valuable, and estimating to verify the accuracy of a result is a good activity to encourage such reflection. Estimating to check answers also emphasizes that results obtained in different ways should agree and, more generally, that mathematics makes sense.

In *Kindergarten* through *Third Grade Everyday Mathematics,* children are often asked to make estimates to check their answers obtained from either paper-and-pencil or calculator methods. Sometimes they are asked to estimate before calculating in order to let the calculated answer verify their estimating skills. More often, they estimate after calculation in order to check the reasonableness of the answer.

Children should be encouraged to estimate answers in problem situations in which exact answers are unnecessary or not justified. Because many people are uncomfortable with estimates, it is important to discuss the differences between exact and estimated answers and to identify situations in which an estimate is good enough or even makes more sense than an exact answer. For example, *I have 75¢. I want to buy an eraser for 29¢ and a notebook for 39¢. Do I have enough money?* Sharing strategies can help children develop their estimation skills. Children should become aware that there is no single "correct" estimate; the purpose of estimation is to find a reasonable answer, not the exact answer.

This kind of interaction is worth your setting aside two or more 10–15 minute periods each week in addition to the basic lessons, at least at the beginning of the school year. Continue until children feel comfortable sharing their strategies and are able to talk about them fluently and listen to one another attentively.

16.1.2 Extreme Numbers

Children are interested in very large and very small numbers, which *Everyday Mathematics* calls *extreme numbers.* They appear in exact and estimated counts such as the populations of countries, stars in galaxies, hairs on a head, cells in the brain, and the national debt. Extreme numbers also appear in measurements such as the distances between galaxies, years since the dinosaurs, the area of a continent, and the speed of light.

Extreme numbers are difficult for many people to understand, so relating them to familiar counts or measures can help. For example, it takes about 60 city blocks to cover one square mile. That means it would take about 6 million city blocks to cover the 104,000 square miles recorded as the area of Colorado (104,000 square miles assumes that Colorado is flat). Comparisons of a smaller, familiar measure to a larger, somewhat unfathomable one and vice versa are useful applications of ratio comparison and similarity.

It can be difficult to compare large numbers to each other. Many people can visualize a comparison of 1 to 1,000 by comparing a 1-cm cube to a 10-cm by 10-cm by 10-cm block. However, comparing 1,000,000 to 1,000,000,000 may not be quite as easy, even if the 1-cm cube is considered to represent 1,000,000.

Working with extreme numbers illustrates the need for estimating and approximating. Extreme numbers may need to be estimated if the things with which they are associated cannot be accurately counted, if they are measurements, or if the number is a large product or a small quotient. For example, in third grade, children are exposed to numbers in the millions when they encounter population figures.

In many situations, the numbers are so large that exact counts or accurate measurements cannot be obtained. *The number of books in a large library at the end of a day is exact, but how would it be determined? How many grains of sand are on a beach? What is the population of*

In Grades 4 through 6, students look at ratio comparisons of extreme numbers. For example, they study 1 billion as 1,000 *times* 1 million, not as 1,000 *more than* 1 million, as many people think it is. Students are also introduced to the concept of *order of magnitude,* in which a ratio of two numbers is expressed as a power of 10.

NOTE: Some scientists call a 10-times change in value a *magnitude* increase. A *magnitude estimate* is an estimate of whether a count, measure, or result of an operation is in the tens, hundreds, thousands, ten-thousands, and so on.

chapter 16

 perspective

In Grades 4 through 6, students extend the place-value system beyond millions and explore the relative sizes of millions, billions, and trillions. They also compare large numbers by rounding to a consistent place value and by writing the results in exponential notation.

the United States? Although the Census Bureau attempts to count every person in the United States every 10 years, census takers may miss people, count incorrectly, or make other errors.

Taking samples and using statistics often give good estimates of large counts. In *Everyday Mathematics,* children explore many different ways of estimating large counts and measurements using surveys, polls, and experiments. Through class discussions, they are also encouraged to cultivate a healthy skepticism for claims that are based on such estimates.

16.1.3 Estimates in Calculations

Ballpark estimates make calculations easier when exact answers are not needed. For example, when you plan a trip, estimates of the costs of driving and flying are easier to compare than are exact values. Your thinking might be as follows: *The trip will be about 800 miles, my automobile gets about 25 miles per gallon, and gasoline costs about $3.10 per gallon; but there will be two days' extra driving and the motel will cost $120 and meals on the road about $60. On the other hand, the cheapest way to fly costs about $350, and I'll need to rent a car at the destination for five days at $80 per day . . ..*

Even with calculators and computers taking much of the work out of computation, estimating may make things a lot easier with no important loss in the quality of the answers. In fact, answers derived using estimates may be more reasonable and more realistic than exact answers, as in planning a car trip.

For situations in which exact answers are required and a calculator is used to find them, estimation can help check the results. Most of us have heard the story about the cashier at the fast-food restaurant who entered the price for an item incorrectly but couldn't tell that the total was incorrect. This story is often used to support the argument that people depend too much on machines and, therefore, that calculators should be banned from the classroom and children should master the traditional paper-and-pencil algorithms.

This argument misses the point entirely. Few people would want the cashier to stop using a machine and do the work on paper. What the cashier needs are estimation skills to check whether the machine total is reasonable. If it isn't, then it should be recalculated. In the cashier's defense, many traditional mathematics curricula don't teach estimation skills in conjunction with arithmetic operations. In fact, such skills are sometimes reviled as being merely trial and error. *Everyday Mathematics,* on the other hand, sees these skills as an integral component of a comprehensive and balanced approach to computation. Children are encouraged to compute either exactly or approximately, working mentally, with paper and pencil, or with a calculator, depending on what is most appropriate for each situation.

16.2 Approximation and Rounding

Estimation is a reasoned guess at an unknown or unknowable value. *Rounding* is a technique to approximate *known* numbers. Three common rounding algorithms and their uses are described below. Each one requires you to first pick a *target place value* for the rounded number.

- *Round up* This algorithm is used to *overapproximate* a value.

Example: A school bus holds 28 children. How many school buses should be scheduled to take 300 children on a field trip?

Solution: The target is a *whole number* of buses.

300/28 → 10 R20

The quotient 10 R20 means that 10 buses would leave 20 children behind, so 11 buses must be ordered.

- *Round down* This algorithm is used to *underapproximate* a value.

Example: An elevator manufacturer tests the maximum weight an elevator can hold and finds that the cable breaks at an average of 2,023.5 pounds. What should the posted weight limit be?

Solution: The target is usually *hundreds of pounds,* although this varies.

Round down to be safe. Perhaps the limit should be posted as 1,500 pounds.

- *Round to the nearest* This algorithm is intended to be as fair as possible. The traditional version says to round up if the digit to the right of the target place is 5 or greater and to round down if the digit is less than 5.

Example: What is 17.688 centimeters rounded to the nearest tenth of a centimeter?

Solution: The target is *tenths.*

The digit to the right of the 6 in the tenths place is an 8. $8 > 5$, so round up to 17.7 centimeters.

When writing approximations, the symbol ≈ means *is approximately equal to*. So in the last example, the solution could be written $17.688 \approx 17.7$.

Often, numbers are rounded to make them easier to work with. Usually, you round either up or down to a number that is close to a known number but easier to work with, where "close" and "easier"

chapter 16

are determined by the context of a problem. In the following example, rounding makes estimation easier.

Example: You want to buy 4 cans of tennis balls that cost \$4.57 a can. Estimate the least number of dollar bills you need in order to pay for your purchase.

Solution 1: Rounding up to \$5 per can, a reasonable estimate for the cost of 4 cans is $4 \times \$5 = \$20$. However, because you rounded up, you will definitely not need more than \$20. So 20 \$1 bills will be enough.

Solution 2: Rounding down to \$4.50 per can, a closer estimate to the cost of 4 cans is \$18, because $4 \times \$4.50 = \$18$. However, $4 \times \$4.57$ is a bit more than \$18, so you will need at least 19 \$1 bills.

Both solutions are good applications of rounding. Which solution is right? Although the second solution of \$19 is closer to the exact cost of \$18.28 than the first solution of \$20, it is not necessarily a better estimate. In class, you might discuss both solutions and compare them to each other. Children may realize that to estimate a result to a nearest dollar, they don't necessarily round to the nearest dollar first.

NOTE: Both the Texas Instruments TI-108 and Casio SL-450 that the authors used while writing this edition of *Everyday Mathematics* round down. For more information, see Section 3.1.1: Calculators.

All calculators round decimals to fit the display screen. Some 4-function calculators use the round-to-the-nearest algorithm, but most round down. Most scientific calculators round to the nearest value of the place at the far right of the display. Almost all calculators hold more digits accurately in memory than they display. Understanding the principles and effects of rounding is important when using a calculator.

NOTE: Most scientific calculators have a *fix* feature that lets you set (fix) the number of decimal places your calculator displays. For example, you can set it to round to hundredths when doing calculations involving money and always see values rounded to the nearest penny. If you have such a calculator, see your owner's manual for instructions.

A Note on Significant Digits and Precision

The important, yet difficult, topic of *significant digits* is treated informally in *Everyday Mathematics* but is not taught explicitly. The basic idea is that computation cannot yield a result that is more precise than the least precise count or measure in the computation, as indicated by the *significant,* or meaningful, digits in the counts or measures. For example:

- If one length is measured to the nearest centimeter (say 15 cm), a second to the nearest half-centimeter (say 4.5 cm), and a third to the nearest millimeter (say 2.8 cm), their sum is best reported to the nearest centimeter (22 cm).
- If a rectangular wall is 3.6 meters by 4.8 meters, multiplication gives the area as 17.28 square meters. However, each dimension has only two significant digits, so the area to two significant digits is 17 square meters.
- If the population of a city is estimated to the nearest thousand and the population of a second city to the nearest ten-thousand, the difference in population of the cities should be estimated to the nearest ten-thousand.

The smallest interval on the scale of any measuring tool establishes the *precision* of the tool. The precision establishes the number of significant digits allowable in measurements using the tool. For example, a standard foot-long ruler typically has a smallest interval of $\frac{1}{16}$ inch. So the most precise measure using such a ruler is the nearest $\frac{1}{16}$ inch, and all calculations with measures from that ruler should be rounded to the nearest $\frac{1}{16}$ inch. If there is a metric scale on the other side of the ruler with a smallest interval of a millimeter, then the precision on that scale is 1 millimeter.

A ruler with $\frac{1}{16}$-inch precision on the right side and 1-millimeter precision on the left

16.3 Mental Arithmetic

Although people frequently associate mental arithmetic with estimation, it is also useful for finding exact answers. In many situations, an exact answer is required but a calculator is not available and *mental arithmetic* is a convenient alternative. Even most paper-and-pencil algorithms for finding exact answers involve mental arithmetic. Paper-and-pencil division, for example, is likely to require mental addition, multiplication, and subtraction.

In *Everyday Mathematics,* children practice mental arithmetic to learn useful techniques; to develop flexible thinking; and to gain *fact power,* or the automatic recall of basic addition/subtraction and multiplication/division facts. These skills contribute to children's *number sense,* which includes a flexible understanding both of numbers and of operations on those numbers. *Everyday Mathematics* also emphasizes number sense because calculators and computers have actually increased the importance of estimation and mental arithmetic in daily life. Complicated paper-and-pencil computation has become relatively less important in everyday life and in the curriculum, while mental arithmetic and skillful use of calculators have become relatively more important.

For more information, see Section 16.3.2: Basic Facts and Fact Power and Section 16.4: Number Sense and Mathematical Connections.

An important part of being a flexible problem solver is to add continually to a personal tool kit of mental-arithmetic skills. Some of these mental-arithmetic skills should become automatic so they can be used reflexively, almost without thinking.

Mental-arithmetic skills are developed throughout the *Everyday Mathematics* curriculum as an integral part of the program. Each lesson in first through sixth grades begins with a brief set of oral or slate exercises called Mental Math and Reflexes. In Kindergarten through Grade 3, *Minute Math* and *Minute Math+* provide many activities for practicing mental arithmetic and problem-solving skills. In *Everyday Mathematics,* problems to be solved without calculators are identified with a no-calculator icon. Whenever children use calculators, they need to verify that the calculator answer makes sense.

A no-calculator icon

Strategy sharing is vitally important throughout *Everyday Mathematics.* Perhaps the most important part of learning mental-arithmetic skills is to have children share their solution strategies after they solve a problem. Sharing strategies requires children to verbalize their thinking, thus making them conscious of a process

For more information, see Section 18.4.2: Sharing Children's Strategies and Solutions.

that is often intuitive. Children also get insights into alternative approaches from their classmates and develop creative and flexible thinking processes. Importantly, children learn that common sense applies to mathematics and that they can solve difficult problems by themselves.

16.3.1 Mental-Calculation Strategies

There are many strategies and techniques for mental arithmetic. Some are formally introduced in *Everyday Mathematics,* and children develop others on their own. Children are exposed to many techniques, learn how they work, master a few, and build some into reflexes. A few examples of strategies follow. All may be justified mathematically, but we describe them here briefly in terms that you may hear in the classroom.

- *Round* Techniques include rounding, as appropriate, to the nearest ten, hundred, thousand, and so on, and computing with rounded numbers. For example, 647 + 284 is approximately 600 + 300 = 900, or perhaps 650 + 280 = 930.
- *Adjust the numbers* A sum is unchanged if one addend is increased by a given amount and the other addend is decreased by the same amount. For example, in 86 + 37, think *86 + 4 = 90 and 37 − 4 = 33, so 90 + 33 = 123.* This is called the *opposite-change rule for addition.*

  A similar rule is the *same-change rule for subtraction:* a difference is unchanged if the same amount is added to or subtracted from both the minuend and the subtrahend. For example, in 54 − 37, think *37 + 3 = 40 and 54 + 3 = 57, so 57 − 40 = 17.*
- *Look for easy combinations* For example, in 17 + 25 + 3 + 15, add 17 and 3 *(20)* and 25 and 15 *(40).* So 17 + 25 + 3 + 15 = 20 + 40 = 60.
- *Estimate, then adjust* An approximate answer is obtained first and then adjusted to make it more accurate. For example, 647 + 284 is approximately 640 + 280 *(920);* then add 7 + 4 *(11)* to that sum *(920 + 11 = 931).*
- *For multiplication of whole numbers (only), attach zeros* To multiply by a multiple of 10, 100, 1,000, and so on, multiply the nonzero part of the factors and append as many zeros to the result as there are zeros in the factors. For example, in 12 × 300, think *12 × 3 = 36 with 2 zeros is 3,600.*
- *For division of whole numbers (only), cross out zeros* To divide multiples of 10, 100, 1,000, and so on, cross out the same number of ending zeros in the divisor as in the dividend. For example, in 4,500 ÷ 50 cross out 1 zero in each number and get 4,50∅ ÷ 5∅ = 450 ÷ 5 = 90.
- *Estimate magnitude* As a useful check for answers found another way, ask *Is a reasonable answer in the tens? hundreds? thousands?*

Miscellaneous Strategies

- To multiply a whole number by 10, append one zero to the number; to multiply by 100, append two zeros.
- To multiply a decimal by 10, move the decimal point one place to the right; to multiply a decimal by 100, move the decimal point two places to the right. Append zeros as necessary.
- To divide a decimal by 10, move the decimal point one place to the left; to divide a decimal by 100, move the decimal point two places to the left. Append zeros as necessary.
- To rename a decimal as a percent, move the decimal point two places to the right and append a percent sign; reverse the process to rename a percent as a decimal. Append zeros as necessary.
- To multiply a whole number by 5, multiply by 10 and find half of the result.
- To determine whether a number is divisible by 3, find the sum of its digits. If the sum is divisible by 3, then the number is divisible by 3. For example: 117 is divisible by 3, because the sum of the digits, 9, is divisible by 3; 117 is also divisible by 9 because the sum of the digits is divisible by 9.
- To multiply a 2-digit number by 11, add the two digits and write the sum between the two digits. For example, to multiply 11×34, add the two digits in 34 and place the sum between the 3 and 4. So $3 + 4 = 7$, and $11 \times 34 = 374$.

  To multiply 11×69, add the two digits in 69. Because $6 + 9 = 15$, add a 1 to the first digit and place a 5 between 7 and 9. So $11 \times 69 = 759$.

16.3.2 Basic Facts and Fact Power

Automatically knowing basic number facts is as important to learning mathematics as knowing words by sight is to reading. This has not gone unnoticed among educational researchers. Benjamin Bloom (1986) has written at length on the importance of *automaticity* as part of any complex talent and *Everyday Mathematics* co-creator Max Bell has long emphasized the importance of number-fact reflexes. Children are often told that habits, good and bad, come from doing something over and over until they do it without thinking. Developing basic number-fact reflexes can be likened to developing good habits.

In *Everyday Mathematics,* good fact habits are called *fact power.* In Grades 1 through 3, children keep fact power tables of the facts they know. The grades in which *Everyday Mathematics* activities help children gain fact power for each of the four basic arithmetic operations are shown in the table on the next page. For each operation, easier facts are introduced, explored using a variety of strategies, and practiced before harder facts are introduced, usually in the next grade.

Grade-Level Development of Children's Fact Power	K	1	2	3	4
Addition					
Easy facts					
Hard facts					
Subtraction					
Easy facts					
Hard facts					
Multiplication					
Easy facts					
Hard facts					
Division					
Easy facts					
Hard facts					

Each bar in this table represents the *Everyday Mathematics* grade levels during which children continuously gain a higher degree of fact power, from introduction and exploration of new facts with manipulatives to automatic recall (automaticity) in which facts are easily recalled from long-term memory. In the middle of this process, children develop their own strategies and learn new strategies for calculating mentally. The goal is to increase children's proficiency using favorite strategies that can help them gain automaticity. For example, easier facts are made more automatic through their application to learning the harder facts; that is, 8 + 7 may be seen as 1 less than the "easier" double 8 + 8.

As children share their strategies, encourage them to articulate what they are doing and to learn new ways of thinking about facts from you and their classmates. They practice their strategies in Mental Math and Reflex activities, in games, in Math Boxes, and in the context of solving number stories and other problems. The next two sections explain more ways that *Everyday Mathematics* helps children gain proficiency through continual practice.

By the end of the school year, most second graders should know the basic addition and subtraction facts automatically. In third and fourth grades, the emphasis shifts to learning the multiplication and division facts. Although some children may not know all these facts, they should be well on their way to achieving this goal by the end of fourth grade.

16.3.3 Fact Practice

Practicing the facts traditionally involves pages and pages of drills. This can be tedious and can lead children to dislike mathematics. Teachers of *Everyday Mathematics* have reported great success using these alternative approaches.

Choral Drills

Beginning in first grade, children participate in many short drills that review small groups of facts written on the board. To hold everyone's interest, you can vary the drill over a period of several days by playing with the numbers, formats, and speed. You might, for example, work with doubles such as $3 + 3$ and $5 + 5$ for several days and then advance to near doubles such as $3 + 4$ and $5 + 6$. A good time to do the drills is just after a break such as lunch or recess.

Double-9 Dominoes

Double-9 dominoes are wonderful concrete models of the addition/subtraction facts through $9 + 9$ and $18 - 9$. Dominoes help children visualize the facts as well as develop an understanding of the meanings of addition and subtraction and the relationship between the two operations. Many suggestions for using dominoes for basic-facts work are included in the *Teacher's Lesson Guide.*

Labels

Because numbers in real life nearly always occur in some context, *Everyday Mathematics* recommends that you and the children select *labels for the day* to use with fact practice. The kinds and numbers of labels you need depend on the operations being used. In addition and subtraction, only one label is needed. For example, on one day choose the label *pencils* and read the problem $7 + 9 = ?$ as 7 pencils + 9 pencils = ? pencils.

In multiplication and division, two or three related labels are needed. For example, one day you might use *cartons, pounds per carton,* and *pounds* so that the problem $5 \times 8 = \_$ becomes 5 cartons × 8 pounds per carton = _ pounds. Sometimes it makes sense for the two factors in multiplication to have the same label. For example, when finding an area, 5 feet × 8 feet = 40 square feet.

Post the labels and refer to them occasionally as children practice the facts. The labels of the day reinforce the idea that numbers refer to something real and useful. Keep the labels simple. They can be true-to-life or fanciful, serious or silly. They can be units of measure such as centimeters, minutes, and pounds or countable objects such as cats, hats, and ribbons. Although the main purpose for using labels is to keep numbers from becoming too abstract, labels are also important in other curriculum areas, especially reading, the sciences, and language arts.

Fact Families and Fact Triangles

A *fact family* is a collection of four related facts linking two inverse operations. For example, the following four equations symbolize the fact family relating 8, 9, and 17 by addition and subtraction.

$$8 + 9 = 17 \qquad 9 + 8 = 17$$
$$17 - 9 = 8 \qquad 17 - 8 = 9$$

NOTE: Technically, the Commutative Property of Addition is illustrated by the equation $8 + 9 = 9 + 8$. Because $8 + 9 = 17$ and $17 = 9 + 8$, then $8 + 9 = 9 + 8$ by the Transitive Property of Equality (if $a = b$ and $b = c$, then $a = c$).

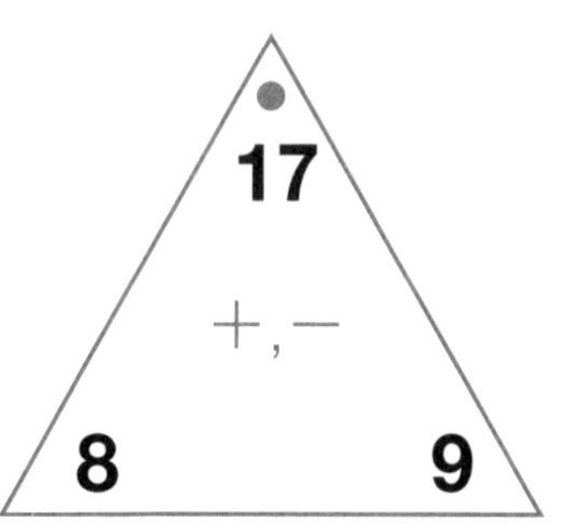

An addition/subtraction Fact Triangle

By fifth grade, *Everyday Mathematics* fact families are extended further as students learn equivalent values for decimals, fractions, and percents.

You may recognize that the two addition facts in this family taken together are an instance of the Commutative Property of Addition. Although *Everyday Mathematics* does not require children to learn mathematical names for properties, it is handy to have a name for occasional use. The *turn-around rule for addition* is the name used in *Everyday Mathematics* for the Commutative Property of Addition.

Everyday Mathematics calls properties of arithmetic *shortcuts,* and the four facts in a fact family are all related by shortcuts. A major reason for teaching fact families is to give children different options when solving problems that are new or difficult. By recalling a shortcut, a child can reword or rewrite the problem in a more meaningful way. For example, when faced with $7 - 3 = ?$, a first grader may think, *Hmm, lemme think. What plus 3 is 7? Ah, that's easy, it's 4.*

Fact Triangles are the *Everyday Mathematics* version of flash cards. Fact Triangles are more effective than traditional flash cards because they emphasize fact families. An addition/subtraction Fact Triangle has two addends and a sum; a multiplication/division Fact Triangle has two factors and a product. A Fact Triangle for the $8 + 9 = 17$ fact family is shown in the margin.

Fact Triangles are best employed in a cooperative-learning situation. One player covers a corner with a finger and the other player gives a fact that has the hidden number as an answer. For example, one player might cover up the 8 in an {8, 9, 17} addition/subtraction Fact Triangle. The other player might say "$17 - 9 = 8$." Fact Triangles can also be sorted into known/unknown facts or by a strategy such as doubles, near doubles, + 1, and + 2 to make for efficient practice. Because these activities are easy to do at home, Fact Triangles are strongly recommended as Home Links.

First Grade Everyday Mathematics uses Fact Triangles to establish and emphasize addition/subtraction fact families through $9 + 9$. In second grade, the addition/subtraction fact families are developed and multiplication/division Fact Triangles are introduced. In third grade, children get both addition/subtraction and multiplication/division Fact Triangles. In Kindergarten through Grade 3, a useful long-term project is to have students write the four number models in the fact family on the back of each Fact Triangle. Also, in all grades, new facts are usually introduced through concrete manipulations, drawings, games, and connections to previously known facts.

Fact Extensions

Fact extensions are powerful mental-arithmetic strategies for all operations with larger numbers. For example:

- If children know $3 + 4 = 7$, they also know $30 + 40 = 70$, $70 - 30 = 40$, and $300 + 400 = 700$.
- If children know $6 \times 5 = 30$, they also know $60 \times 5 = 300$, $600 \times 5 = 3{,}000$, and $3{,}000 \div 600 = 5$.

Fact extensions are introduced in first grade and are extended throughout the program.

16.3.4 Games for Fact Practice

Frequent practice is necessary in order for children to build and maintain strong mental-arithmetic skills and reflexes. Although drill has its place, much of the practice in *Everyday Mathematics* is in game format. Games are not merely attractive add-ons but essential parts of the complete *Everyday Mathematics* program.

In "Playing games and real mathematics," Ainley (1988) writes,

> The most effective mathematical games are those in which the structure and rules of the game are based on mathematical ideas, and where winning the game is directly related to understanding this mathematics. (p. 241)

All grades of *Everyday Mathematics* include games that have been developed to help children learn specific arithmetic and other skills at an appropriate developmental level. Some, in fact, are so targeted to the development of certain skills that once a child becomes proficient, the game is no longer necessary.

Drill and games should not be viewed as competitors for class time, nor should games be thought of as time-killers or rewards. In fact, games satisfy many, if not most, standard drill objectives with many built-in options. Drill tends to become tedious and, therefore, gradually loses its effectiveness. Games relieve the tedium because children enjoy them. Indeed, children often wish to continue to play games during their free time, lunch, and even recess.

Arithmetic practice through games is also recommended to help you deal with individual differences in children's motivations and abilities. Seckinger, Mitchel, and Lemire (1989) found that games improve children's attitudes about mathematics as well as improve achievement among low achievers. Alternatively, Johnson (2000) advocates using mathematical games with gifted children, who tend to invent new rules or increase difficulty of games on their own. Researchers such as Wolpert (1996) also support games or other play to encourage automaticity of arithmetic skills by learning-disabled children.

Drill exercises aim primarily at building fact and operation skills. Practice through games shares these objectives, but at the same time, games often reinforce calculator skills, logical thinking, geometric intuition, and intuition about probability and chance because many games involve randomly generated numbers.

Using games to practice number skills also greatly reduces the need for worksheets. Because the numbers in most games are generated randomly, the games can be played over and over without repeating the same problems. Many of the *Everyday Mathematics* games come with variations that allow players to progress from easy to more challenging versions. Games, therefore, offer an almost unlimited source of practice material.

NOTE: Cognitive and educational psychologists have long supported children's playing games in school. For a concise summary, see *Theories of Childhood: An Introduction to Dewey, Montessori, Erickson, Piaget and Vygotsky* by C. G. Mooney. A full reference can be found on page 201.

NOTE: The federal and some state education departments advocate children playing mathematics games in school and at home. The U.S. Department of Education (2004) places high value on games in *Helping Your Child Learn Mathematics.* A full reference can be found on page 201. The New York State Department of Education has recommended games along with concrete objects, number lines, and other approaches for more than 25 years. For more information on New York's position, see this Web site: www.emsc.nysed.gov/ciai/mst/math.html

▶ 16.4 Number Sense and Mathematical Connections

It is perhaps the single greatest goal of *Everyday Mathematics* that children completing the program acquire number sense. People with *number sense:*

- Have good mental-arithmetic skills as well as reliable algorithms and procedures for finding results they can't produce mentally;
- Are flexible in thinking about numbers and arithmetic and will look for shortcuts to make their efforts as efficient as possible;
- Can use their number and arithmetic skills to solve problems in everyday situations;
- Are familiar with a variety of ways to communicate their strategies and results;
- Can recognize unreasonable results when they see them in their own work, in everyday situations, or in the media.

Number sense develops only with wide mathematical experience, including instruction and practice in specific techniques. But good number sense also depends on attitudes and beliefs, especially the belief that mathematics makes sense. People with good number sense expect their mathematical knowledge to connect with the rest of what they know, including their common sense and whatever they know about the situation at hand. Number sense thus depends on making connections between various kinds of mathematical knowledge and between mathematics and other subjects.

Everyday Mathematics helps children develop number sense in the contexts of data analysis, geometry, and elementary explorations of functions and sequences. In *Everyday Mathematics,* children make connections across mathematical topics and come to view mathematics as a coherent, consistent discipline rather than a hodgepodge of disconnected procedures and skills.

Number sense also involves making connections between mathematics and other subjects in the curriculum. Many activities in *Everyday Mathematics* are designed to show how number sense applies to science, social studies, and geography. Throughout *Everyday Mathematics* there are connections between mathematics and history, including both the history of mathematics and how mathematics has shaped human endeavors.

Everyday Mathematics also connects mathematics to the community through efforts to share the authors' commitment to number sense with children's families and other caregivers. Family Letters explain how *Everyday Mathematics* introduces children not only to the traditional mathematics people expect but also to a richer mathematics curriculum that older family members may not have experienced. Home Links enable parents or guardians to see the kinds of mathematics their children do in school and pass along some interesting ideas for family involvement as well.

References and Resources on Estimation, Mental Arithmetic, and Number Sense

Ainley, J. (1988). "Playing games and real mathematics." In Pimm, D. (Ed.) *Mathematics, Teachers and Children.* London: Hodder and Stoughton.

Bell, M., and Usiskin, Z. (1983). *Applying Arithmetic.* Chicago: University of Chicago. Available in three parts from Educational Resources Information Center (ERIC): ED 264087, ED 264088, and ED 264089.

Bloom, B. (1986). "Automaticity: The Hands and Feet of Genius." *Educational Leadership (43)5,* pp. 70–77.

Kamii, C., and DeVries, R. (1980). *Group games in early education: Implications of Piaget's theory.* Washington, DC: National Association for the Education of Young Children.

Mooney, C. G. (2000). *Theories of Childhood: An Introduction to Dewey, Montessori, Erickson, Piaget and Vygotsky.* St. Paul, MN: Redleaf.

Office of Intergovernmental and Interagency Affairs. (2004). *Helping Your Child Learn Mathematics.* Washington, DC: U.S. Department of Education.

Peters, S. (1998). "Playing games and learning mathematics: The results of two intervention studies." *International Journal of Early Years Education (6)1,* pp. 49–58.

Schoen, H. L., and Zweng, M. J. (1986). *Estimation and Mental Computation: 1986 Yearbook.* Reston, VA: National Council of Teachers of Mathematics.

Steen, L. (Ed.) (1997). *Why Numbers Count: Quantitative Literacy for Tomorrow's America.* New York: College Entrance Examination Board.

Wolpert, G. (1996). *The Educational Challenges Inclusion Study.* New York: National Down Syndrome Society.

17 Patterns, Sequences, Functions, and Algebra

Contents

Patterns can be found in sounds, in movements, in shapes, in numbers, in graphs, and in data. Indeed, patterns can be found almost anywhere. Patterns are especially important in mathematics. Some people even define mathematics as the science of patterns.

Most of mathematics deals with patterns that are predictable. This means that objects, colors, or numbers are arranged so that you can predict what comes next. You can "see" or continue such patterns; and in many cases, it is possible to find a rule that underlies a given pattern. The first part of this chapter deals with such patterns, including sequences and functions.

The second part of the chapter discusses uses of variables and how to read and write open number sentences. It closes with a brief description of some informal ways to solve open sentences.

Patterns and algebra are closely related. Pattern activities involve many mathematical processes that are fundamental in algebra. Among these are looking for patterns; making, testing, and proving conjectures about patterns; and representing patterns in several ways. Looking for patterns helps children develop modeling skills, which are crucial to many applications of algebra. By making and justifying conjectures about patterns, children develop habits of generalization and verification that will serve them well in algebra and beyond. Finally, working with multiple representations for functions, such as function machines, tables, rules, graphs, words, and symbols, helps children to build the conceptual understanding that will eventually support the symbol-manipulation skills so necessary for success in algebra.

17.1 Patterns, Sequences, and Functions

Most of the patterns in *Everyday Mathematics* are either *visual patterns,* such as those found in colored manipulatives, geometric shapes, and data or coordinate graphs, or *number patterns,* such as those found in sequences and functions.

17.1.1 Visual Patterns

A major aim of *Everyday Mathematics* is for children to become aware of patterns of shapes and colors in their environment. Many pattern-recognition activities help children focus on geometric properties of shapes. Three examples follow.

- Make a pattern with craft sticks and ask your partner what comes next.

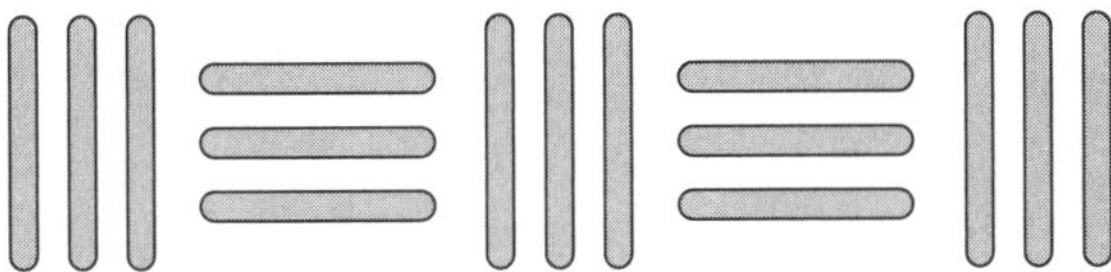

  This type of sequence involves an understanding of the beauty and symmetry of parallel line segments and right-angle turns. What comes next, a horizontal triplet or a repetition of the first five triplets?

- Look at this pattern and describe what comes next.

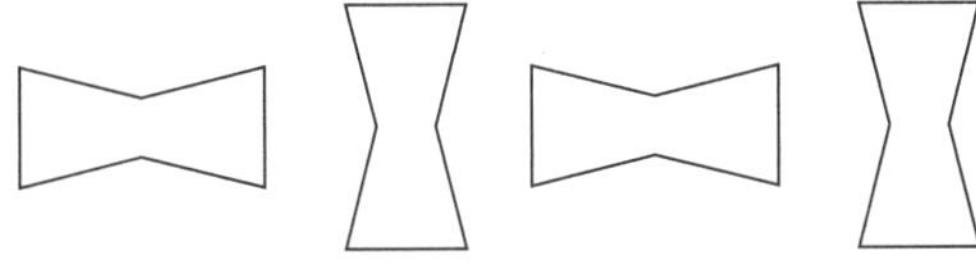

  This puzzle introduces children to a sequence of concave hexagons, each of which is a 90° turn of the previous one. Or is it a slide of the first two repeated over and over? Or is it one sequence of horizontally oriented shapes with another sequence of vertically oriented ones spliced in? Without the need for formal names of the shapes or definitions of the slides and turns involved, this kind of activity helps children become aware of relationships of 2-dimensional objects and how those relationships can be described.

For more information, see Section 13.6: Geometric Relations.

- Color the diamond pattern with three colors.

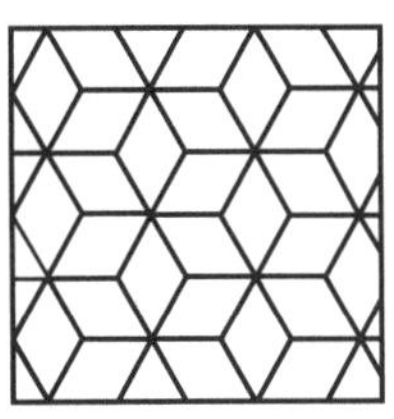

  This pattern is a *tessellation.* Without knowing any of the names of the shapes, young children can explore some rather sophisticated relations of polygons in the plane. In this example, the result suggests a pattern of stacked 3-dimensional cubes.

For more on the illusion of the cube, see Section 13.5.4: Connecting 2-D and 3-D.

Everyday Mathematics engages children in many other activities with visual patterns. Patterns around the classroom or school include covers on fluorescent lights, panes in windows, wires or slats in fences, milk cartons in crates, floor and ceiling tiles, and patterns in magazine and

chapter 17

newspaper pictures and advertisements. Home Links encourage children to find patterns at home and bring in examples. Visual patterns also appear frequently in Math Boxes and in *Minute Math+*.

17.1.2 Odd and Even Number Patterns

For centuries people have studied number patterns in a branch of mathematics called *number theory*. This section discusses perhaps the simplest of these patterns, *odd* and *even* numbers.

KEVIN: Odd numbers are neat. They always have a middle.

FATHER: What?

KEVIN: See (pointing to the third of five sticks in a row), always something in the middle. But with even numbers (removing the third stick from the row), there is just a space in the middle.

Odd and even numbers are simple, but exploring them can lead children to generalizations that are of fundamental importance in number theory. For example, it is easy to observe that pairing odd numbers of things always leaves one left over. Building on this simple observation, some children discover relationships such as the following:

- The sum of any two even numbers is even (there are no leftover pieces).
- The sum of an even number and an odd number is odd (the leftover piece remains).
- The sum of any two odd numbers is even (the leftovers pair up).
- The statements are still true if *positive difference* is substituted for *sum*. For example, the positive difference of any two even numbers is even.

Similar relationships exist for the products of odd and even numbers, although children are less likely to discover these relationships on their own. A product is even if at least one of the factors is even. If none of the factors is even, then the product is odd. For example, $3 \times 7 \times 5$ is odd because all the factors are odd. $27 \times 3 \times 4$ is even because one of the factors is even.

Odd numbers of people or things are often seen as a nuisance. An odd number of people cannot be assigned equally to two different teams. Similarly, two people cannot equally share an odd number of unbreakable objects, such as marbles. On the other hand, it is easier to find the middle value, or median, of an odd number of data values because an even number of values has no single middle value.

Making generalizations based on observations of patterns is fundamental to mathematics and science. When children discover and "prove" simple relationships about odd and even numbers, they are learning powerful ways of thinking that will serve them throughout their mathematical careers.

17.1.3 Sequences

A *number sequence* is a list of numbers. Many sequences are important enough to have names:

- Whole numbers: 0, 1, 2, 3, 4, 5, 6, . . .
- Odd numbers: 1, 3, 5, 7, 9, 11, . . .
- Even numbers: 2, 4, 6, 8, 10, 12, . . .
- Prime numbers: 2, 3, 5, 7, 11, 13, . . .
- Square numbers: 1, 4, 9, 16, 25, 36, . . .

Sequences of numbers are similar to visual patterns in that both number sequences and shape or color sequences often have a *rule* that governs what the next number or object in the sequence is. For number sequences, the rule may involve one or more arithmetic operations. For example, the counting numbers can be generated by starting with 1 and then repeatedly applying the rule "Add 1." The even numbers can be generated by starting with 2 and then applying the rule "Add 2."

Many number sequences can be linked to visual patterns. The square numbers, for example, can be modeled by a sequence of square arrays. The even numbers and triangular numbers can also be modeled by sequences of dot patterns. The interplay of number sequences and visual patterns is fertile ground for investigations in elementary school mathematics.

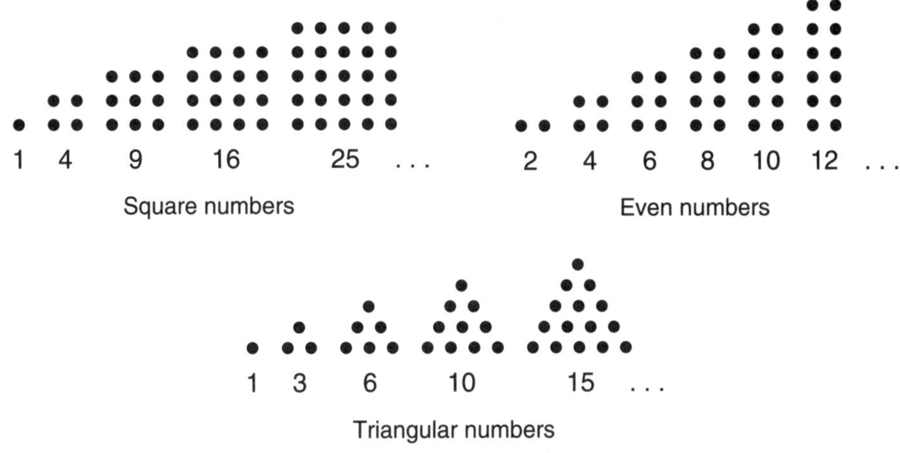

Patterns in many number sequences are accessible to children of any age. Starting in *First Grade Everyday Mathematics,* children use Frames-and-Arrows diagrams to invent or extend sequences or to find a rule or rules for a given sequence.

Frames and Arrows

Frames-and-Arrows diagrams consist of a sequence of frames connected by arrows. Each frame contains a number; each arrow represents a rule that determines which number goes in the next frame. The numbers in a Frames-and-Arrows diagram form a sequence; the arrow rule(s) represent the mathematical structure that generates the sequence. Frames-and-Arrows diagrams are also called *chains.* A simple example of a Frames-and-Arrows diagram for the rule "Add 1" is shown below.

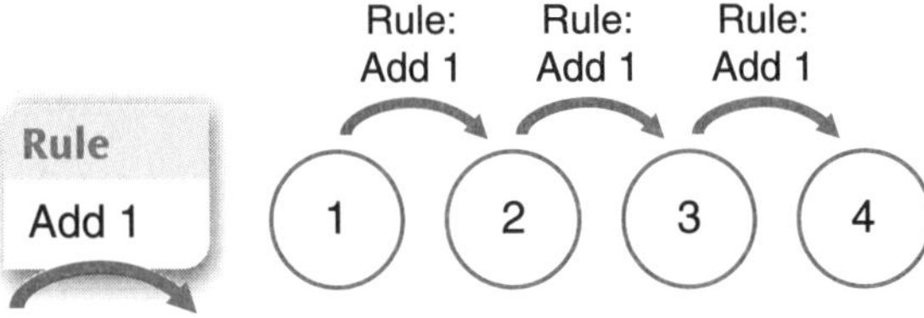

NOTE: There are many possible rules for any given Frames-and-Arrows problem, although most people usually agree on a "best" one. For example, the rule "Add 4" is equivalent to "Add two 2s." Children are not expected to invent or even understand equivalent rules in these problems, so don't emphasize it. But be careful not to dismiss correct alternatives that you or others may not think are "best."

In Frames-and-Arrows problems, some information is missing. Several types are described here.

- A rule is given. Some of the frames are empty. Fill in the blank frames.

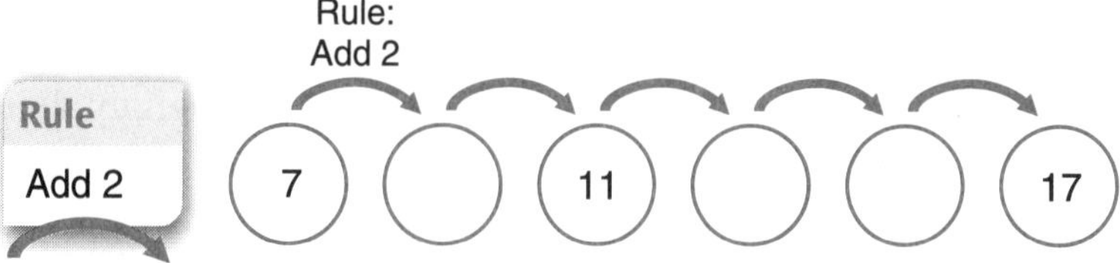

Solution: Write 9, 13, and 15 in the blank frames.

- The frames are filled in. A rule is missing. Find a rule.

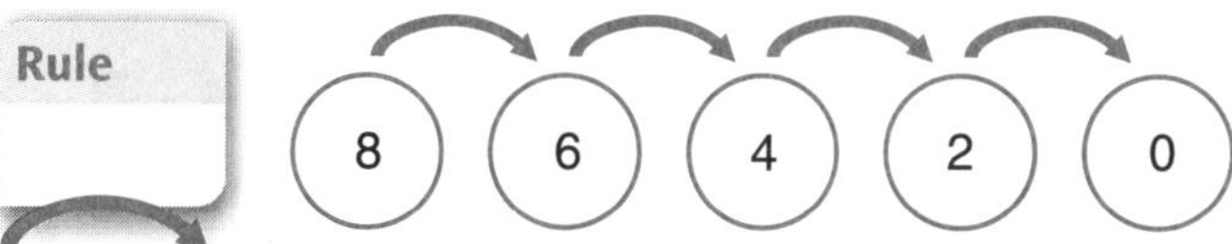

Solution: A rule is "Subtract 2," "Minus 2," or "– 2."

- Some of the frames are empty. A rule is missing. Find a rule and fill in the empty frames.

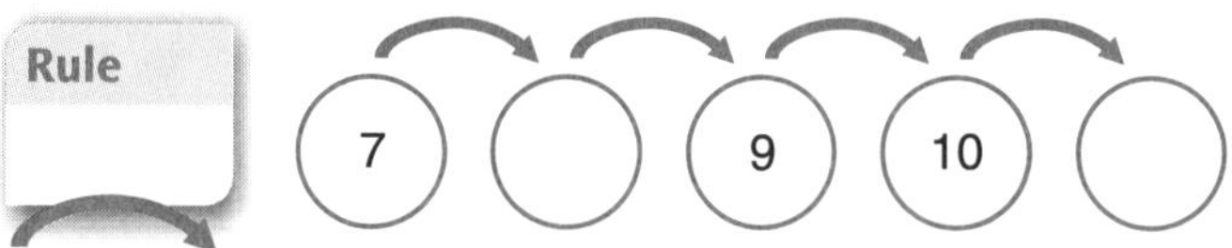

Solution: A rule is "Add 1." Write 8 and 11 in the empty frames.

A chain can have more than one arrow rule, and different rules need different arrows. In the following problem , a black arrow means + 3 and a colored arrow means + 2.

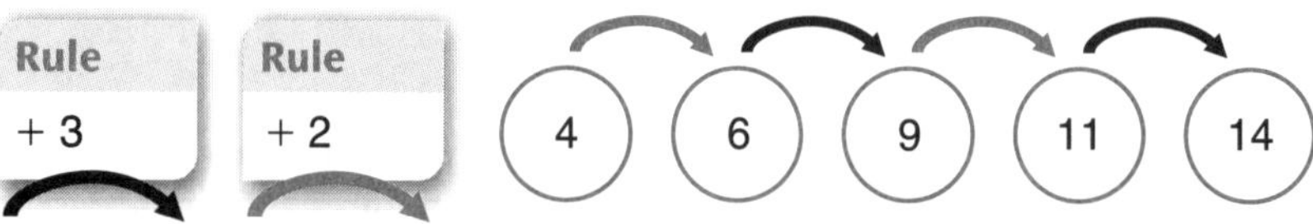

In the next example, the rules are given and the frames are filled in, but the arrows between frames are missing:

- Draw the arrows in the proper positions.

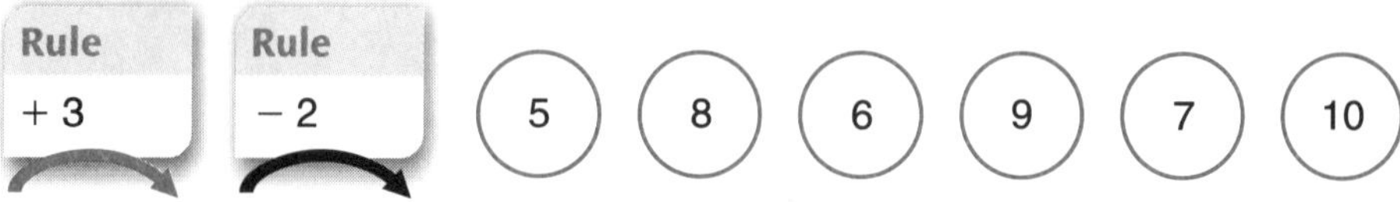

Solution: Draw a + 3 arrow from 5 to 8, from 6 to 9, and from 7 to 10. Draw a – 2 arrow from 8 to 6 and from 9 to 7.

The Frames-and-Arrows format is easily grasped by children and is highly flexible. *Everyday Mathematics* encourages you and the children to devise your own Frames-and-Arrows problems.

Incomplete Number Lines

In first and second grades, number lines are used to keep track of days of the school year and to help with counting. Beginning in *First Grade Everyday Mathematics,* number lines are also used in a variation of Frames and Arrows. Children are given a number line with a sequence of blanks to fill in or tick marks to label.

Like Frames-and-Arrows diagrams, *incomplete number lines* involve sequences in a different format. The scale of the number line, that is, the distance between ticks, corresponds to the rule that governs the sequence. Introduce incomplete-number-line problems using whole numbers and the rule "Add 1." Examples of two general types of problems are given below.

- Given two boundary points on a number line with scale 1, fill in the blanks.

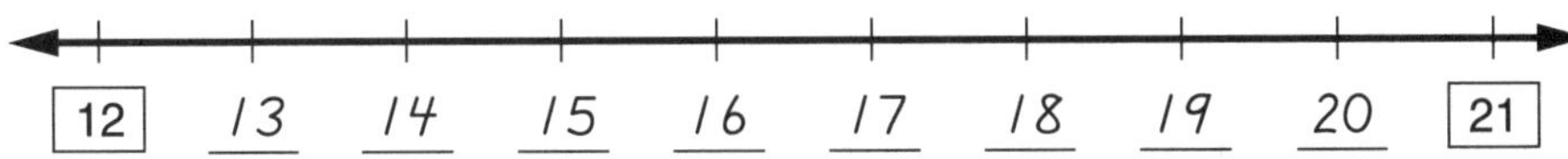

Note that the rule does not actually need to be stated in this type of problem because the number of intervals between the boundary points determines the scale.

- Given one or two numbers on a number line with scale 1, fill in the blanks in either direction. This encourages practice with both counting up and counting down.

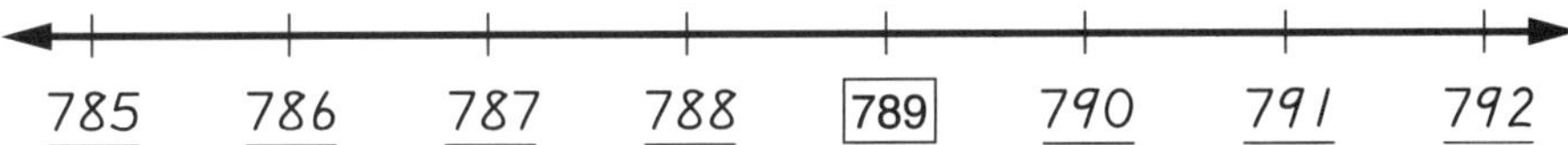

Note that in the second type of problem, children could use a scale other than 1. For example, they could decide to count by 10s, which would lead to the values 749 through 819. Don't push children to understand this early on, but don't penalize any child who realizes the possibilities. If you don't want to open this door for the children, be sure to label at least two tick marks on the given number line. The labeled points need not be consecutive. The best procedure for creating such problems is to complete the entire line and then erase all but one or two numbers to ensure that the problem you create will have a reasonable answer.

After children are comfortable with how incomplete number lines work, you can introduce scales other than 1 into problems so that children practice more sophisticated counting techniques. Eventually you can vary the problems to include fractions, decimals, and negative numbers. Some variations include the following:

- Given part of a number line on which two boundary points are labeled with whole numbers, skip count to fill in whole-number labels for points between the given points.

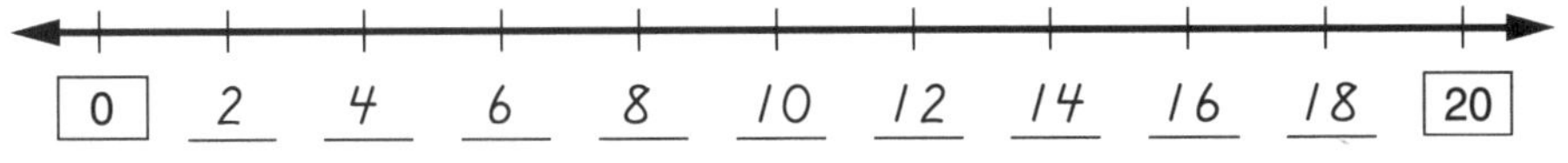

NOTE: Children can use their calculators to skip count while filling in some incomplete number lines, allowing them to use "harder" numbers. For more information, see Section 11.3: Algorithms on Calculators.

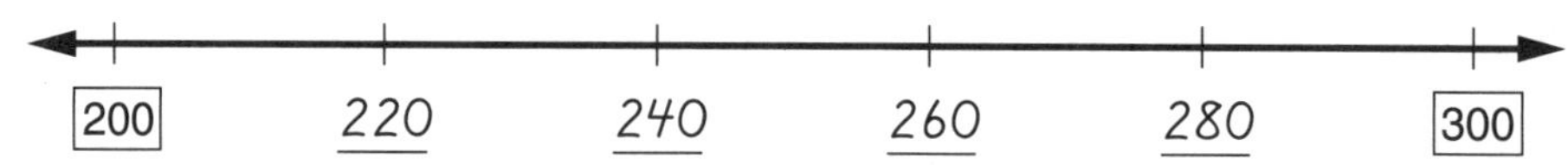

- Fill in missing labels on number lines with decimals or fractions.

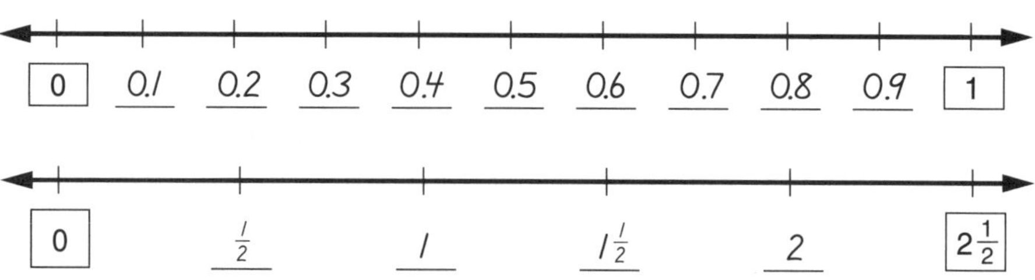

- Extend the number line to the left of 0.

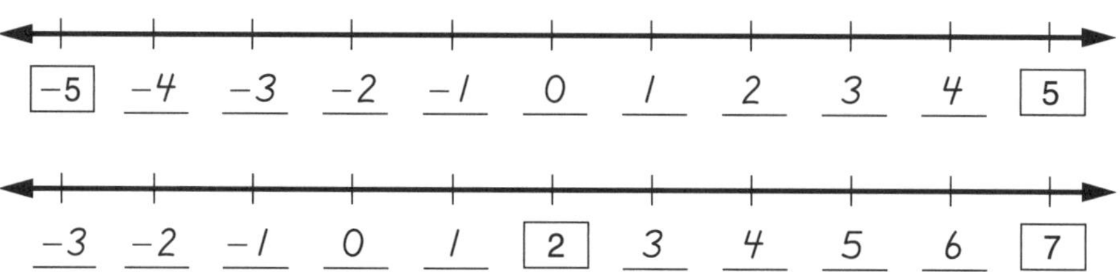

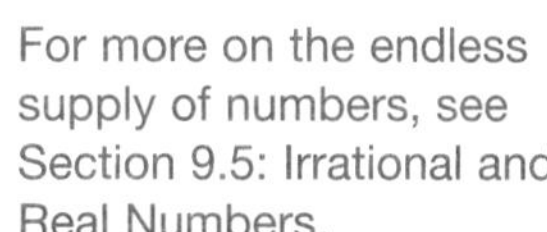
For more on the endless supply of numbers, see Section 9.5: Irrational and Real Numbers.

As the last two number lines demonstrate, these approaches can be used for any number system. Also consider open-ended problems in which only one tick mark is labeled, but be prepared for a variety of scale choices. As this work with number lines continues, children may discover the amazing fact that between any two points or numbers, there is always another point or number. The number line is thus doubly infinite. The entire number line contains infinitely many numbers, but even the smallest interval between two numbers also contains infinitely many numbers.

Teaching with Sequences

Many Frames-and-Arrows and incomplete-number-line problems have been incorporated into *First* through *Third Grade Everyday Mathematics.* Once you introduce these kinds of problems, use them often. Many different frame shapes are used for the Frames-and-Arrows routines. This helps children understand that it is the number sequence and its rules, not the shapes of the frames, that are important. A blackline master with a blank chain is included in *Math Masters* for you and the children to create your own Frames-and-Arrows problems.

Rules for sequence problems can become increasingly complicated. Toward the end of first grade, for example, you might use rules such as "Double," "Double and add 1," or "Take half of" for Frames and Arrows, and use numbers in the hundreds in incomplete number lines. Toward the end of third grade, rules might include "Multiply by 10" or "Add $1.25," with numbers in the thousands and negative numbers on number lines.

Although number lines do not necessarily have to be labeled with *arithmetic sequences,* that is, sequences that involve adding or subtracting a constant from left to right, *Everyday Mathematics* suggests using this convention in problems. Other scales are possible, however, and variations should not be considered wrong. Such scales are called *nonlinear scales* because they do not involve constant, or linear, change.

Scales on radio dials, for example, are nonlinear.

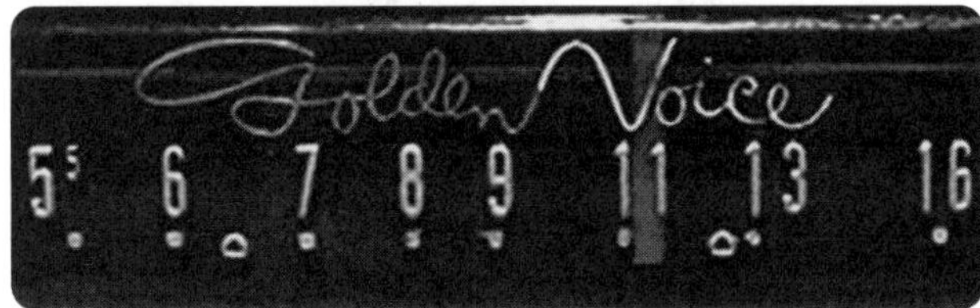

A radio dial with a nonlinear scale

Scientists sometimes use nonlinear scales such as powers of 10 to simplify graphs of relationships such as the effects of compound interest.

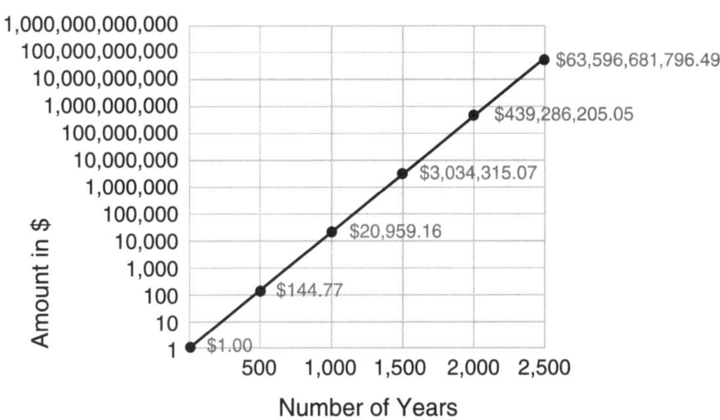

A graph with a nonlinear scale

17.1.4 Functions

Function is one of those everyday words that mathematicians use in a special way. This section begins with descriptions of how *Everyday Mathematics* approaches this powerful idea in ways that even Kindergartners can understand. The mathematical definition of function follows that idea, along with a discussion of the many ways functions can be represented or modeled.

Function Machines

A *function machine* is an imaginary device that receives inputs and generates outputs. For example, the function machine in the margin takes an *input* number and *outputs* its double.

Children can imagine putting a number into this machine, waiting a moment, and then getting its double out. If a 1 is put in, then a 2 comes out. If a 5 is put in, then a 10 comes out. Whatever number goes in, twice that number comes out.

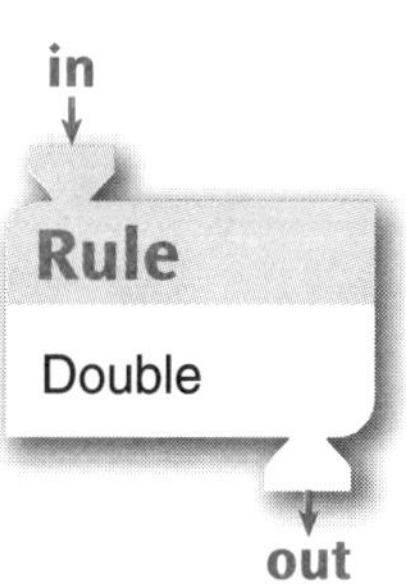

A doubling machine

chapter 17

The inputs and outputs from a function machine can be recorded in a *function table*. Each row in the table holds an *ordered pair* in which the first number is the input and the second number is the output. Here is a table for the doubling function machine.

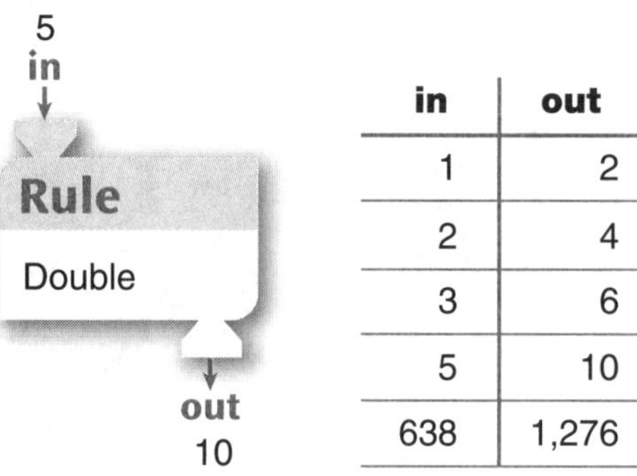

in	out
1	2
2	4
3	6
5	10
638	1,276

A doubling function

An important feature of a function machine is that it *always* gives the same output for a given input number. If two rows in an input-output table have the same number in the input column, then they must also have the same number in the output column.

Often, every input number has a different output number as in the doubling machine, but this is not required. For example, a function machine might always output the same number, no matter what is put in. Such functions are called *constant functions* and are perfectly legitimate, if a bit dull.

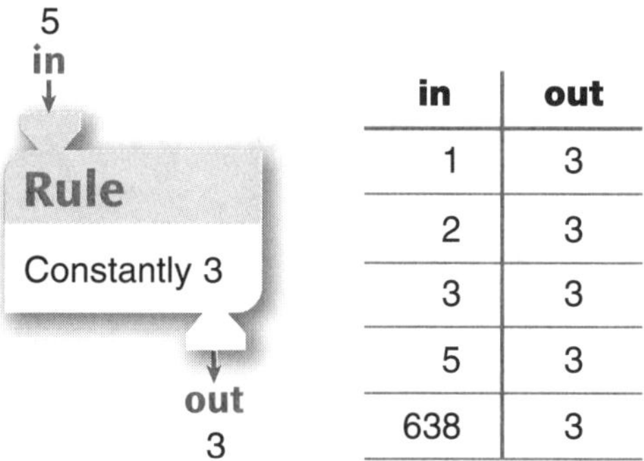

in	out
1	3
2	3
3	3
5	3
638	3

A constant function

A function machine captures the key features of most of the functions that are studied in pre-college mathematics, in which there are a set of inputs, a set of outputs, and a rule associating each input with exactly one output.

In *Kindergarten* through *Third Grade Everyday Mathematics,* function machines and function tables help children visualize how a rule associates each input value with an output value. A principal activity for developing this concept further is called "What's My Rule?"

"What's My Rule?"

Simple "What's My Rule?" games begin in *Kindergarten Everyday Mathematics.* The first games are attribute or rule activities that sort children into a specified group. For example, children with hook-and-loop fasteners on their shoes belong to the group while children with other types of fasteners do not. You sort the children without revealing your rule, and the children have to guess what the sorting rule is.

In first through third grades, this idea is extended to sorting numbers. For example, you might draw a circle on the board and begin writing even numbers in the circle and odd numbers outside the circle. The children say numbers and try to guess where they go. Once they can reliably predict which numbers belong in the circle, they propose rules for the sorting. This can be repeated for other rules such as 1-digit numbers, numbers with zero in the ones place, and numbers between 20 and 30.

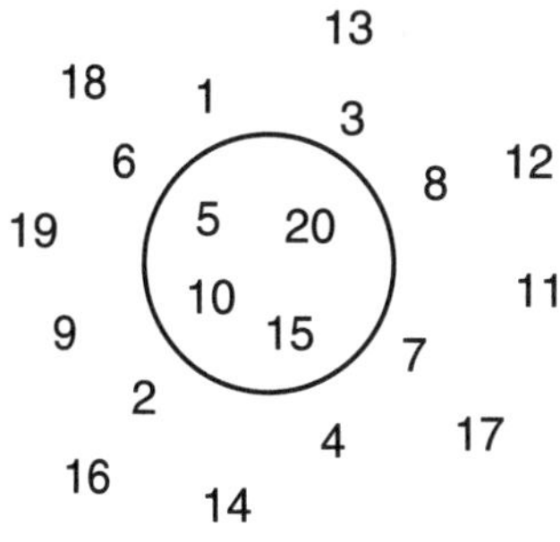

"What's My Rule?"

"What's My Rule?" activities are eventually extended to include problems in which pairs of numbers are given and the task is to find a rule that relates the numbers in each pair. The same rule has to work for every pair. If the first number is input to a function machine, the second number is output. The problem is to identify a function machine's rule. The pairings can be displayed in a table of values.

Generally, in a "What's My Rule?" problem, two of the three parts of a function (input, output, and rule) are known. The goal is to find the unknown part. There are three basic types of problems:

- The rule and some input numbers are known. Give the corresponding output numbers.

in	out
39	
54	
163	

39
in
Rule
+ 10
out
?

- The rule and some output numbers are known. Give the corresponding input numbers.

in	out
	6
	10
	20

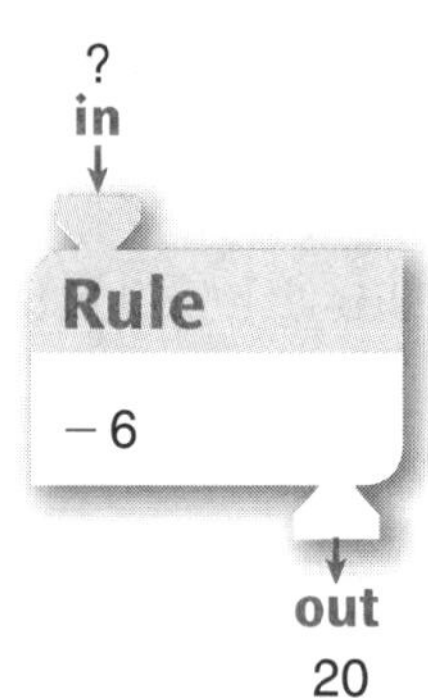

- Some input and output numbers are known. Give a rule.

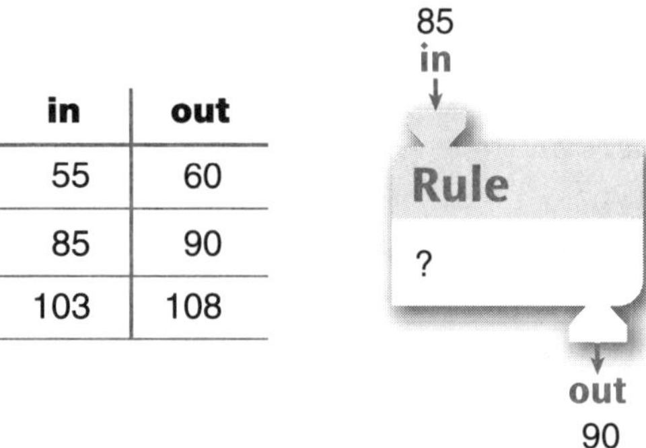

in	out
55	60
85	90
103	108

You can combine more than one type of problem in a single table. For example, you could give a partially completed table with an unknown rule. If you give enough input and output clues, children can fill in blanks as well as figure out a rule, as in the problem below.

in	out
15	25
4	14
7	
	63

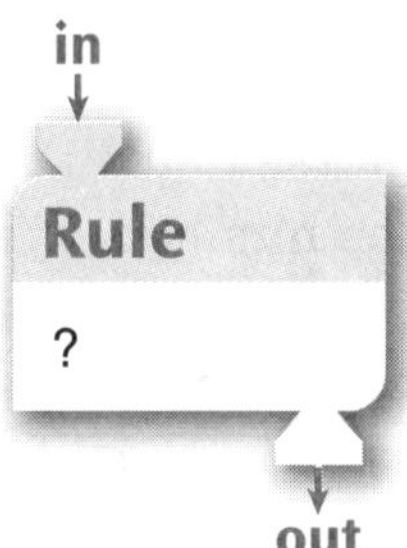

What Is a Function?

Like many ideas in mathematics, the concept of a function is simple, yet powerful. Also like many ideas in mathematics, the definition of function seems at first to be rather odd. According to a dictionary of mathematics, "A *function* is a set of ordered pairs (x,y) in which each value of x is paired with exactly one value of y." A few examples may help clarify what this means:

- Doubling: {(1,2), (2,4), (3,6), (4,8), . . .}
- Squaring: {(1,1), (2,4), (3,9), (4,16), . . .}
- Adding 1: {(1,2), (2,3), (3,4), (4,5), . . .}

In each of these sets of ordered pairs, the first number is paired with exactly one second number. According to the definition, then, each of these sets is a function.

This definition applies to all the functions discussed so far in this chapter, but you will note that there is no mention of a rule. *The pairings in a function don't have to follow any rule.* The only requirement is that *each* first value has to be paired with *exactly one* second value. For example, you have a function if you pair each whole number less than 100 with any other whole number less than 100.

- A function with no rule: {(0,10), (1,82), (2,15), (3,74), . . ., (99,17), (100,92)}

Such a function may not be very useful, but it is still a legitimate function. A more interesting example of a function with no rule is one that takes a date as the input and gives the closing price of IBM stock as the output. If you could find a rule for such a function, you could get rich quickly. Unfortunately, economists have proved that no such rule can exist. The only way to find the closing price of IBM stock on a future date is to wait and see what it is.

NOTE: A rule pairing a date with the closing price of IBM stock can't exist. If such a rule did exist, someone would figure it out, then buy or sell stock to take advantage of the information, and by doing so, invalidate the rule.

In *Everyday Mathematics,* children do not explore functions without rules. Most interesting functions are interesting because they have rules. So all the functions in the program are associated with rules that are either given or may be deduced. To keep the rules interesting to children, the authors based many of them in real-life situations.

Along with no mention of rules, the mathematical definition of a function does not mention numbers. In fact, *functions do not have to involve numbers at all*—just a set of paired inputs and outputs. A function might take polygons in and output a name based on number of sides, (triangle, quadrangle, pentagon, and so on). Another function might take triangles in and output a name based on angles (acute, right, or obtuse). All that is required for a function is a set of ordered pairs (*input, output*)—in which every input has exactly one output.

Many real-world situations may remind you of functions. A bathroom scale is a function machine; when you stand on it, it outputs your weight. A gasoline pump has a built-in function machine, in which the input is an amount of gasoline pumped and the output is a total cost including tax. One way to think about science is as a search for functions that relate real-world variables.

Sequences can also be considered to be functions. Some sequences are *iterative* functions, in which an output comes from applying a rule to the previous output, that is, to the previous number, or *term,* in the sequence, rather than to an independent input value. For example, to get the next even number, just add 2 to the previous even number. Other sequences are not iterative because there is no rule that gives the next term from the previous terms. In a sequence of closing prices for IBM stock, knowing the previous term or terms is not enough to determine the next term.

Another way to think of sequences as functions is to number, or *index,* the terms. For example, indexing a sequence of even numbers beginning with 2 led to the table at the right. The indices can be thought of as input values and the even numbers in the sequence as the output. Thinking of a sequence in this way can sometimes lead you to a rule that will give any term in the sequence without having to find all the previous terms. From the table, it appears that a rule to find the nth even number is to simply double n.

in	out
1	2
2	4
3	6
4	8
5	10

In *Everyday Mathematics,* sequences are not treated as functions. It's easier to think of sequences as lists of numbers, often with a rule for generating the next term, as in Frames-and-Arrows diagrams. However, activities with sequences are quite helpful for developing children's understanding of functions.

NOTE: Functions are not restricted to a single input variable and a single output variable. For example, a function with two input variables and one output variable is a *set of ordered triples*—perhaps the number of gallons of gasoline and the price per gallon as the inputs and total cost as the output. *Everyday Mathematics* is restricted to functions with only two variables.

For more information about these four representations, see Section 18.2: Problem Representations.

Representing Functions

In *Everyday Mathematics*, children approach functions *concretely, pictorially, verbally,* and *symbolically.* Children see *concrete* representations in activities such as sorting objects according to some measure or attribute, lining up by height, or ordering pattern blocks by shape. All of these concrete activities include patterns that lead to functions.

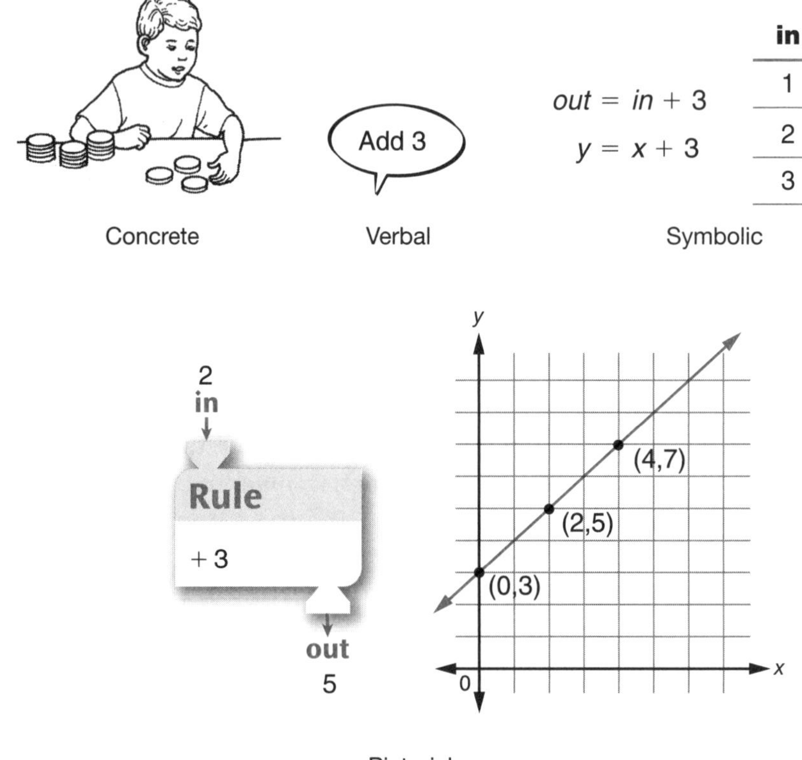

Four representations of functions

Verbal representations of functions include rules like "Double" or "Add 5." Verbal representations can often be made more concise by using *symbolic* representations like + 3 or *out* = *in* + 3 or $y = x + 3$, where x is input and y is output. The symbolic representation of functions as equations is explored extensively in fourth through sixth grades.

Frames-and-Arrows problems, incomplete number lines, and function machines are *pictorial* representations of functions and sequences. In Grade 3, children get their first exposure to coordinate graphs of functions when they plot ordered pairs on a coordinate grid. Graphs are particularly important pictorial representations that are investigated extensively in *Fourth* through *Sixth Grade Everyday Mathematics.*

Function tables, or tables of values, are an important kind of representation of functions in *Kindergarten* through *Third Grade Everyday Mathematics* and beyond. A table is sort of a cross between a pictorial and a symbolic representation. Many functions in real life are given as tables, such as those that fill the sports and business sections of a newspaper. For example, the input could be the name of a baseball team and the output the team batting average on the date of the newspaper. Many sports standings, financial tables, weather tables, and the like may represent functions. A great deal of the tabular information in almanacs and other reference books may also represent functions.

17.2 Algebra and Uses of Variables

Most adults in the United States probably remember algebra as a junior or senior high school course devoted to learning how to manipulate equations containing variables. But algebra is actually far more than just symbol manipulation. Algebra can be thought of as generalized arithmetic, as a set of powerful problem-solving procedures, as a study of numeric relations, or as a study of the structure of mathematics. The authors of *Everyday Mathematics* believe these are all valid descriptions of algebra. Accordingly, although the formal study of algebraic syntax is not appropriate for most elementary school children, *Everyday Mathematics* includes many activities involving algebra.

NOTE: For more on the place of algebra in the elementary school curriculum, see *The Ideas of Algebra, K–12,* edited by Art Coxford and Al Shulte. A full reference can be found on page 219.

Algebra is a branch of mathematics that deals with variables and operations on variables. As soon as first graders encounter problems like $8 + \_ = 12$ they are thinking algebraically because the blank is a kind of variable. Later in *Everyday Mathematics,* children experience variables as *unknowns* ($5 + x = 8$), in *formulas* ($A = lw$), in statements of mathematical *properties* ($a + b = b + a$), and in functions ($y = x + 5$). All of these experiences with variables prepare children for eventual success in algebra.

Algebra has important links to the pattern, sequences, and functions strand, as well as to the problem-solving thread in *Everyday Mathematics.* The diagram below identifies the four representations that are featured in the program to model problems: concrete, verbal, pictorial, and symbolic. To represent problems symbolically, children need to understand the usefulness of algebraic notation and variables.

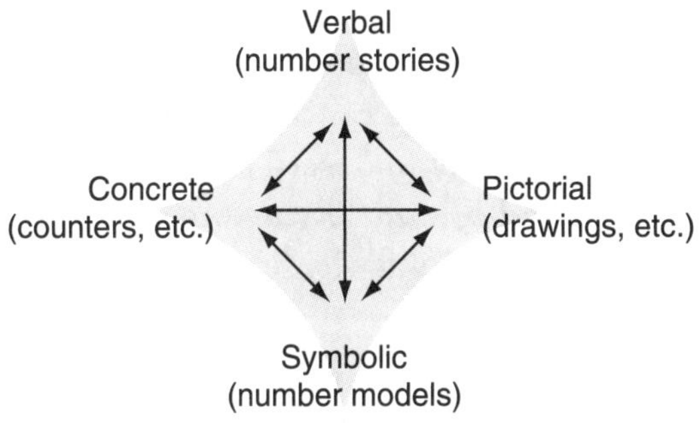

Four problem-solving representations

For more information, see Section 18.2: Problem Representations and Section 17.1.4: Functions.

17.2.1 Uses of Variables

A *variable* is a letter or other symbol that stands for a number. In *Kindergarten* through *Third Grade Everyday Mathematics,* variables are primarily *unknowns* in open number sentences as described in the next section. The other four sections are included to advise you on how variables are used in later grades of the program and beyond.

Variables as Unknowns

As children write number sentences to fit problem situations, they often find that they need to represent numbers that are *unknown.* For example, the problem *There are 24 children in our class, but today only 18 are here. How many are not here?* might be modeled using any of these three equations using ? as the variable:

24 − ? = 18   18 + ? = 24   24 − 18 = ?

Alternatively, a *letter*, a *blank*, or a *box* can be used to indicate the unknown number:

$24 - n = 18$ 18 + __ = 24   24 − 18 = □

All four of the symbols ?, n, ___, and □ are variables.

Introducing the term *variable* in *Kindergarten* through *Third Grade Everyday Mathematics* is unnecessary because variables are used primarily as unknowns in open sentences. Also, in sentences such as $5 + n = 13$, the unknown is a single number that doesn't vary, so explaining the root of the word variable (*vary*) is not helpful.

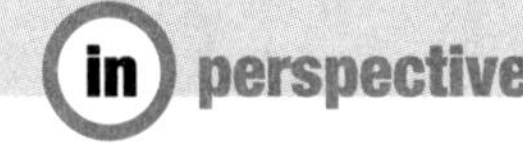

Students in Grades 4 through 6 use more than one unknown when they write and interpret open sentences for "What's My Rule?" problems or geometric formulas.

Besides being used to represent single unknown numbers such as x in $x + 6 = 12$, variables can represent more than a single unknown number in certain situations. For example, *I'm thinking of a number less than 10* can be modeled as $x < 10$, which has the whole-number solutions 0, 1, . . ., 9, and many more solutions if fractions, decimals, or negative numbers are allowed.

There can also be more than one unknown in situations modeled by equations. For example, *What pairs of whole numbers have 8 as their sum?* can be modeled as $m + n = 8$. Solutions are the pairs 0 and 8, 1 and 7, 2 and 6, and so on.

Students use area and volume formulas for many geometric figures in *Fourth* through *Sixth Grade Everyday Mathematics.*

For more information, see Section 1.3.6: Unit Boxes.

Variables in Formulas

A *formula* uses variables to state concisely a relationship that would otherwise require many words to describe. For example, *The area of a rectangle can be found by multiplying the length of the rectangle times the width* may be written as the formula $A = l \times w$, or simply $A = lw$.

It is important to keep track of the units associated with the variables in formulas and to make sure that those units are consistent with the relationship expressed by the formula. For example, an area formula for a rectangle will not give a correct result if the length is measured in feet and the width in meters. In Grades 1 through 3, children use unit boxes to help them develop the habit of thinking about units.

In formulas with three variables, such as $A = lw$, if the values of any two variables are known, the value of the third variable can be calculated. A similar rule applies to relationships expressed with a greater number of variables; if a formula has n variables, then knowing values for $n - 1$ of them lets you calculate the remaining value.

Variables in Properties of Numbers and Operations

Variables are also used to express basic mathematical *properties.* For example, the *turn-around rule for addition* says that adding two numbers in either order results in the same sum. Expressed with variables, the turn-around rule is $a + b = b + a$, or, more formally, "For any two numbers a and b, $a + b = b + a$."

NOTE: A less child-friendly name for the turn-around rule for addition is the Commutative Property of Addition.

Variables in Functions

An important use of variables in higher mathematics is to write *functions.* Simply defined, a function is a rule that gives a certain output for a given input. For example, "Add 2" is a simple function relating a set of input numbers with a set of output numbers. Using variables, this function can be written *output* = *input* + 2 or $y = x + 2$, where x represents a number in the input set and y represents the corresponding number in the output set.

In *Kindergarten* through *Third Grade Everyday Mathematics,* children explore functions through function machines and by playing "What's My Rule?"

For more information, see Section 17.1.4: Functions.

In fourth through sixth grades, students make tables of values for functions such as $y = x + 2$. Then they graph the ordered pairs from the table and connect the points to get a picture of the relationship, in this case, a line.

Variables as Storage Locations

In computer programs, variables serve as names for *memory locations* where values are stored. Computer variables may consist of more than one letter; often they name the quantity being stored. For example, *price* might name the location of the current price of an item. INPUT *price* in some computer languages means to place a value into the storage location *price.* To find a price plus 8% sales tax, the computer could calculate 1.08 * *price,* where * means multiply.

17.2.2 Reading and Writing Open Sentences

Just as English words are more meaningful when they are in sentences, mathematical symbols are more meaningful in number sentences. And just as proper punctuation and grammar make written English easy to read, rules and conventions for reading and writing number sentences ease mathematical communication.

Number sentences such as $10 = 7 + 3$, $12 \div n = 6$, and $14 > 3$ have a left-hand side, a relation symbol, and a right-hand side. Symbols for numbers, unknowns, and operations can appear on either side of the relation symbol. Each side of a number sentence is a *numerical expression.* In the sentences above, 10, $7 + 3$, $12 \div n$, 6, 14, and 3 are expressions. In practice, however, single numbers are usually just called "numbers" and expressions usually include one or more operations.

Equations are number sentences in which the relation symbol is =, meaning *equals* or *is equal to.*

chapter 17

Inequalities are number sentences in which the relation symbol is one of the following:

$<$ (*is less than*)	$\leq$ (*is less than or equal to*)
$>$ (*is greater than*)	$\geq$ (*is greater than or equal to*)
$\neq$ (*is not equal to*)	$\approx$ (*is approximately equal to*)

A number phrase with a variable but no relation symbol, such as $3 + y$, is called an *algebraic expression* or simply an *expression.* A single number, called a *constant,* or a product of a constant and one or more variables is a *term* of an expression. Terms are operated on in expressions, if they are not the whole expression itself. For example, in the expression $75 + 3x$, the terms are 75 and $3x$. In $y = 3x$, the expression $3x$ is also a term.

An *open sentence* is a number sentence that is neither true nor false because it contains a variable or unknown. Examples are $14 = t - 9$ and $81 + c < 100$. Any number can replace the variable. A number that makes an open sentence *true* is called a *solution* of the sentence. The process of determining a value or values for a variable that make a number sentence true is called *solving the sentence.*

In *Everyday Mathematics,* children in first grade encounter unknowns in situation diagrams. These diagrams display the numbers in number stories so that the quantitative relationships are easier to understand. For example, a parts-and-total diagram models the problem below. The empty cell in a diagram represents the unknown, or the variable.

Total		
?		
Part	Part	Part
12	8	5

> Twelve fourth graders, 8 third graders, and 5 first graders are on a bus. How many students in all are on the bus?

First-grade teachers are encouraged to write open sentences to model number stories using blanks or question marks for variables. For the example above, a teacher might write $12 + 8 + 5 = \_\_$ or $? = 12 + 8 + 5$. Beginning in second grade, children write their own open sentences using blanks and question marks. In fourth grade, students use letter variables.

in perspective

Open sentences with inequalities are introduced in fourth grade. The terms *expression* and *equation* are introduced in fifth grade. In fifth and sixth grades, students begin to solve open number sentences using algebraic manipulations. Various forms of variables and names for open sentences are used so students become familiar with a variety of mathematical symbols and with algebraic language.

17.2.3 Solving Open Sentences

In *Kindergarten* through *Third Grade Everyday Mathematics,* number models are used primarily to represent quantities and relationships in number stories and to help children understand them. For example, before solving a number story like *Marie has $5. She wants to go to a movie that costs $8. How much more does she need?* a child might write the number model $5 + ? = 8$. The model shows the relationships between the quantities in the story and suggests finding the answer by counting up or thinking of an addition fact. After solving the story, the child might write $5 + 3 = 8$ to summarize his work. Learning to use number models to represent number stories helps children learn the mathematical symbol system that is the foundation of algebra.

In later grades, more complicated equations are treated informally through such puzzles as *I am the number* m *in* $6 + 5 \times m = 16$. *What number am I?* Solving this puzzle requires knowing that the order of operations dictates that m be multiplied by 5 before 6 is added. Children are encouraged to clarify this by rewriting the number sentence as $6 + (5 \times m) = 16$. Children solve such puzzles by trial and error or by working backward. Solving equations by formal algebraic manipulations is not part of *Kindergarten* through *Third Grade Everyday Mathematics.*

in perspective

Beginning in *Fifth Grade Everyday Mathematics,* students are introduced to a pan-balance metaphor for solving equations. The example below models $3x + 14 = 23$. The metaphor is first presented concretely, with objects of different weights distributed on both sides of a pan balance and children attempting to keep the balance level while removing weights. This leads to applying the same operation to both sides of an equation to obtain a form in which a solution is more obvious.

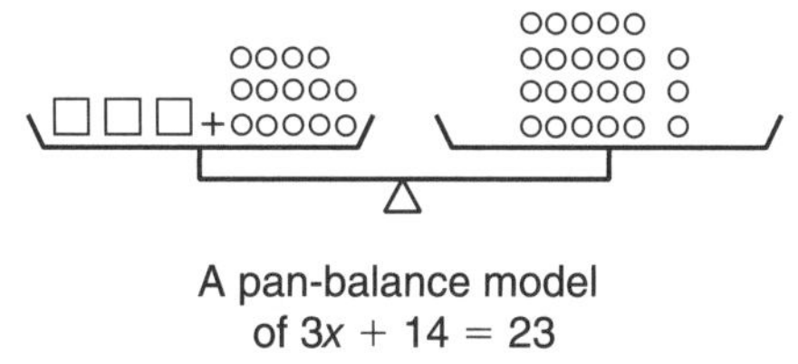

A pan-balance model of $3x + 14 = 23$

References and Resources for Patterns, Sequences, Functions, and Algebra

Coxford, A. F., and Shulte, A. P. (1988). *The Ideas of Algebra, K–12: 1988 Yearbook.* Reston, VA: National Council of Teachers of Mathematics.

Friedlander, A., and Tabach, M. (2001). “Promoting Multiple Representations in Algebra.” In Cuoco, A. A., and Curcio, F. R. (Eds.) *The Roles of Representation in School Mathematics: 2001 Yearbook.* Reston, VA: National Council of Teachers of Mathematics.

Kalchman, M., and Koedinger, K. R. (2005). “Teaching and Learning Functions.” In Donovan, M., and Bransford, J. (Eds.) *How Students Learn: History, Mathematics, and Science in the Classroom.* Washington, DC: The National Academies Press.

Problem Solving

Contents

chapter 18

In 1977, the National Council of Supervisors of Mathematics issued a position paper on basic skills. The first basic skill listed was *problem solving:* "Learning to solve problems is the principal reason for studying mathematics" (NCSM, 1977, p. 20). Ever since, problem solving has remained at the top of the school mathematics agenda.

This chapter is about problem solving and how *Everyday Mathematics* teaches it. It first examines different definitions of problem solving and explains what problem solving means in *Everyday Mathematics.* This is followed by a discussion of ways mathematical ideas can be represented (concretely, pictorially, verbally, and symbolically) and what such representations have to do with problem solving. Next is an explanation of what mathematical modeling is and its relationship to problem solving. The chapter closes with details about teaching problem solving in *Everyday Mathematics* and a list of resources to help you learn more about this important mathematical thread.

18.1 What Is Problem Solving?

In elementary school mathematics books, *problem solving* often refers only to finding answers to printed "word problems." But problem solving is much more than that. In the NCSM position paper cited above, problem solving is defined as "the process of applying previously acquired knowledge to new and unfamiliar situations." In *Principles and Standards for School Mathematics,* the National Council of Teachers of Mathematics (NCTM) states that problem solving "is finding a way to reach a goal that is not immediately attainable" (NCTM, 2000, p. 116). In his classic book *How to Solve It,* George Polya wrote, "Solving a problem is finding the unknown means to a distinctly conceived end" (1988, p. 1).

These broader definitions of problem solving are not restricted to arithmetic and certainly not to arithmetic "word problems." Central to all of them is the idea that solution methods are not known in advance. A problem is not a problem if the problem solver knows exactly what to do right away. "Problems" for which the solution method is known ahead of time are simply exercises.

NOTE: A comprehensive curriculum like *Everyday Mathematics* must include many exercises so children can practice essential skills. But they are not genuine problems in the sense implied here.

In *Everyday Mathematics,* problem solving is broadly conceived. Number stories, the program's version of word problems, have their place, but problem solving permeates the entire curriculum. Children solve problems both in purely mathematical contexts, such as "What's My Rule?" tables, and in real situations from the classroom and everyday life. Children also create and solve problems using information from the materials, from you, and from their own experiences and imaginations.

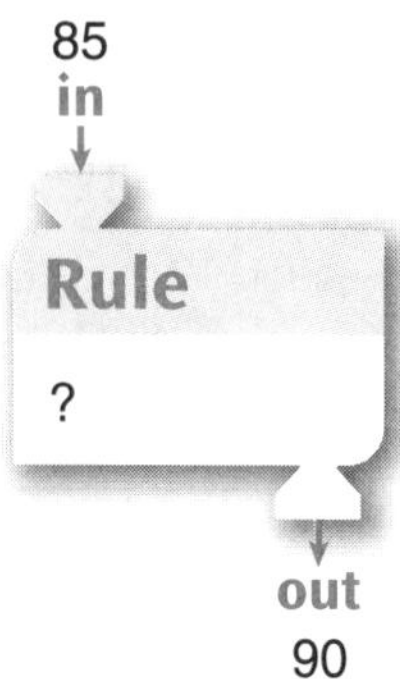

in	out
55	60
85	90
103	108

A "What's My Rule?" problem

Everyday Mathematics defines problem solving as "the process of modeling everyday situations to find solutions using tools from mathematics." Mathematical modeling is discussed in detail in Section 18.3, but, in a nutshell, it means that expert problem solvers generally do one or more of these things:

- Identify what the problem is;
- Analyze what is known and seek out further data as necessary;
- Play with the data to discover patterns and meaning;
- Identify and apply mathematical techniques to find a solution;
- Look back after finding a solution to ask whether it makes sense and whether the method can be applied to other problems.

18.2 Problem Representations

Often a key step in solving a problem is simply looking at it in the right way. Consider the problem *How many handshakes are there when five people shake hands with one another?* Some ways to solve this problem are listed here.

NOTE: In mathematics, the word *solution* has two related meanings. One meaning is *the answer.* The other is *how the answer was obtained.* Usually the context makes clear which meaning is intended, but you may find it useful to call a final result an "answer" and the method used to get the result the "solution."

- Find five people and have them shake hands, being careful to count each handshake. This approach is, to say the least, not very convenient.
- Make a list. If the people are represented by the letters A, B, C, D, and E, the handshakes could be listed as follows: A-B, A-C, A-D, A-E, B-C, B-D, B-E, C-D, C-E, and D-E. Although this is practical for five people, it could be troublesome for larger numbers, as you might make a mistake in listing all the handshakes.
- Draw a picture of a pentagon with all its diagonals. Each corner stands for a person, and each line connecting two people stands for a handshake. Finding a mistake in such a figure may be easier than finding one in a long list, although it might be a nuisance to draw the figure for a large number of people.

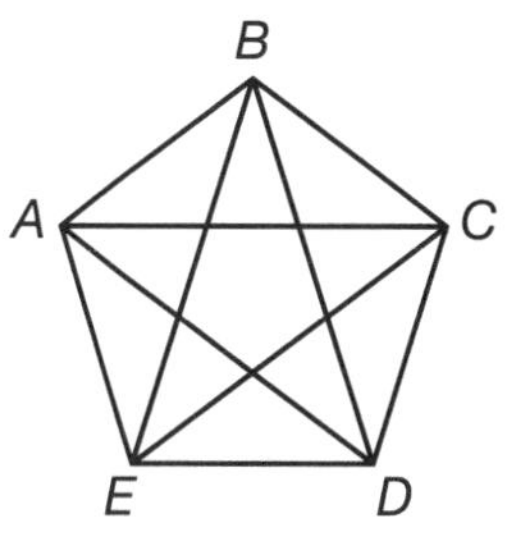

Each of these solutions to the handshake problem depends on a different way of approaching, or representing, the problem. One way used real people; another involved a list; the third made use of a drawing. Different ways of approaching a problem are called *problem representations.*

Everyday Mathematics focuses on four problem representations: *concrete, verbal, pictorial,* and *symbolic.* Suppose, for example, you need a dozen eggs to make egg salad, but when you take the eggs out of the refrigerator, you drop the carton on the floor. That's a *concrete* situation. A *verbal* description might make certain details explicit, such as *Oh no! I broke seven of them!* A *pictorial* representation like the one in the margin could show the unfortunate eggs, and symbolically, you could write the number model $12 - 7 = 5$.

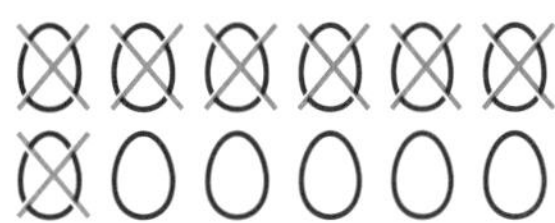

For examples of four problem representations of functions, see Section 17.1.4: Functions.

These varieties of problem representations are diagrammed below. Note that double-headed arrows connect each kind of representation with each of the other kinds. Children and adults are likely to use all of these representations at one time or another, depending on the situation at hand.

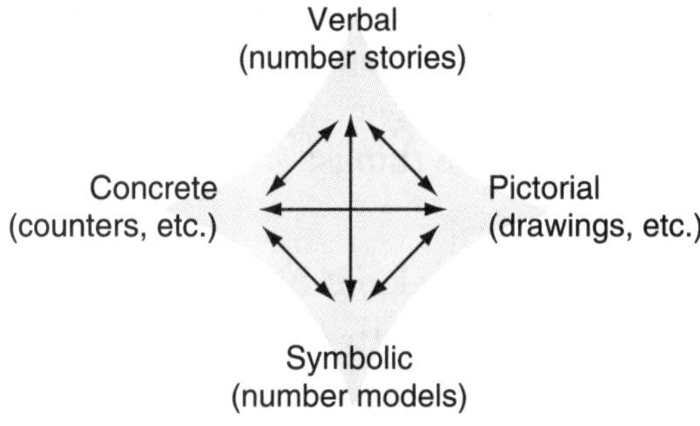

Four problem-solving representations

Representations are used both to give problems and to model solutions. Different children have different talents for, and preferences among, the representations, so all children benefit from repeated exposures to all four types. One of the aims of *Everyday Mathematics* is to increase children's facility with a variety of representations.

Another objective in *Everyday Mathematics* is to help children make easy translations among various ways of representing problems. Representations are closely related to solution strategies; translating a problem into another representation is often a key to solving it. Discussion of different representations and solutions exposes children to methods they may like to try and reinforces the important message that there are many ways to solve problems.

As you discuss problems and solutions with children, compare various representations and ask for translations from one to another. For example:

- Ask children to draw a picture for a problem given in words.
- If a child solves $25 + 36$ by counting up on a number grid, ask her to solve $35 + 42$ by just thinking about the grid rather than by using an actual grid.
- Ask children to translate a situation diagram into an open number sentence with a ? or __ for the unknown.

in perspective

In Grades 4 through 6, students extend their use of symbolic representations by writing and solving open sentences and their use of pictorial representations by drawing and interpreting coordinate graphs.

NOTE: Individual differences are likely to lead some children, and even teachers, to favor some representations over others. For example, ELL or hearing-impaired children may be less likely to favor verbal representations. Be careful not to over-emphasize the need for all children to explore all the representations.

By encouraging multiple representations and translations among representations, you can help children develop into more powerful problem solvers.

As you observe children working with various representations, you can also determine their problem-solving strengths and weaknesses. In turn, this can help you tailor activities to meet individual needs. For example, you might observe that a certain child always uses counters to solve problems. This might lead you to suggest drawing a simple picture of the counters. Or a child who is adept at drawing pictures might benefit from a suggestion to try using a number grid.

NOTE: Using pictures to represent problems and solutions can be especially helpful for children who are having difficulty with other representations. Use simple pictures and diagrams to illustrate classroom discussions as much as possible.

For more information on problem representations, see *The Roles of Representation in School Mathematics* edited by Cuoco and Curcio (2001). A full reference is on page 230.

18.3 Mathematical Modeling

A *mathematical model* is something mathematical that corresponds to something in the real or imaginary world. A sphere is a model for a basketball. The number sentence $22 + 1 = 23$ is a model for the number of children in a classroom when a new student arrives. The equation $d = (5 \text{ hours}) \times (50 \text{ miles/hour})$ is a model for the distance a car travels in 5 hours at 50 mph; and the formula $d = rt$ is a model linking distance, rate (speed), and time more generally. Specialists in science and industry spend much of their time building and testing mathematical models of real-world systems. Some people do mathematical modeling whenever they use mathematics to solve a problem.

NOTE: The word *model* can also refer to something in the real world that illustrates something mathematical. In this sense, a basketball is a model of a sphere. When people speak of mathematical modeling, however, the model is the mathematical object and the thing that is modeled is something in the real or hypothetical world.

Put another way, *mathematical modeling* is a process of translating a real or hypothetical situation into mathematical language. After the translation, a solution is found using mathematical techniques. Then the result is translated back into the real or hypothetical world as the answer to the original problem. This process is illustrated in the margin.

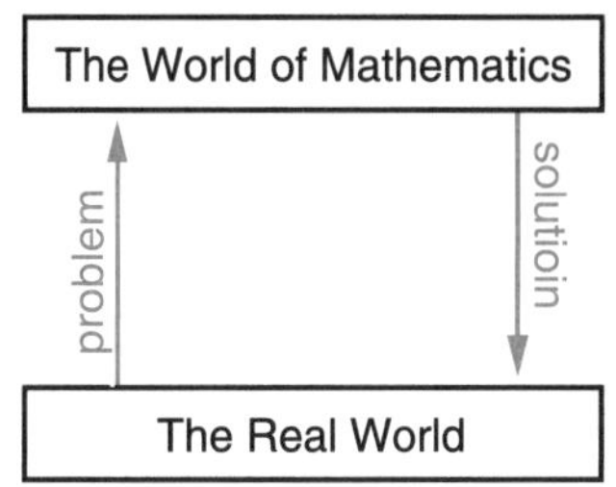

Mathematical modeling

Yet the figure in the margin probably oversimplifies the process. Mathematical modeling is often more complicated and is likely to involve some or all of the following stages:

- Formulate or confront a problem. Try to understand your problem. What do you want to find out? Imagine what the answer would look like if you had one.
- Study the information that is given and seek additional data as necessary. Discard unnecessary information. Sort the data you have.
- Explore the data. Represent the data in various ways, perhaps by drawing a picture, making a graph, or writing a number model. Play with the data.
- Do the math. Do the arithmetic, algebra, geometry, data analysis, or whatever else is necessary to find an answer.
- Check the answer to see if it makes sense. Compare your answer to someone else's or to an answer you obtain in another way. Think about the method you used. Can the same method be used to solve other problems? Is there another method that would work for this problem? Compare various solutions and methods.

These stages of the mathematical-modeling process are summarized in the diagram on the next page.

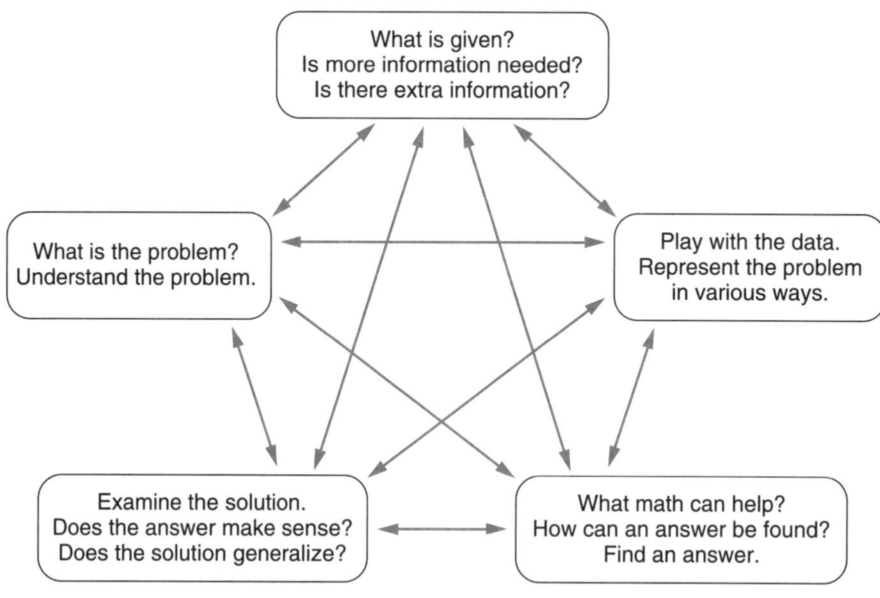

Stages in the mathematical-modeling process

NOTE: In *Everyday Mathematics,* the problem-solving process often begins with information from a journal or *Student Reference Book* page. Children use the information to make up their own problems, which they or their classmates solve.

The process of mathematical modeling can actually begin anywhere and go anywhere. The arrows in the figure above illustrate this. For example, mathematical modeling often begins with data. Suppose you are a baseball fan and are studying tables of baseball statistics. As you explore the data, you might notice that it appears that in inter-league games, National League teams win more often than American League teams. This might lead you to ask whether this is actually true. By finding the total number of wins for each league, you might find that the National League does win more often. If you wished, you could test your conclusion by making a prediction about the next set of inter-league games.

This baseball situation involves all five stages of the mathematical-modeling process. Sometimes, only a few of the stages are involved. An expert problem solver, or a child for that matter, might see a solution to a problem instantly and simply have to check that it's correct. Sometimes it may be necessary to cycle repeatedly among the stages—play with the data, find more data, play with the new data, and so on—before finding a solution.

Mathematical modeling involves *abstraction.* For example, the number model $100 - 79 = 21$ is an abstraction of buying a 79¢ granola bar with a dollar bill. The modeling process involves both a real situation and an abstract mathematical model of that situation. Even a mathematical model that uses concrete physical objects, such as base-10 blocks, is abstract in the sense that it omits many details of the original situation. Because it is abstract, a single mathematical model can fit many different real-world situations. For example, the formula for the area of a rectangle, $A = lw$ (area A equals length l times width w), applies to all real-world rectangles. This versatility is part of what makes mathematics such a powerful problem-solving tool.

However, because they are abstract, mathematical models can become disconnected from the situation they are meant to model. Sometimes, children work their way through a mathematical process, arrive at an answer that makes no sense, and are completely unconcerned that they have produced nonsense. Making frequent connections between the real situation and the abstract model can help keep the process on track. Encourage children to ask themselves questions to keep the modeling process grounded: *What does this number refer to? What does this graph say about the problem situation? Does this solution make sense?*

One reason for making ballpark estimates is to keep the problem-solving process on track. If a solution doesn't agree with the estimate, then something is wrong either with the estimate or with the solution. Making ballpark estimates helps reinforce connections between mathematical abstractions and real-world situations.

18.4 Teaching Problem Solving

Often when you are trying to learn something complicated, it is a good idea to focus on just one part of the whole. A pianist might play a difficult passage over and over again; a chef might practice making a *roux* until it's just right; a golfer might spend hours working on 8-foot putts. Practicing just one part at a time helps develop component skills that are essential for mastery of the entire complex activity, whether it's piano playing, cooking, or golfing.

As the mathematical-modeling-process diagram illustrates, problem solving is a complicated activity that can be broken down into parts, such as formulating problems and playing with data, each of which children can practice separately. Many of the exercises in *Everyday Mathematics* aim to provide practice in specific parts of the problem-solving process. For example, children become skilled at counting, measuring, calculating, estimating, looking up information, and many other skills that are useful in solving problems. During their years in school, children thus learn how to be effective in each separate stage of the mathematical-modeling process.

Such instruction is effective in teaching children how to manage each individual stage of the process, but successful problem solving in real life requires experience in navigating among the stages, just as cooking a fine meal requires successfully orchestrating many separate steps. It may take years of experience to become proficient at navigating among the stages. Knowing when to abandon an approach that's not working and go back to playing with the data, for example, is a skill that develops with experience.

As children progress through *Everyday Mathematics,* they confront or pose problems that are more interesting and less routine, that make use of more sophisticated skills and concepts, and that require more complicated navigation through the mathematical-modeling process.

18.4.1 Number Stories

Everyday Mathematics aims to help children deal with real, age-appropriate problems. The authors' research shows that young children have impressive but largely untapped problem-solving abilities.

One way *Everyday Mathematics* works to expand these abilities is through the use of number stories.

Number stories are stories that involve numbers and one or more explicit or implicit questions. For example:

- *I have 7 crayons in my desk. Carrie gave me 8 more crayons. How many crayons do I have in all? There are 15 crayons in all.*
- *I have 7 crayons in my desk. Carrie gave me 8 more crayons. Now I have 15 crayons in all.*

Number stories may be written, oral, pictorial, or even dramatic. They may be created by you or by the children. Stories may arise spontaneously from classroom situations or be designed to practice specific problem-solving techniques. For example you might tell a rate story in order to introduce or practice using a rate diagram.

in perspective

Beginning in fourth grade, students also write and tell stories based on reference materials, sections of the *Student Reference Book,* including the World Tour and American Tour sections, and data from experiments they perform.

Starting with *Kindergarten Everyday Mathematics,* children create number stories based on everyday experiences. In Kindergarten through Grade 3, many of the children's stories are based on journal pages that present a range of numerical data related to real situations such as animal measures, shopping for groceries, and vending machines.

Problem posing, that is, making up problems, is a part of the problem-solving process that is often ignored in school mathematics; yet identifying and defining the problem is often the crucial first step toward a solution. Problem posing also leads to a high level of enthusiasm and involvement because children feel they have ownership of the problems they themselves create. Because the information presented tends to cover a wide range of difficulty, all members of the class have opportunities to participate.

Children enjoy hearing and telling number stories. You might consider devoting an occasional language arts lesson to working with number stories. Creating, sharing, and discussing number stories can help develop children's communication and listening skills as well as their problem-solving abilities. The careful reading required for solving number stories helps children develop skills that will serve them well when they deal with technical text in later years.

Number stories provide a bridge from natural to symbolic language. Children in Kindergarten and Grade 1 can be helped across that bridge if you follow these steps:

- Introduce number stories using a situation that is familiar to the children. Keep the stories short and the language simple. Be aware that when children tell their own stories, this is not always easy to do. Draw pictures or diagrams whenever possible to illustrate the stories. Modeling with concrete objects is effective with all ages and essential with younger children.
- Begin to include occasional mathematical terms in your comments on children's stories. For example, *You told an addition story. You had 5 candies and then you added 3 more.*

- Begin writing number models beneath your illustrations as you discuss the stories. Connect the numbers and relation symbols in the number models to quantities and actions in the stories. For example, *This 5 is for the candies you started with. + 3 means you got 3 more, 8 tells how many you ended up with, and = means that 8 is the same as 5 and 3 more.* Help children understand how the symbols fit the problem situation. Explain that symbols let them write a number story quickly and easily. *If you write it in words, it takes a long time and might fill the board.*
- Children may begin writing number models to fit stories. Often more than one number model can fit a given number story. Some first-grade children may begin to use diagrams for parts-and-total, change, and comparison stories, although this is not expected until second grade.

Many first-grade teachers report that children enjoy trying to put their stories into words. For many children, it appears that skill at writing stories develops later than the ability to write number models using +, −, and =. But by second grade, most children are able to write number stories. Younger children can tell or dictate stories before they can write them, or they can draw pictures and write a few words or numbers for their stories.

perspective

By fourth grade, students consistently use variables in number models for number stories.

In all grades, writing provides opportunities for students to analyze their own thinking, to reflect upon their thoughts, and to organize information for themselves. It also gives you a great additional way to assess students' understanding of ideas and concepts.

Children use a variety of methods to solve one another's number stories, but *Everyday Mathematics* encourages using mental arithmetic whenever possible. This does not mean restricting children to doing the arithmetic entirely in their heads. Instead, children should develop a variety of flexible solution strategies that use whatever means are familiar and comfortable, such as manipulatives, jumps on a number line, doodles, diagrams, and calculators. The emphasis is on solving problems in the children's own ways, on being open to a variety of approaches, and on choosing the approach that is most appropriate for a particular problem situation.

18.4.2 Sharing Children's Strategies and Solutions

Research indicates that children develop a variety of problem-solving strategies if they are given the opportunity to share their ideas with their peers. If this sharing takes place in an open, receptive environment, children will learn that inventing creative, innovative ways of solving problems is acceptable in mathematics. The practice of gathering together to share solutions after individual or group problem solving continues throughout *Everyday Mathematics.*

For more information, see "Exploring Mathematics through Talking and Writing" by Whitin and Whitin (2000). A full reference is on page 230.

Number stories are an excellent context for developing habits of sharing. Children can share their strategies, both correct and incorrect. They can record their solutions on the board, illustrating with pictures and number models. Children develop a better understanding of various mathematical processes when asked to think and strategize rather than when they are merely asked to repeat the steps of a standard written algorithm.

Discussing children's solutions can be extremely valuable, but care should be taken to ensure that children are not embarrassed if their efforts fall short. Children with correct answers are usually happy to share their models and their strategies with the class, but discussing incorrect answers can also be very instructive. Here are several suggestions for dealing with wrong answers:

- Emphasize that it is OK to make mistakes. In fact, errors are inevitable. What is *not* OK is failing to learn from one's mistakes.
- Frame discussions of incorrect solutions by saying, *Some children in last year's class did* _____ [Describe the incorrect approach.] *Why do you think they did that? How would you help them see their mistake?*
- Emphasize that answers obtained using different methods should agree, so if there is not agreement, something must be wrong. Encourage children to resolve the dilemma.
- Compare and contrast different strategies and help children see advantages and disadvantages of each. An incorrect method may have some good ideas that can be used to improve another method.

At the beginning of each school year, *Everyday Mathematics* includes specific occasions for children to share strategies and solutions. Many other opportunities materialize over the course of the year. With practice, children eventually become comfortable sharing their strategies and are able to talk about them freely and fluently, listen to one another attentively, and revise their own strategies and adopt new ones based on these discussions.

18.4.3 Problem-Solving Strategies for Beginners

The diagram of the mathematical-modeling process shown on page 224 fits what experts actually do when they solve problems but is too complicated to be of much help for beginners. On the other hand, many elementary school mathematics textbooks include long lists of strategies and tips; but these lists are often little help even with simple real-life problems and are essentially useless for dealing with complicated problems on public policy and the workplace.

Children need a guide that is more useful than a list of tips but simpler than a diagram of expert behavior. To this end, *Kindergarten* through *Third Grade Everyday Mathematics* outlines general guidelines for managing problem solving, such as those in the margin.

Guide to Solving Number Stories

1. What do you know from reading the story?
2. What do you want to find out?
3. What do you need to do? Do it, and then record what you did.
4. If you can, write a number model that fits the problem.
5. Answer the question.
6. Check. Ask *Does my answer make sense? How do I know?*

Because problems from everyday life are usually complicated, the first need is often to simplify the situation and figure out exactly what is known and what is to be found out. For example, problem situations in daily life often contain many irrelevant numbers. Sometimes relevant numbers are missing and must be inferred or derived from what is known. Often, the problem solver must deal not only with just a few counts or measures but also with large sets of data. Considerable effort may be required to make the data consistent in format and to devise a display that suggests useful patterns or interesting questions. The process seldom follows one predictable step after another.

18.4.4 Results from *Everyday Mathematics* Teachers

Teachers who have used the approach to problem solving that is integrated into *Everyday Mathematics* report very positive results, as have researchers and program evaluators who have studied problem solving in the program. These teachers and researchers find that children develop strong, flexible, and independent calculation skills and problem-solving strategies. After using mental arithmetic with interesting number stories and relatively small numbers, children become able to operate with much larger numbers than they would typically have been able to handle. Children also develop an understanding of various mathematical processes that many children do not attain when using standard written algorithms.

Blair Chewning, an *Everyday Mathematics* teacher from Virginia, provides an example of the powerful results that this approach can yield. Ms. Chewning read an article in the *Richmond Times-Dispatch* with the headline "State, national math scores add up to poor report card." The picture painted was bleak, charging that on a recent national mathematics test, 40% of eighth-grade students failed to perform at even a basic level. The following problem was given as an example of a "basic" problem for grade 8:

> Jill needs to earn $45 for a class trip. She earns $2 each day on Mondays, Tuesdays, and Wednesdays. She earns $3 each day on Thursdays, Fridays, and Saturdays. She does not work on Sundays. How many weeks will it take her to earn $45?

Ms. Chewning was teaching second grade at the time, using *Everyday Mathematics,* and decided to see how her children would handle this problem. This is what she reported:

> Every single student attempted the problem, which was presented as optional. Such risk-takers they have become! Two children, using mental math only, presented me with the correct answer by the time I had completed writing the number story on the board. A total of 82% of the children, using a variety of strategies (see page 230), successfully solved the problem in less than five minutes. Of the three children who struggled, two were right on track, making only minor computational errors, and the third achieved success after extensive trial and error.
>
> Needless to say, I was astounded. While I had expected them to be successful to some extent, I had not anticipated the speed and comfort with which they approached the task.

Thank you, *Everyday Mathematics*. The skills your program fosters empowered my second graders to soar higher than they or their teacher thought possible. They wore the "hats" of eighth graders quite proudly that day and would seem to suggest that our math future is anything but bleak.

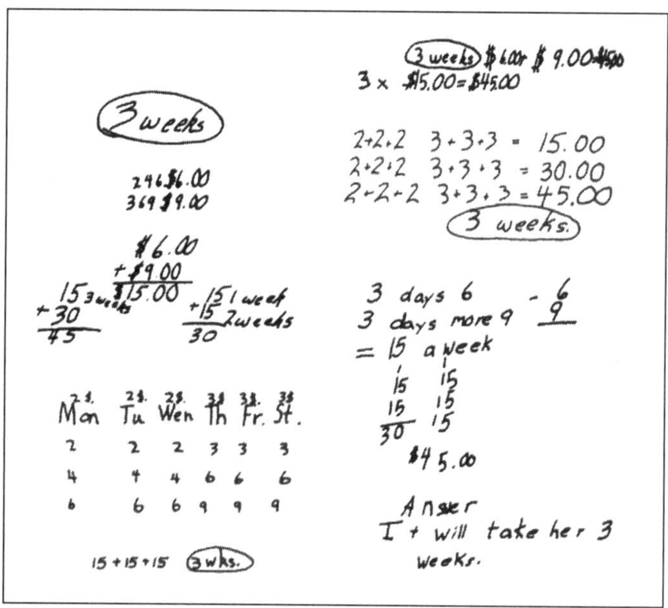

References and Resources on Problem Solving

Cuoco, A. A., and Curcio, F. R. (2001). *The Roles of Representation in School Mathematics: 2001 Yearbook.* Reston, VA: National Council of Teachers of Mathematics.

National Council of Supervisors of Mathematics. (1977). Position paper on basic skills. *Arithmetic Teacher 25 (1)*, pp. 19-22.

National Council of Supervisors of Mathematics. (1988). *Essential mathematics for the 21st century: The position of the National Council of Supervisors of Mathematics.* Minneapolis, MN: Author.

National Council of Teachers of Mathematics. (1980). *An Agenda for Action: Recommendations for School Mathematics of the 1980s.* Reston, VA: Author.

National Council of Teachers of Mathematics. (1989). *Curriculum and Evaluation Standards for School Mathematics.* Reston, VA: Author.

National Council of Teachers of Mathematics. (2000). *Principles and Standards for School Mathematics.* Reston, VA: Author.

Polya, George. (1988). *How to Solve It.* Princeton, NJ: Princeton University Press.

Whitin, D.J., and Whitin, P. (2000). "Exploring Mathematics through Talking and Writing." In Burke, M., and Curcio, F.R. (Eds.) *Learning Mathematics for a New Century: 2000 Yearbook.* Reston, VA: National Council of Teachers of Mathematics.

Glossary

This glossary contains words and phrases from *First* through *Third Grade Everyday Mathematics.* To place the definitions in broader mathematical contexts, most entries also refer to sections in this *Teacher's Reference Manual*. In a definition, terms in italics are defined elsewhere in the glossary.

absolute value The distance between a number and 0 on a *number line.* The absolute value of a positive number is the number itself, and the absolute value of a negative number is the *opposite* of the number. The absolute value of 0 is 0. The symbol for the absolute value of n is $|n|$.

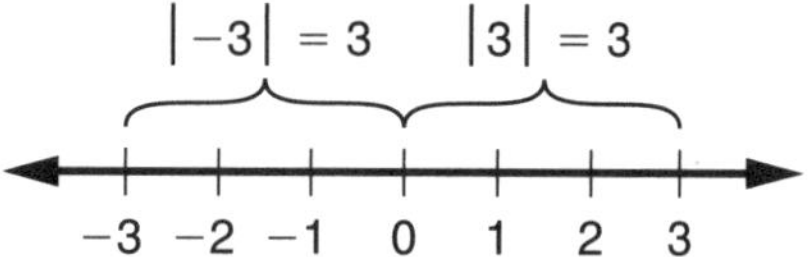

accurate As correct as possible according to an accepted standard. For example, an accurate measure or count is one with little or no error. See *precise* and Section 16.2: Approximation and Rounding.

acre A U.S. customary unit of *area* equal to 43,560 square feet. An acre is roughly the size of a football field. A square mile is 640 acres. See the Tables of Measures and Section 14.4: Area.

acute angle An *angle* with a measure less than 90°. See Section 13.4.1: Angles and Rotations.

Acute angles

acute triangle A *triangle* with three acute angles. See Section 13.4.2: Polygons (n-gons).

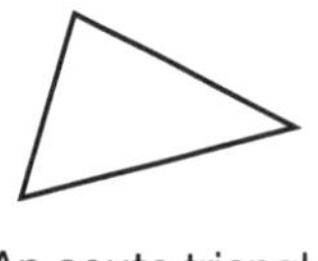

An acute triangle

addend Any one of a set of numbers that are added. For example, in $5 + 3 + 1$, the addends are 5, 3, and 1.

addition fact Two 1-digit numbers and their sum, such as $9 + 7 = 16$. See *arithmetic facts* and Section 16.3.3: Fact Practice.

addition/subtraction use class In *Everyday Mathematics,* situations in which addition or subtraction is used. These include *parts-and-total, change*, and *comparison* situations. See Section 10.2.1: Addition and Subtraction Use Classes.

additive inverses Two numbers whose sum is 0. Each number is called the additive inverse, or *opposite,* of the other. For example, 3 and −3 are additive inverses because $3 + (-3) = 0$.

adjacent angles Two *angles* with a common *side* and *vertex* that do not otherwise overlap.

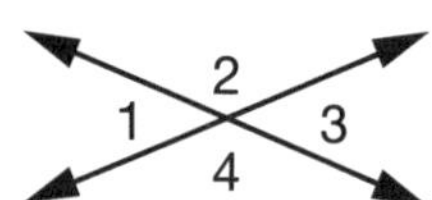

Angles 1 and 2, 2 and 3, 3 and 4, and 4 and 1 are pairs of adjacent angles.

adjacent sides Same as *consecutive sides.*

algebra (1) The use of letters of the alphabet to represent numbers in *equations, formulas,* and rules. (2) A set of rules and properties for a number system. (3) A school subject, usually first studied in eighth or ninth grade. See Section 17.2: Algebra and Uses of Variables.

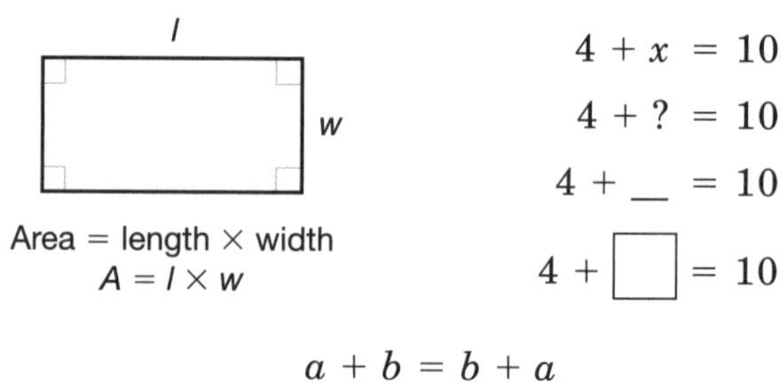

Formulas, equations, and properties using algebra

algebraic expression An *expression* that contains a *variable.* For example, if Maria is 2 inches taller than Joe and if the variable M represents Maria's height, then the algebraic expression $M - 2$ represents Joe's height. See *algebra* and Section 17.2: Algebra and Uses of Variables.

algebraic order of operations Same as *order of operations.*

algorithm A set of step-by-step instructions for doing something, such as carrying out a computation or solving a problem. The most common algorithms are those for basic arithmetic computation, but there are many others. Some mathematicians and many computer scientists spend a great deal of time trying to find more efficient algorithms for solving problems. See Chapter 11: Algorithms.

altitude (1) In *Everyday Mathematics,* same as *height* of a figure. (2) Distance above sea level. Same as *elevation.*

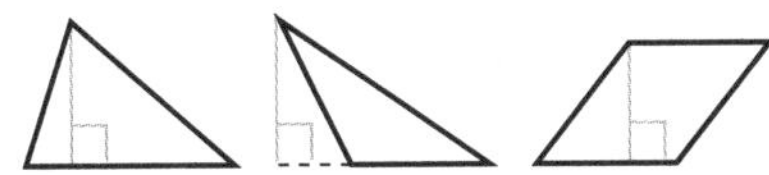

Altitudes of 2-D figures are shown in blue.

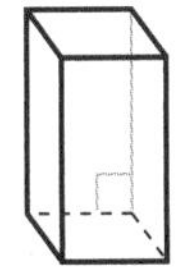

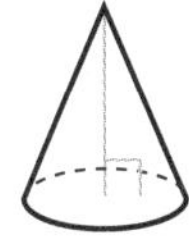

Altitudes of 3-D figures are shown in blue.

A.M. The abbreviation for *ante meridiem,* meaning "before the middle of the day" in Latin. From midnight to noon.

analog clock (1) A clock that shows the time by the positions of the hour and minute hands. (2) Any device that shows time passing in a continuous manner, such as a sundial. Compare to *digital clock.* See Section 15.2.1: Clocks.

An analog clock

-angle A suffix meaning *angle,* or corner.

angle A figure formed by two *rays* or two *line segments* with a common *endpoint* called the *vertex* of the angle. The rays or segments are called the *sides* of the angle. An angle is measured in degrees between 0 and 360. One side of an angle is the *rotation* image of the other side through a number of degrees. Angles are named after their vertex point alone as in $\angle A$ below; or by three points, one on each side and the vertex in the middle as in $\angle BCD$ below. See *acute angle, obtuse angle, reflex angle, right angle, straight angle,* and Section 13.4.1: Angles and Rotations.

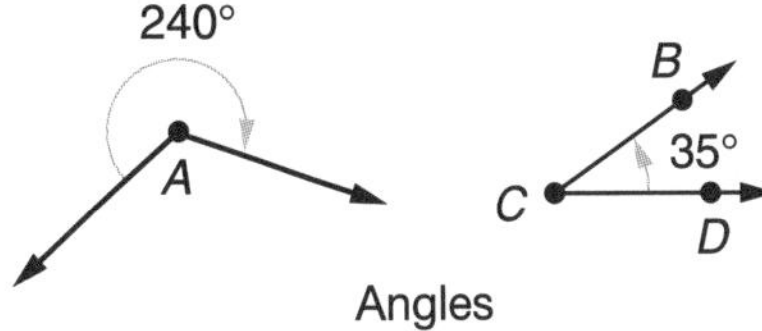

Angles

apex In a *pyramid* or *cone,* the *vertex* opposite the *base.* In a pyramid, all the nonbase faces meet at the apex. See Section 13.5.2: Polyhedrons and Section 13.5.3: Solids with Curved Surfaces.

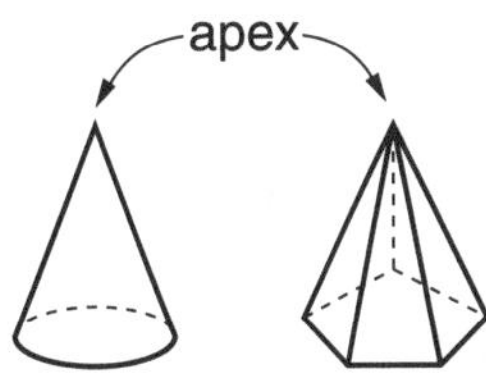

approximately equal to (≈) A symbol indicating an *estimate* or approximation to an exact value. For example, $\pi \approx 3.14$. See Section 16.2: Approximation and Rounding.

arc of a circle A part of a *circle* between and including two *endpoints* on the circle. For example, the endpoints of the *diameter* of a circle define an arc called a *semicircle.* An arc is named by its endpoints.

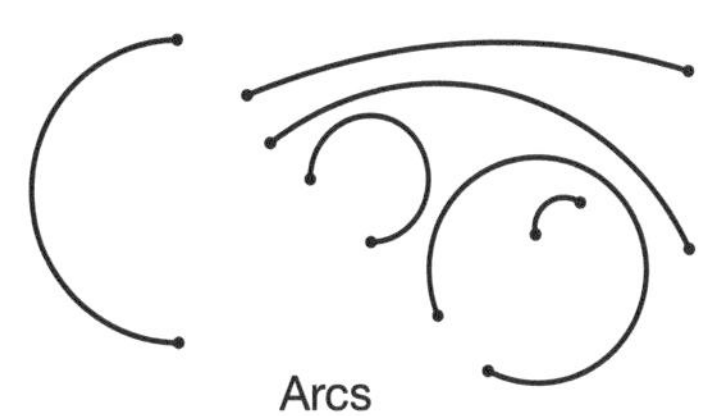

Arcs

area The amount of *surface* inside a *2-dimensional figure.* The figure might be a triangle or rectangle in a plane, the curved surface of a cylinder, or a state or country on Earth's surface. Commonly, area is measured in *square units* such as square miles, square inches, or square centimeters. See Section 14.4: Area.

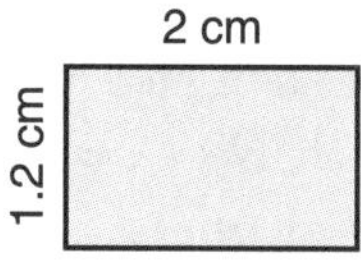

A rectangle with area 1.2 cm × 2 cm = 2.4 cm^2

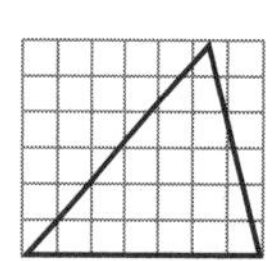

A triangle with area 21 square units

The area of the United States is about 3,800,000 square miles.

area model (1) A model for multiplication in which the *length* and *width of a rectangle* represent the *factors,* and the *area* of the rectangle represents the *product.* See Section 10.2.2: Multiplication and Division Use Classes.

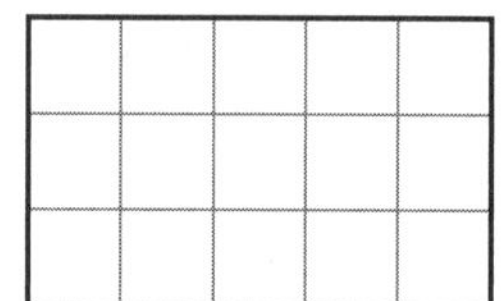

Area model for 3 × 5 = 15

(2) A model showing fractions as parts of a whole. The *whole* is a region, such as a circle or a rectangle, representing the *ONE,* or *unit whole.* See Section 9.3.2: Uses of Fractions.

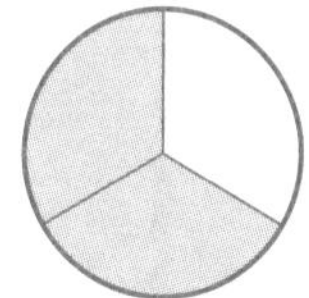

Area model for $\frac{2}{3}$

arithmetic facts The addition facts (whole-number *addends* 9 or less); their inverse subtraction facts; multiplication facts (whole-number *factors* 9 or less); and their inverse division facts, except there is no division by zero. There are

100 addition facts: 0 + 0 = 0 through 9 + 9 = 18
100 subtraction facts: 0 − 0 = 0 through 18 − 9 = 9
100 multiplication facts: 0 × 0 = 0 through 9 × 9 = 81
90 division facts: 0 ÷ 1 = 0 through 81 ÷ 9 = 9

See *extended facts, fact extensions, fact power,* and Section 16.3.2: Basic Facts and Fact Power.

arm span Same as *fathom.*

array (1) An arrangement of objects in a regular *pattern,* usually rows and columns. (2) A *rectangular array.* In *Everyday Mathematics,* an array is a rectangular array unless specified otherwise. See Section 10.2.2: Multiplication and Division Use Classes and Section 14.4: Area.

arrow rule In *Everyday Mathematics,* an operation that determines the number that goes into the next frame in a *Frames-and-Arrows* diagram. There may be more than one arrow rule per diagram. See Section 17.1.4: Functions.

arrows In *Everyday Mathematics,* the links representing the *arrow rule(s)* in a *Frames-and-Arrows* diagram. See Section 17.1.4: Functions.

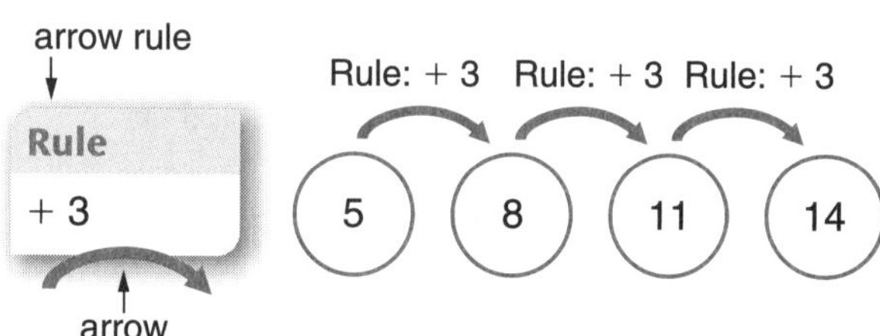

Associative Property of Addition A property of addition that three numbers can be added in any order without changing the sum. For example, (4 + 3) + 7 = 4 + (3 + 7) because 7 + 7 = 4 + 10.

In symbols:

For any numbers *a, b,* and *c,*
$(a + b) + c = a + (b + c)$.

Subtraction is not associative. For example, (4 − 3) + 7 ≠ 4 − (3 + 7) because 8 ≠ −6.

Glossary

Associative Property of Multiplication A property of multiplication that three numbers can be multiplied in any order without changing the product. For example, $(4 \times 3) \times 7 = 4 \times (3 \times 7)$ because $12 \times 7 = 4 \times 21$.

In symbols:
For any numbers a, b, and c,
$(a \times b) \times c = a \times (b \times c)$.

Division is not associative. For example, $(8 \div 2) \div 4 \neq 8 \div (2 \div 4)$ because $1 \neq 16$.

attribute A feature of an object or common feature of a set of objects. Examples of attributes include size, shape, color, and number of sides. Same as *property.*

attribute blocks A set of blocks in which each block has one each of four *attributes* including color, size, thickness, and shape. The blocks are used for attribute identification and sorting activities. Compare to *pattern blocks.*

autumnal equinox The first day of autumn, when the sun crosses the plane of Earth's equator and day and night are about 12 hours each. "Equinox" is from the Latin *aequi-* meaning "equal" and *nox* meaning "night." Compare to *vernal equinox.*

average A typical value for a set of numbers. In everyday life, average usually refers to the *mean* of the set, found by adding all the numbers and dividing the sum by the number of numbers. In statistics, several different averages, or *landmarks,* are defined, including *mean, median,* and *mode.* See Section 12.2.4: Data Analysis.

axis of a coordinate grid Either of the two *number lines* used to form a *coordinate grid.* Plural is axes. See Section 15.3: Coordinate Systems.

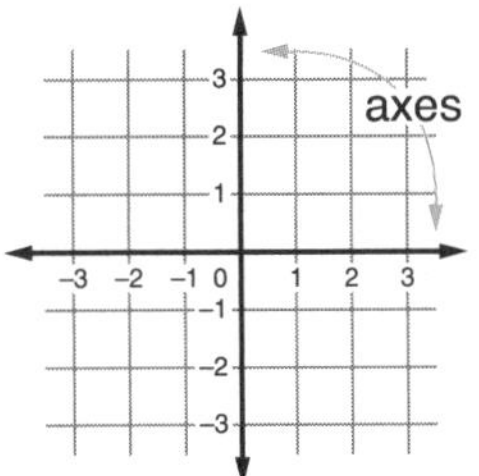

axis of rotation A line about which a solid figure rotates.

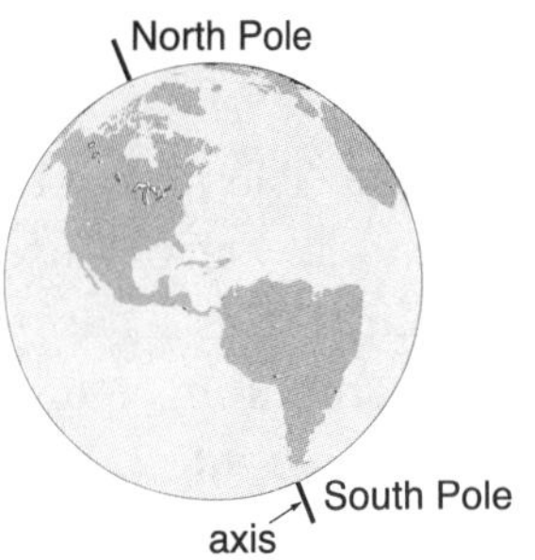

B

ballpark estimate A rough *estimate;* "in the ballpark." A ballpark estimate can serve as a check of the reasonableness of an answer obtained through some other procedure, or it can be made when an exact value is unnecessary or impossible to obtain. See Section 16.1: Estimation.

bank draft A written order for the exchange of money. For example, $1,000 bills are no longer printed so $1,000 bank drafts are issued. People can exchange $1,000 bank drafts for smaller bills, perhaps ten $100 bills.

bar graph A graph with horizontal or vertical bars that represent data. See Section 12.2.3: Organizing and Displaying Data.

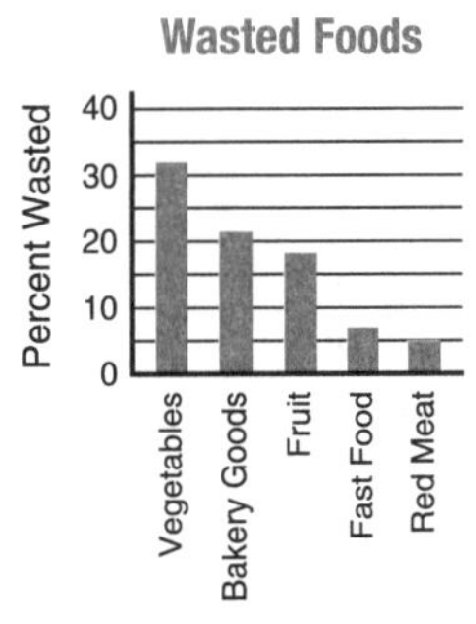

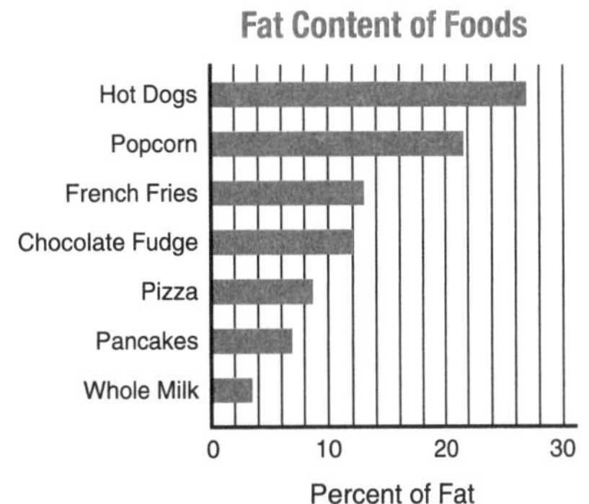

Glossary

base (in exponential notation) A number that is raised to a *power*. For example, the base in 5^3 is 5. See *exponential notation* and Section 10.1.1: Arithmetic Symbols.

base of a number system The foundation number for a *numeration* system. For example, our usual way of writing numbers uses a *base-10 place-value* system. In programming computers or other digital devices, bases of 2, 8, 16, or other powers of 2 are more common than base 10. See Section 9.2.1: Numeration and Place Value.

base of a parallelogram (1) The side of a *parallelogram* to which an *altitude* is drawn. (2) The length of this side. The area of a parallelogram is the base times the *altitude* or height perpendicular to it. See *height of a parallelogram* and Section 13.4.2: Polygons (n-gons).

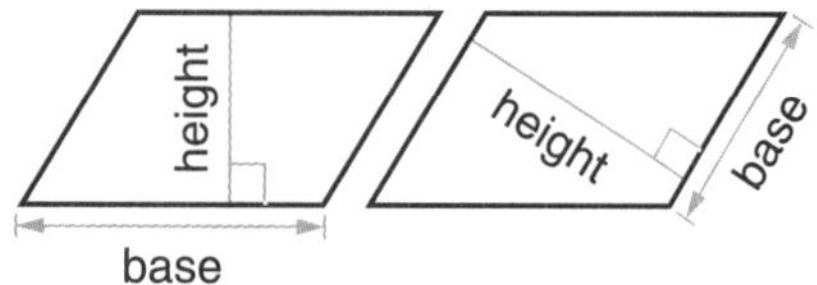

base of a prism or cylinder Either of the two parallel and congruent *faces* that define the shape of a *prism* or *cylinder.* In a cylinder, the base is a circle. See *height of a prism or cylinder,* Section 13.5.2: Polyhedrons, and Section 13.5.3: Solids with Curved Surfaces.

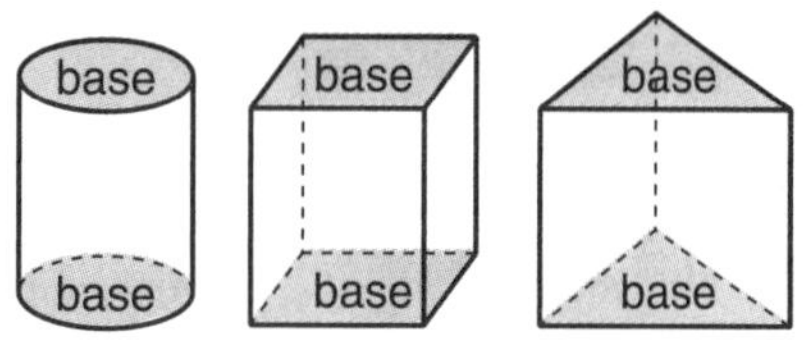

base of a pyramid or cone The *face* of a pyramid or cone that is opposite its *apex*. The base of a cone is a circle. See *height of a pyramid or cone,* Section 13.5.2: Polyhedrons, and Section 13.5.3: Solids with Curved Surfaces.

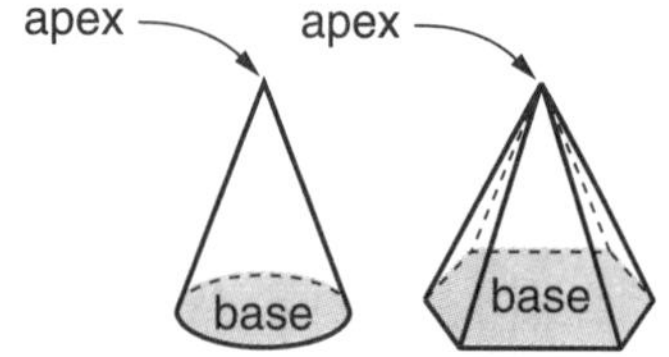

base of a rectangle (1) One of the sides of a *rectangle*. (2) The length of this side. The area of a rectangle is the base times the *altitude* or height. See *height of a rectangle* and Section 13.4.2: Polygons (n-gons).

base of a triangle (1) Any side of a *triangle* to which an *altitude* is drawn. (2) The length of this side. The area of a triangle is half the base times the altitude or height. See *height of a triangle* and Section 13.4.2: Polygons (n-gons).

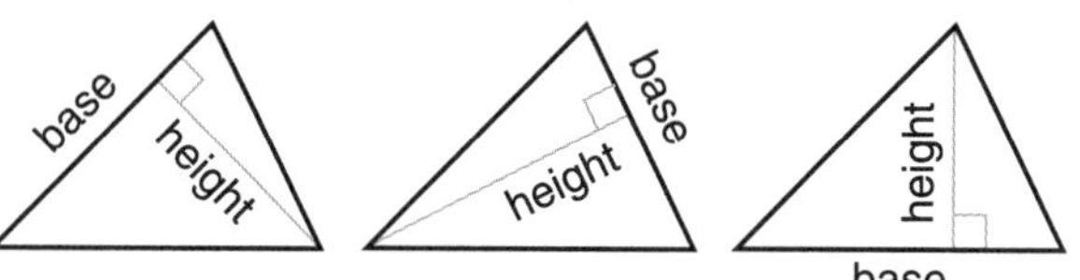

base ten Our system for writing numbers that uses only the 10 symbols 0, 1, 2, 3, 4, 5, 6, 7, 8, and 9, called *digits.* You can write any number using one or more of these 10 digits, and each digit has a value that depends on its place in the number (its *place value*). In the base-ten system, each place has a value 10 times that of the place to its right, and 1 tenth the value of the place to its left. See Section 9.2.1: Numeration and Place Value.

base-10 blocks A set of blocks to represent ones, tens, hundreds, and thousands in the *base-10 place-value* system. In *Everyday Mathematics,* the unit block, or *cube,* has 1-cm edges; the ten block, or *long,* is 10 unit blocks in length; the hundred block, or *flat,* is 10 longs in width; and the thousand block, or *big cube,* is 10 flats high. See *long, flat,* and *big cube* for photos of the blocks. See *base-10 shorthand* and Section 9.7.1: Base-10 Blocks.

Glossary

base-10 shorthand In *Everyday Mathematics,* a written notation for *base-10 blocks*. See Section 9.7.1: Base-10 Blocks.

Base-10-Block Shorthand

Name	Block	Shorthand
cube		
long		
flat		
big cube		

benchmark A count or measure that can be used to evaluate the reasonableness of other counts, measures, or estimates. A benchmark for land area is that a football field is about one acre. A benchmark for length is that the width of an adult's thumb is about one inch. See Section 14.1: Personal Measures.

big cube In *Everyday Mathematics,* a *base-10 block* cube that measures 10-cm by 10-cm by 10-cm. A big cube consists of one thousand 1-cm cubes. See Section 9.7.1: Base-10 Blocks.

A big cube

bisect To divide a segment, angle, or figure into two parts of equal measure. See *bisector.*

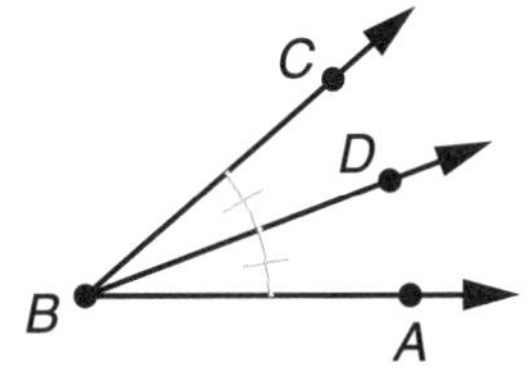

Ray *BD* bisects angle *ABC*.

bisector A *line, segment,* or *ray* that divides a segment, an angle, or a figure into two parts of equal measure. See *bisect.*

braces See *grouping symbols.*

brackets See *grouping symbols.*

broken-line graph Same as *line graph.*

C

calendar (1) A *reference frame* to keep track of the passage of time. Many different calendars exist, including the Gregorian calendar currently used by most of the Western world, the Hebrew calendar, and the Islamic calendar. See Section 15.2.2: Calendars. (2) A practical model of the reference frame, such as the large, reusable Class Calendar in *First* through *Third Grade Everyday Mathematics.* See Section 5.2: Class Calendar. (3) A schedule or listing of events.

August 2007

Sunday	Monday	Tuesday	Wednesday	Thursday	Friday	Saturday
			1 Dr's appt. 3:00	2	3	4
5	6	7	8	9	10	11
12	13 Mom's b-day	14	15	16	17	18
19	20	21	22	23	24	25
26	27	28	29	30	31	

calibrate (1) To divide or mark a measuring tool with gradations such as the degree marks on a *thermometer.* (2) To test and adjust the accuracy of a measuring tool.

capacity (1) The amount of space occupied by a *3-dimensional figure.* Same as *volume.* (2) Less formally, the amount a container can hold. Capacity is often measured in units such as quarts, gallons, cups, or liters. See Section 14.5: Volume (Capacity). (3) The maximum weight a scale can measure. See Section 14.10.3: Scales and Balances.

Celsius A *temperature scale* on which pure water at sea level freezes at 0° and boils at 100°. The Celsius scale is used in the metric system. A less common name for this scale is centigrade because there are 100 units between the freezing and boiling points of water. Compare to *Fahrenheit.* See Section 15.1.1: Temperature Scales.

census An official count of population and the recording of other demographic data such as age, gender, income, and education.

cent A penny; $\frac{1}{100}$ of a dollar. From the Latin word *centesimus,* which means "a hundredth part." See Section 14.9: Money.

cent- A prefix meaning 100, as in *century* or centennial.

center of a circle The point in the plane of a *circle* equally distant from all points on the circle. See Section 13.4.3: Circles and Pi (π).

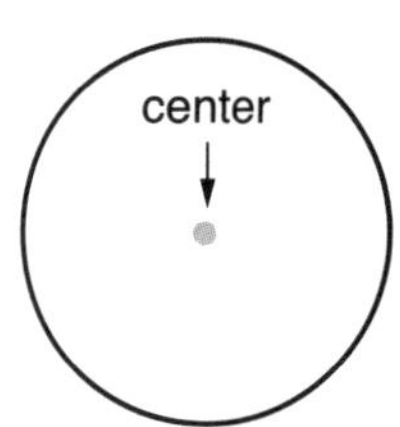

center of a sphere The point equally distant from all points on a *sphere.* See Section 13.5.3: Solids with Curved Surfaces.

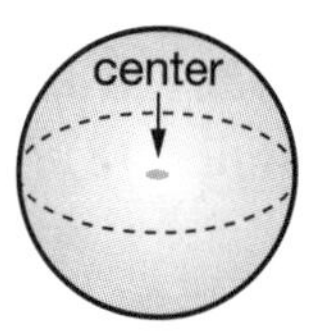

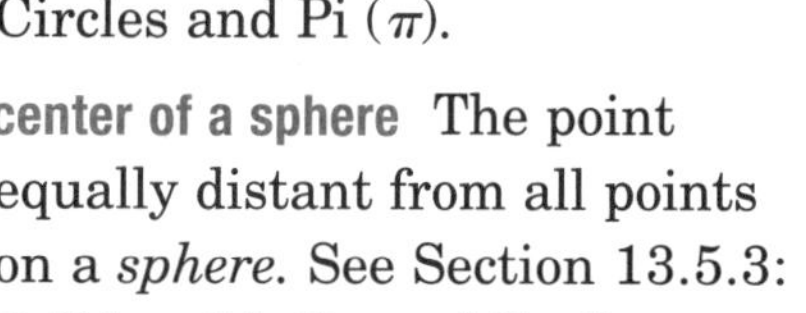

centi- A prefix meaning 1 hundredth.

centimeter (cm) A metric unit of *length* equivalent to 10 millimeters, $\frac{1}{10}$ of a decimeter, and $\frac{1}{100}$ of a meter. See the Tables of Measures and Section 14.2.2: Metric System.

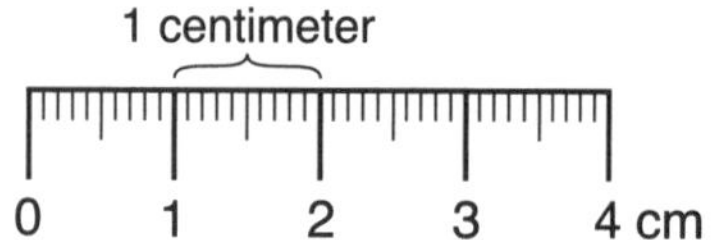

century One hundred years.

chance The possibility that an *outcome* will occur in an uncertain *event.* For example, in flipping a coin there is an equal chance of getting HEADS or TAILS. See Section 12.1.2: The Language of Chance.

change diagram A diagram used in *Everyday Mathematics* to model situations in which quantities are either increased or decreased by addition or subtraction. The diagram includes a starting quantity, an ending quantity, and an amount of change. See *situation diagram* and Section 10.2.1: Addition and Subtraction Use Classes.

A change diagram for 14 − 5 = 9

change-to-less story A *number story* about a change situation in which the ending quantity is less than the starting quantity. For example, a story about spending money is a change-to-less story. Compare to *change-to-more story.* See Section 10.2.1: Addition and Subtraction Use Classes.

change-to-more story A *number story* about a change situation in which the ending quantity is more than the starting quantity. For example, a story about earning money is a change-to-more story. Compare to *change-to-less story.* See Section 10.2.1: Addition and Subtraction Use Classes.

circle The set of all points in a *plane* that are equally distant from a fixed point in the plane called the *center* of the circle. The distance from the center to the circle is the *radius* of the circle. The *diameter* of a circle is twice its radius. Points inside a circle are not part of the circle. A circle together with its interior is called a disk or a circular region. See Section 13.4.3: Circles and Pi (π).

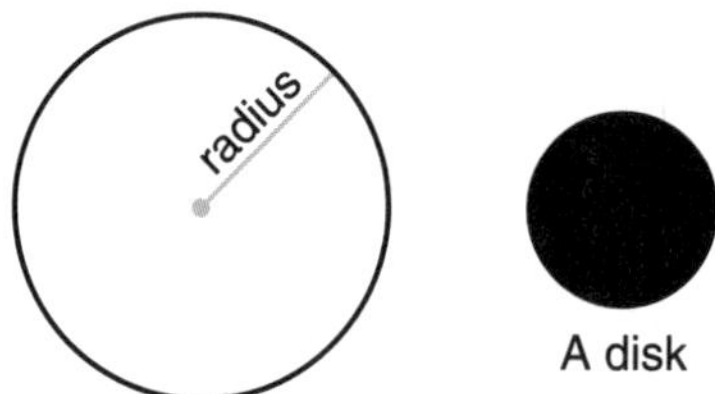

circle graph A graph in which a *circle* and its interior are divided into *sectors* corresponding to parts of a set of data. The whole circle represents the whole set of data. Same as *pie graph* and sometimes called a pie chart. See Section 12.2.3: Organizing and Displaying Data.

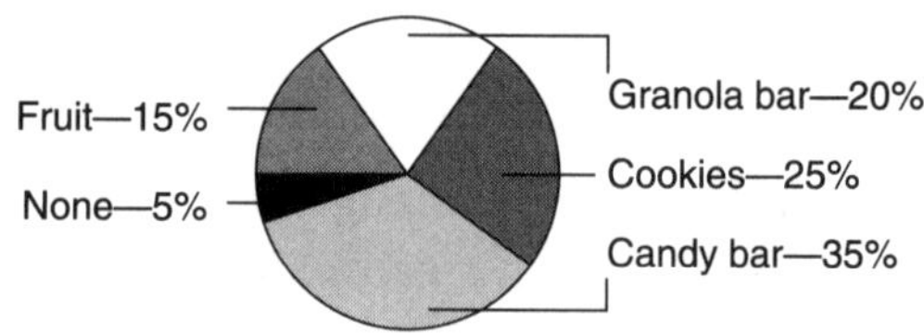

circumference The distance around a circle; its *perimeter.* The circumference of a sphere is the circumference of a circle on the sphere with the same center as the sphere. See Section 13.4.3: Circles and Pi (π) and Section 13.5.3: Solids with Curved Surfaces.

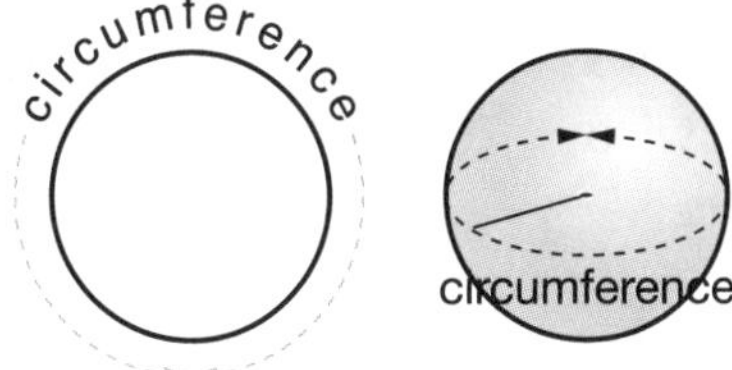

Class Data Pad In *Everyday Mathematics,* a large pad of paper used to store and recall data collected throughout the year. The data can be used for analysis, graphing, and generating number stories. See Section 5.3: Class Data Pad.

clockwise rotation The direction in which the hands move on a typical *analog clock;* a turn to the right.

column A vertical arrangement of objects or numbers in an *array* or a table.

column addition An addition *algorithm* in which the addends' digits are first added in each place-value column separately, and then 10-for-1 trades are made until each column has only one digit. Lines may be drawn to separate the place-value columns. See Section 11.2.1: Addition Algorithms.

common denominator A nonzero number that is a multiple of the *denominators* of two or more fractions. For example, the fractions $\frac{1}{2}$ and $\frac{2}{3}$ have common denominators 6, 12, 18, and other multiples of 6. Fractions with the same denominator already have a common denominator.

common factor A *factor* of each of two or more counting numbers. For example, 4 is a common factor of 8 and 12. See *factor of a counting number.*

Commutative Property of Addition A property of addition that two numbers can be added in either order without changing the sum. For example, $5 + 10 = 10 + 5$. In *Everyday Mathematics,* this is called a *turn-around fact,* and the two Commutative Properties are called *turn-around rules.*

In symbols:

For any numbers a and b, $a + b = b + a$.

Subtraction is not commutative. For example, $8 - 5 \neq 5 - 8$ because $3 \neq -3$. See Section 16.3.3: Fact Practice.

Commutative Property of Multiplication A property of multiplication that two numbers can be multiplied in either order without changing the product. For example, $5 \times 10 = 10 \times 5$. In *Everyday Mathematics,* this is called a *turn-around fact,* and the two Commutative Properties are called *turn-around rules.*

In symbols:

For any numbers a and b, $a \times b = b \times a$.

Division is not commutative. For example, $10 \div 5 \neq 5 \div 10$ because $2 \neq \frac{1}{2}$. See Section 16.3.3: Fact Practice.

comparison diagram A diagram used in *Everyday Mathematics* to model situations in which two quantities are compared by addition or subtraction. The diagram contains two quantities and their difference. See *situation diagram* and Section 10.2.1: Addition and Subtraction Use Classes.

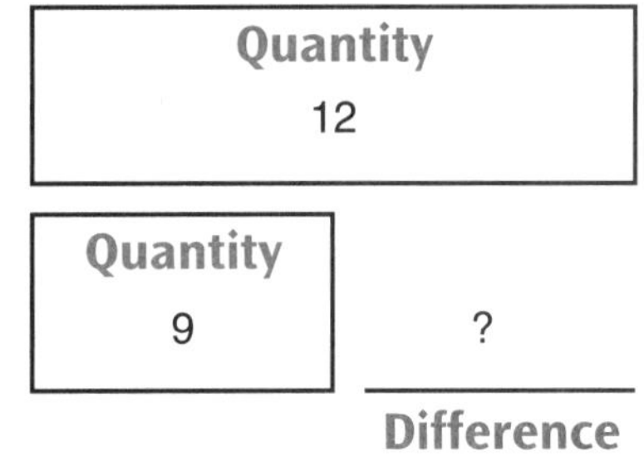

A comparison diagram for 12 = 9 + ?

comparison story A *number story* about the difference between two quantities. Comparison situations can lead to either addition or subtraction depending on whether one of the compared quantities or the difference between them is unknown. See Section 10.2.1: Addition and Subtraction Use Classes.

complement of a number *n* (1) In *Everyday Mathematics,* the difference between *n* and the next higher multiple of 10. For example, the complement of 4 is 10 − 4 = 6 and the complement of 73 is 80 − 73 = 7. (2) The difference between *n* and the next higher power of 10. In this definition, the complement of 73 is 100 − 73 = 27.

complementary angles Two *angles* whose measures add to 90°. Complementary angles do not need to be *adjacent*. Compare to *supplementary angles*.

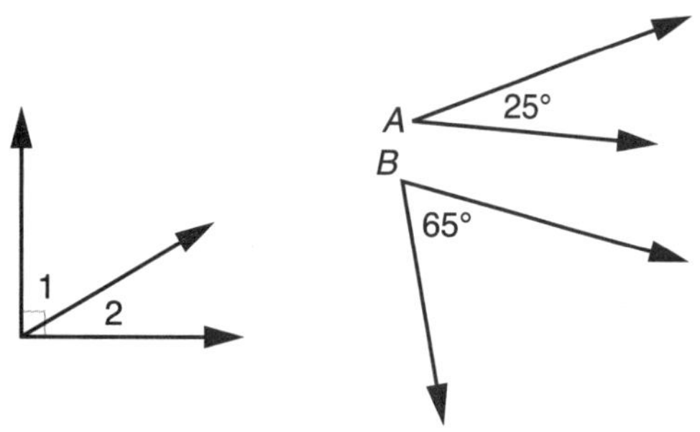

∠1 and ∠2 and ∠*A* and ∠*B* are pairs of complementary angles.

composite number A *counting number* greater than 1 that has more than two *factors*. For example, 10 is a composite number because it has four factors: 1, 2, 5, and 10. A composite number is divisible by at least three whole numbers. Compare to *prime number*.

concave polygon A *polygon* on which there are at least two points that can be connected with a *line segment* that passes outside the polygon. For example, segment *AD* is outside the hexagon between *B* and *C*. Informally, at least one vertex appears to be "pushed inward." At least one interior angle has measure greater than 180°. Same as *nonconvex polygon*. Compare to *convex polygon*. See Section 13.4.2: Polygons (*n*-gons).

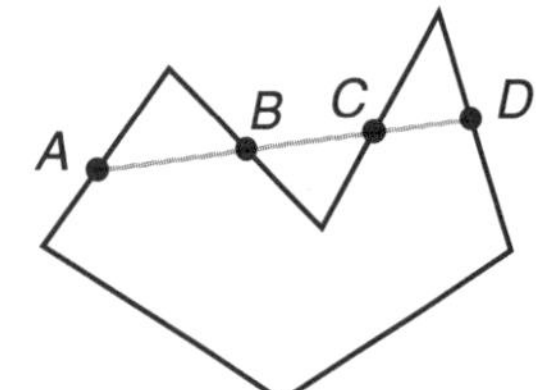

A concave polygon

concentric circles *Circles* that have the same center but radii of different lengths.

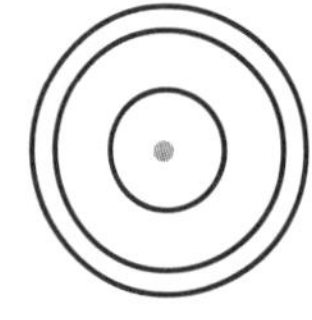

Concentric circles

cone A *geometric solid* with a circular *base,* a vertex *(apex)* not in the *plane* of the base, and all of the line segments with one endpoint at the apex and the other endpoint on the circumference of the base. See Section 13.5.3: Solids with Curved Surfaces.

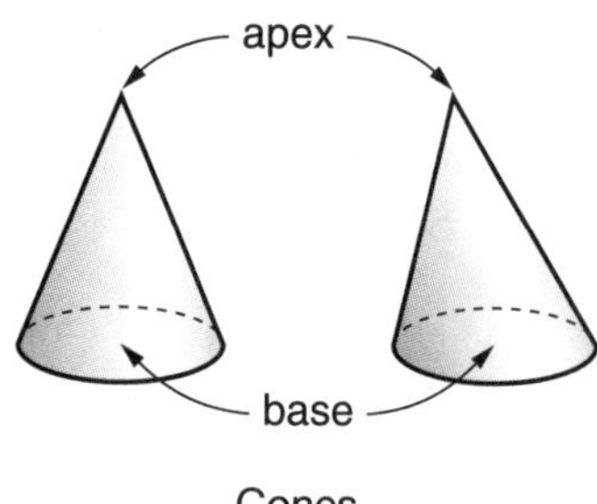

Cones

congruent figures (≅) Figures having the same size and shape. Two figures are congruent if they match exactly when one is placed on top of the other after a combination of slides, flips, and/or turns. In diagrams of congruent figures, the corresponding congruent sides may be marked with the same number of hash marks. The symbol ≅ means "is congruent to." See Section 13.6.2: Congruence and Similarity.

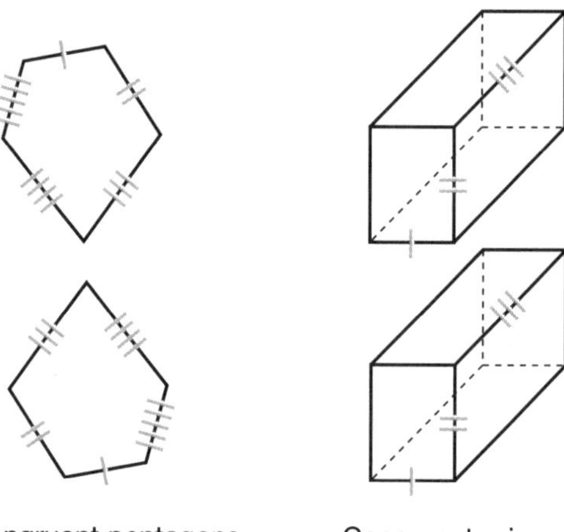

Congruent pentagons Congruent prisms

consecutive Following one after another in an uninterrupted order. For example, A, B, C, and D are four consecutive letters of the alphabet; 6, 7, 8, 9, and 10 are five consecutive whole numbers.

consecutive angles Two *angles* in a *polygon* with a common side.

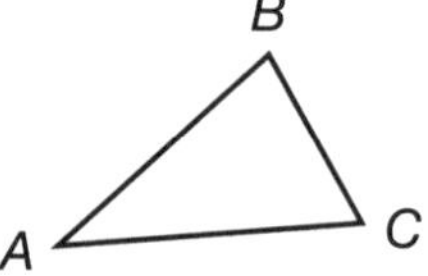

Angles *A* and *B*, *B* and *C*, and *C* and *A* are pairs of consecutive angles.

consecutive sides (1) Two *sides* of a *polygon* with a common *vertex.* (2) Two sides of a *polyhedron* with a common *edge.* Same as *adjacent sides.*

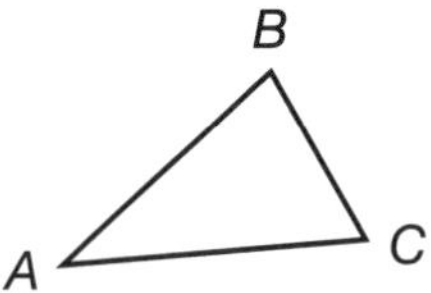

Sides *AB* and *BC*, *BC* and *CA*, and *CA* and *AB* are pairs of consecutive sides.

consecutive vertices The vertices of *consecutive angles* in a polygon.

constant A quantity that does not change. For example, the ratio of the circumference of a circle to its diameter is the famous constant π. In $x + 3 = y$, 3 is a constant.

contour line A curve on a map through places where a measurement such as temperature, elevation, air pressure, or growing season is the same. Contour lines often separate regions that have been differently colored to show a range of conditions. See *contour map.*

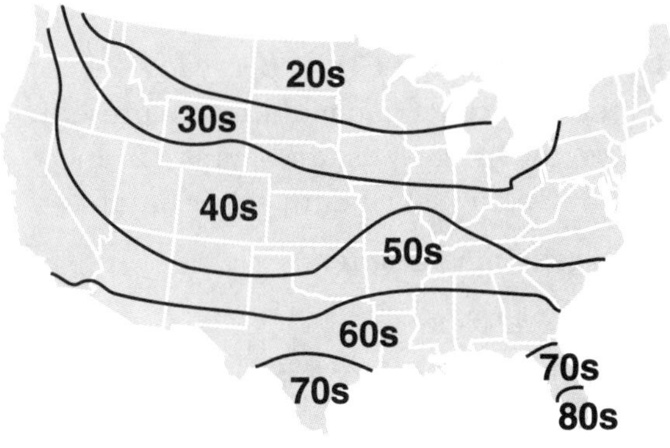

A temperature contour map

contour map A map that uses *contour lines* to indicate areas having a particular feature, such as elevation or temperature.

conversion fact A fixed relationship such as 1 yard = 3 feet or 1 inch = 2.54 centimeters that can be used to convert measurements within or between systems of measurement. See Section 14.2.3: Converting between Measures.

convex polygon A *polygon* on which no two points can be connected with a line segment that passes outside the polygon. Informally, all vertices appear to be "pushed outward." Each angle in the polygon measures less than 180°. Compare to *concave polygon.* See Section 13.4.2: Polygons (*n*-gons).

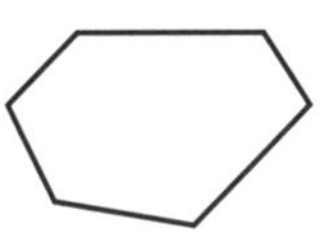

A convex polygon

coordinate (1) A number used to locate a point on a *number line;* a point's distance from an *origin.* (2) One of the numbers in an *ordered pair* or triple that locates a point on a *coordinate grid* or in coordinate space, respectively. See Section 9.7.2: Number Grids, Scrolls, and Lines and Section 15.3: Coordinate Systems.

coordinate grid (rectangular coordinate grid) A *reference frame* for locating points in a plane by means of *ordered pairs* of numbers. A rectangular coordinate grid is formed by two number lines that intersect at *right angles* at their *zero points.* See Section 15.3.2: Coordinate Grids.

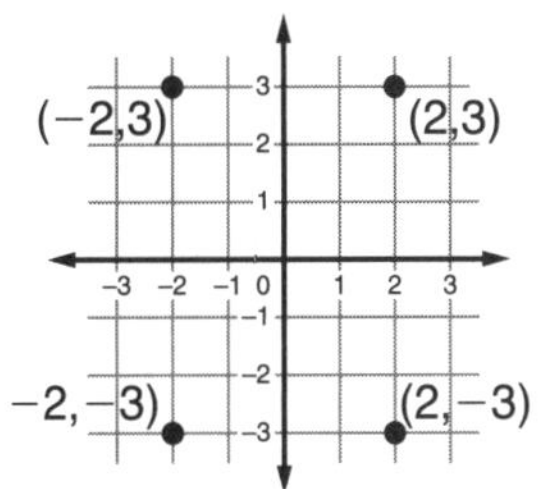

A coordinate grid

corner Same as *vertex.*

counterclockwise rotation Opposite the direction in which the hands move on a typical *analog clock;* a turn to the left.

counting numbers The numbers used to count things. The set of counting numbers is {1, 2, 3, 4, . . .}. Sometimes 0 is included, but not in *Everyday Mathematics.* Counting numbers are in the sets of *whole numbers, integers, rational numbers,* and *real numbers,* but each of these sets include numbers that are not counting numbers. See Section 9.2.2: Plain and Fancy Counting.

counting-up subtraction A subtraction *algorithm* in which a difference is found by counting or otherwise adding up from the smaller number to the larger number. For example, to calculate 87 − 49, start at 49, add 30 to reach 79, and then add 8 more to reach 87. The difference is 30 + 8 = 38. See Section 11.2.2: Subtraction Algorithms.

cross section A shape formed by the intersection of a *plane* and a *geometric solid.*

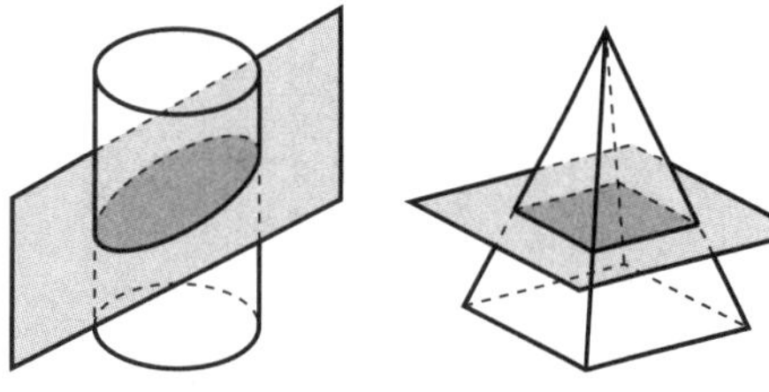

Cross sections of a cylinder and a pyramid

cube (1) A *regular polyhedron* with 6 square faces. A cube has 8 *vertices* and 12 *edges.* See Section 13.5.2: Polyhedrons.

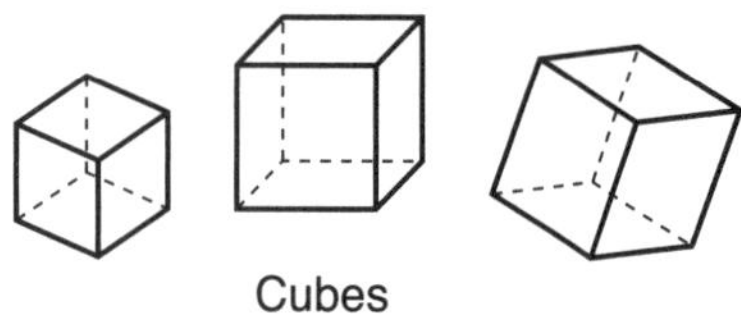

Cubes

(2) In *Everyday Mathematics,* the smaller cube of the *base-10 blocks,* measuring 1 cm on each edge. See Section 9.7.1: Base-10 Blocks.

cubic centimeter (cc or cm^3) A metric unit of *volume* or *capacity* equal to the volume of a cube with 1-cm edges. 1 cm^3 = 1 milliliter (mL). See the Tables of Measures and Section 14.5: Volume (Capacity).

cubic unit A unit such as cubic centimeters, cubic inches, cubic feet, and cubic meters used to measure *volume* or *capacity.* See Section 14.5: Volume (Capacity).

cubit An ancient unit of *length,* measured from the point of the elbow to the end of the middle finger. The cubit has been standardized at various times between 18 and 22 inches. The Latin word *cubitum* means "elbow." See Section 14.1: Personal Measures.

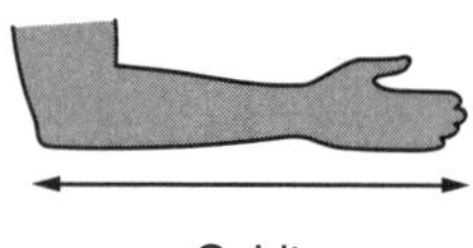

Cubit

cup (c) A U.S. customary unit of *volume* or *capacity* equal to 8 fluid ounces or $\frac{1}{2}$ pint. See the Tables of Measures and Section 14.5: Volume (Capacity).

curved surface A 2-dimensional surface that does not lie in a plane. *Spheres, cylinders,* and *cones* each have one curved surface. See Section 13.5.3: Solids with Curved Surfaces.

customary system of measurement In *Everyday Mathematics,* same as *U.S. customary system of measurement.*

cylinder A *geometric solid* with two congruent, parallel circular regions for *bases* and a curved *face* formed by all the segments with an endpoint on each circle that are parallel to a segment with endpoints at the centers of the circles. Also called a circular cylinder. See Section 13.5.3: Solids with Curved Surfaces.

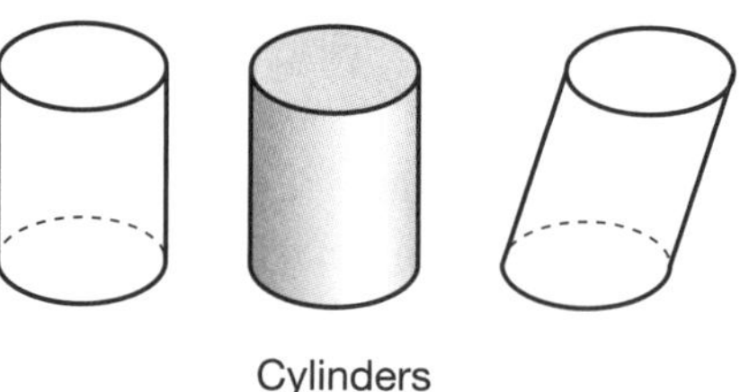

Cylinders

data Information that is gathered by counting, measuring, questioning, or observing. Strictly, data is the plural of *datum,* but data is often used as a singular word. See Section 12.2: Data Collection, Organization, and Analysis.

data bank (1) In *Third Grade Everyday Mathematics,* a collection of data sets presented in posters, tables, graphs, and maps. (2) In general, any established data set or database.

deca- A prefix meaning ten.

decade Ten years.

decagon A 10-sided polygon. See Section 13.4.2: Polygons (*n*-gons).

deci- A prefix meaning 1 tenth.

decimal (1) In *Everyday Mathematics,* a number written in standard *base-10* notation containing a decimal point, such as 2.54. (2) Any number written in standard base-10 notation. See *repeating decimal, terminating decimal,* and Section 9.3.1: Fraction and Decimal Notation.

decimal notation In *Everyday Mathematics,* same as *standard notation.*

decimal point A mark used to separate the ones and tenths places in *decimals.* A decimal point separates dollars from cents in *dollars-and-cents notation.* The mark is a dot in the U.S. customary system and a comma in Europe and some other countries.

decimeter (dm) A metric unit of *length* equivalent to $\frac{1}{10}$ meter, or 10 centimeters.

degree (°) (1) A unit of measure for *angles* based on dividing a *circle* into 360 equal parts. Lines of latitude and longitude are measured in degrees, and these degrees are based on angle measures. See Section 13.4.1: Angles and Rotations.
(2) A unit for measuring *temperature*. See *degree Celsius, degree Fahrenheit,* and Section 15.1.1: Temperature Scales.
The symbol ° means degrees of any type.

degree Celsius (°C) The *unit interval* on *Celsius* thermometers and a metric unit for measuring *temperatures*. Pure water at sea level freezes at 0°C and boils at 100°C. See Section 15.1.1: Temperature Scales.

degree Fahrenheit (°F) The *unit interval* on *Fahrenheit* thermometers and a U.S. customary unit for measuring *temperatures*. Pure water at sea level freezes at 32°F and boils at 212°F. A saturated salt solution freezes at 0°F. See Section 15.1.1: Temperature Scales.

denominator The nonzero divisor b in a fraction $\frac{a}{b}$ and a/b. In a *part-whole fraction,* the denominator is the number of equal parts into which the *whole,* or *ONE,* has been divided. Compare to *numerator*. See Section 9.3.1: Fraction and Decimal Notation.

diagonal (1) A *line segment* joining two nonconsecutive vertices of a *polygon*. See Section 13.4.2: Polygons (n-gons). (2) A segment joining two nonconsecutive vertices on different faces of a polyhedron.

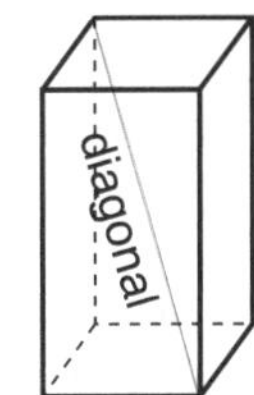

(3) A line of objects or numbers from upper left to lower right or from lower left to upper right, in an *array* or a table.

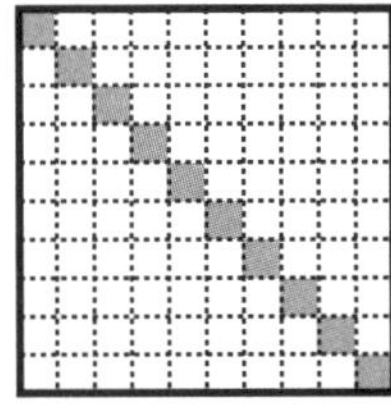

A diagonal of an array

diameter (1) A *line segment* that passes through the center of a *circle* or *sphere* and has endpoints on the circle or sphere. (2) The length of such a segment. The diameter of a circle or sphere is twice the *radius*. See Section 13.4.3: Circles and Pi (π) and Section 13.5.3: Solids with Curved Surfaces.

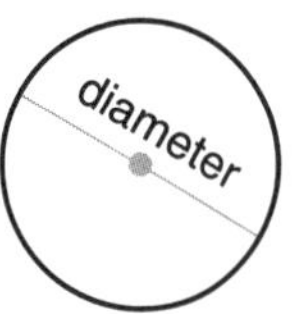

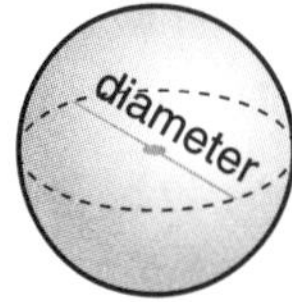

difference The result of subtracting one number from another. For example, the difference of 12 and 5 is $12 - 5 = 7$.

digit (1) Any one of the symbols 0, 1, 2, 3, 4, 5, 6, 7, 8, and 9 in the *base-10* numeration system. For example, the numeral 145 is made up of the digits 1, 4, and 5. (2) Any one of the symbols in any number system. For example, A, B, C, D, E, and F are digits along with 0 through 9 in the base-16 notation used in some computer programming.

digital clock A clock that shows the time with numbers of hours and minutes, usually separated by a colon. This display is discrete, not continuous, meaning that the display jumps to a new time after a minute delay. Compare to *analog clock.* See Section 15.2.1: Clocks.

A digital clock

dimension (1) A measure along one direction of an object, typically length, width, or height. For example, the dimensions of a box might be 24-cm by 20-cm by 10-cm. (2) The number of *coordinates* necessary to locate a point in a geometric space. For example, a line has one dimension because one coordinate uniquely locates any point on the line. A plane has two dimensions because an *ordered pair* of two coordinates uniquely locates any point in the plane. See Section 13.1: Dimension.

Distributive Property of Multiplication over Addition A property relating multiplication to a sum of numbers by distributing a *factor* over the terms in the sum. For example, $2 \times (5 + 3) = (2 \times 5) + (2 \times 3) = 10 + 6 = 16$.

In symbols:

For any numbers a, b, and c:

$a \times (b + c) = (a \times b) + (a \times c)$

or $a(b + c) = ab + ac$

Distributive Property of Multiplication over Subtraction A property relating multiplication to a difference of numbers by distributing a *factor* over the terms in the difference. For example, $2 \times (5 - 3) = (2 \times 5) - (2 \times 3) = 10 - 6 = 4$.

In symbols:

For any numbers a, b, and c:

$a \times (b - c) = (a \times b) - (a \times c)$

or $a(b - c) = ab - ac$

dividend The number in division that is being divided. For example, in $35 \div 5 = 7$, the dividend is 35.

divisor
dividend → 35/5 = 7 ← quotient

divisor
dividend → $40 \div 8 = 5$ ← quotient

quotient → 3
divisor → $12\overline{)36}$ ← dividend

divisibility rule A shortcut for determining whether a counting number is *divisible by* another counting number without actually doing the division. For example, a number is divisible by 5 if the *digit* in the ones place is 0 or 5. A number is divisible by 3 if the sum of its digits is divisible by 3.

divisibility test A test to see if a *divisibility rule* applies to a particular number.

divisible by If the larger of two *counting numbers* can be divided by the smaller with no remainder, then the larger is divisible by the smaller. For example, 28 is divisible by 7, because $28 \div 7 = 4$ with no remainder. If a number n is divisible by a number d, then d is a *factor* of n. Every counting number is divisible by itself.

division symbols The number a divided by the number b is written in a variety of ways. In *Everyday Mathematics,* $a \div b$; a/b and $\frac{a}{b}$ are the most common notations, while $b\overline{)a}$ is used to set up the traditional long-division algorithm. $a{:}b$ is sometimes used in Europe, [÷] is common on calculators, and [/] is common on computer keyboards. See Section 10.1.1: Arithmetic Symbols.

divisor In division, the number that divides another number, the *dividend.* For example, in $35 \div 7 = 5$, the divisor is 7. See the diagram under the definition of *dividend.*

dodecahedron A *polyhedron* with 12 faces. If each face is a regular pentagon, it is one of the five *regular polyhedrons*. See Section 13.5.2: Polyhedrons.

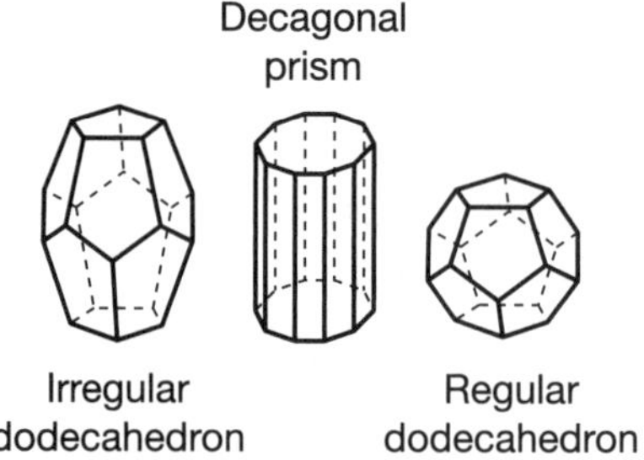

dollar The basic unit in the U.S. monetary system, equal to 100 *cents.*

dollars-and-cents notation The U.S. customary notation for writing amounts of money as a number of dollars and hundredths of dollars *(cents).* The decimal is preceded by the $ symbol, as in $8.98, meaning "eight dollars and 98 cents." See Section 14.9: Money.

double Two times an amount; an amount added to itself.

doubles fact The sum (or product) of a 1-digit number added to (or multiplied by) itself, such as $4 + 4 = 8$ or $3 \times 3 = 9$. A doubles fact does not have a *turn-around fact* partner.

edge (1) Any *side* of a polyhedron's *faces.* (2) A line segment or curve where two surfaces of a geometric solid meet. See Section 13.5.2: Polyhedrons and Section 13.5.3: Solids with Curved Surfaces.

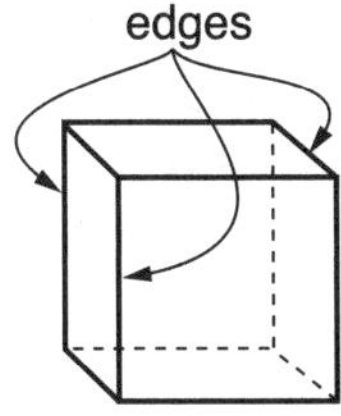

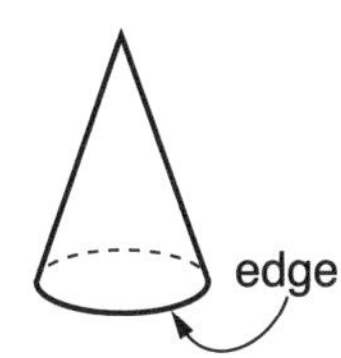

elapsed time The difference in two times. For example, between 12:45 P.M. and 1:30 P.M., 45 minutes have elapsed.

elevation A height above sea level. Same as *altitude (2).*

embedded figure A figure entirely enclosed within another figure.

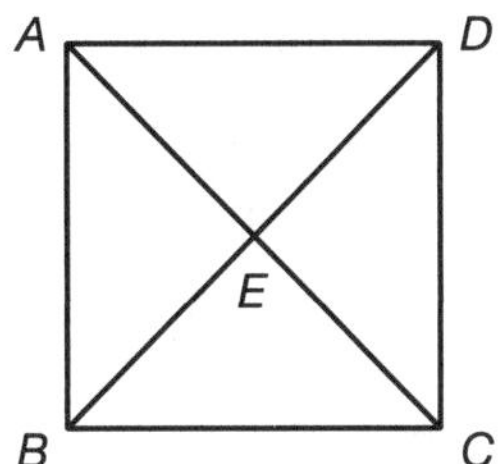

Triangle *ADE* is embedded in square *ADCB*.

endpoint A point at the end of a *line segment, ray,* or *arc.* These shapes are usually named using their endpoints. For example, the segment shown is "segment *TL*" or "segment *LT*."

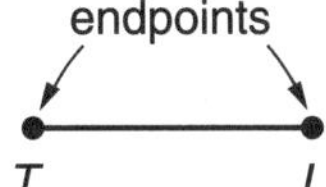

enlarge To increase the size of an object or a figure without changing its shape. Same as *stretch*. See *scale factor* and Section 13.7.2: Stretches and Shrinks.

equal Same as *equivalent.*

equal-grouping story A *number story* in which a quantity is divided into equal groups. The total and size of each group are known. For example, *How many tables seating 4 people each are needed to seat 52 people?* is an equal-grouping story. Often division can be used to solve equal-grouping stories. Compare to *measurement division* and *equal-sharing story* and see Section 10.2.2: Multiplication and Division Use Classes.

equal groups Sets with the same number of elements, such as cars with 5 passengers each, rows with 6 chairs each, and boxes containing 100 paper clips each. See Section 10.2.2: Multiplication and Division Use Classes.

equal-groups notation In *Everyday Mathematics,* a way to denote a number of equal-size groups. The size of each group is shown inside square brackets and the number of groups is written in front of the brackets. For example, 3 [6s] means 3 groups with 6 in each group. In general, *n* [*b*s] means *n* groups with *b* in each group.

equal parts Equivalent parts of a *whole.* For example, dividing a pizza into 4 equal parts means each part is $\frac{1}{4}$ of the pizza and is equal in size to the other 3 parts. See Section 9.3.2: Uses of Fractions.

4 equal parts, each $\frac{1}{4}$ of a pizza

equal-sharing story A *number story* in which a quantity is shared equally. The total quantity and the number of groups are known. For example, *There are 10 toys to share equally among 4 children; how many toys will each child get?* is an equal-sharing story. Often division can be used to solve equal-sharing stories. Compare to *partitive division* and *equal-grouping story.* See Section 10.2.2: Multiplication and Division Use Classes.

equally likely outcomes *Outcomes* of a chance experiment or situation that have the same *probability* of happening. If all the possible outcomes are equally likely, then the probability of an *event* is equal to:

$$\frac{\text{number of favorable outcomes}}{\text{number of possible outcomes}}$$

See *random experiment* and Section 12.1.2: The Language of Chance.

equation A *number sentence* that contains an equal sign. For example, $5 + 10 = 15$ and $P = 2l + 2w$ are equations. See Section 10.1.2: Reading and Writing Number Sentences and Section 17.2.2: Reading and Writing Open Sentences.

equator An imaginary circle around Earth halfway between the North Pole and the South Pole.

equilateral polygon A polygon in which all sides are the same length. See Section 13.4.2: Polygons (*n*-gons).

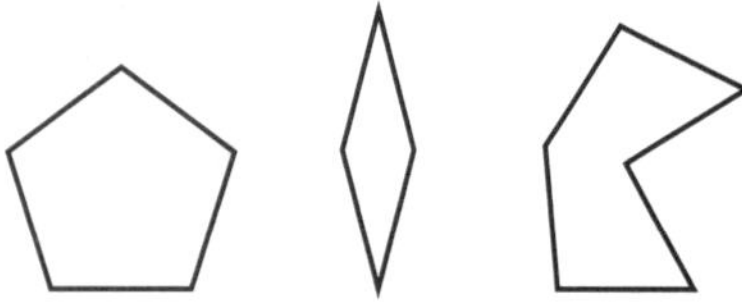

Equilateral polygons

equilateral triangle A *triangle* with all three sides equal in length. Each angle of an equilateral triangle measures 60°, so it is also called an equiangular triangle. See Section 13.4.2: Polygons (*n*-gons).

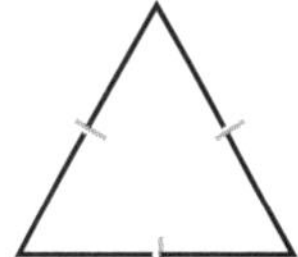

An equilateral triangle

equivalent Equal in value but possibly in a different form. For example, $\frac{1}{2}$, 0.5, and 50% are all equivalent. See Section 9.6.1: Equality.

equivalent equations *Equations* with the same *solution*. For example, $2 + x = 4$ and $6 + x = 8$ are equivalent equations with the common solution 2. See Section 17.2.3: Solving Open Sentences.

equivalent fractions *Fractions* with different *denominators* that name the same number. See Section 9.3.3: Rates and Ratios.

equivalent names Different ways of naming the same number. For example, 2 + 6, 4 + 4, 12 − 4, 18 − 10, 100 − 92, 5 + 1 + 2, eight, VIII, and ~~////~~ /// are all equivalent names for 8. See *name-collection box.*

estimate (1) An answer close to, or approximating, an exact answer. (2) To make an estimate. See Section 16.1: Estimation.

European subtraction A subtraction *algorithm* in which the subtrahend is increased when regrouping is necessary. The algorithm is commonly used in Europe and in certain parts of the United States. See Section 11.2.2: Subtraction Algorithms.

even number (1) A *counting number* that is *divisible by* 2. (2) An *integer* that is divisible by 2. Compare to *odd number* and see Section 17.1.2: Odd and Even Number Patterns.

event A set of possible *outcomes* to an experiment. For example, in an experiment flipping two coins, getting 2 HEADS is an event, as is getting 1 HEAD and 1 TAIL. The *probability* of an event is the chance that the event will happen. For example, the probability that a fair coin will land HEADS up is $\frac{1}{2}$. If the probability of an event is 0, the event is *impossible.* If the probability is 1, the event is *certain.* See Section 12.1: Probability.

expanded notation A way of writing a number as the sum of the values of each *digit.* For example, 356 is 300 + 50 + 6 in expanded notation. Compare to *standard notation, scientific notation,* and *number-and-word notation.*

Explorations In *First* through *Third Grade Everyday Mathematics,* independent or small-group activities that focus on one or more of the following: concept development, manipulatives, data collection, problem solving, games, and skill reviews. See Section 1.2.1: Explorations.

exponent A small raised number used in *exponential notation* to tell how many times the *base* is used as a *factor.* For example, in 5^3, the base is 5, the exponent is 3, and $5^3 = 5 \times 5 \times 5 = 125$. Same as *power.* See Section 10.1.1: Arithmetic Symbols.

exponential notation A way of representing repeated multiplication by the same factor. For example, 2^3 is exponential notation for $2 \times 2 \times 2$. The *exponent* 3 tells how many times the *base* 2 is used as a factor. See Section 10.1.1: Arithmetic Symbols.

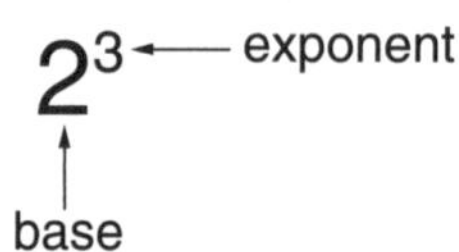

expression (1) A mathematical phrase made up of numbers, *variables, operation symbols,* and/or *grouping symbols*. An expression does not contain *relation symbols* such as =, >, and ≤ . (2) Either side of an *equation* or *inequality*. See Section 10.1.2: Reading and Writing Number Sentences and Section 17.2.2: Reading and Writing Open Sentences.

$2 + 3$

$\sqrt{2ab}$

πr^2

$9x - 2$

Expressions

extended facts Variations of basic *arithmetic facts* involving multiples of 10, 100, and so on. For example, $30 + 70 = 100$, $40 \times 5 = 200$, and $560 \div 7 = 80$ are extended facts. See *fact extensions* and Section 16.3: Mental Arithmetic.

F

face (1) In *Everyday Mathematics,* a flat *surface* on a *3-dimensional figure*. Some special faces are called *bases*. (2) More generally, any 2-dimensional surface on a 3-dimensional figure. See Section 13.5: Space and 3-D Figures.

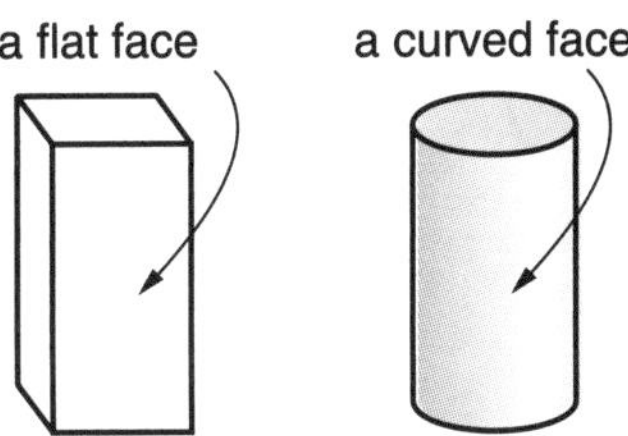

fact extensions Calculations with larger numbers using knowledge of basic *arithmetic facts*. For example, knowing the addition fact $5 + 8 = 13$ makes it easier to solve problems such as $50 + 80 = ?$ and $65 + ? = 73$. Fact extensions apply to all four basic arithmetic operations. See *extended facts* and Section 16.3.3: Fact Practice.

fact family A set of related *arithmetic facts* linking two inverse operations. For example,

$5 + 6 = 11$ $6 + 5 = 11$

$11 - 5 = 6$ $11 - 6 = 5$

are an addition/subtraction fact family. Similarly,

$5 \times 7 = 35$ $7 \times 5 = 35$

$35 \div 7 = 5$ $35 \div 5 = 7$

are a multiplication/division fact family. Same as *number family*. See Section 16.3.3: Fact Practice.

fact habits Same as *fact power*.

fact power In *Everyday Mathematics,* the ability to automatically recall basic *arithmetic facts*. Automatically knowing the facts is as important to arithmetic as knowing words by sight is to reading. Same as *fact habits*. See Section 16.3.2: Basic Facts and Fact Power.

Fact Triangle In *Everyday Mathematics,* a triangular flash card labeled with the numbers of a *fact family* that students can use to practice addition/subtraction and multiplication/division facts. The two 1-digit numbers and their sum or product (marked with a dot) appear in the corners of each triangle. See Section 1.3.1: Fact Families/Fact Triangles.

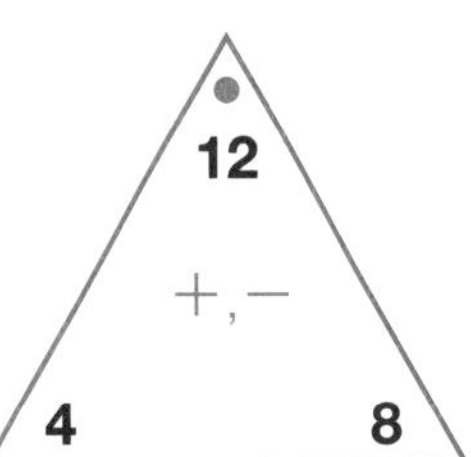

factor (1) Each of the two or more numbers in a *product*. For example, in 6×0.5, 6 and 0.5 are factors. Compare to *factor of a counting number* n. (2) To represent a number as a product of factors. For example, factor 21 by rewriting as 7×3.

factor of a counting number ***n*** A *counting number* whose product with some other counting number equals *n*. For example, 2 and 3 are factors of 6 because $2 \times 3 = 6$. But 4 is not a factor of 6 because $4 \times 1.5 = 6$, and 1.5 is not a counting number.

factor pair Two *factors of a counting number* n whose product is *n*. A number may have more than one factor pair. For example, the factor pairs for 18 are 1 and 18, 2 and 9, and 3 and 6.

factorial (!) A *product* of a whole number and all smaller whole numbers except 0. The symbol ! means "factorial." For example, 3! is read "three factorial" and $3! = 3 \times 2 \times 1 = 6$. Similarly, $4! = 4 \times 3 \times 2 \times 1 = 24$. For any number *n*,

$$n! = n \times (n - 1) \times (n - 2) \times \ldots \times 1.$$

By convention, $0! = 1$.

facts table A chart showing *arithmetic facts*. An addition/subtraction facts table shows addition and subtraction facts. A multiplication/division facts table shows multiplication and division facts.

Glossary

Fahrenheit A *temperature scale* on which pure water at sea level freezes at 32° and boils at 212°. The Fahrenheit scale is widely used in the U.S. but in few other places. Compare to *Celsius.* See *degree Fahrenheit* and Section 15.1.1: Temperature Scales.

fair Free from bias. Each side of a fair die or coin will land up about equally often. Each region of a fair spinner will be landed on in proportion to its area.

fair game A game in which every player has the same chance of winning. See Section 12.1.2: The Language of Chance.

false number sentence A *number sentence* that is not true. For example, $8 = 5 + 5$ is a false number sentence. Compare to *true number sentence*. See Section 10.1.2: Reading and Writing Number Sentences.

fathom A unit of *length* equal to 6 feet, or 2 yards. It is used mainly by people who work with boats and ships to measure depths underwater and lengths of cables. Same as *arm span*. See Section 14.1: Personal Measures.

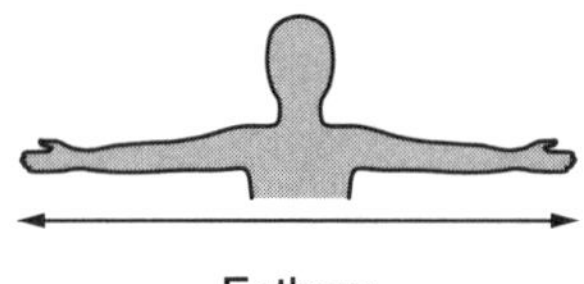

Fathom

figurate numbers Numbers that can be illustrated by specific geometric *patterns. Square numbers* and *triangular numbers* are figurate numbers. See Section 17.1.3: Sequences.

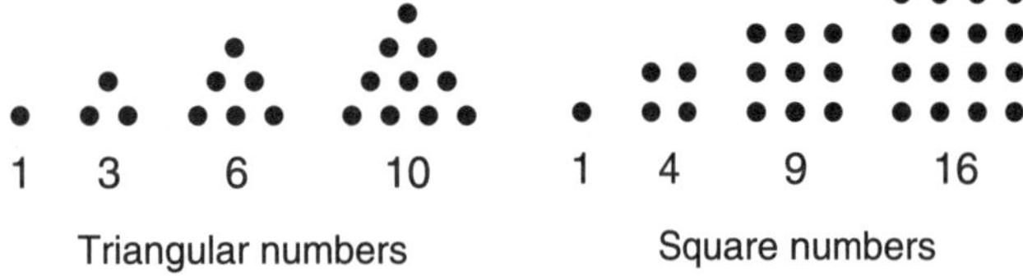

flat In *Everyday Mathematics,* the *base-10 block* consisting of one hundred 1-cm cubes. See Section 9.7.1: Base-10 Blocks.

A flat

flat surface A *surface* contained entirely in one *plane*. See Section 13.4: Planes and Plane Figures and Section 13.5: Space and 3-D Figures.

flip An informal name for a *reflection* transformation. See Section 13.7.1: Flips, Turns, and Slides.

fluid ounce (fl oz) A U.S. customary unit of *volume* or *capacity* equal to $\frac{1}{16}$ of a pint, or about 29.573730 milliliters. Compare to *ounce.* See the Tables of Measures and Section 14.5: Volume (Capacity).

foot (ft) A U.S. customary unit of *length* equivalent to 12 inches, or $\frac{1}{3}$ of a yard. See the Tables of Measures and Section 14.3: Length.

formula A general rule for finding the value of something. A formula is usually an *equation* with quantities represented by letter *variables*. For example, a formula for distance traveled d at a rate r over a time t is $d = r \times t$. The area of a triangle A with base length b and height h is given below. See Section 17.2.1: Uses of Variables.

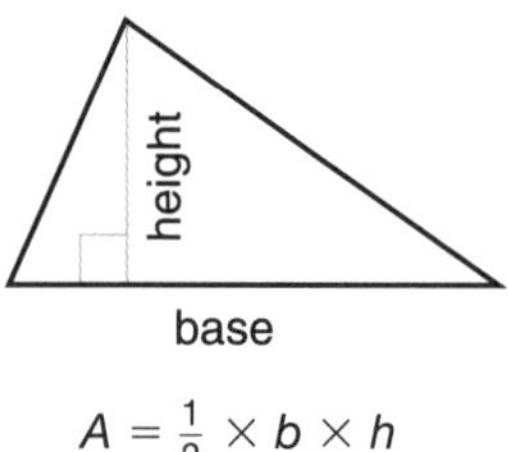

$A = \frac{1}{2} \times b \times h$

fraction (primary definition) A number in the form $\frac{a}{b}$ or a/b, where a and b are *whole numbers* and b is not 0. A fraction may be used to name part of an object or part of a collection of objects, to compare two quantities, or to represent division. For example, $\frac{12}{6}$ might mean 12 eggs divided into 6 groups of 2 eggs each, a ratio of 12 to 6, or 12 divided by 6. See Section 9.3: Fractions, Decimals, Percents, and Rational Numbers.

fraction (other definitions) (1) A fraction that satisfies the previous definition and includes a *unit* in both the *numerator* and *denominator.* For example, the *rates*

$$\frac{50 \text{ miles}}{1 \text{ gallon}} \text{ and } \frac{40 \text{ pages}}{10 \text{ minutes}}$$

are fractions. (2) A number written using a fraction bar, where the fraction bar is used to indicate division. For example,

$$\frac{2.3}{6.5}, \frac{1\frac{4}{5}}{12}, \text{ and } \frac{\frac{3}{4}}{\frac{5}{8}}.$$

fractional part Part of a *whole. Fractions* represent fractional parts of numbers, sets, or objects. See Section 9.3.2: Uses of Fractions.

frames In *Everyday Mathematics,* the empty shapes in which numbers are written in a *Frames-and-Arrows* diagram. See Section 17.1.4: Functions.

Frames and Arrows In *Everyday Mathematics,* diagrams consisting of frames connected by arrows used to represent number *sequences.* Each frame contains a number, and each arrow represents a rule that determines which number goes in the next frame. There may be more than one rule, represented by different-color arrows. Frames-and-Arrows diagrams are also called "chains." See Section 17.1.3: Sequences.

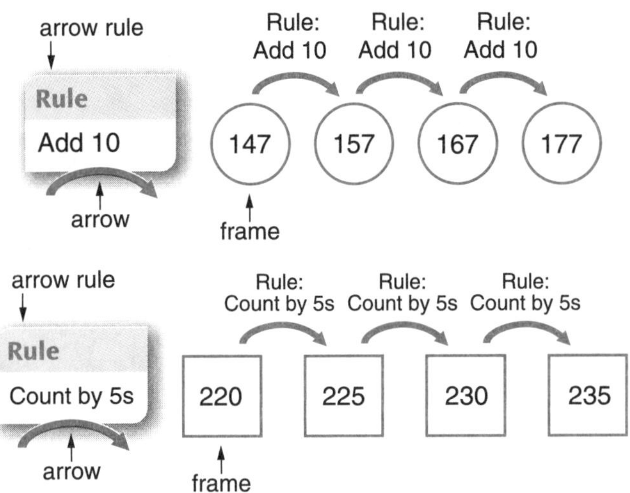

frequency (1) The number of times a value occurs in a set of data. See Section 12.2.3: Organizing and Displaying Data. (2) A number of repetitions per unit of time. For example, the vibrations per second in a sound wave.

frequency graph A graph showing how often each value occurs in a data set. See Section 12.2.3: Organizing and Displaying Data.

Colors in a Bag of Gumdrops

Number of Gumdrops: 0 1 2 3 4 5 6

Red Green Yellow Orange White

frequency table A table in which data are *tallied* and organized, often as a first step toward making a *frequency graph.* See Section 12.2.3: Organizing and Displaying Data.

Color	Number of Gumdrops
red	𝍸
green	𝍸 /
yellow	////
orange	///
white	𝍸

fulcrum (1) The point on a mobile at which a rod is suspended. (2) The point or place around which a lever pivots. (3) The center support of a *pan balance.*

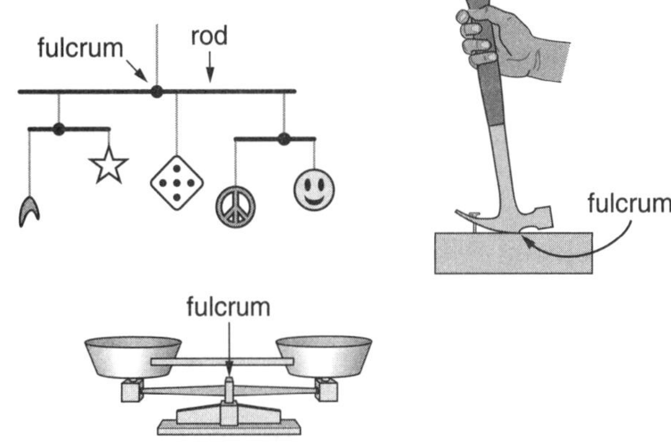

function A set of *ordered pairs* (x,y) in which each value of x is paired with exactly one value of y. A function is typically represented in a table, by points on a coordinate graph, or by a rule such as an *equation.* For example, for a function with the rule "Double," 1 is paired with 2, 2 is paired with 4, 3 is paired with 6, and so on. In symbols, $y = 2 \times x$ or $y = 2x$. See Section 17.1.4: Functions.

Glossary

function machine In *Everyday Mathematics,* an imaginary device that receives inputs and pairs them with *outputs.* For example, the function machine below pairs an input number with its double. See *function* and Section 17.1.4: Functions.

input

Rule

Double

output

in	out
1	2
2	4
3	6
5	10
20	40
300	600

A function machine and function table

furlong A unit of *length* equal to 1 eighth of a mile. Furlongs are commonly used in horse racing.

gallon (gal) A U.S. customary unit of *volume* or *capacity* equal to 4 quarts. See the Tables of Measures and Section 14.5: Volume (Capacity).

generate a random number To produce a *random number* by such methods as drawing a card without looking from a shuffled deck, rolling a fair die, and flicking a fair spinner. In *Everyday Mathematics,* random numbers are commonly generated in games. See Section 12.4.1: Random-Number Generators.

geoboard A manipulative *2-dimensional coordinate system* made with nails or other posts at equally-spaced intervals relative to both axes. Children loop rubber bands around the posts to make polygons and other shapes.

geometric solid The *surface* or surfaces that make up a *3-dimensional figure* such as a prism, pyramid, cylinder, cone, or sphere. Despite its name, a geometric solid is hollow; that is, it does not include the points in its interior. Informally, and in some dictionaries, a solid is defined as both the surface and its interior. See Section 13.5.1: "Solid" Figures.

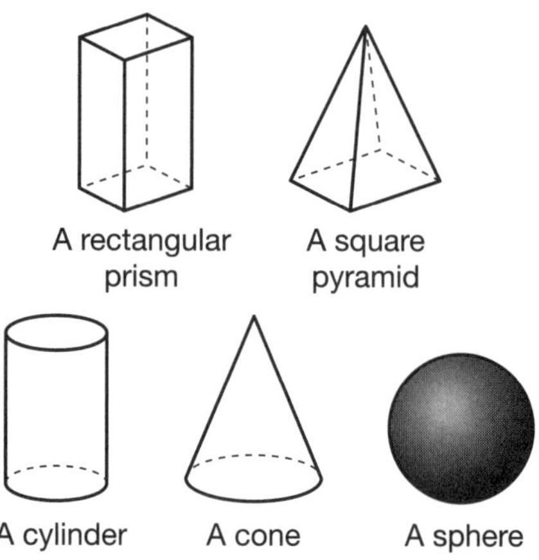

Geometric solids

girth The distance around a 3-dimensional object.

-gon A suffix meaning *angle.* For example, a *hexagon* is a plane figure with six angles.

gram (g) A metric unit of *mass* equal to $\frac{1}{1,000}$ of a kilogram. See the Tables of Measures and Section 14.6: Weight and Mass.

graph key An annotated list of the symbols used in a graph explaining how to read the graph. Compare to *map legend.*

greatest common factor (GCF) The largest *factor* that two or more *counting numbers* have in common. For example, the common factors of 24 and 36 are 1, 2, 3, 4, 6, and 12, and their greatest common factor is 12.

great span The distance from the tip of the thumb to the tip of the little finger (pinkie), when the hand is stretched as far as possible. The great span averages about 9 inches for adults. Same as *hand span.* Compare to *normal span* and see Section 14.1: Personal Measures.

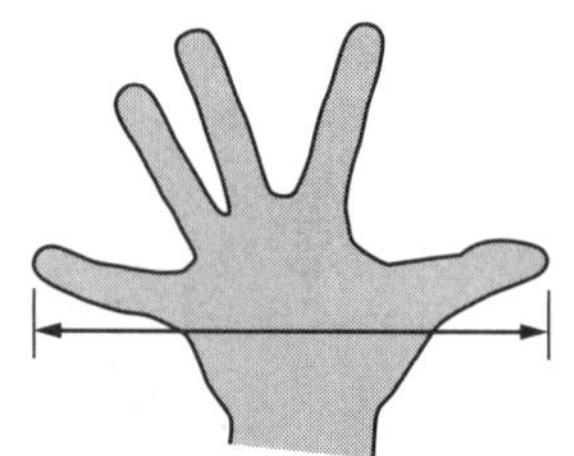

Great span

grouping symbols Parentheses ( ), brackets [ ], braces { }, and similar symbols that define the order in which operations in an *expression* are to be done. *Nested* grouping symbols are groupings within groupings, and the innermost grouping is done first. For example, in $(3 + 4) \times [(8 + 2) \div 5]$, the group $(8 + 2)$ is nested within $[(8 + 2) \div 5]$ and is done first. So $(3 + 4) \times [(8 + 2) \div 5]$ simplifies as follows:

$$(3 + 4) \times [(8 + 2) \div 5]$$
$$(3 + 4) \times [10 \div 5]$$
$$7 \times 2$$
$$14$$

See Section 10.1.2: Reading and Writing Number Sentences.

H

half One of two *equal parts.*

hand span Same as *great span.*

height (1) A perpendicular segment from one *side* of a geometric figure to a parallel side or from a *vertex* to the *opposite side.* (2) The length of this segment. In *Everyday Mathematics,* same as *altitude.* See *height of a parallelogram, height of a rectangle, height of a prism or cylinder, height of a pyramid or cone, height of a triangle,* Section 13.4.2: Polygons (*n*-gons), Section 13.5.2: Polyhedrons, and Section 13.5.3: Solids with Curved Surfaces.

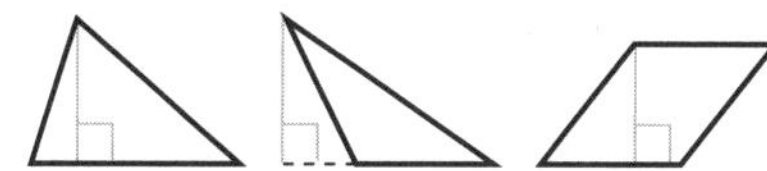

Heights/altitudes of 2-D figures are shown in blue.

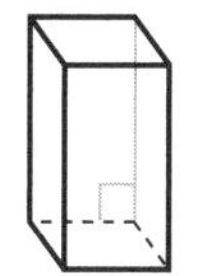

Heights/altitudes of 3-D figures are shown in blue.

height of a parallelogram (1) The *length* of the shortest line segment between a *base of a parallelogram* and the line containing the *opposite side.* The height is perpendicular to the base. (2) The line segment itself. See *altitude, base of a parallelogram,* and Section 13.4.2: Polygons (*n*-gons).

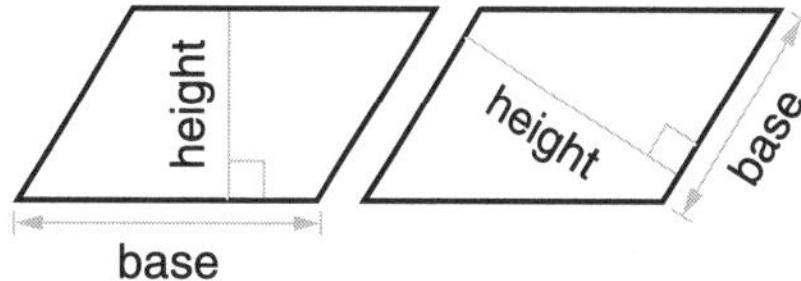

height of a prism or cylinder The *length* of the shortest line segment from a *base of a prism or cylinder* to the plane containing the opposite base. The height is perpendicular to the bases. (2) The line segment itself. See *altitude, base of a prism or cylinder,* and Section 13.5.2: Polyhedrons.

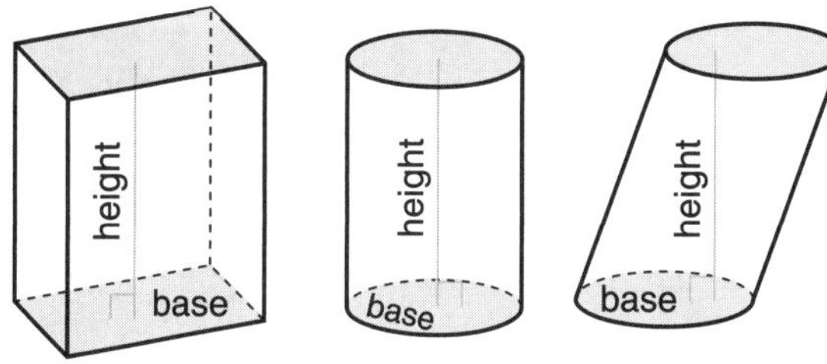

height of a pyramid or cone The *length* of the shortest line segment from the *apex* of a pyramid or cone to the plane containing the *base.* The height is perpendicular to the base. (2) The line segment itself. See *altitude, base of a pyramid or cone,* and Section 13.5.2: Polyhedrons.

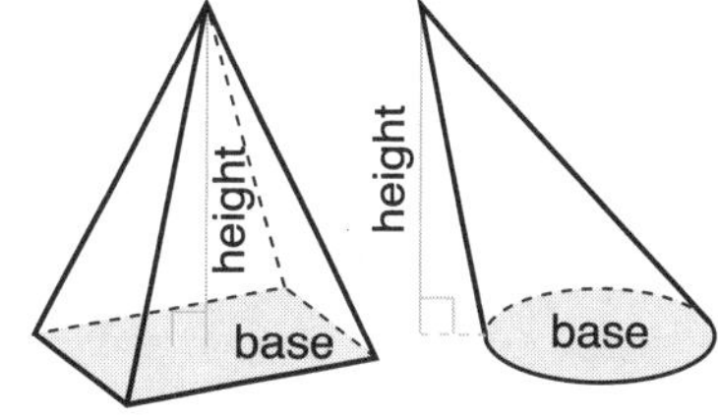

height of a rectangle The *length* of a side perpendicular to a *base of a rectangle.* Same as *altitude* of a rectangle. See Section 13.4.2: Polygons (*n*-gons).

Glossary

height of a triangle The *length* of the shortest segment from a *vertex* of a triangle to the line containing the opposite *side*. The height is perpendicular to the base. (2) The line segment itself. See *altitude, base of a triangle*, and Section 13.4.2: Polygons (*n*-gons).

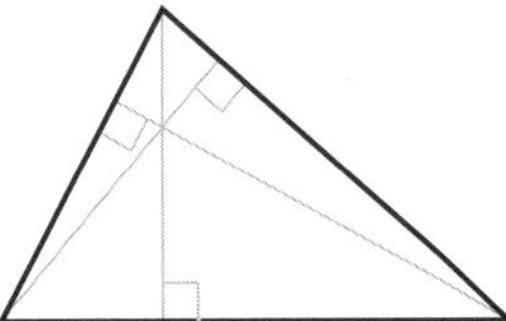

The heights of the triangle are shown in blue.

hemisphere (1) Half of Earth's surface. (2) Half of a *sphere.*

hepta- A prefix meaning seven.

heptagon A 7-sided *polygon*. See Section 13.4.2: Polygons (*n*-gons).

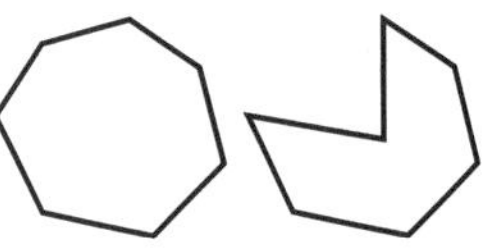

Heptagons

hexa- A prefix meaning six.

hexagon A 6-sided *polygon*. See Section 13.4.2: Polygons (*n*-gons).

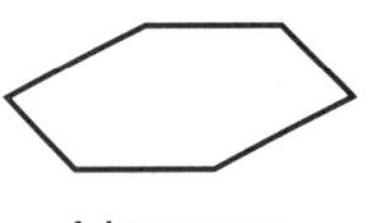

A hexagon

Home Link In *First* through *Third Grade Everyday Mathematics,* a suggested follow-up or enrichment activity to be done at home. See Section 1.2.3: Home Links.

horizon Where the earth and sky appear to meet, if nothing is in the way. The horizon looks like a line when you look out to sea.

horizontal In a left-to-right orientation. Parallel to the *horizon.*

hypotenuse In a *right triangle,* the *side* opposite the *right angle.* See Section 13.4.2: Polygons (*n*-gons).

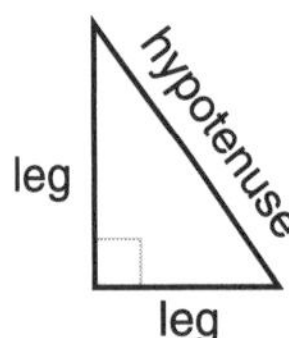

icon A small picture or diagram sometimes used to represent quantities. For example, an icon of a stadium might be used to represent 100,000 people on a *pictograph.* Icons are also used to represent functions or objects in computer operating systems and applications.

icosahedron A *polyhedron* with 20 faces. An icosahedron with equilateral triangle faces is one of the five *regular polyhedrons.* See Section 13.5.2: Polyhedrons.

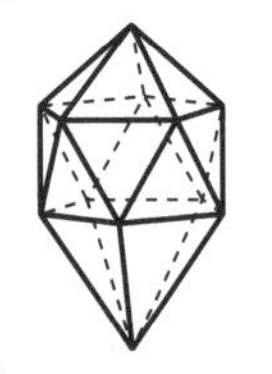

An irregular icosahedron

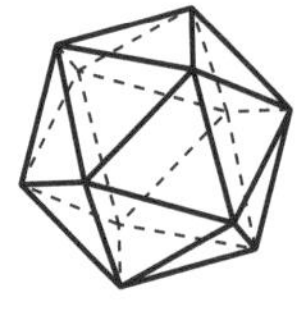

A regular icosahedron

image A figure that is produced by a *transformation* of another figure called the *preimage.* See Section 13.7: Transformations.

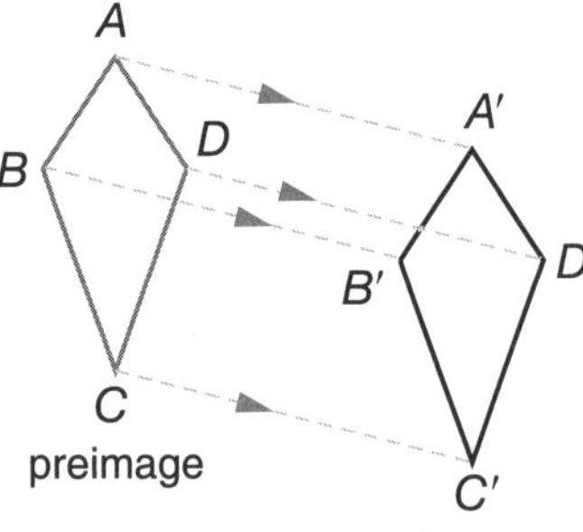

improper fraction A *fraction* with a *numerator* that is greater than or equal to its *denominator.* For example, $\frac{4}{3}$, $\frac{5}{2}$, $\frac{4}{4}$, and $\frac{24}{12}$ are improper fractions. In *Everyday Mathematics,* improper fractions are sometimes called "top-heavy" fractions.

inch (in.) A U.S. customary unit of *length* equal to $\frac{1}{12}$ of a foot and 2.54 centimeters. See the Tables of Measures and Section 14.3: Length.

indirect measurement The determination of heights, distances, and other quantities that cannot be measured directly.

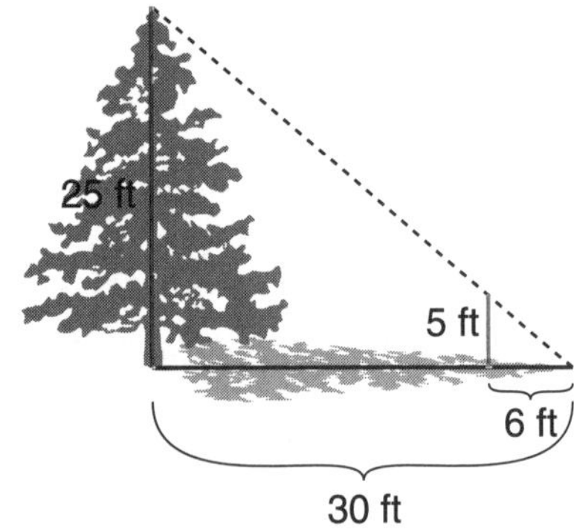

Indirect measurement lets you calculate the height of the tree from the other measures.

inequality A *number sentence* with a *relation symbol* other than =, such as >, <, ≥, ≤, ≠, or ≈. See Section 9.6: Numeric Relations.

input (1) A number inserted into an imaginary *function machine,* which applies a rule to pair the input with an *output.* (2) The values for x in a *function* consisting of *ordered pairs* (x, y). See Section 17.1.4: Functions. (3) Numbers or other information entered into a calculator or computer.

inscribed polygon A *polygon* whose vertices are all on the same *circle.*

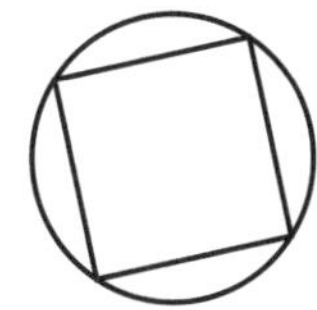

An inscribed square

integer A number in the set {. . ., −4, −3, −2, −1, 0, 1, 2, 3, 4, . . .}. A *whole number* or its *opposite,* where 0 is its own opposite. Compare to *rational number, irrational number,* and *real number.* See Section 9.4: Positive and Negative Numbers.

interior of a figure (1) The set of all points in a *plane* bounded by a closed *2-dimensional figure* such as a *polygon* or *circle*. (2) The set of all points in space bounded by a closed *3-dimensional figure* such as a *polyhedron* or *sphere*. The interior is usually not considered to be part of the figure. See Section 13.4: Planes and Plane Figures and Section 13.5: Space and 3-D Figures.

intersect To share a common point or points.

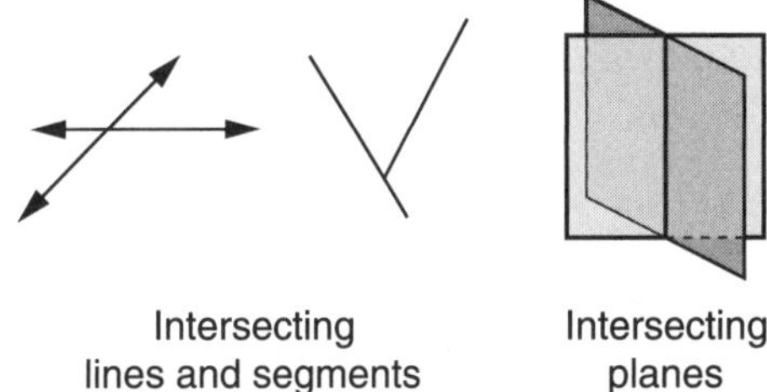

Intersecting lines and segments

Intersecting planes

interval (1) The set of all numbers between two numbers *a* and *b,* which may include one or both of *a* and *b.* (2) The points and their coordinates on a segment of a number line. The interval between 0 and 1 on a number line is the *unit interval.*

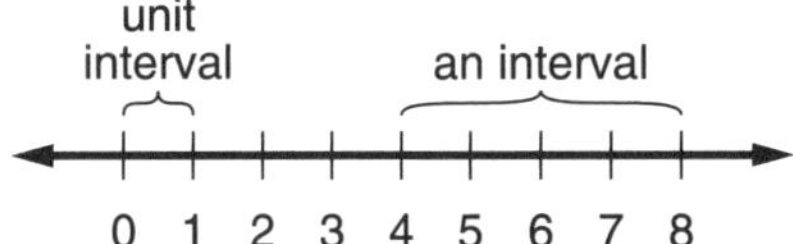

irrational numbers Numbers that cannot be written as *fractions* where both the *numerator* and *denominator* are *integers* and the denominator is not zero. For example, $\sqrt{2}$ and π are irrational numbers. An irrational number can be written as a nonterminating, nonrepeating decimal. For example, $\pi = 3.141592653 \ldots$ continues forever without any known pattern. The number 1.10100100010000 . . . is irrational because its pattern does not repeat. See Section 9.5: Irrational and Real Numbers.

isometry transformation A *transformation* in which the *preimage* and *image* are *congruent. Reflections* (flips), *rotations* (turns), and *translations* (slides) are isometry transformations, while a *size-change* (stretch or shrink) is not. Although the size and shape of the figures in an isometry transformation are the same, their orientations may be different. From the Greek *isometros* meaning "of equal measure." See Section 13.7.1: Flips, Turns, and Slides.

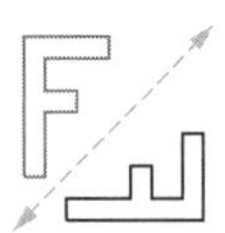

A reflection (flip)

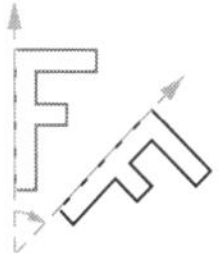

A rotation (turn)

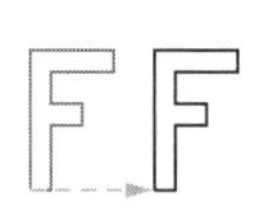

A translation (slide)

isosceles trapezoid A *trapezoid* whose nonparallel sides are the same length. Pairs of base angles have the same measure. See Section 13.4.2: Polygons (*n*-gons).

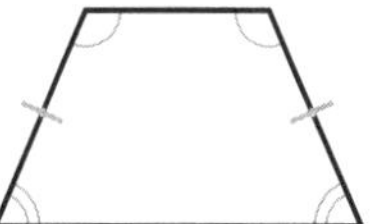

An isosceles trapezoid

isosceles triangle A *triangle* with at least two sides equal in length. Angles opposite the congruent sides are congruent to each other. See Section 13.4.2: Polygons (*n*-gons).

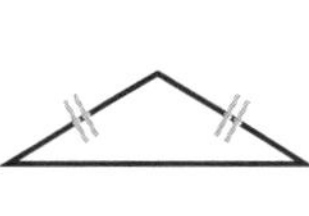

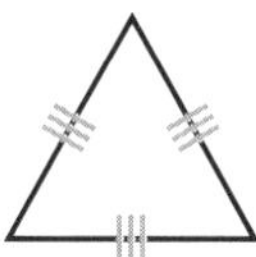

Isosceles triangles

J

juxtapose To represent multiplication in an *expression* by placing *factors* side by side without a multiplication symbol. At least one factor is a *variable.* For example, $5n$ means $5 \times n,$ and ab means $a \times b.$ See Section 10.1.1: Arithmetic Symbols.

K

key sequence The order in which calculator keys are pressed to perform a calculation. See Section 3.1.1: Calculators.

kilo- A prefix meaning 1 thousand.

kilogram A metric unit of *mass* equal to 1,000 grams. The international standard kilogram is a 39 mm diameter, 39 mm high *cylinder* of platinum and iridium kept in the International Bureau of Weights and Measures in Sèvres, France. A kilogram is about 2.2 pounds. See the Tables of Measures and Section 14.6: Weight and Mass.

kilometer A metric unit of *length* equal to 1,000 meters. A kilometer is about 0.62 mile. See the Tables of Measures and Section 14.3: Length.

kite A *quadrilateral* with two distinct pairs of adjacent sides of equal length. In *Everyday Mathematics,* the four sides cannot all have equal length; that is, a *rhombus* is not a kite. The diagonals of a kite are *perpendicular.* See Section 13.4.2: Polygons (*n*-gons).

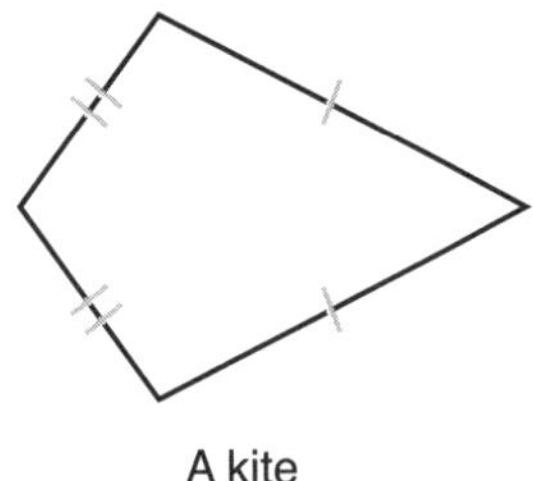

A kite

label A descriptive word or phrase used to put a number or numbers in context. Labels encourage children to associate numbers with real objects. Flags, snowballs, and scary monsters are examples of labels. See Section 10.2: Use Classes and Situation Diagrams.

landmark In *Everyday Mathematics,* a notable feature of a *data* set. Landmarks include the *median, mode, mean, maximum, minimum,* and *range.* See Section 12.2.4: Data Analysis.

lattice multiplication A very old *algorithm* for multiplying multidigit numbers that requires only basic multiplication facts and addition of 1-digit numbers in a lattice diagram. See Section 11.2.3: Multiplication Algorithms.

least common denominator (LCD) The *least common multiple* of the denominators of every fraction in a given collection. For example, the least common denominator of $\frac{1}{2}$, $\frac{4}{5}$, and $\frac{3}{8}$ is 40.

least common multiple (LCM) The smallest number that is a *multiple* of two or more given numbers. For example, common multiples of 6 and 8 include 24, 48, and 72. The least common multiple of 6 and 8 is 24.

left-to-right subtraction A subtraction *algorithm* that works from the left decimal place to the right in several steps. For example, to solve 94 − 57, first calculate 94 − 50 to obtain 44 and then calculate 44 − 7 to obtain 37. The method is especially suited to mental arithmetic. See Section 11.2.2: Subtraction Algorithms.

leg of a right triangle Either *side* of the *right angle* in a *right triangle*; a side that is not the *hypotenuse*. See Section 13.4.2: Polygons (*n*-gons).

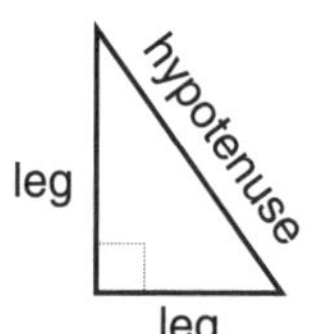

length The distance between two points on a *1-dimensional figure.* For example, the figure might be a line segment, arc, or a curve on a map modeling a hiking path. Length is measured in units such as inches, kilometers, and miles. See Section 14.3: Length.

length of a rectangle Typically, but not necessarily, the longer dimension of a *rectangle.*

like fractions *Fractions* with equal *denominators.*

line In *Everyday Mathematics*, a 1-dimensional straight path that extends forever in opposite directions. A line is named using two points on it or with a single, italicized lower-case letter such as *l*. In formal Euclidean geometry, line is an undefined geometric term. See Section 13.3: Lines, Segments, and Rays.

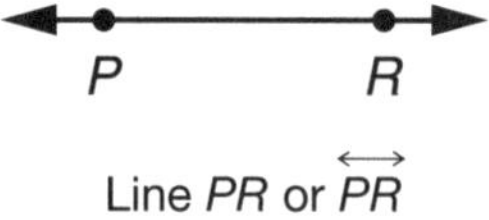

Line *PR* or $\overleftrightarrow{PR}$

line graph A graph in which *data* points are connected by *line segments*. Same as *broken-line graph*. See Section 12.2.3: Organizing and Displaying Data.

line of reflection (mirror line) (1) In *Everyday Mathematics,* a line halfway between a figure and its *reflection* image in a plane. (2) The *perpendicular bisector* of the line segments connecting points on a figure with their corresponding points on its reflection image. Compare to *line of symmetry.* See Section 13.7.1: Flips, Turns, and Slides.

line of symmetry A line that divides a figure into two parts that are *reflection* images of each other. A figure may have zero, one, or more lines of symmetry. For example, the numeral 2 has no lines of symmetry, a square has four lines of symmetry, and a circle has infinitely many lines of symmetry. Also called a symmetry line. See Section 13.8.1: Line Symmetry.

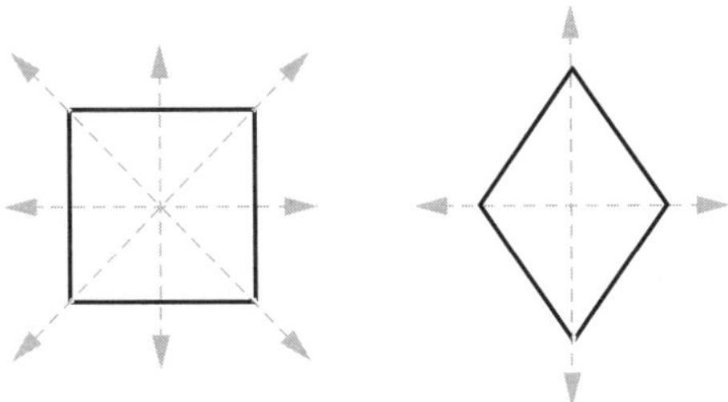

Lines of symmetry are shown in blue.

line plot A sketch of data in which check marks, Xs, or other symbols above a labeled line show the frequency of each value. See Section 12.2.3: Organizing and Displaying Data.

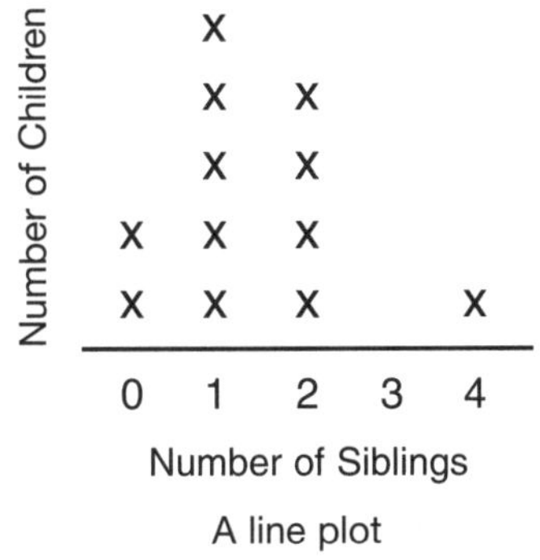

A line plot

line segment A part of a *line* between and including two points called *endpoints* of the segment. Same as *segment*. A line segment is often named by its endpoints. See Section 13.3: Lines, Segments, and Rays.

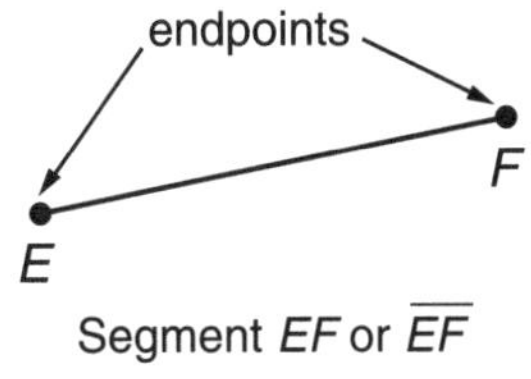

Segment *EF* or $\overline{EF}$

line symmetry A figure has line symmetry if a line can be drawn that divides it into two parts that are *reflection* images of each other. See *line of symmetry* and Section 13.7.1: Flips, Turns, and Slides.

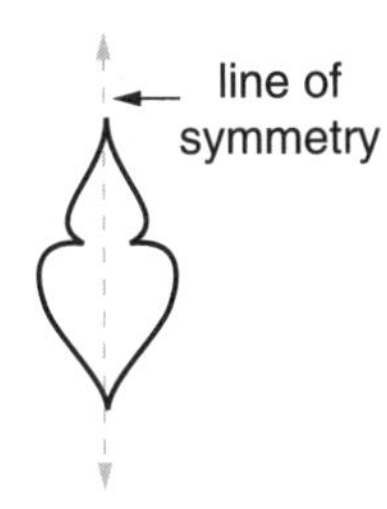

liter (L) A metric unit of *volume* or *capacity* equal to the volume of a cube with 10-cm-long edges. 1 L = 1,000 mL = 1,000 cm^3. A liter is a little larger than a quart. See the Tables of Measures and Section 14.5: Volume (Capacity).

long In *Everyday Mathematics*, the *base-10 block* consisting of ten 1-cm cubes. Sometimes called a "rod." See Section 9.7.1: Base-10 Blocks.

A long

long-term memory *Memory in a calculator* used by keys with an M on them, such as M- and M+. Numbers in long-term memory are not affected by calculations with keys without an M, which use *short-term memory*. See Section 3.1.1: Calculators.

lowest terms of a fraction Same as *simplest form of a fraction*.

magnitude estimate A rough *estimate* of whether a number is in the tens, hundreds, thousands, or other powers of 10. For example, the U.S. national debt per person is in the tens of thousands of dollars. In *Everyday Mathematics,* children give magnitude estimates for problems such as *How many dimes are in $200?* or *How many halves are in 30?* Same as *order-of-magnitude estimate*. See Section 16.1.3: Estimates in Calculations.

map direction symbol A symbol on a map that identifies north, south, east, and west. Sometimes only north is indicated. See Section 15.4: Maps.

map legend (map key) A diagram that explains the symbols, markings, and colors on a map.

map scale The *ratio* of a distance on a map, globe, or drawing to an actual distance. For example, 1 inch on a map might correspond to 1 real-world mile. A map scale may be shown on a segment of a number line, given as a ratio of distances such as $\frac{1}{63,360}$ or 1:63,360 when an inch represents a mile, or by an informal use of the = symbol such as "1 inch = 1 mile." See Section 15.4.2: Map and Model Scales.

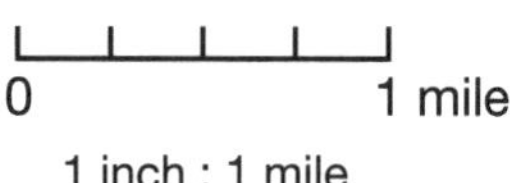

1 inch : 1 mile

mass A measure of the amount of matter in an object. Mass is not affected by gravity, so it is the same on Earth, the moon, or anywhere else in space. Mass is usually measured in grams, kilograms, and other metric units. Compare to *weight*. See Section 14.6: Weight and Mass.

Math Boxes In *Everyday Mathematics,* a collection of problems to practice skills. Math Boxes for each lesson are in the *Math Journal.* See Section 1.2.4: Math Boxes.

Math Journal In *Everyday Mathematics,* a place for students to record their mathematical discoveries and experiences. Journal pages give models for conceptual understanding, problems to solve, and directions for individual and small-group activities.

Math Master In *Everyday Mathematics,* a page ready for duplicating. Most masters support children in carrying out suggested activities. Some masters are used more than once during the school year.

Math Message In *Everyday Mathematics,* an introductory activity to the day's lesson that children complete before the lesson starts. Messages may include problems to solve, directions to follow, sentences to complete or correct, review exercises, or reading assignments. See Section 1.2.5: Math Messages.

maximum The largest amount; the greatest number in a set of data. Compare to *minimum.* See Section 12.2.4: Data Analysis.

mean For a set of numbers, their sum divided by the number of numbers. Often called the *average* value of the set. Compare to other data *landmarks median* and *mode*. See Section 12.2.4: Data Analysis.

measurement division A term for the type of division used to solve an *equal-grouping story* such as *How many tables seating 4 people each are needed for 52 people?* Same as *quotitive division.* Compare to *partitive division.* See Section 10.2.2: Multiplication and Division Use Classes.

measurement unit The reference unit used when measuring. Examples of basic units include inches for *length,* grams for *mass* or *weight,* cubic inches for *volume* or *capacity,* seconds for *elapsed time,* and degrees Celsius for change of temperature. Compound units include square centimeters for area and miles per hour for speed. See Section 14.2: Measurement Systems.

median The middle value in a set of data when the data are listed in order from smallest to largest or vice versa. If there is an even number of data points, the median is the *mean* of the two middle values. Compare to other data *landmarks mean* and *mode*. See Section 12.2.4: Data Analysis.

memory in a calculator Where numbers are stored in a calculator for use in later calculations. Most calculators have both a *short-term memory* and a *long-term memory*. See Section 3.1.1: Calculators.

mental arithmetic Computation done by people "in their heads," either in whole or in part. In *Everyday Mathematics,* students learn a variety of mental-calculation strategies to develop automatic recall of basic facts and *fact power.* See Section 16.3: Mental Arithmetic.

Mental Math and Reflexes In *Everyday Mathematics,* exercises at three levels of difficulty at the beginning of lessons for students to get ready to think about math, warm-up skills they need for the lesson, continually build mental-arithmetic skills, and help you assess individual strengths and weaknesses. See Section 1.2.6: Mental Math and Reflexes.

meter (m) The basic metric unit of *length* from which other metric units of length are derived. Originally, the meter was defined as $\frac{1}{10,000,000}$ of the distance from the North Pole to the equator along a meridian passing through Paris. From 1960 to 1983, the meter was redefined as 1,630,763.73 wavelengths of orange-red light from the element krypton. Today, the meter is defined as the distance light travels in a vacuum in $\frac{1}{299,792,458}$ second. One meter is equal to 10 decimeters, 100 centimeters, or 1,000 millimeters. See Section 14.3: Length.

metric system A measurement system based on the *base-ten* (decimal) numeration system and used in most countries and by virtually all scientists around the world. Units for *length* include millimeter, centimeter, meter, and kilometer; units for *mass* and *weight* include gram and kilogram; units for *volume* and *capacity* include milliliter and liter; and the unit for *temperature* change is degrees Celsius. See the Tables of Measures and Section 14.2.2: Metric System.

middle value Same as *median*.

midpoint A point halfway between two other points. The midpoint of a line segment is the point halfway between the endpoints.

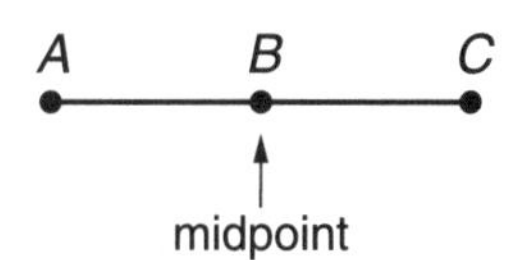

mile (mi) A U.S. customary unit of *length* equal to 5,280 feet, or 1,760 yards. A mile is about 1,609 meters.

milli- A prefix meaning thousandth.

milliliter (mL) A metric unit of *volume* or *capacity* equal to $\frac{1}{1,000}$ of a liter, or 1 cubic centimeter. See Section 14.5: Volume (Capacity).

millimeter (mm) A metric unit of *length* equal to $\frac{1}{10}$ of a centimeter, or $\frac{1}{1,000}$ of a meter. See Section 14.3: Length.

millisecond (ms or msec) A unit of time equal to $\frac{1}{1,000}$ of a second.

minimum The smallest amount; the smallest number in a set of data. Compare to *maximum.* See Section 12.2.4: Data Analysis.

minuend In subtraction, the number from which another number is subtracted. For example, in $19 - 5 = 14$, the minuend is 19. Compare to *subtrahend.*

mirror image Same as *reflection* image.

mixed number A number that is written using both a *whole number* and a *fraction.* For example, $2\frac{1}{4}$ is a mixed number equal to $2 + \frac{1}{4}$.

modal Of or relating to the *mode.*

mode The value or values that occur most often in a set of data. Compare to other *landmarks median* and *mean.* See Section 12.2.4: Data Analysis.

modified repeated addition A multiplication *algorithm* based on adding a to itself b times to find $a \times b$. One of the factors is separated into parts and the partial products of the other factor and those parts are then added. For example, to compute 67×53, think of 10 [67s] as 670 and add five of them to get 50×67. Then add the remaining 3 [67s] to the result. See Section 11.2.3: Multiplication Algorithms.

modified U.S. traditional multiplication A multiplication *algorithm* in which the traditional algorithm is enhanced by introducing 0s into the blanks to maintain the logic of the process and to help avoid sloppy alignment of partial products. See Section 11.2.3: Multiplication Algorithms.

multiple of a number *n* (1) A product of n and a *counting number.* For example, the multiples of 7 are 7, 14, 21, 28, ... (2) A product of n and an *integer.* For example, the multiples of 7 are . . ., −21, −14, −7, 0, 7, 14, 21, ...

multiples of equal groups A *multiple* of a rate in an *equal-grouping* situation. For example, *How many balloons are there altogether in 6 packages with 20 balloons per package?* is a multiple-of-an-equal-groups problem. See Section 10.2.2: Multiplication and Division Use Classes.

multiplication/division use class In *Everyday Mathematics,* a situation in which multiplication or division is used. These include *equal grouping/sharing, arrays and area, rates and ratio, scaling,* and *Cartesian product* situations. See Section 10.2.2: Multiplication and Division Use Classes.

multiplication/division diagram A diagram used in *Everyday Mathematics* to model situations in which a total number is made up of equal-size groups. The diagram contains a number of groups, a number in each group, and a total number. Also called a multiplication diagram for short. See *situation diagram* and Section 10.2.2: Multiplication and Division Use Classes.

rows	chairs per row	total chairs
15	25	?

A multiplication/division diagram

multiplication fact The product of two 1-digit numbers, such as $6 \times 7 = 42$. See *arithmetic facts* and Section 16.3.2: Basic Facts and Fact Power.

multiplication symbols The number a multiplied by the number b is written in a variety of ways. Many mathematics textbooks and *Second* and *Third Grade Everyday Mathematics* use $\times$ as in $a \times b$. Beginning in fourth grade, *Everyday Mathematics* uses $*$ as in $a * b$. Other common symbols are a dot as in $a \bullet b$ and by *juxtaposition* as in ab, which is common in formulas and in algebra courses. See Section 10.1.1: Arithmetic Symbols.

multiplicative inverses Same as *reciprocals.*

name-collection box In *Everyday Mathematics,* a diagram that is used for collecting *equivalent names* for a number. See Section 1.3.3: Name-Collection Boxes.

25
37 − 12
20 + 5
HHH HHH HHH HHH HHH
twenty-five
veinticinco

natural numbers In *Everyday Mathematics,* same as *counting numbers.*

negative numbers Numbers less than 0; the opposites of the *positive numbers,* commonly written as a positive number preceded by a −. Negative numbers are plotted left of 0 on a horizontal number line or below 0 on a vertical number line. See Section 9.4: Positive and Negative Numbers.

negative rational numbers *Rational numbers* less than 0; the opposites of the *positive rational numbers.* For example, −24, −2.333 . . ., and $-\frac{5}{8}$ are negative rational numbers. See Section 9.4: Positive and Negative Numbers.

nested parentheses Parentheses within parentheses in an *expression.* Expressions are evaluated from within the innermost parentheses outward. See *grouping symbols* for an example and Section 10.1.2: Reading and Writing Number Sentences.

net score The final score of a turn or game after all calculations have been completed.

net weight The *weight* of the contents of a container, excluding the weight of the container.

***n*-gon** Same as *polygon,* where n is the number of sides. Polygons that do not have special names like squares and pentagons are usually named using n-gon notation, such as 13-gon or 100-gon.

nona- A prefix meaning nine.

nonagon A 9-sided *polygon.*

nonconvex polygon Same as *concave polygon.*

normal span The distance from the end of the thumb to the end of the index (first) finger of an outstretched hand. For estimating lengths, many people can adjust this distance to approximately 6 inches or 15 centimeters. Same as *span.* Compare to *great span.* See Section 14.1: Personal Measures.

***n*-to-1 ratio** A ratio of a number n to 1. Every ratio $a{:}b$ can be converted to an n-to-1 ratio by dividing a by b. For example, a ratio of 3 to 2 is a ratio of $3 \div 2 = 1.5$ or a 1.5-to-1 ratio.

number-and-word notation A notation consisting of the *significant digits* of a number and words for the place value. For example, 27 billion is number-and-word notation for 27,000,000,000.

number family Same as *fact family.*

number grid In *Everyday Mathematics,* a table in which *consecutive* numbers are arranged in *rows,* usually 10 *columns* per row. A move from one number to the next within a *row* is a change of 1; a move from one number to the next within a *column* is a change of 10. See Section 9.7.2: Number Grids, Scrolls, and Lines.

−9	−8	−7	−6	−5	−4	−3	−2	−1	0
1	2	3	4	5	6	7	8	9	10
11	12	13	14	15	16	17	18	19	20
21	22	23	24	25	26	27	28	29	30
31	32	33	34	35	36	37	38	39	40
41	42	43	44	45	46	47	48	49	50
51	52	53	54	55	56	57	58	59	60
61	62	63	64	65	66	67	68	69	70
71	72	73	74	75	76	77	78	79	80
81	82	83	84	85	86	87	88	89	90
91	92	93	94	95	96	97	98	99	100
101	102	103	104	105	106	107	108	109	110

A number grid

number-grid puzzle In *Everyday Mathematics,* a piece of a *number grid* in which some, but not all, of the numbers are missing. Students use number-grid puzzles to practice place-value concepts.

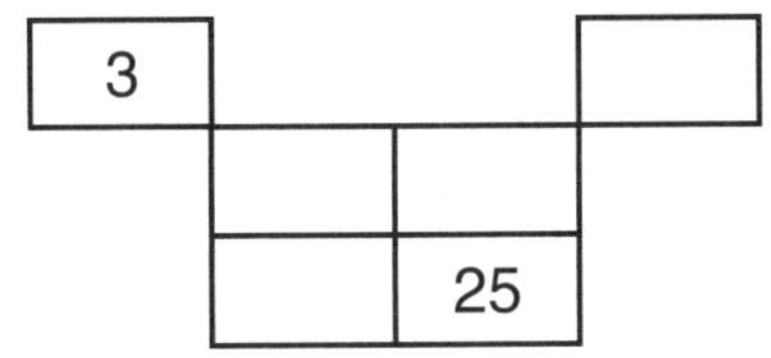

A number-grid puzzle

number line A line on which points are indicated by *tick marks* that are usually at regularly spaced intervals from a starting point called the *origin*, the *zero point*, or simply 0. Numbers are associated with the tick marks on a *scale* defined by the *unit interval* from 0 to 1. See Section 9.7.2: Number Grids, Scrolls, and Lines.

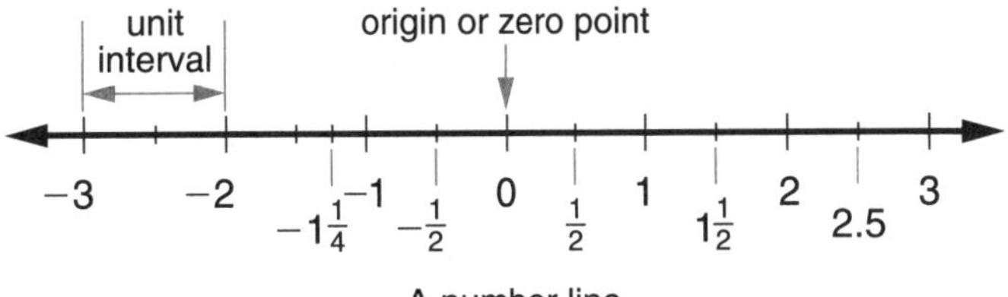

A number line

number model A *number sentence, expression,* or other representation that models a *number story* or situation. For example, the story *Sally had $5, and then she earned $8* can be modeled as the number sentence 5 + 8 = 13, as the expression 5 + 8, or by

$$\begin{array}{r} 5 \\ +\ 8 \\ \hline 13 \end{array}$$

See Section 10.1: Number Sentences and Number Models and Section 18.3: Mathematical Modeling.

number scroll In *Everyday Mathematics,* a series of *number grids* taped together. See Section 9.7.2: Number Grids, Scrolls, and Lines.

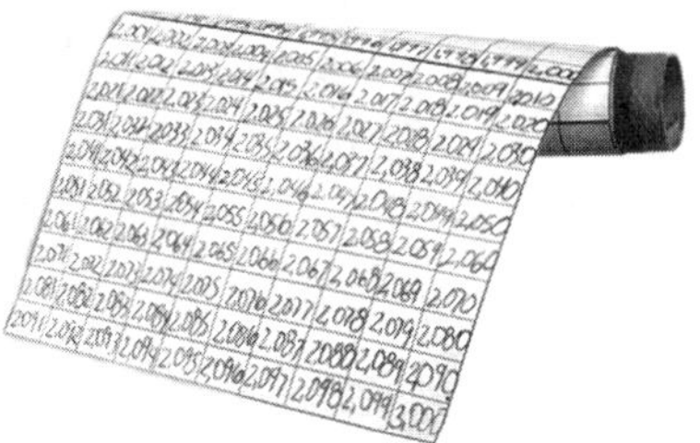

A number scroll

number sentence Two *expressions* with a *relation symbol*. See Section 10.1: Number Sentences and Number Models.

$5 + 5 = 10$ $\quad$ $16 \leq a \times b$

$2 - ? = 8$ $\quad$ $a^2 + b^2 = c^2$

Number sentences

Glossary

number sequence A list of numbers, often generated by a rule. In *Everyday Mathematics*, students explore number sequences using *Frames-and-Arrows* diagrams. See Section 17.1.3: Sequences.

1, 2, 3, 4, 5, . . . 1, 4, 9, 16, 25, . . .

1, 2, 1, 2, 1, . . . 1, 3, 5, 7, 9, . . .

Number sequences

number story A story that involves numbers and one or more explicit or implicit questions. For example, *I have 7 crayons in my desk. Carrie gave me 8 more crayons. Now I have 15 crayons in all* is a number story. See Section 18.4.1: Number Stories.

numeral A word, symbol, or figure that represents a number. For example, six, VI, 卌/, and 6 are all numerals that represent the same number.

numeration A method of numbering or of reading and writing numbers. In *Everyday Mathematics,* numeration activities include counting, writing numbers, identifying equivalent names for numbers in *name-collection boxes,* exchanging coins such as 5 pennies for 1 nickel, and renaming numbers in computation. See Section 9.2.1: Numeration and Place Value.

numerator The dividend a in a fraction $\frac{a}{b}$ or a/b. In a part-whole *fraction,* in which the *whole* (the *ONE* or *unit whole*) is divided into a number of equal parts, the numerator is the number of equal parts being considered. Compare to *denominator*. See Section 9.3.1: Fraction and Decimal Notation.

O

obtuse angle An *angle* with measure between 90° and 180°. See Section 13.4.1: Angles and Rotations.

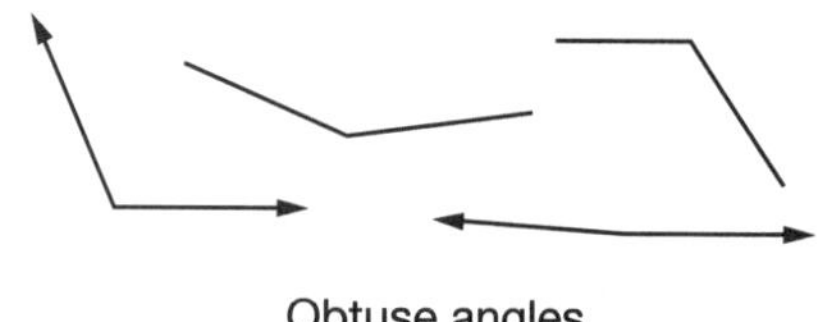

Obtuse angles

obtuse triangle A *triangle* with an angle measuring more than 90°. See Section 13.4.2: Polygons (n-gons).

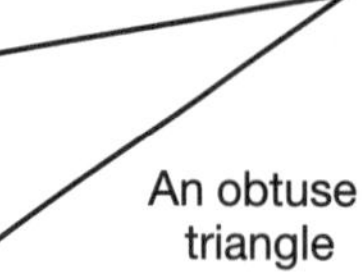

An obtuse triangle

octa- A prefix meaning eight.

octagon An 8-sided *polygon*. See Section 13.4.2: Polygons (n-gons).

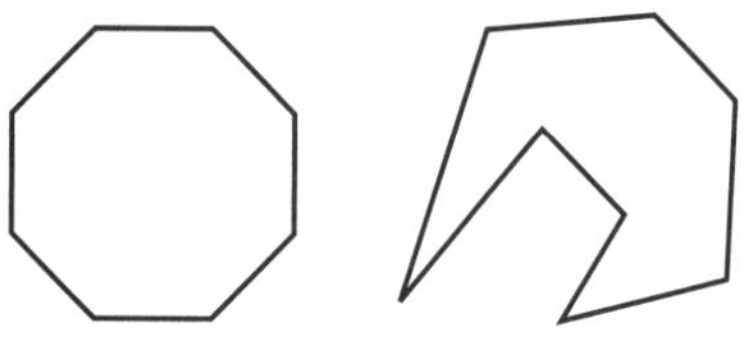

Octagons

octahedron A *polyhedron* with 8 faces. An octahedron with 8 *equilateral triangle* faces is one of the five *regular polyhedrons.* See Section 13.5.2: Polyhedrons.

odd number A *counting number* that is not *divisible by* 2. Compare to *even number.* See Section 17.1.2: Odd and Even Number Patterns.

ONE In *Everyday Mathematics,* same as *whole* or *unit whole.*

1-dimensional (1-D) coordinate system A *reference frame* in which any point on a *1-dimensional figure* can be located with one *coordinate* relative to the origin of a number line. Compare to *2-dimensional* and *3-dimensional coordinate systems*. See Section 15.3.1: Number Grids, Scrolls, and Lines.

1-dimensional (1-D) figure A figure such as a line segment, arc, or part of a curve that has length but no width or depth. Compare to *2-* and *3-dimensional figures.* See Section 13.1: Dimension.

open sentence A *number sentence* with one or more *variables*. An open sentence is neither true nor false. For example, $9 + \_ = 15$, $? - 24 < 10$, and $7 = x + y$ are open sentences. See Section 17.2.2: Reading and Writing Open Sentences.

operation A rule performed on one or more mathematical objects such as numbers, *variables,* or *expressions* to produce another mathematical object. Addition, subtraction, multiplication, and division are the four basic arithmetic operations. Taking a square root, squaring a number, and multiplying both sides of an *equation* by the same number are also operations. In *Everyday Mathematics,* students learn about many operations along with several procedures, or *algorithms,* for carrying them out. See Chapter 10: Operations and Number Models.

operation symbol A symbol used in *expressions* and *number sentences* to stand for a particular mathematical operation. Symbols for common arithmetic operations are:

addition	+
subtraction	−
multiplication	×, *, •
division	÷, /
powering	^

See Section 10.1: Number Sentences and Number Models.

opposite angle in a triangle The *angle* opposite a *side* of a *triangle* that is not one of the sides of the angle.

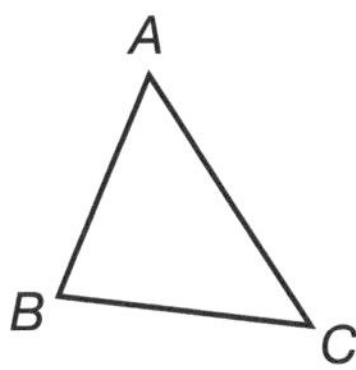

Angle *C* is opposite side *AB*.

opposite angles in a quadrilateral Two *angles* in a *quadrilateral* that do not share a side.

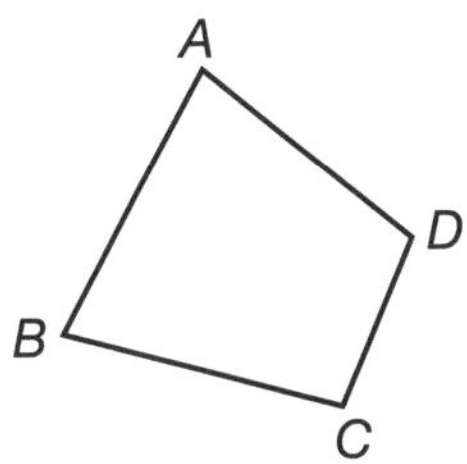

Angles *A* and *C* and angles *B* and *D* are pairs of opposite angles.

opposite-change rule for addition An addition *algorithm* in which a number is added to one *addend* and subtracted from the other addend. Compare to *same-change rule for subtraction*. See Section 11.2.1: Addition Algorithms.

opposite of a number *n* A number that is the same distance from 0 on a number line as *n*, but on the opposite side of 0. In symbols, the opposite of a number *n* is $-n$ and, in *Everyday Mathematics*, OPP(n). If *n* is a negative number, $-n$ is a positive number. For example, the opposite of -5 is 5. The sum of a number *n* and its opposite is zero; $n + -n = 0$. Same as *additive inverse*.

opposite side in a triangle The *side* opposite an *angle* of a *triangle* that is not a side of the angle.

opposite sides in a quadrilateral Two *sides* in a *quadrilateral* that do not share a *vertex*.

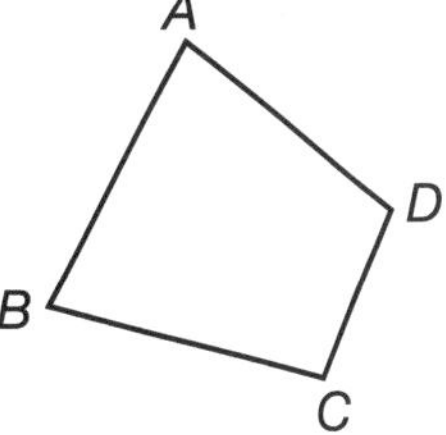

Sides *AB* and *DC* and sides *BC* and *AD* are pairs of opposite sides.

order-of-magnitude estimate Same as *magnitude estimate*.

order-of-magnitude increase A 10-times change in a value. Sometimes simply called a magnitude increase. See Section 16.1.2: Extreme Numbers.

order of operations Rules that tell the order in which operations in an *expression* should be carried out. The conventional order of operations is:

1. Do operations inside *grouping symbols*. Work from the innermost set of grouping symbols outward. Inside grouping symbols, follow Rules 2–4.
2. Calculate all expressions with *exponents*.
3. *Multiply* and *divide* in order from left to right.
4. *Add* and *subtract* in order from left to right.

For example:

$$\begin{aligned} 5^2 + (3 \times 4 - 2) \div 5 &= 5^2 + (12 - 2) \div 5 \\ &= 5^2 + 10 \div 5 \\ &= 25 + 10 \div 5 \\ &= 25 + 2 \\ &= 27 \end{aligned}$$

Same as *algebraic order of operations*. See Section 10.1.2: Reading and Writing Number Sentences.

Glossary

ordered pair (1) Two numbers, or *coordinates,* used to locate a point on a *rectangular coordinate grid.* The first coordinate x gives the position along the horizontal axis of the grid, and the second coordinate y gives the position along the vertical axis. The pair is written (x,y). See Section 15.3: Coordinate Systems. (2) Any pair of objects or numbers in a particular order.

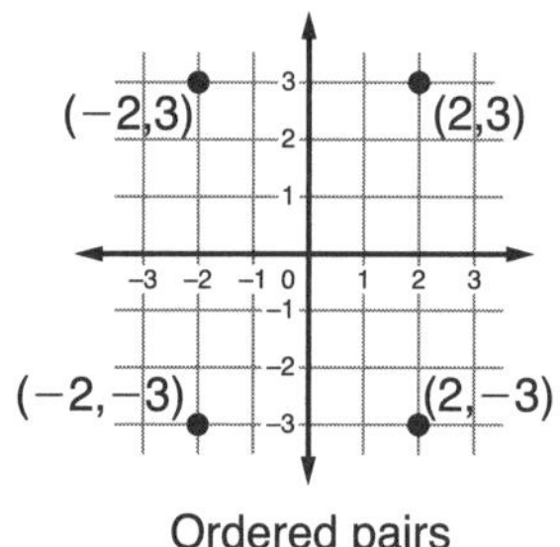

Ordered pairs

orders of magnitude Positive powers of 10 including 10, 100, 1,000, and so on. See *order-of-magnitude increase* and Section 16.1.2: Extreme Numbers.

ordinal number The position or order of something in a *sequence,* such as first, third, or tenth. Ordinal numbers are commonly used in dates, as in "May fifth" instead of "May five." See Section 9.2.3: Ordinal Numbers.

origin The *zero point* in a *coordinate system*. On a number line, the origin is the point at 0. On a coordinate grid, the origin is the point (0,0) where the two axes intersect. See Section 15.3: Coordinate Systems.

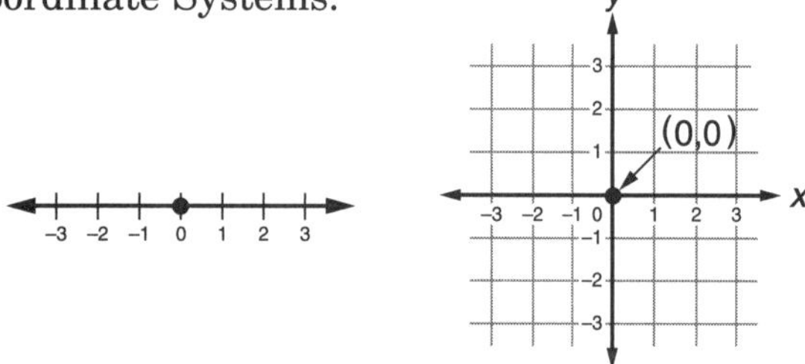

The points at 0 and (0,0) are origins.

ounce (oz) A U.S. customary unit of *weight* equal to $\frac{1}{16}$ of a pound or about 28.35 grams. Compare to *fluid ounce*. See the Tables of Measures and Section 14.6: Weight and Mass.

outcome A possible result of a chance experiment or situation. For example, HEADS and TAILS are the two possible outcomes of flipping a coin. See *event, equally likely outcomes,* and Section 12.1.2: The Language of Chance.

output (1) A number paired to an *input* by an imaginary *function machine* applying a rule. (2) The values for y in a *function* consisting of ordered pairs (x,y). See Section 17.1.4: Functions. (3) Numbers or other information displayed by calculator or computer.

P

pan balance A device used to weigh objects or compare their *weights*. See Section 14.10.3: Scales and Balances.

parallel lines *Lines* in a *plane* that never meet. Two parallel lines are always the same distance apart. *Line segments* or *rays* on parallel lines are parallel to each other. See Section 13.6.1: Perpendicular and Parallel.

parallel planes *Planes* in space that never meet. Two parallel planes are always the same distance apart. A figure in one plane is parallel to the other plane. Polygons in one plane are said to be parallel to polygons in the other plane. However, 1-dimensional shapes such as lines, segments, and rays in one plane are not necessarily parallel to 1-dimensional shapes in a parallel plane. See Section 13.6.1: Perpendicular and Parallel.

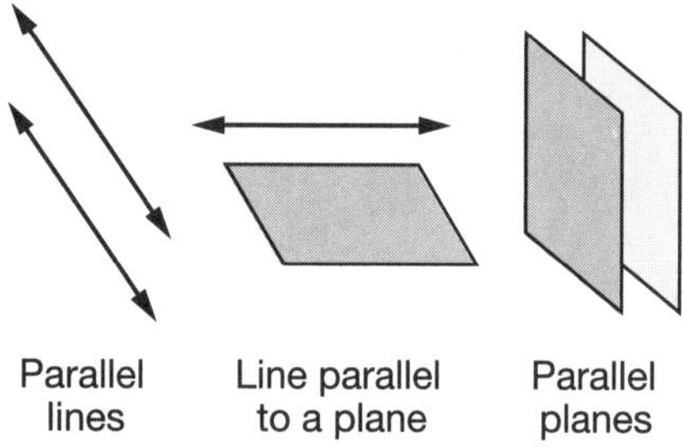

parallelogram A *quadrilateral* with two pairs of parallel sides. *Opposite sides* of a parallelogram have the same length and *opposite angles* have the same measure. All rectangles are parallelograms, but not all parallelograms are rectangles because parallelograms do not necessarily have right angles. See Section 13.4.2: Polygons (n-gons).

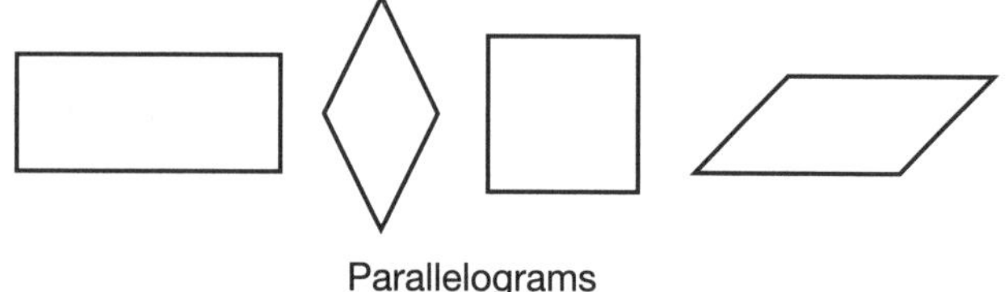
Parallelograms

parentheses See *grouping symbols.*

partial-differences subtraction A subtraction *algorithm* in which separate differences are computed for each place value of the numbers and then added to get a final difference. See Section 11.2.2: Subtraction Algorithms.

partial-products multiplication A multiplication *algorithm* in which partial products are computed by multiplying the value of each digit in one factor by the value of each digit in the other factor. The final product is the sum of the partial products. See Section 11.2.3: Multiplication Algorithms.

partial-sums addition An addition *algorithm* in which separate sums are computed for each place value of the numbers and then added to get a final sum. See Section 11.2.1: Addition Algorithms.

partitive division A term for the type of division used to solve an *equal-sharing story* such as *If $10 is shared by 4 people, how much does each person get?* Compare to *measurement division.* See Section 10.2.2: Multiplication and Division Use Classes.

parts-and-total diagram In *Everyday Mathematics,* a diagram used to model problems in which two or more quantities (parts) are combined to get a total quantity. See *situation diagram* and Section 10.2.1: Addition and Subtraction Use Classes.

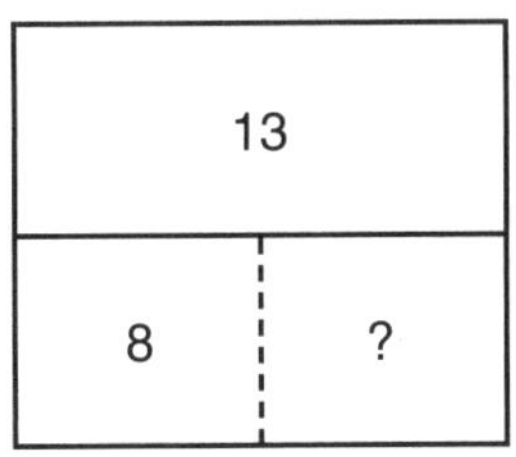

Total
13
Part 8
Part ?

Parts-and-total diagrams for 13 = 8 + ?

parts-and-total story A *number story* in which a whole is made up of distinct parts. For example, *There are 15 girls and 12 boys in Mrs. Dorn's class. How many students are there in all?* is a parts-and-total story. In other stories, the total and one or more parts may be known and the last part unknown. See Section 10.2.1: Addition and Subtraction Use Classes.

pattern A repetitive order or arrangement. In *Everyday Mathematics,* students mainly explore visual and number patterns in which elements are arranged so that what comes next can be predicted. See Section 17.1: Patterns, Sequences, and Functions.

Pattern-Block Template In *First* through *Third Grade Everyday Mathematics,* a sheet of plastic with geometric shapes cut out, used to draw patterns and designs. See Section 13.10.1: Pattern-Block Template.

pattern blocks A set of *polygon*-shaped blocks of varying sizes in which smaller blocks can be placed on larger blocks to show fractional parts. The blocks are used for geometric-shape identification and fraction activities. Compare to *attribute blocks.*

penta- A prefix meaning five.

pentagon A 5-sided *polygon.* See Section 13.4.2: Polygons (n-gons).

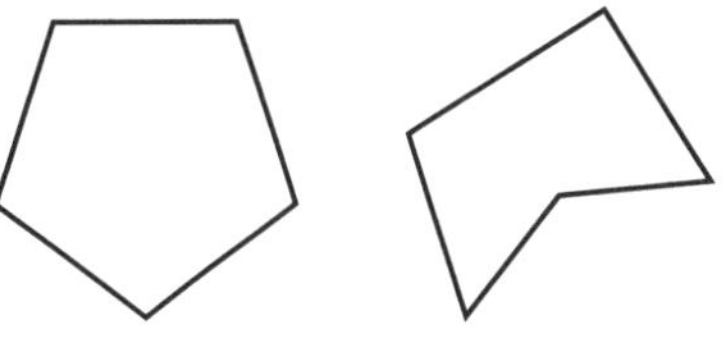

Pentagons

per For each, as in *ten chairs per row* or *six tickets per family.*

per capita For each person. Often used to describe an *average* of a data set, as in *The per-capita debt for U.S. citizens in July 2005 was $26,451.95.*

percent (%) Per hundred, for each hundred, or out of a hundred. $1\% = \frac{1}{100} = 0.01$. For example, *48% of the students in the school are boys* means that, on average, 48 of every 100 children in the school are boys. See Section 9.3.4: Percents.

perimeter The distance around the boundary of a *2-dimensional figure*. The perimeter of a *circle* is called its *circumference*. A formula for the perimeter P of a *rectangle* with length l and width w is $P = 2 \times (l + w)$. Perimeter comes from the Greek words for "around measure." See Section 14.3: Length.

perpendicular ($\perp$) Two *lines* or two *planes* that intersect at *right angles. Line segments* or *rays* that lie on perpendicular lines are perpendicular to each other. The symbol $\perp$ means "is perpendicular to." See Section 13.6.1: Perpendicular and Parallel.

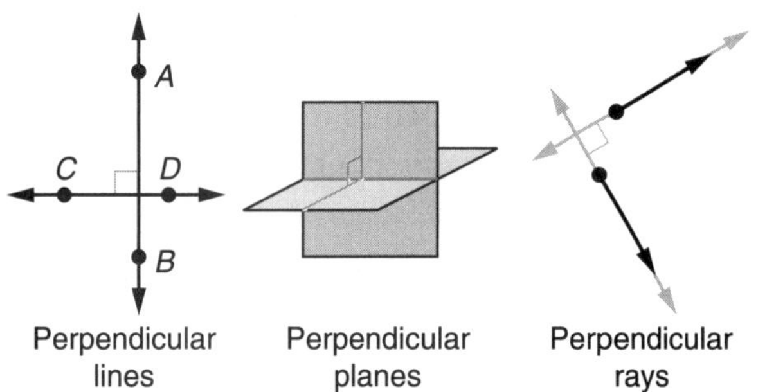

Perpendicular lines | Perpendicular planes | Perpendicular rays

perpendicular bisector A *line, ray,* or *segment* that *bisects* a line segment at a *right angle.*

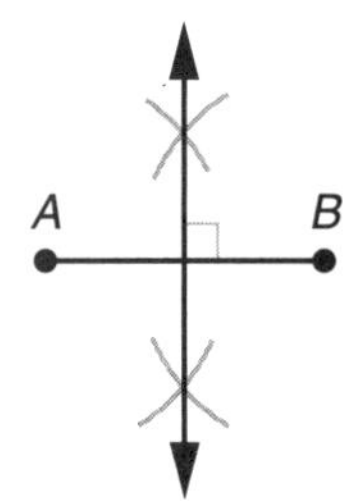

Construction of a perpendicular bisector of $\overline{AB}$

personal-measurement reference A convenient approximation for a standard unit of measurement. For example, many people have thumbs that are approximately one inch wide. See Section 14.1: Personal Measures.

perspective drawing A drawing that realistically represents a 3-dimensional object on a 2-dimensional surface. See Section 13.5.4: Connecting 2-D and 3-D.

pi (π) The ratio of the *circumference* of a circle to its *diameter.* Pi is also the ratio of the area of a circle to the square of its radius. Pi is the same for every circle and is an *irrational number* that is approximately equal to 3.14. The symbol π is the sixteenth letter of the Greek alphabet. See page 67 for the first 1,832 digits of π, and Section 13.4.3: Circles and Pi (π).

pictograph A graph constructed with pictures or symbols. See Section 12.2.3: Organizing and Displaying Data.

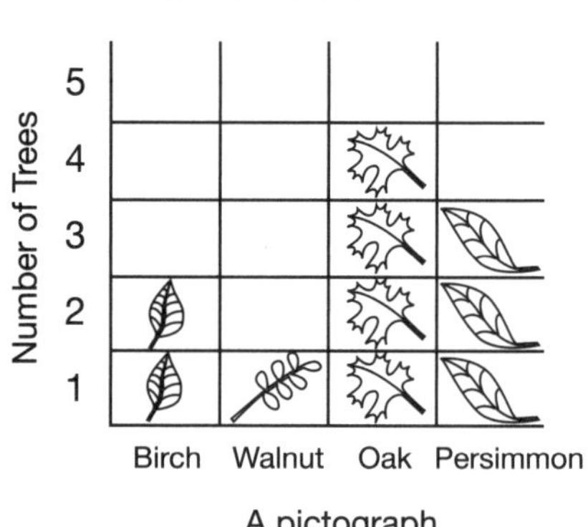

A pictograph

pie graph Same as *circle graph.*

pint (pt) A U.S. customary unit of *volume* or *capacity* equal to 2 cups, or 16 fluid ounces. A handy saying to remember is *A pint's a pound the world around,* meaning that a pint of water weighs about 1 pound. See the Tables of Measures and Section 14.5: Volume (Capacity).

place value A system that gives a *digit* a value according to its position, or place, in a number. In our standard, *base-ten* (decimal) system for writing numbers, each place has a value 10 times that of the place to its right and 1 tenth the value of the place to its left. See Section 9.2.1: Numeration and Place Value.

thousands	hundreds	tens	ones	.	tenths	hundredths

A place-value chart

plane In *Everyday Mathematics,* a *2-dimensional* flat surface that extends forever in all directions. In formal Euclidean geometry, plane is an undefined geometric term. See Section 13.4: Planes and Plane Figures.

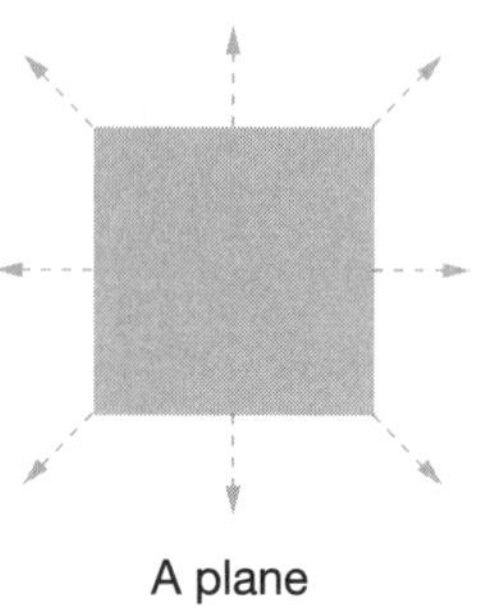

A plane

plane figure A *2-dimensional figure* that is entirely contained in a single *plane*. For example, triangles, squares, pentagons, circles, and parabolas are plane figures; lines, rays, cones, cubes, and prisms are not. See Section 13.4: Planes and Plane Figures.

P.M. The abbreviation for *post meridiem,* meaning "after the middle of the day" in Latin. From noon to midnight.

point In *Everyday Mathematics,* an exact location in space. Points are usually labeled with capital letters. In formal Euclidean geometry, point is an undefined geometric term. See Section 13.2: Points.

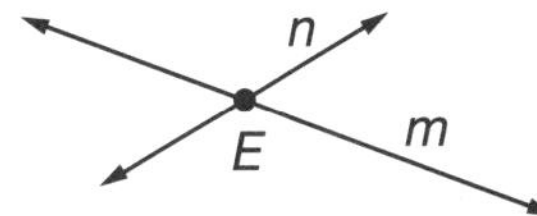

Lines *m* and *n* intersect at point *E*.

poly- A prefix meaning many.

polygon A *2-dimensional figure* formed by three or more line segments (*sides*) that meet only at their endpoints (*vertices*) to make a closed path. The sides may not cross one another. See Section 13.4.2: Polygons (*n*-gons).

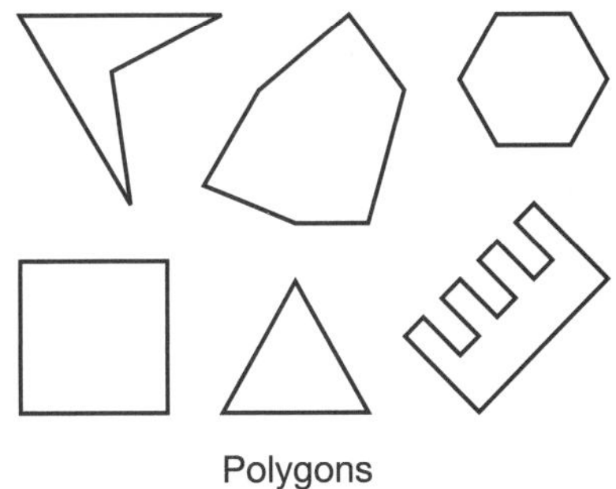

Polygons

polyhedron A *3-dimensional figure* formed by *polygons* with their interiors (*faces*) and having no holes. Plural is polyhedrons or polyhedra. See Section 13.5.2: Polyhedrons.

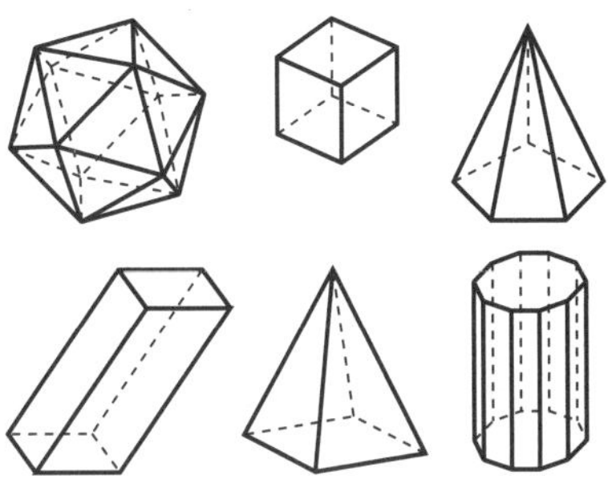

Polyhedrons

population (1) The total number of people living within a defined geographic region. (2) In data collection, the group of people or objects that is the focus of study. Large populations are often studied by picking a representative *random sample* from the population. See Section 12.2.2: Collecting and Recording Data.

population density The number of people living in a defined geographic region, usually given as a *rate,* such as *876 people per square mile.*

positive numbers Numbers greater than 0; the opposites of the *negative numbers.* Positive numbers are plotted to the right of 0 on a horizontal number line or above 0 on a vertical number line. See Section 9.4: Positive and Negative Numbers.

positive rational numbers *Rational numbers* greater than 0; the opposites of the negative *rational numbers*. For example, 7, $\frac{4}{3}$, $\frac{1}{1,000}$, 0.01, 8.125, and 5.111 . . . are positive rational numbers. See Section 9.4: Positive and Negative Numbers.

poster In *Everyday Mathematics,* a page displaying a collection of illustrated numerical data. A poster may be used as a source of data for developing *number stories.*

pound (lb) A U.S. customary unit of *weight* equal to 16 ounces and defined as 0.45359237 kilograms. See the Tables of Measures and Section 14.6: Weight and Mass.

power Same as *exponent.*

power of a number A *product of factors* that are all the same; the result of a^b for any numbers a and b. For example, $5^3 = 5 \times 5 \times 5 = 125$ is read "5 to the third power" or "the third power of 5" because 5 is a factor 3 times. See *exponential notation* and Section 10.1.1: Arithmetic Symbols.

precipitation Condensed atmospheric moisture that falls to the ground, including rain, snow, and hail. In the United States, rainfall is typically measured in inches. Snow and hail are first melted and then measured like rain.

precise Exact or accurate.

precise calculations The more accurate measures or other data are, the more *precise* any calculations using those numbers can be. See *significant digits* and Section 16.2: Approximation and Rounding.

precise measures The smaller the *scale* of a measuring tool, the more *precise* a measurement can be. For example, a measurement to the nearest inch is more precise than a measurement to the nearest foot. A ruler with $\frac{1}{16}$-inch markings can be more precise than a ruler with only $\frac{1}{4}$-inch markings, depending on the skill of the person doing the measuring.

predict In mathematics, to say what will happen in the future based on experimental data or theoretical calculation.

preimage The original figure in a *transformation*. Compare to *image*. See Section 13.7: Transformations.

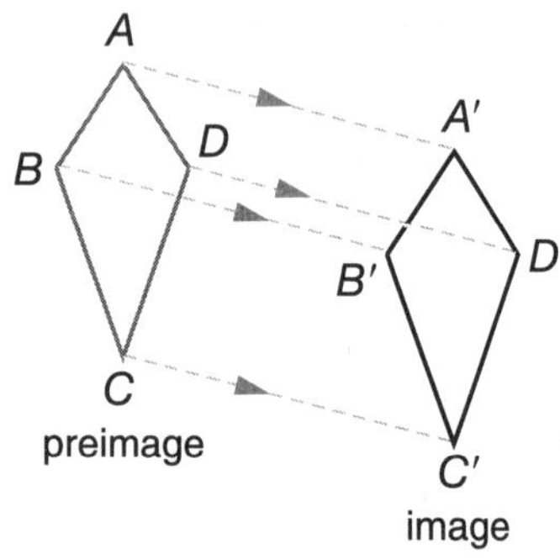

prime factorization A *counting number* written as a product of *prime-number* factors. Every counting number greater than 1 has a unique prime factorization. For example, the prime factorization of 24 is $2 \times 2 \times 2 \times 3$.

prime number A *counting number* greater than 1 that has exactly two whole-number factors, 1 and itself. For example, 7 is a prime number because its only factors are 1 and 7. The first five prime numbers are 2, 3, 5, 7, and 11. Also simply called primes. Compare to *composite number.*

prism A *polyhedron* with two parallel and congruent polygonal regions for *bases* and lateral *faces* formed by all the line segments with endpoints on corresponding edges of the bases. The lateral faces are all parallelograms. Lateral faces intersect at lateral *edges*. In a *right prism,* the lateral faces are rectangular. Prisms get their names from the shape of their bases. See Section 13.5.2: Polyhedrons.

A triangular prism

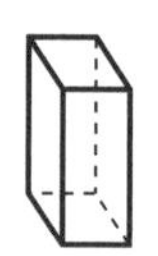
A rectangular prism

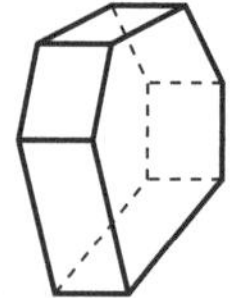
A hexagonal prism

probability A number from 0 through 1 giving the likelihood that an *event* will happen. The closer a probability is to 1, the more likely the event is to happen. The closer a probability is to 0, the less likely the event is to happen. For example, the probability that a fair coin will show HEADS is $\frac{1}{2}$. See Section 12.1: Probability.

product The result of multiplying two numbers, called *factors*. For example, in $4 \times 3 = 12$, the product is 12.

Project In *Everyday Mathematics,* a thematic activity to be completed in one or more days by small groups or by a whole class. Projects often involve collecting and analyzing data and are usually cross-curricular in nature. See Section 1.2.9: Projects.

proper factor Any *factor of a counting number* except the number itself. For example, the factors of 10 are 1, 2, 5, and 10, and the proper factors of 10 are 1, 2, and 5.

proper fraction A *fraction* in which the numerator is less than the denominator. A proper fraction is between -1 and 1. For example, $\frac{3}{4}$, $-\frac{2}{5}$, and $\frac{12}{24}$ are proper fractions. Compare to *improper fraction. Everyday Mathematics* does not emphasize these distinctions.

property (1) A generalized statement about a mathematical relationship such as the *Distributive Property of Multiplication over Addition*. (2) Same as *attribute*.

protractor A tool used for measuring or drawing *angles.* A half-circle protractor can be used to measure and draw angles up to 180°. A full-circle protractor can be used to measure and draw angles up to 360°.

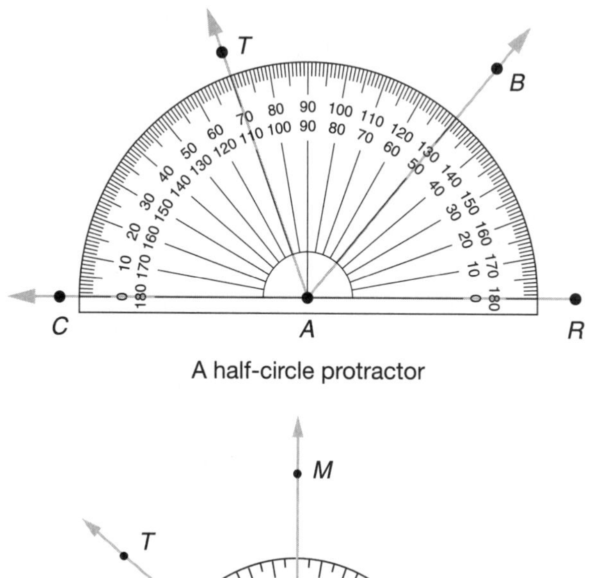

A half-circle protractor

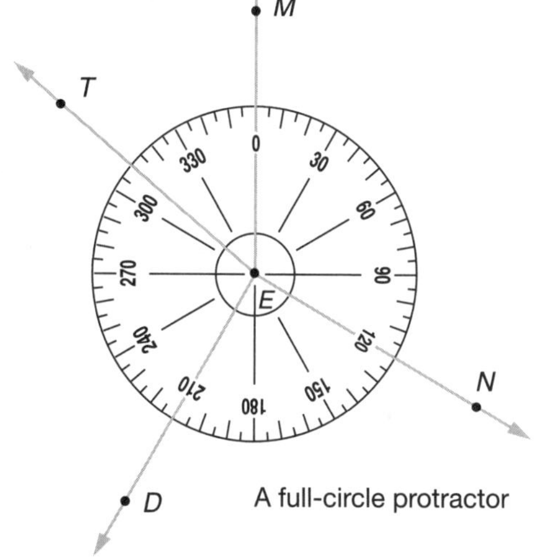

A full-circle protractor

pyramid A *polyhedron* made up of any polygonal region for a *base,* a vertex *(apex)* not in the plane of the base, and all of the line segments with one endpoint at the apex and the other on an edge of the base. All faces except perhaps the base are triangular. Pyramids get their name from the shape of their base. See Section 13.5.2: Polyhedrons.

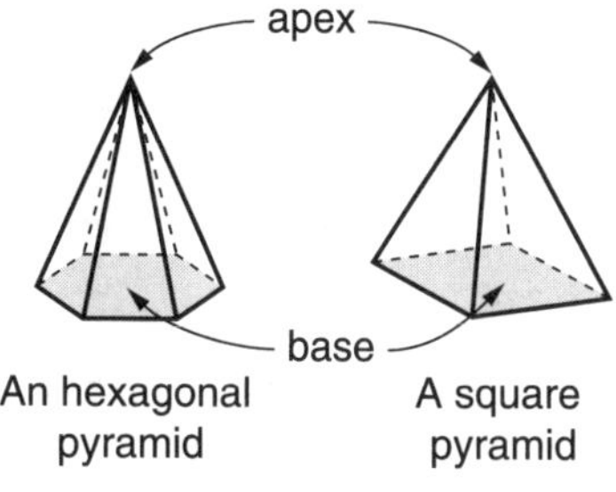

quad- A prefix meaning four.

quadrangle Same as *quadrilateral.*

quadrant One of the four sections into which a *rectangular coordinate grid* is divided by the two axes. The quadrants are typically numbered I, II, III, and IV counterclockwise beginning at the upper right.

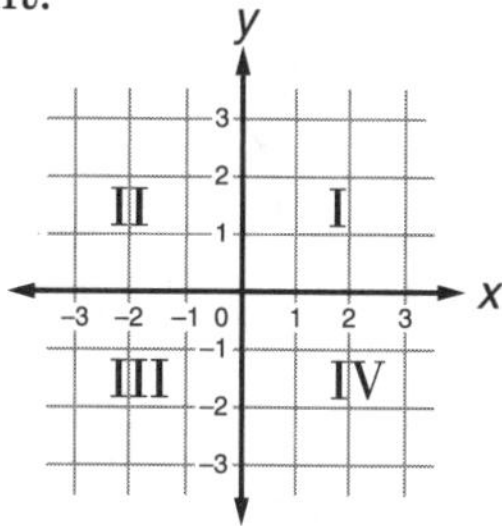

quadrilateral A 4-sided *polygon.* See *square, rectangle, parallelogram, rhombus, kite, trapezoid,* and Section 13.4.2: Polygons (*n*-gons).

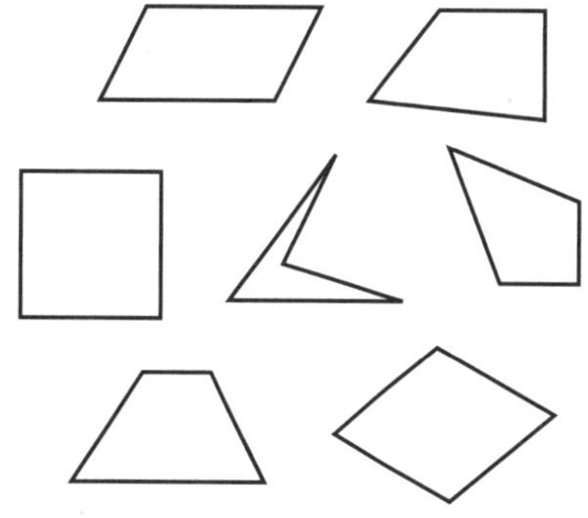
Quadrilaterals

quadruple Four times an amount.

quart A U.S. customary unit of *volume* or *capacity* equal to 32 fluid ounces, 2 pints, or 4 cups. See the Tables of Measures and Section 14.5: Volume (Capacity).

quotient The result of dividing one number by another number. For example, in $10 \div 5 = 2$, the quotient is 2.

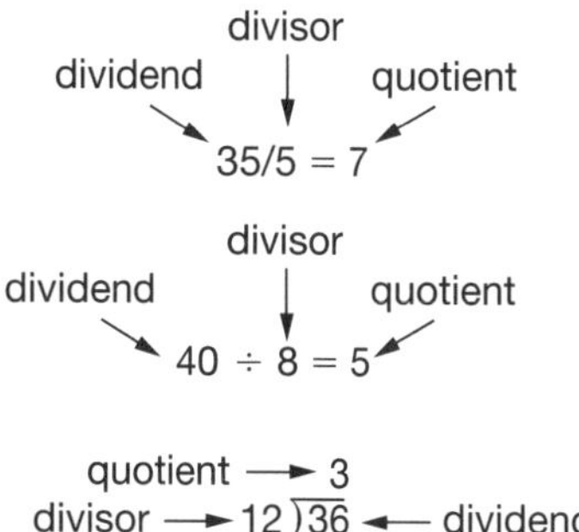

quotitive division Same as *measurement division.*

radius (1) A *line segment* from the center of a circle (or sphere) to any point on the *circle* (or *sphere*). (2) The length of this line segment. The length of a radius is half the length of a *diameter.* Plural is radiuses or radii. See Section 13.4.3: Circles and Pi (π).

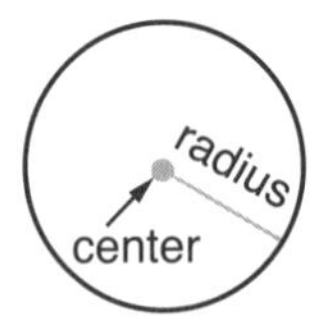

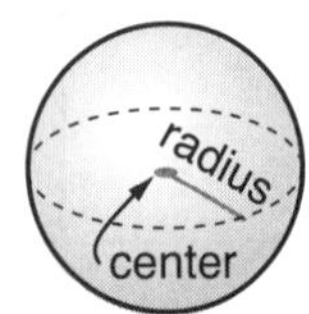

random draw Taking an object from a set of objects in which each object has an *equally likely* chance of being chosen. For example, drawing a card from a deck and drawing a domino from a bag of dominos are random draws. See Section 12.1.2: The Language of Chance.

random experiment An experiment in which all *outcomes* are *equally likely.* No one outcome is more predictable than any other. See Section 12.1.2: The Language of Chance.

random number A number produced by a *random experiment,* such as rolling a die or spinning a spinner. For example, rolling a fair die produces random numbers because each of the six possible numbers 1, 2, 3, 4, 5, and 6 has the same chance of coming up. See Section 12.1.2: The Language of Chance.

random sample A *sample* that gives all members of the *population* the same chance of being selected. See Section 12.2.2: Collecting and Recording Data.

range The *difference* between the *maximum* and the *minimum* in a set of data. Used as a measure of the spread of the data. See Section 12.2.4: Data Analysis.

rate A comparison by division of two quantities with different *units.* For example, traveling 100 miles in 2 hours is an average rate of $\frac{100 \text{ mi}}{2 \text{ hr}}$, or 50 miles per hour. Compare to *ratio.* See Section 9.3.3: Rates and Ratios and Section 10.2.2: Multiplication and Division Use Classes.

rate diagram A diagram used in *Everyday Mathematics* to model *rate* situations. The diagram includes two quantities and the rate comparing them. See *situation diagram* and Section 10.2.2: Multiplication and Division Use Classes.

rows	chairs per row	chairs
6	4	?

A rate diagram

rate-multiplication story A *number story* in which one quantity is a *rate* times another quantity. A typical rate is *speed,* which multiplied by a time traveled gives distance traveled. There are many other rates such as price per pound or hours per person. For example, *8 people work a total of 20 hours. What is the average number of work hours per person?* is a rate-multiplication story. See Section 10.2.2: Multiplication and Division Use Classes.

rate table A display of *rate* information. In a rate table, the fractions formed by the two numbers in each column are *equivalent fractions.* For example, $\frac{35}{1} = \frac{70}{2}$ in the table below. See Section 10.2.2: Multiplication and Division Use Classes.

miles	35	70	105	140	175	210
gallons	1	2	3	4	5	6

rate unit A compound *unit* for a *rate.* For example, *miles per hour, dollars per pound,* and *words per minute* are rate units. See Section 9.3.3: Rates and Ratios.

ratio A comparison by division of two quantities with the same *units.* Ratios can be fractions, decimals, percents, or stated in words. Ratios can also be written with a colon between the two numbers being compared. For example, if a team wins 3 games out of 5 games played, the ratio of wins to total games is $\frac{3}{5}$, 3/5, 0.6, 60%, 3 to 5, or 3:5 (read "three to five"). Compare to *rate.* See Section 9.3.3: Rates and Ratios.

rational counting Counting using one-to-one matching. For example, counting a number of chairs, people, or crackers. See Section 9.2.2: Plain and Fancy Counting.

rational numbers Numbers that can be written in the form $\frac{a}{b}$, where *a* and nonzero *b* are *integers*. The decimal form of a rational number either terminates or repeats. For example, $\frac{2}{3}$, $-\frac{2}{3}$, 0.5, 20.5, and 0.333 . . . are rational numbers. See Section 9.3: Fractions, Decimals, Percents, and Rational Numbers.

ray A part of a *line* starting at the ray's *endpoint* and continuing forever in one direction. A ray is often named by its endpoint and another point on it. See Section 13.3: Lines, Segments, and Rays.

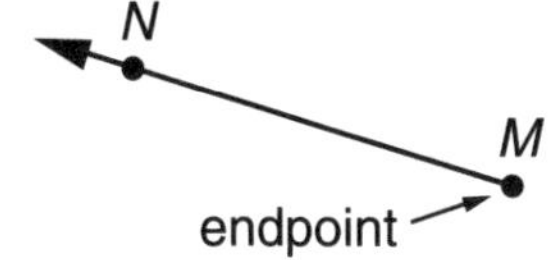

Ray *MN* or $\overrightarrow{MN}$

***r*-by-*c* array** A rectangular arrangement of elements with *r* rows and *c* elements per row. Among other things, an *r*-by-*c* array models *r* sets with *c* objects per set. Although listing rows before columns is arbitrary, it is in keeping with the order used in matrix notation, which students will study later.

real numbers All *rational* and *irrational numbers;* all numbers that can be written as decimals. For every real number there is a corresponding point on a number line, and for every point on the number line there is a real number. See Section 9.5: Irrational and Real Numbers.

reciprocals Two numbers whose product is 1. For example, 5 and $\frac{1}{5}$, $\frac{3}{5}$ and $\frac{5}{3}$, and 0.2 and 5 are pairs of reciprocals. Same as *multiplicative inverses*.

rectangle A *parallelogram* with all *right angles.* See Section 13.4.2: Polygons (*n*-gons).

rectangular array An arrangement of objects in *rows* and *columns* that form a *rectangle*. All rows have the same number of objects, and all columns have the same number of objects. See r-*by*-c *array* and Section 10.2.2: Multiplication and Division Use Classes.

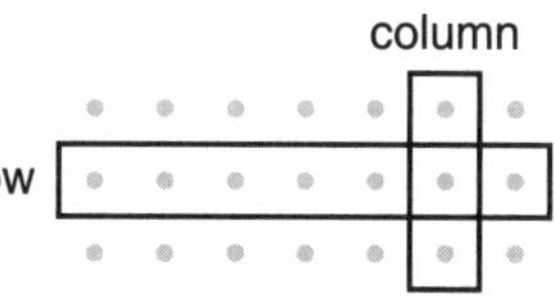

A rectangular array

rectangular coordinate grid (1) In *Everyday Mathematics,* same as *coordinate grid.* (2) A coordinate grid with perpendicular *axes.* See Section 15.3: Coordinate Systems.

rectangular prism A *prism* with rectangular *bases.* The four faces that are not bases are either *rectangles* or *parallelograms.* For example, a shoe box models a rectangular prism in which all sides are rectangles. See Section 13.5.2: Polyhedrons.

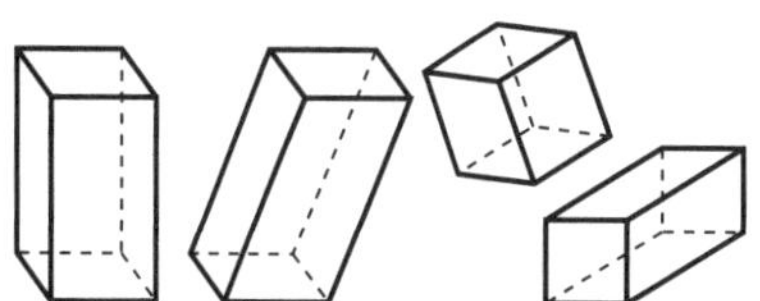

Rectangular prisms

rectangular pyramid A *pyramid* with a rectangular *base*. See Section 13.5.2: Polyhedrons.

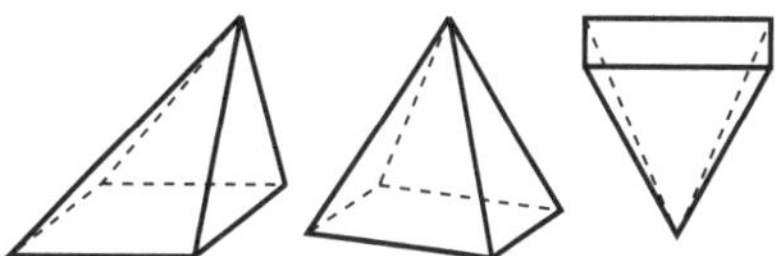

Rectangular pyramids

reduce To decrease the size of an object or figure without changing its shape. Same as *shrink.* See *scale factor* and Section 13.7.2: Stretches and Shrinks.

reduce a fraction To rewrite a fraction in a *simpler form.* See *simplest form of a fraction.*

reference frame A system for locating numbers within a given context, usually with reference to an *origin* or *zero point.* For example, number lines, clocks, calendars, temperature scales, and maps are reference frames. See Chapter 15: Reference Frames.

reflection A *transformation* in which the *image* of a figure is a mirror image of the figure over a *line of reflection*. Each point *A* on the figure and its corresponding point *A′* on the image are the same distance from the line of reflection on a line perpendicular to it. Informally called a *flip.* See Section 13.7.1: Flips, Turns, and Slides.

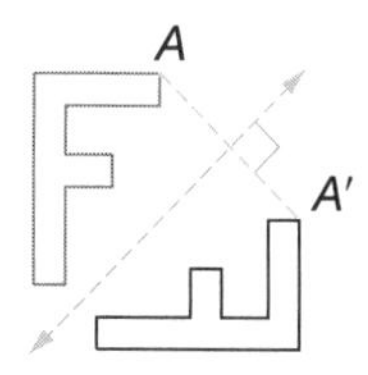

A reflection

Glossary

reflex angle An *angle* with a measure between 180° and 360°. See Section 13.4.1: Angles and Rotations.

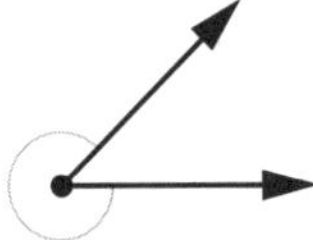

A reflex angle

regular polygon A *polygon* in which all *sides* are the same length and all *angles* have the same measure. See Section 13.4.2: Polygons (*n*-gons).

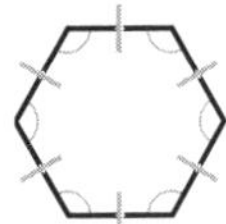 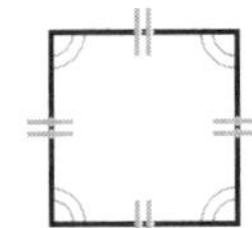 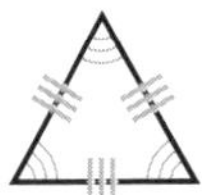

Regular polygons

regular polyhedron A *polyhedron* whose faces are all *congruent regular polygons* and in which the same number of faces meet at each *vertex*. The five regular polyhedrons, known as the Platonic solids, are shown below.

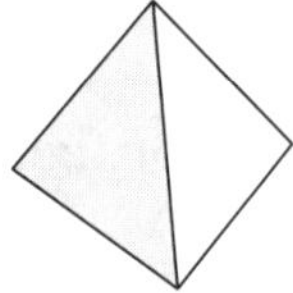

A tetrahedron (4 equilateral triangles)

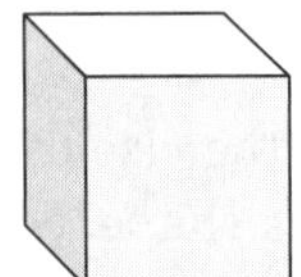

A cube (6 squares)

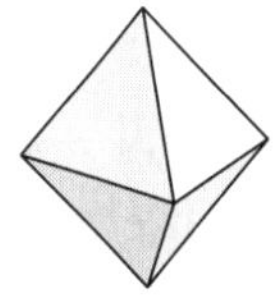

An octahedron (8 equilateral triangles)

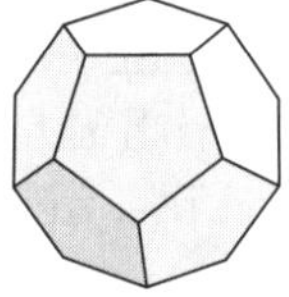

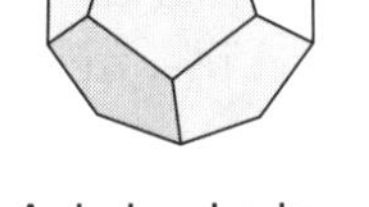

A dodecahedron (12 regular pentagons)

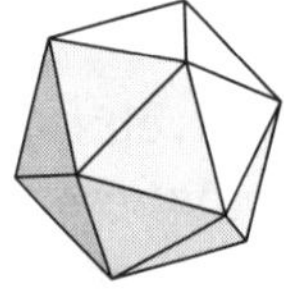

An icosahedron (20 equilateral triangles)

regular tessellation A *tessellation* of one *regular polygon*. The only three regular tessellations are shown below.

 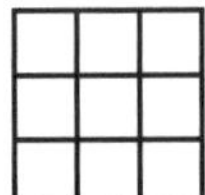 

Samples of the three regular tessellations

relation symbol A symbol used to express a relationship between two quantities. See Section 10.1.2: Reading and Writing Number Sentences.

Relation	Meaning
=	is equal to
≠	is not equal to
$<$	is less than
$>$	is greater than
≤	is less than or equal to
≥	is greater than or equal to
≈	is approximately equal to

remainder An amount left over when one number is divided by another number. For example, in 16 ÷ 3 → 5 R1, the *quotient* is 5 and the remainder R is 1. See Section 10.1.1: Arithmetic Symbols.

repeating decimal A *decimal* in which one *digit* or a group of digits is repeated without end. For example, 0.3333. . . and $0.\overline{147}$ are repeating decimals. Compare to *terminating decimal*. See Section 9.3.1: Fraction and Decimal Notation.

rhombus A *parallelogram* with all sides the same length. All rhombuses are parallelograms. Every square is a rhombus, but not all rhombuses are squares. Also called a diamond. Plural is rhombuses or rhombi. See Section 13.4.2: Polygons (*n*-gons).

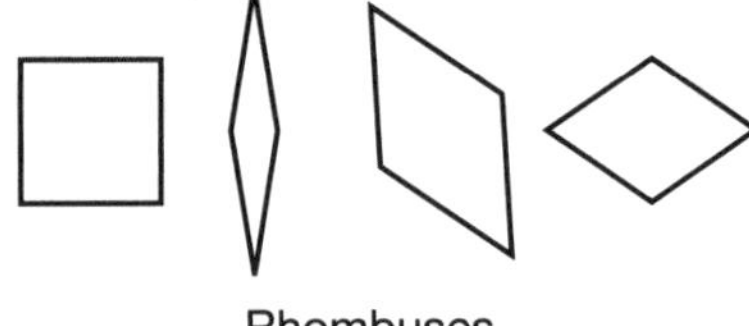

Rhombuses

right angle A 90° *angle*. See Section 13.4.1: Angles and Rotations.

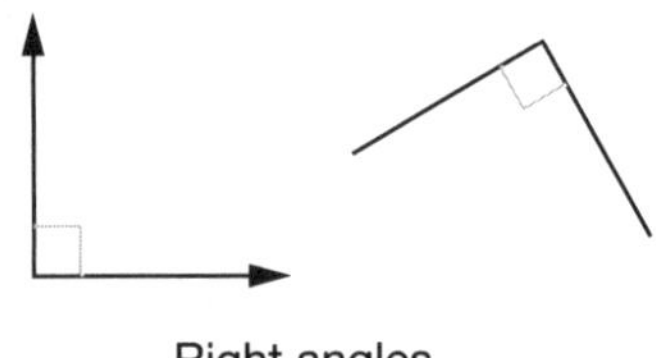

Right angles

right cone A *cone* whose *base* is perpendicular to the line segment joining the *apex* and the center of the base. See Section 13.5.3: Solids with Curved Surfaces.

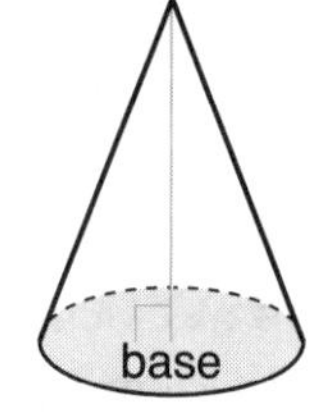

A right circular cone

right cylinder A *cylinder* whose *bases* are perpendicular to the line segment joining the centers of the bases. See Section 13.5.3: Solids with Curved Surfaces.

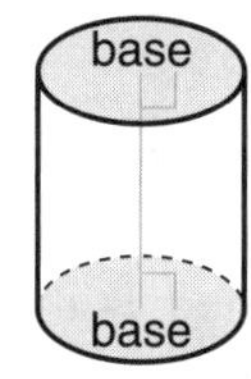

A right circular cylinder

right prism A *prism* whose *bases* are perpendicular to all of the *edges* that connect the two bases. See Section 13.5.2: Polyhedrons.

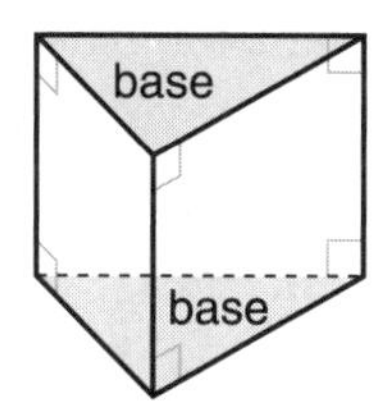

A right triangular prism

right triangle A *triangle* with a *right angle*. See Section 13.4.2: Polygons (*n*-gons).

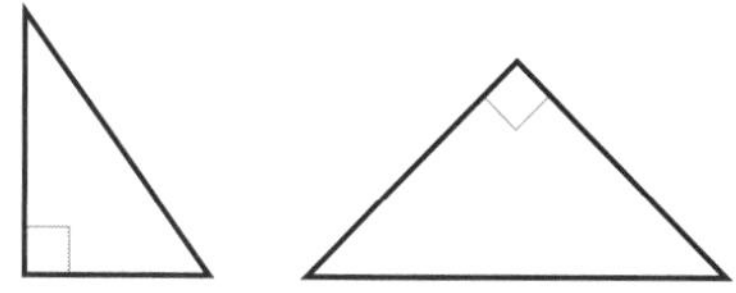
Right triangles

Roman numerals Letters that are used alone and in combination to represent numbers in an ancient Roman system of *numeration*. Roman numerals are found on clocks, building cornerstones, preliminary pages in books, movie copyright dates, and other places.

Roman Numerals

I = 1	X = 10	C = 100
II = 2	XX = 20 (2 tens)	CC = 200
III = 3	XXX = 30 (3 tens)	CCC = 300
IV = 4	XL = 40 (50 less 10)	CD = 400
V = 5	L = 50	D = 500
VI = 6	LX = 60 (50 plus 10)	CM = 900
VII = 7	LXX = 70 (50 plus 20)	M = 1,000
VIII = 8	LXXX = 80 (50 plus 30)	$\overline{X}$ = 10,000
IX = 9	XC = 90 (100 less 10)	$\overline{C}$ = 100,000
		∞ = 100,000,000 or infinity

rotation (1) A point *P′* is a rotation *image* of a point *P* around a center of rotation *C* if *P′* is on the *circle* with center *C* and radius *CP*. If all the points in one figure are rotation images of all the points in another figure around the same center of rotation and with the same angle of rotation, the figures are rotation images. The center can be inside or outside of the original image. Informally called a *turn*. See Section 13.7.1: Flips, Turns, and Slides. (2) If all points on the image of a *3-dimensional figure* are rotation images around a point on a line called the axis of rotation, then the image is a rotation image of the original figure.

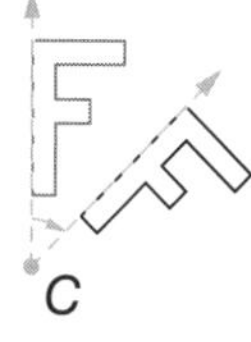

A rotation

rotation symmetry A figure has rotation symmetry if it is the *rotation* image of itself after less than a 360° turn around a center or axis of rotation. See Section 13.8.2: Other Symmetries.

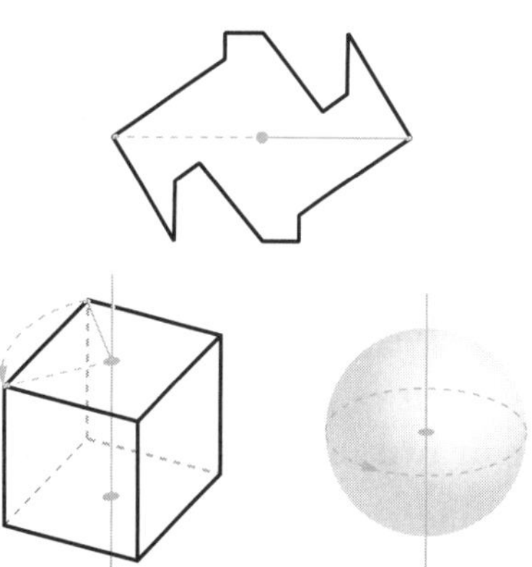
Shapes with rotation symmetry

rote counting Reciting a string of number words by rote, without understanding their significance. See *skip counting* and Section 9.2.2: Plain and Fancy Counting.

round (1) To approximate a number to make it easier to work with, or to make it better reflect the precision of the data. "Rounding up" means to approximate larger than the actual value. "Rounding down" means to approximate smaller than the actual value. See *round to the nearest* and Section 16.2: Approximation and Rounding. (2) Circular in shape.

round to the nearest To *round* a number up or down in a particular decimal place, depending on which approximation is closer to the actual value. See Section 16.2: Approximation and Rounding.

row A horizontal arrangement of objects or numbers in an *array* or table.

same-change rule for subtraction A subtraction *algorithm* in which the same number is added to or subtracted from both numbers. See Section 11.2.2: Subtraction Algorithms.

sample A part of a *population* intended to represent the whole population. See *random sample* and Section 12.2.2: Collecting and Recording Data.

scale (1) The relative size of something. (2) Same as *scale factor.* (3) A tool for measuring *weight.* See Section 14.6: Weight and Mass.

scale of a map Same as *map scale.*

scale of a number line The *unit interval* on a number line or measuring device. The scales on this ruler are 1 millimeter on the left side and $\frac{1}{16}$ inch on the right side. See Section 9.7.2: Number Grids, Scrolls, and Lines.

scale drawing A drawing of an object in which all parts are drawn to the same *scale* to the object. For example, architects and builders use scale drawings traditionally called blueprints. A map is a scale drawing of a geographical region. See *scale factor* and Section 15.4.2: Map and Model Scales.

A woodpecker (8 in.) to $\frac{1}{4}$ scale

scale factor (1) The *ratio* of lengths on an *image* and corresponding lengths on a *preimage* in a *size change*. Same as *size-change factor*. See Section 13.7.2: Stretches and Shrinks. (2) The ratio of lengths in a *scale drawing* or *scale model* to the corresponding lengths in the object being drawn or modeled. See Section 15.4.2: Map and Model Scales.

scale model A model of an object in which all parts are made to the same *scale* to the object. For example, many model trains or airplanes are scale models of actual vehicles. See *scale factor* and Section 15.4.2: Map and Model Scales.

scalene triangle A *triangle* with sides of three different lengths. The three angles of a scalene triangle have different measures. See Section 13.4.2: Polygons (*n*-gons).

scientific calculator A calculator that can display numbers using *scientific notation.* Scientific calculators follow the *algebraic order of operations* and can calculate a *power of a number,* a *square root,* and several other functions beyond simple 4-function calculators. Some scientific calculators let you enter and do arithmetic with *fractions.* See Section 3.1.1: Calculators.

scientific notation A way of writing a number as the product of a *power* of 10 and a number that is at least 1 and less than 10. Scientific notation allows you to write large and small numbers with only a few symbols. For example, in scientific notation, 4,300,000 is 4.3×10^6, and 0.00001 is 1×10^{-5}. *Scientific calculators* display numbers in scientific notation. Compare to *standard notation* and *expanded notation*.

second (s or sec) (1) A unit of time defined as $\frac{1}{31{,}556{,}925.9747}$ of the tropical year at midnight Eastern Time on New Year's Day, 1900. There are 60 seconds in a minute. (2) An *ordinal number* in the sequence *first, second, third, . . .*.

sector A region bounded by and including an *arc* and two *radii* of a circle. A sector resembles a slice of pizza. *Circle graphs* are made with sectors corresponding to parts of a data set. Also called a wedge.

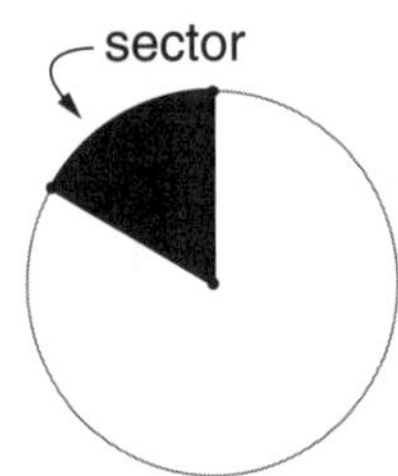

segment Same as *line segment.*

semicircle (1) Half of a *circle.* (2) Half of a circle and the *diameter* between the endpoints of the arc. Sometimes the interior of this closed figure is also included. See *circle* and Section 13.4.3: Circles and Pi (π).

A semicircle

sequence A list of numbers, often with an underlying rule that may be used to generate subsequent numbers in the list. *Frames-and-Arrows* diagrams are used to represent sequences. See Section 17.1.3: Sequences.

set A collection or group of objects, numbers, or other items.

short-term memory *Memory in a calculator* used to store values for immediate calculation. Short-term memory is usually cleared with a (C), (AC), (Clear), or similar key. Compare to *long-term memory.* See Section 3.1.1: Calculators.

shrink Same as *reduce.*

side (1) One of the *line segments* that make up a *polygon.* (2) One of the *rays* or *segments* that form an *angle.* (3) One of the *faces* of a *polyhedron.*

significant digits The *digits* in a number that convey useful and reliable information. A number with more significant digits is more *precise* than a number with fewer significant digits. In general, calculations should not produce results with more significant digits than the original numbers. See *scientific notation* and Section 16.2: Approximation and Rounding.

similar figures Figures that have the same shape, but not necessarily the same size. Compare to *congruent.* See Section 13.6.2: Congruence and Similarity.

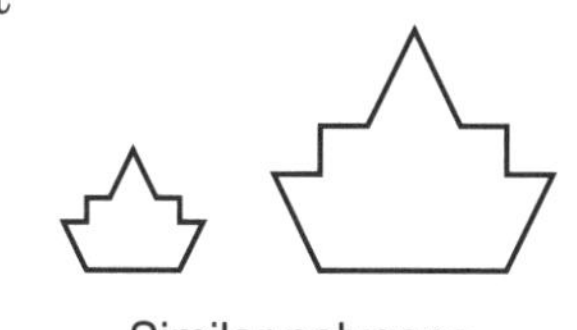
Similar polygons

simpler form of a fraction A *fraction* renamed as an *equivalent fraction* with a smaller numerator and smaller denominator. To put a fraction in simpler form, divide both the numerator and the denominator by a common factor greater than 1. For example, divide the numerator and the denominator of $\frac{18}{24}$ by 2 to get the simpler form $\frac{9}{12}$.

simplest form of a fraction A *fraction* that cannot be renamed in *simpler form.* Same as *lowest terms of a fraction. A mixed number* is in simplest form if its fractional part is in simplest form.

simplify a fraction To write a fraction in *simplest form.*

situation diagram A diagram used to organize information in a problem situation in one of the *addition/subtraction* or *multiplication/division use classes.* See Section 10.2: Use Classes and Situation Diagrams.

size change A *transformation* in which the *image* of a figure is an enlargement (*stretch*) or reduction (*shrink*) of the original figure by a given *scale factor.* See Section 13.7.2: Stretches and Shrinks.

size-change factor Same as *scale factor.*

skip counting *Rote counting* by intervals, such as by twos, fives or tens. See Section 9.2.2: Plain and Fancy Counting.

slanted cylinder, cone, prism, or pyramid A *cylinder, cone, prism,* or *pyramid* that is not a *right cylinder, right cone, right prism,* or *right pyramid.*

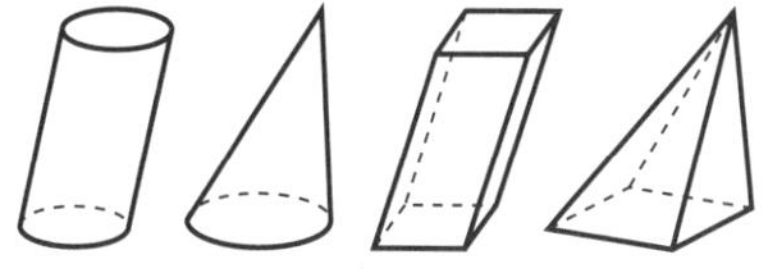
A slanted cylinder, cone, prism, and pyramid

slate A lap-size (about 8-inch by 11-inch) chalkboard or whiteboard that children use in *Everyday Mathematics* for recording responses during group exercises and informal group assessments. See Section 1.2.10: Slates.

slide An informal name for a *translation.* See Section 13.7.1: Flips, Turns, and Slides.

solution of an open sentence A value or values for the *variable(s)* in an *open sentence* that make the sentence true. For example, 7 is a solution of $5 + n = 12$. Although equations are not necessarily open sentences, the solution of an open sentence is commonly referred to as a solution of an equation. See Section 17.2.3: Solving Open Sentences.

solution of a problem (1) The method by which an answer to a problem is obtained. (2) The answer to a problem. See Chapter 18: Problem Solving.

solution set The set of all *solutions of an open sentence*. For example, the solution set of $x^2 = 25$ is {5, −5} because substituting either 5 or −5 for x makes the sentence true.

span Same as *normal span*.

speed A *rate* that compares distance traveled with the time taken to travel that distance. For example, if a car travels 100 miles in 2 hours, then its average speed is $\frac{100 \text{ mi}}{2 \text{ hr}}$, or 50 miles per hour. See Section 9.3.3: Rates and Ratios.

sphere The set of all points in space that are an equal distance from a fixed point called the *center of the sphere*. The distance from the center to the sphere is the *radius* of the sphere. The *diameter* of a sphere is twice its radius. Points inside a sphere are not part of the sphere. See Section 13.5.3: Solids with Curved Surfaces.

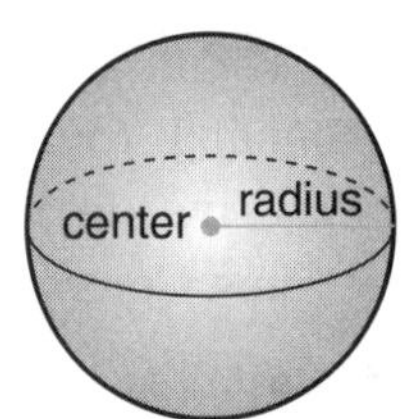

A sphere

square A *rectangle* with all sides of equal length. All angles in a square are *right angles*. See Section 13.4.2: Polygons (*n*-gons).

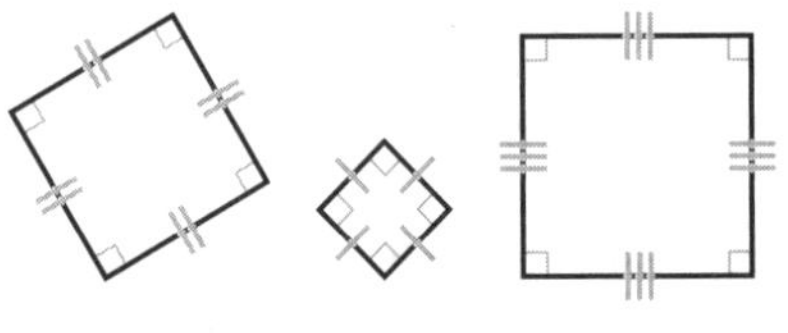
Squares

square array A rectangular *array* with the same number of *rows* as *columns*. For example, 16 objects will form a square array with 4 objects in each row and 4 objects in each column. See Section 10.2.2: Multiplication and Division Use Classes.

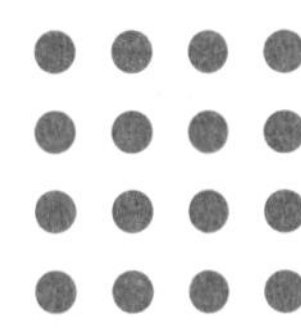
A square array

square corner Same as a *right angle*.

square numbers *Figurate numbers* that are the product of a *counting number* and itself. For example, 25 is a square number because 25 = 5 × 5. A square number can be represented by a *square array* and as a number squared, such as $25 = 5^2$. See Section 10.1.1: Arithmetic Symbols and Section 17.1.3: Sequences.

square of a number *n* The product of n and itself, commonly written n^2. For example, $81 = 9 \times 9 = 9^2$ and $3.5^2 = 3.5 \times 3.5 = 12.25$. See Section 10.1.1: Arithmetic Symbols.

square pyramid A *pyramid* with a square *base*. See Section 13.5.2: Polyhedrons.

square root of a number *n* A number that multiplied by itself is n, commonly written $\sqrt{n}$. For example, 4 is a square root of 16, because 4 × 4 = 16. Normally, square root refers to the positive square root, but the *opposite* of a positive square root is also a square root. For example, −4 is also a square root of 16 because −4 × −4 = 16.

square unit A unit to measure *area*. A model of a square unit is a square with each side a related unit of *length*. For example, a square inch is the area of a square with 1-inch sides. Square units are often labeled as the length unit squared. For example, 1 cm^2 is read "1 square centimeter" or "1 centimeter squared." See Section 14.4: Area.

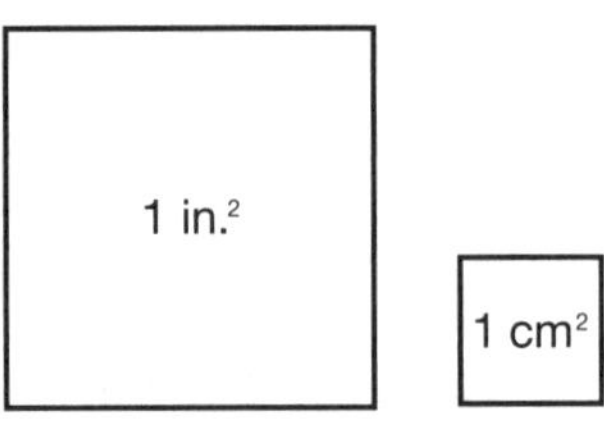

Square units

standard notation Our most common way of representing *whole numbers, integers,* and *decimals*. Standard notation is *base-ten place-value* numeration. For example, standard notation for three hundred fifty-six is 356. Same as *decimal notation*. See Section 9.2.1: Numeration and Place Value and Section 9.3.1: Fraction and Decimal Notation.

standard unit A unit of measure that has been defined by a recognized authority, such as a government or a standards organization. For example, *inches, meters, miles, seconds, pounds, grams,* and *acres* are all standard units. See Section 14.2: Measurement Systems.

straight angle A 180° *angle.* See Section 13.4.1: Angles and Rotations.

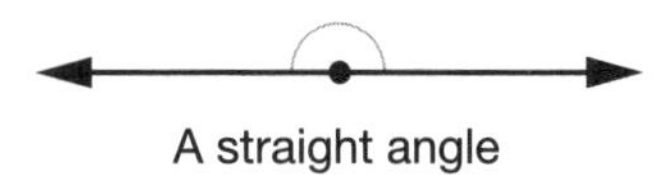

A straight angle

straightedge A tool used to draw *line segments.* Strictly speaking, a straightedge does not have a measuring *scale* on it, so ignore the marks if you use a ruler as a straightedge.

stretch Same as *enlarge.*

substitute (1) To replace one thing with another. (2) To replace *variables* with numbers in an *expression* or *formula*. For example, substituting $b = 4.5$ and $h = 8.5$ in the formula $A = b \times h$ gives $A = 4.5 \times 8.5 = 38.25$. See Section 17.2.1: Uses of Variables.

subtrahend The number being taken away in a subtraction problem. For example, in $15 - 5 = 10$, the subtrahend is 5.

sum The result of adding two or more numbers. For example, in $5 + 3 = 8$, the sum is 8. Same as *total.*

summer solstice The longest day of the year, when the sun is farthest north of Earth's equator. The number of hours of daylight depends on the latitude of a location. In Colorado, the summer solstice averages a little less than 16 hours of daylight. Compare to *winter solstice.*

supplementary angles Two angles whose measures add to 180°. Supplementary angles do not need to be *adjacent*. Compare to *complementary angles.*

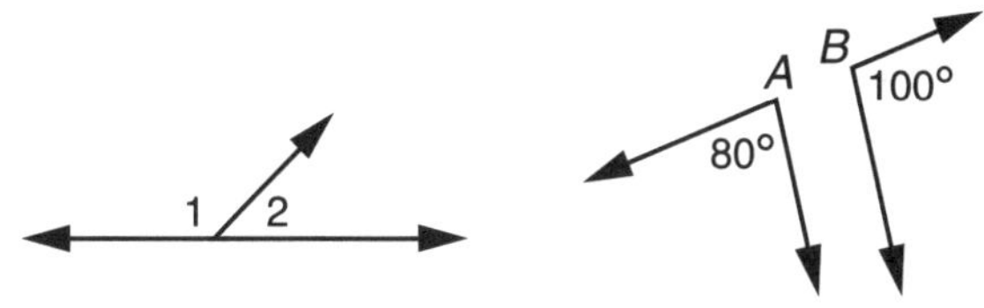

∠1 and ∠2 and ∠A and ∠B are two pairs of supplementary angles.

surface (1) The boundary of a 3-dimensional object. The part of an object that is next to the air. Common surfaces include the top of a body of water, the outermost part of a ball, and the topmost layer of ground that covers Earth. See Section 13.5: Space and 3-D Figures. (2) Any 2-dimensional layer, such as a *plane* or a face of a *polyhedron.*

surface area The *area* of the *surface* of a *3-dimensional figure.* The surface area of a polyhedron is the sum of the areas of its faces.

survey A study that collects *data.* Surveys are commonly used to study "demographics" such as people's characteristics, behaviors, interests, and opinions. See Section 12.2.2: Collecting and Recording Data.

symmetric figure A figure that exactly matches with its *image* under a *reflection* or *rotation.* See *line symmetry, rotation symmetry,* and Section 13.8: Symmetry.

symmetry The balanced distribution of points over a line or around a point in a *symmetric figure.* See *line symmetry, rotation symmetry,* and Section 13.8: Symmetry.

A figure with line symmetry

A figure with rotation symmetry

tally (1) To keep a record of a count, commonly by making a mark for each item as it is counted. (2) The mark used in a count. Also called "tally mark" and "tick mark." See Section 12.2.2: Collecting and Recording Data.

tally chart A table to keep track of a *tally,* typically showing how many times each value appears in a set of data.

temperature How hot or cold something is relative to another object or as measured on a standardized *scale* such as *degrees Celsius* or *degrees Fahrenheit.* See Section 15.1: Temperature.

template In *Everyday Mathematics,* a sheet of plastic with geometric shapes cut out of it, used to draw patterns and designs. See Section 13.10.1: Pattern-Block Template.

term (1) In an *algebraic expression,* a number or a product of a number and one or more *variables.* For example, in the equation $5y + 3k = 8$, the terms are $5y$, $3k$, and 8. The 8 is a *constant* term, or simply a *constant,* because it has no variable part. See Section 17.2.2: Reading and Writing Open Sentences. (2) An element in a *sequence.* In the sequence of square numbers, the terms are 1, 4, 9, 16, and so on.

terminating decimal A *decimal* that ends. For example, 0.5 and 0.125 are terminating decimals. See Section 9.3.1: Fraction and Decimal Notation.

tessellate To make a *tessellation;* to tile a surface.

tessellation A pattern of shapes that covers a surface completely without overlaps or gaps. Same as a *tiling.*

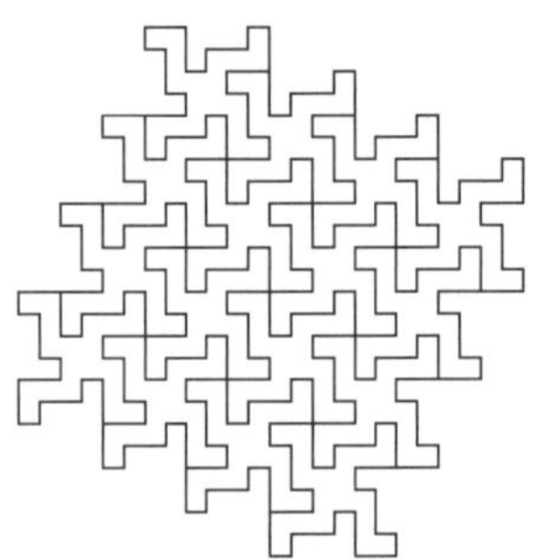

A tessellation

tetrahedron A *polyhedron* with 4 faces. A tetrahedron is a *triangular pyramid.* See Section 13.5.2: Polyhedrons.

theorem A mathematical statement that can be proved to be true. For example, the Pythagorean theorem states that if the *legs of a right triangle* have lengths a and b and the *hypotenuse* has length c, then $a^2 + b^2 = c^2$. The Pythagorean theorem has been proven in hundreds of ways over the past 2,500 years.

thermometer A tool used to measure *temperature* in *degrees* according to a fixed scale. The most common scales are *Celsius* and *Fahrenheit.* See Section 15.1.2: Thermometers.

3-dimensional (3-D) coordinate system A *reference frame* in which any point on a *3-dimensional figure* can be located with three *coordinates* relative to the *origin* of three axes intersecting perpendicularly at their origins in space. Compare to *1-* and *2-dimensional coordinate systems.* See Section 15.3: Coordinate Systems.

3-dimensional (3-D) figure A figure whose points are not all in a single *plane.* Examples include *prisms, pyramids,* and *spheres,* all of which have length, width, and height. See Section 13.1: Dimension.

tick marks (1) Marks showing the *scale* of a number line or ruler. (2) Same as *tally (2).*

tile A shape used in a *tessellation.* A tessellation of only one tile is called a "same-tile tessellation."

tiling Same as *tessellation.*

timeline A *number line* showing when events took place. In some timelines the *origin* is based on the context of the events being graphed, such as the birth date of the child's life graphed below. The origin can also come from another reference system, such as the year A.D. in which case the scale below might cover the years 2000 through 2005. See Section 15.2.3: Timelines.

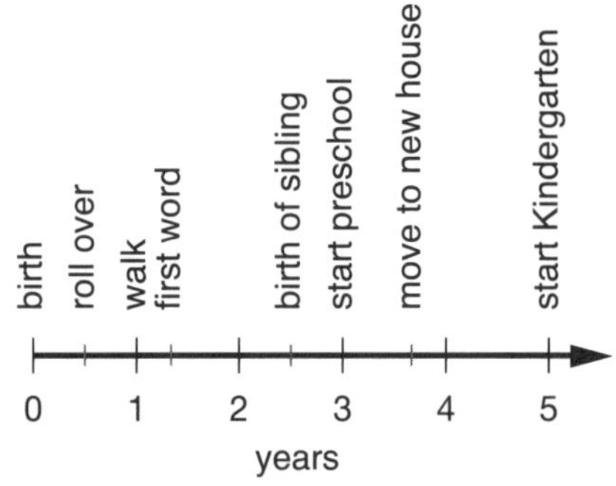

A timeline of a child's milestones

toggle A key on a calculator that changes back and forth between two displays each time it is pressed. For example, on some calculators [+/-] toggles between a number and its *opposite.* See Section 3.1.1: Calculators.

tool kit In *First* through *Third Grade Everyday Mathematics,* a bag or a box containing a calculator, measuring tools, and manipulatives often used by children in the program.

top-heavy fraction Same as *improper fraction.*

total Same as *sum.*

trade-first subtraction A subtraction *algorithm* in which all necessary trades between places in the numbers are done before any subtractions are carried out. Some people favor this algorithm because they can concentrate on one thing at a time. See Section 11.2.2: Subtraction Algorithms.

transformation An operation on a geometric figure (the *preimage*) that produces a new figure (the *image*). The study of transformations is called transformation geometry. Transformations are often based on rules for how points behave, as in the translation below. Although the preimage does not actually move under a transformation, it is convenient to think and talk about transformations as moving a figure from one place to another and sometimes changing its size or shape. So *Everyday Mathematics* encourages using informal terms such as *flip, turn,* and *slide.* See *isometry transformation, reflection, rotation, translation, size change* and Section 13.7: Transformations.

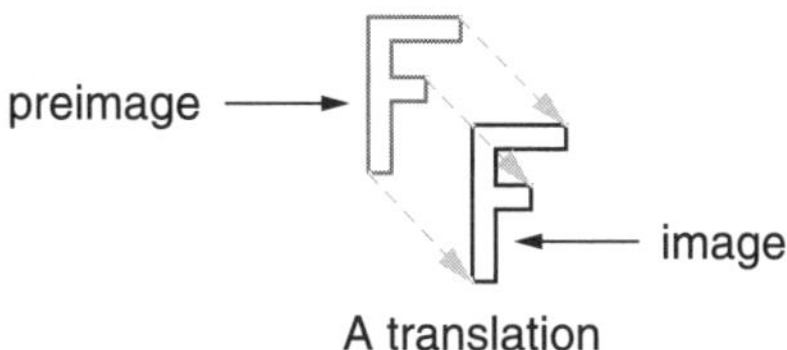

A translation

translation A *transformation* in which every point in the *image* of a figure is at the same distance in the same direction from its corresponding point in the figure. Informally called a *slide*. See *transformation* for an example and Section 13.7.1: Flips, Turns, and Slides.

trapezoid A *quadrilateral* that has exactly one pair of *parallel* sides. In *Everyday Mathematics,* both pairs of sides cannot be parallel; that is, a parallelogram is not a trapezoid. See Section 13.4.2: Polygons (*n*-gons).

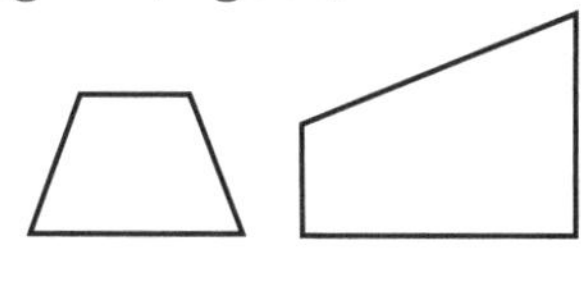

Trapezoids

tri- A prefix meaning three, as in tricycle.

triangle A 3-sided polygon. See *equilateral triangle, isosceles triangle, scalene triangle, acute triangle, right triangle, obtuse triangle,* and Section 13.4.2: Polygons (*n*-gons).

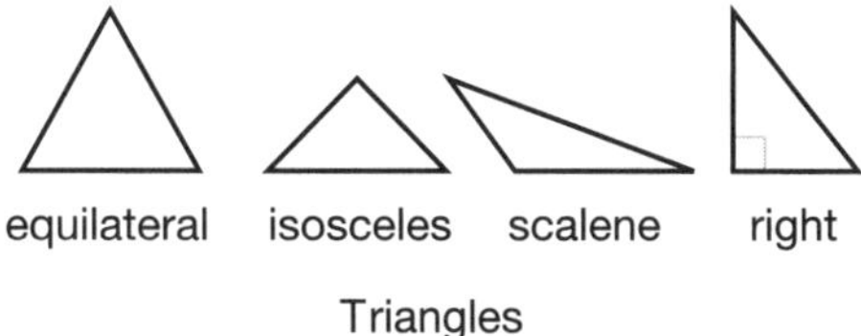

Triangles

triangular numbers *Figurate numbers* that can be shown by triangular arrangements of dots. The triangular numbers are {1, 3, 6, 10, 15, 21, 28, 36, 45, . . .}. See Section 17.1.3: Sequences.

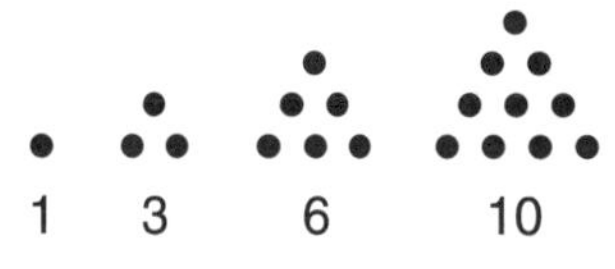

Triangular numbers

triangular prism A *prism* whose bases are triangles. See Section 13.5.2: Polyhedrons.

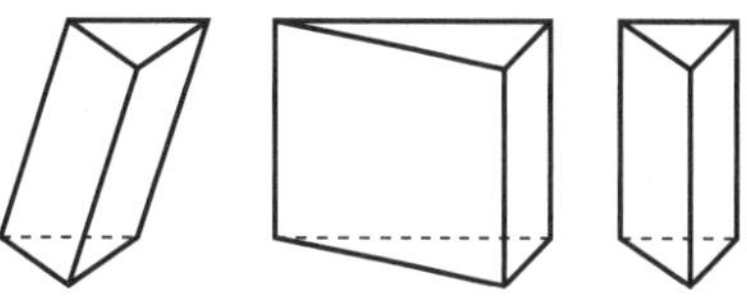

Triangular prisms

triangular pyramid A *pyramid* in which all *faces* are *triangles,* any one of which is the *base.* A regular tetrahedron has four *equilateral triangles* for faces and is one of the five *regular polyhedrons.* See Section 13.5.2: Polyhedrons.

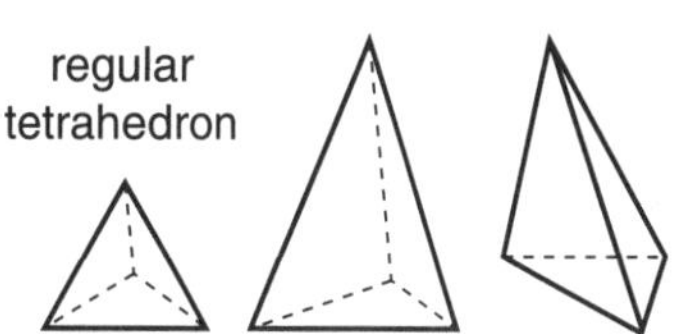

Triangular pyramids

true number sentence A *number sentence* stating a correct fact. For example, $75 = 25 + 50$ is a true number sentence. See Section 10.1.2: Reading and Writing Number Sentences.

truncate (1) In a *decimal,* to cut off all *digits* after the decimal point or after a particular place to the right of the decimal point. For example, 12.345 can be truncated to 12.34, 12.3, or 12. *Integers* cannot be truncated. Same as rounding down in places to the right of the decimal point. See *round* and Section 16.2: Approximation and Rounding. (2) Informally, to cut off a part of a solid figure.

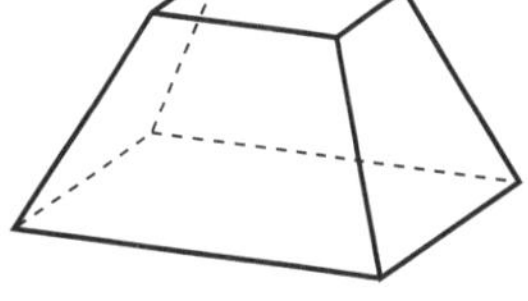

A truncated pyramid

turn An informal name for a *rotation.*

turn-around facts A pair of multiplication (or addition) facts in which the order of the factors (or addends) is reversed. For example, $3 \times 9 = 27$ and $9 \times 3 = 27$ are turn-around multiplication facts, and $4 + 5 = 9$ and $5 + 4 = 9$ are turn-around addition facts. There are no turn-around facts for subtraction or division. Turn-around facts are instances of the *Commutative Properties of Addition* and *Multiplication.* See Section 16.3.2: Basic Facts and Fact Power.

turn-around rule A rule for solving addition and multiplication problems based on the *Commutative Properties of Addition* and *Multiplication.* For example, if you know that $6 \times 8 = 48$, then, by the turn-around rule, you also know that $8 \times 6 = 48$.

2-dimensional (2-D) coordinate system A reference frame in which any point on a *2-dimensional figure* can be located with an *ordered pair* of coordinates relative to the *origin* of two intersecting perpendicular axes in space. Compare to *1-* and *3-dimensional coordinate systems.* See Section 15.3: Coordinate Systems.

2-dimensional (2-D) figure A figure whose points are all in one *plane* but not all on one *line.* Examples include polygons and circles, all of which have length and width but no height. See Section 13.1: Dimension.

U

unfair game A game in which every player does not have the same chance of winning. See Section 12.1.2: The Language of Chance.

unit A label used to put a number in context. In measuring *length,* for example, inches and centimeters are units. In a problem about 5 apples, apple is the unit. In *Everyday Mathematics,* students keep track of units in *unit boxes.* See Section 10.2.1: Addition and Subtraction Use Classes.

unit box In *Everyday Mathematics*, a box displaying the *unit* for the numbers in the problems at hand. See Section 1.3.6: Unit Boxes.

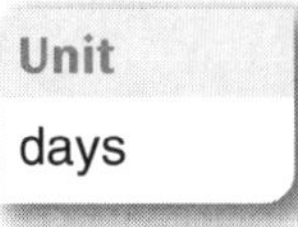

A unit box

unit fraction A *fraction* whose *numerator* is 1. For example, $\frac{1}{2}, \frac{1}{3}, \frac{1}{12}, \frac{1}{8}$, and $\frac{1}{20}$ are unit fractions. Unit fractions are especially useful in converting among units within measurement systems. For example, because 1 foot = 12 inches you can multiply a number of inches by $\frac{1}{12}$ to convert to feet. See Section 14.2.3: Converting between Measures.

unit interval The *interval* between 0 and 1 on a *number line.*

unit price The price for one item or *per* unit of measure. For example, the unit price of a 5-ounce package of onion powder selling for \$2.50 is \$0.50 per ounce. In recent years, grocery stores have begun posting unit prices to help consumers compare prices of different brands of a similar product or different size containers of the same product. See Section 14.2.3: Converting between Measures.

unit ratio Same as *n*-to-1 ratio.

unit whole Same as *whole* or *ONE.*

U.S. customary system The measuring system used most often in the United States. Units for *length* include inch, foot, yard, and mile; units for *weight* include ounce and pound; units for *volume* or *capacity* include cup, pint, quart, gallon, and cubic units; and the main unit for *temperature* change is degrees Fahrenheit. See Section 14.2.1: U.S. Customary System.

use class In *Everyday Mathematics,* a problem situation that one of the basic arithmetic operations can be used to solve. Students use *situation diagrams* to help model problems from the different use classes. See *addition/subtraction use classes, multiplication/division use classes,* and Section 10.2: Use Classes and Situation Diagrams.

V

variable A letter or other symbol that represents a number. A variable can represent a single number, as in $5 + n = 9$, because only $n = 4$ makes the sentence true. A variable can also stand for many different numbers, as in $x + 2 < 10$, because any number x less than 8 makes the sentence true. In *formulas* and *properties,* variables stand for all numbers. For example, $a + 3 = 3 + a$ for all numbers a. See Section 17.2.1: Uses of Variables.

vernal equinox The first day of spring, when the sun crosses the plane of Earth's equator and day and night are about 12 hours each. "Equinox" is from the Latin *aequi-* meaning "equal" and *nox* meaning "night." Compare to *autumnal equinox.*

vertex The point at which the *rays* of an angle, the *sides* of a polygon, or the *edges* of a polyhedron meet. Plural is vertexes or vertices. In *Everyday Mathematics,* same as *corner.* See Section 13.4: Planes and Plane Figures and Section 13.5: Space and 3-D Figures.

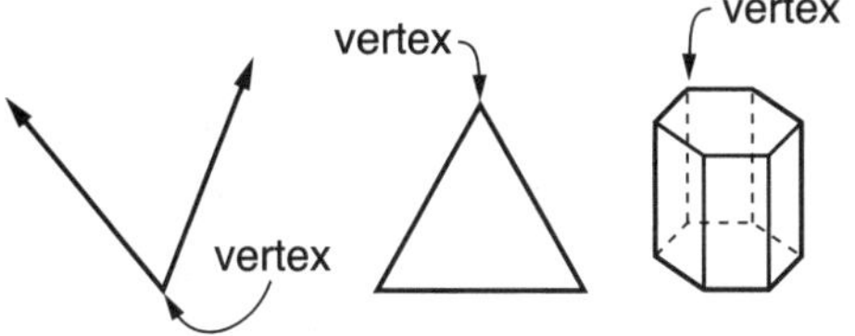

vertical Upright; perpendicular to the *horizon.* Compare to *horizontal.*

volume (1) The amount of space occupied by a *3-dimensional figure.* Same as *capacity.* (2) Less formally, the amount a container can hold. Volume is often measured in cubic units, such as cm^3, cubic inches, or cubic feet. See Section 14.5: Volume (Capacity).

weight A measure of how heavy something is; the force of gravity on an object. An object's *mass* is constant, but it weighs less in weak gravity than in strong gravity. For example, a person who weighs 150 pounds in San Diego weighs about 23 pounds on the moon. See Section 14.6: Weight and Mass.

"What's My Rule?" problem In *Everyday Mathematics,* a problem in which two of the three parts of a *function* (*input, output,* and rule) are known, and the third is to be found out. See Section 17.1.4: Functions.

input

Rule

?

output

in	out
4	2
7	5
12	10
8	

A "What's My Rule?" problem

whole An entire object, collection of objects, or quantity being considered in a problem situation; 100%. Same as *ONE* and *unit whole.* See Section 9.3.2: Uses of Fractions.

whole numbers The *counting numbers* and 0. The set of whole numbers is {0, 1, 2, 3, . . .}.

width of a rectangle The *length* of one side of a *rectangle* or rectangular object, typically the shorter side.

winter solstice The shortest day of the year, when the sun is farthest south of Earth's equator. The number of hours of daylight depends on the latitude of a location. In Colorado, the winter solstice averages a little more than 9 hours of daylight. Compare to *summer solstice.*

yard (yd) A U.S. customary unit of *length* equal to 3 feet, or 36 inches. To Henry I of England, a yard was the distance from the tip of the nose to the tip of the middle finger. In *Everyday Mathematics,* it is from the center of the chest to the tip of the middle finger. See the Tables of Measures and Section 14.1: Personal Measures.

zero fact In *Everyday Mathematics:* (1) The *sum* of two 1-digit numbers when one of the *addends* is 0, as in $0 + 5 = 5$. If 0 is added to any number, there is no change in the number. Same as the additive identity. (2) The product of two 1-digit numbers when one of the factors is 0, as in $4 \times 0 = 0$. The product of a number and 0 is always 0.

zero point Same as *origin.*

General Reference

Symbols

Symbols	
$+$	plus or positive
$-$	minus or negative
$*, \times$	multiplied by
$\div, /$	divided by
$=$	is equal to
$\neq$	is not equal to
$<$	is less than
$>$	is greater than
$\leq$	is less than or equal to
$\geq$	is greater than or equal to
$\approx$	is approximately equal to
x^n, x^n	nth power of x
$\sqrt{x}$	square root of x
%	percent
$a{:}b$, a/b, $\frac{a}{b}$	ratio of a to b or a divided by b or the fraction $\frac{a}{b}$
a [bs]	a groups, b in each group
$n \div d \rightarrow a$ Rb	n divided by d is a with remainder b
{ }, ( ), [ ]	grouping symbols
∞	infinity
$n!$	n factorial
$^\circ$	degree
(a,b)	ordered pair
$\overleftrightarrow{AS}$	line AS
$\overline{AS}$	line segment AS
$\overrightarrow{AS}$	ray AS
⌐	right angle
$\perp$	is perpendicular to
$\parallel$	is parallel to
$\triangle ABC$	triangle ABC
$\angle ABC$	angle ABC
$\angle B$	angle B
$\cong$	is congruent to
$\sim$	is similar to
$\equiv$	is equivalent to
$\lvert n \rvert$	absolute value of n

Prefixes

Prefixes			
uni-	one	tera-	trillion (10^{12})
bi-	two	giga-	billion (10^9)
tri-	three	mega-	million (10^6)
quad-	four	kilo-	thousand (10^3)
penta-	five	hecto-	hundred (10^2)
hexa-	six	deca-	ten (10^1)
hepta-	seven	uni-	one (10^0)
octa-	eight	deci-	tenth (10^{-1})
nona-	nine	centi-	hundredth (10^{-2})
deca-	ten	milli-	thousandth (10^{-3})
dodeca-	twelve	micro-	millionth (10^{-6})
icosa-	twenty	nano-	billionth (10^{-9})

Constants

Constants	
Pi (π)	3.14159 26535 89793
Golden Ratio (ϕ)	1.61803 39887 49894
Radius of Earth at equator	6,378.388 kilometers 3,963.34 miles
Circumference of Earth at equator	40,076.59 kilometers 24,902.44 miles
Velocity of sound in dry air at 0°C	331.36 m/sec 1087.1 ft/sec
Velocity of light in a vacuum	2.997925×10^{10} cm/sec

The Order of Operations

1. Do operations inside grouping symbols following Rules 2–4. Work from the innermost set of grouping symbols outward.
2. Calculate all expressions with exponents.
3. Multiply and divide in order from left to right.
4. Add and subtract in order from left to right.

Tables of Measures

Metric System

Units of Length

1 kilometer (km)	= 1,000 meters (m)
1 meter	= 10 decimeters (dm)
	= 100 centimeters (cm)
	= 1,000 millimeters (mm)
1 decimeter	= 10 centimeters
1 centimeter	= 10 millimeters

Units of Area

1 square meter (m^2)	= 100 square decimeters (dm^2)
	= 10,000 square centimeters (cm^2)
1 square decimeter	= 100 square centimeters
1 are (a)	= 100 square meters
1 hectare (ha)	= 100 ares
1 square kilometer (km^2)	= 100 hectares

Units of Volume and Capacity

1 cubic meter (m^3)	= 1,000 cubic decimeters (dm^3)
	= 1,000,000 cubic centimeters (cm^3)
1 cubic centimeter	= 1,000 cubic millimeters (mm^3)
1 kiloliter (kL)	= 1,000 liters (L)
1 liter	= 1,000 milliliters (mL)

Units of Mass and Weight

1 metric ton (t)	= 1,000 kilograms (kg)
1 kilogram	= 1,000 grams (g)
1 gram	= 1,000 milligrams (mg)

System Equivalents (Conversion Factors)

1 inch ≈ 2.5 cm (2.54)	1 liter ≈ 1.1 quarts (1.057)
1 kilometer ≈ 0.6 mile (0.621)	1 ounce ≈ 28 grams (28.350)
1 mile ≈ 1.6 kilometers (1.609)	1 kilogram ≈ 2.2 pounds (2.21)
1 meter ≈ 39 inches (39.37)	1 hectare ≈ 2.5 acres (2.47)

Body Measures

1 *digit* is about the width of a finger.

1 *hand* is about the width of the palm and thumb.

1 *span* is about the distance from the tip of the thumb to the tip of the first (index) finger of an outstretched hand.

1 *cubit* is about the length from the elbow to the tip of the extended middle finger.

1 *yard* is about the distance from the center of the chest to the tip of the extended middle finger of an outstretched arm.

1 *fathom* is about the length from fingertip to fingertip of outstretched arms. Also called an arm span.

U.S. Customary System

Units of Length

1 mile (mi)	= 1,760 yards (yd)
	= 5,280 feet (ft)
1 yard	= 3 feet
	= 36 inches (in.)
1 foot	= 12 inches

Units of Area

1 square yard (yd^2)	= 9 square feet (ft^2)
	= 1,296 square inches (in^2)
1 square foot	= 144 square inches
1 acre	= 43,560 square feet
1 square mile (mi^2)	= 640 acres

Units of Volume and Capacity

1 cubic yard (yd^3)	= 27 cubic feet (ft^3)
1 cubic foot	= 1,728 cubic inches (in^3)
1 gallon (gal)	= 4 quarts (qt)
1 quart	= 2 pints (pt)
1 pint	= 2 cups (c)
1 cup	= 8 fluid ounces (fl oz)
1 fluid ounce	= 2 tablespoons (tbs)
1 tablespoon	= 3 teaspoons (tsp)

Units of Mass and Weight

1 ton (T)	= 2,000 pounds (lb)
1 pound	= 16 ounces (oz)

Units of Time

1 century	= 100 years
1 decade	= 10 years
1 year (yr)	= 12 months
	= 52 weeks (plus one or two days)
	= 365 days (366 days in a leap year)
1 month (mo)	= 28, 29, 30, or 31 days
1 week (wk)	= 7 days
1 day (d)	= 24 hours
1 hour (hr)	= 60 minutes
1 minute (min)	= 60 seconds (s or sec)

1–3 Games Correlation Chart

				Skill and Concept Areas									
Game	**Grade 1 Lesson**	**Grade 2 Lesson**	**Grade 3 Lesson**	**Numeration**	**Mental Math**	**Basic Facts**	**Operations**	**Patterns**	**Geometry**	**Money**	**Time**	**Probability**	**Calculator**
Addition Card Draw		12-5			●	●	●						
Addition Spin	*	4-2			●	●	●						
Addition Top-It	6-1	1-4	1-4	●	●	●	●						
Angle Race			6-9		●		●		●				
Animal Weight Top-It	5-5			●	●	●	●						
Array Bingo			9-6	●	●	●	●						
Attribute Train Game	7-2								●				
Base-10 Decimal Exchange			5-8	●									
Base-10 Exchange	5-3	3-4		●									
Baseball Multiplication			4-7		●	●	●						
Baseball Multiplication (Advanced Version)			4-7		●	●	●						
Basketball Addition		7-3			●	●	●						
Beat the Calculator (Addition)	5-11	2-2	1-9		●	●	●						●
Beat the Calculator (Multiplication)		11-8	4-5		●	●	●				●		●
Before and After	3-1			●									
The Block-Drawing Game			8-2					●				●	
Bunny Hop	1-5			●									
Coin-Dice	3-12									●			
Coin Exchange	6-10									●			
Coin Top-It	2-13	1-4	1-10	●						●			
Decimal Solitaire			5-10	●				●					
Difference Game	5-7	2-12			●	●	●			●			
Digit Game	5-1	3-1		●									
Dime-Nickel-Penny Grab	3-13			●			●			●			
Division Arrays			4-3		●	●	●						
Dollar Rummy		3-5		●	●	●	●						
Domino Top-It	3-14	1-4		●	●	●	●						
Doubles or Nothing		2-3		●	●	●	●						
Equivalent Fractions Game		8-5	8-5	●									
Equivalent Fractions Game (Advanced Version)			8-5	●									
Fact Extension	*	4-8			●	●	●						
Fact Power Game	6-4				●	●	●						
Factor Bingo			9-6	●	●	●	●						
Finding Factors			9-6		●	●	●						
Fingers			11-3									●	
Fraction Top-It		8-6	8-6	●									
Fraction Top-It (Advanced)			8-6	●									
High Roller	2-12	3-7		●	●	●	●						
Hit the Target	*	7-2											●
Less Than You!			1-3	●	●	●	●						
Make My Design	7-1								●				
Making Change		3-8		●						●			
Memory Addition/Subtraction			10-8		●	●	●						●
Missing Terms			*		●	●	●						

1–3 Games Correlation Chart *continued*

Game	Grade 1 Lesson	Grade 2 Lesson	Grade 3 Lesson	Numeration	Mental Math	Basic Facts	Operations	Patterns	Geometry	Money	Time	Probability	Calculator
				Skill and Concept Areas									
Money Exchange Game		1-5		●						●			
Monster Squeeze	1-2			●									
Multiplication Bingo			7-3		●	●	●						
Multiplication Draw			11-6		●	●	●						
Multiplication Top-It			10-7	●	●	●	●						
Name That Number	*	2-9	1-6		●	●	●						
Nickel-Penny Grab	2-11			●			●			●			
Number-Grid Difference	*	2-12	1-8	●		●	●	●					
Number-Grid Game	9-2			●			●						
Number-Line Squeeze		1-1	1-1	●									
Number Top-It		1-11		●									
Number Top-It (5-Digit Numbers)			5-2	●									
Number Top-It (7-Digit Numbers)			5-3	●									
Number Top-It (Decimals)			5-10	●									
One-Dollar Exchange	8-2									●			
$1, $10, $100 Exchange Game	10-4			●	●					●			
Penny-Dice Game	1-3			●						●			
Penny-Dime-Dollar Exchange		3-2		●						●			
Penny Grab	2-8	6-2		●			●			●			
Penny-Nickel-Dime Exchange	5-13									●			
Penny-Nickel Exchange	2-10	1-5								●			
Penny Plate	2-8	1-6			●	●							
Pick-a-Coin		10-3	*							●			●
Quarter-Dime-Nickel-Penny Grab	6-9			●			●			●			
Robot Game			6-3						●				
Rock, Paper, Scissors	1-8											●	
Roll to 100			2-1		●	●	●						
Rolling for 50	2-1			●									
Shading Shapes			6-5					●	●				
Shaker Addition Top-It	4-12				●	●	●						
Soccer Spin		7-8	11-3		●			●				●	
Spinning for Money		3-2	1-11	●						●			
Spinning to Win			11-4									●	
Subtraction Top-It	*	*	3-7	●	●	●	●						
Target: 50			2-7	●	●	●	●						
Three Addends		6-1	*		●	●	●						
3, 2, 1 Game	8-5				●	●	●						
Tic-Tac-Toe Addition		10-5			●	●	●						
Time Match	4-4										●		
Top-It	1-6			●									
Touch-and-Match Quadrangles		5-6	6-5						●				
Trading Money			9-7	●									
Tric-Trac	6-8				●	●	●						

Index